The Lean-Agile Way

Unleash business results in the digital era with value stream management

Cecil 'Gary' Rupp

Richard Knaster

Steve Pereira

Al Shalloway

<packt>

The Lean-Agile Way

Group Product Manager: Aaron Tanna
Publishing Product Manager: Uzma Sheerin
Senior Content Development Editor: Rosal Colaco
Book Project Manager: Prajakta Naik
Technical Editor: Vidhisha Patidar
Copy Editor: Safis Editing
Indexer: Pratik Shirodkar
Production Designer: Gokul Raj S.T
DevRel Marketing Coordinators: Deepak Kumar

First published: August 2024

Production reference:1090824

Published by Packt Publishing Ltd.
Grosvenor House
11 St Paul's Square
Birmingham
B3 1RB, UK

ISBN 978-1-83546-187-7

www.packtpub.com

Foreword

Imagine if, at every step of your transformation journey, you have access to the world's most seasoned experts. They guide you to effortlessly avoid the dragons around each corner, secure alignment with every key stakeholder, and continually support your doubling and then quadrupling the productivity of your organization. Envision the effect that this would have on business outcomes, on the happiness of your teams, and on the trajectory of your career. Now consider that all of the wisdom this expert was leveraging was clearly defined and written down in a canonical work combining Lean, Agile, and Value Stream Management (VSM) best practices. This knowledge base is precisely what lies before you in *The Lean-Agile Way*.

We are constantly seeking expertise to help guide us with both near-term decisions and long-term investments on our journey. Most of us have already tried to get transformation advice from the current breed of Large Language Models (LLMs) and have experienced the disappointment of overly generic and superfluous advice. The LLMs are not to blame. The challenge is that our industry has continued creating new ways to apply and evolve Lean principles to a new era of digital innovation and AI.

I recently ran some experiments feeding content from my 2018 *Project to Product* book to cutting-edge LLMs. I found the answers and guidance lacking relative to my experience in the domain, largely because the supplementary levels of detail were missing in the answers. What delighted me most about *The Lean-Agile Way* is that it fills these gaps with both a comprehensive and concise body of knowledge that is missing from other resources available today. This book provides an unprecedented level of detail, implementation guidance models, and expanded frameworks and concepts to accelerate business outcomes with VSM. If you are seeking a summary of the knowledge needed to thrive in the era of AI and digital, hit pause on that last chat session or podcast and dig deep into this book.

The knowledge shared here will eventually be more broadly disseminated and surface in online resources and AI assistants over the coming years. However, I do not think that anyone involved in digital innovation and transformation can wait that long. Industry reports such as **State of DevOps** [1] and the **2023 Project to Product State of the Industry** [2] make it clear that organizations that have already mastered the Lean-Agile operating model are pulling away from the average and delivering orders of magnitude more value to their stakeholders. We need our leaders and teams to gain mastery of the concepts in *The Lean-Agile Way*, and to train our own neural networks on the pattern language that is concisely laid out in this book.

I was recently involved in a large organization's high-stakes reorganization of its engineering teams. The consultant leading the effort was top-tier and had more industry experience running large engineering organizations than most. They ingested data from countless interviews, org charts, financial metrics, and Agile and DevOps tools. The lengthy assessment provided numerous insights into gaps in talent, team sizing issues, and leadership rebalancing opportunities. One of the key recommendations was to move several teams under a very seasoned engineering leader who was particularly well respected according to the interviews. However, when the assessment readout was contrasted with the flow metrics for the leader's value streams, the data showed that the rate of flow was less than a tenth of other top engineering leaders' teams. Executing that recommendation would have likely slowed delivery in a precipitous way and made the entire reorganization take a backward step in productivity. However, the consultancy had no clear framework or tooling to surface this problem as their practice did not consider value streams.

Without the instrumentation and metrics detailed in *The Lean-Agile Way*, which demonstrate that the visibility of siloed organizational structures is ineffective without integrating value stream flow (see *Chapter 6*), the reorganization would have overlooked value stream dynamics and failed. This example is just one of the many conceptual models that the authors provide in this book.

In the past few years, we have seen a growing body of literature on product-oriented operational models and value streams. *The Lean-Agile Way* stands out as it is deeply rooted in the long history of Lean and builds clearly and explicitly on the foundations and empirical work done by others over the past decades. This book provides a refreshing departure from the superficial trends often seen in the industry, such as the reliance on blogs, whitepapers, and shallow guidance.

One notable example is the Spotify model, which, while innovative and aspirational, lacked sufficient grounding in empirical evidence. In 2017, Spotify made a data-driven decision to evolve away from this model, highlighting the importance of adaptability and continuous improvement. This contrasts with the ongoing struggles many enterprises face when rigidly implementing the original framework without considering necessary adaptations.

Thanks to the four authors' profound depth and wealth of practical experience in our field, key topics missed by many others are covered here, ranging from framing value streams with business context to modeling flow economics. In addition to building on the literature and state-of-the-art methods and tools, the authors fill some critical gaps in today's understanding of VSM implementation.

To help you turn theory into practice, *The Lean-Agile Way* provides a thorough implementation roadmap and step-by-step guide. This clarity is critical as too many organizations continue to get stuck on experimentation with VSM rather than achieving the massive productivity gains that result from a deliberate and well-structured deployment. The authors' focus on applying a team of team's emphasis on Lean-Agile work is of particular relevance as the other challenge that countless organizations experience is a failure to operationalize effectively above the team level.

Other vital contributions unique to this book include the E9 VSM process, approaches to nesting and managing supporting value streams, synchronizing value streams, combining VSM with Wardley mapping, and integrating platform value streams. In *Chapter 10*, the authors delve into how organizations can harness the volumes of data available to enhance decision-making and action-taking within a lean-Agile enterprise. They also introduce and expand on two key new frameworks, BLAST and BASE. These frameworks facilitate transitioning your organization from simple MVPs to a continuous flow of minimal valuable increments (MVIs), structuring business value backlogs, coordinating at the team-of-teams level, and operationalizing in an iterative approach to delivering business value via minimal valuable releases (MVRs).

To bring all these concepts together in an actionable way, *The Lean-Agile Way* then tackles what I think is one of the most poorly understood but most critical aspects of success: modeling, understanding, measuring, and improving your value stream network. While a more complex concept, it is distilled clearly with an implementation roadmap that, if followed, is sure to help your business thrive in a matter of months if not weeks. Finally, some excellent case studies conclude this sound and profound contribution to our industry.

I hope that you enjoy *The Lean-Agile Way* as much as I did and use it to advance your organization, your team, and your career!

—Mik Kersten, CTO at Planview, Inc.

1. Google Cloud. (2023). Accelerate State of DevOps Report. DevOps Research and Assessment (DORA). Retrieved from `https://dora.dev/research/2023/dora-report/`

2. Corp. (2023). The 2023 Project to Product State of the Industry Report: Benchmarking the operating model shift for digital innovation. Planview, Inc. `https://info.planview.com/project-to-product-state-of-the-industry-_report_vsm_en_reg.html`

Contributors

About the authors

Cecil 'Gary' Rupp is a Lean-Agile consultant and practitioner with more than two decades of executive-level experience in delivering software-based solutions. With SAFe® SPC, LeSS Practitioner, CSM, CSPO, and PMP certifications, he specializes in managing large software development and enterprise application integration programs involving multiple product delivery teams and is often brought in to get failing software delivery programs back on track. Gary is the author of four books emphasizing Lean-Agile practices and has trained over 600 IT specialists, managers, and executives in applying these practices to support enterprise business transformations. His passion is helping organizations profitably deliver customer value through software.

Richard Knaster has over 30 years of experience in software and systems development and has led large-scale Lean-Agile transformations for over 20 years. He is a SAFe® Fellow, SPCT, and a methodologist. He previously worked for Scaled Agile as a Principal Contributor to SAFe® on the Framework team. He is the author of Value Stream Management for the Digital Age eBook and co-author of the Amazon best-selling book, *SAFe Distilled* book series. Richard is a global keynote speaker and has written several white papers on SAFe® and Technology Business Management. He is the Chief Scientist for Value Stream Management for Agile Rising where he shares his deep expertise in Value Stream Management, Lean Portfolio Management, and SAFe®. Richard is also a Bain & Company Advisor and has held several executive roles in various industries, including CIO, CTO, and Director of Product Development.

Steve Pereira is a value stream consultant with over two decades of experience in tech. He specializes in helping teams define and optimize their value streams. He's helped dozens of organizations of all sizes across many industries improve their software delivery performance. Steve is a former startup CTO, systems and release engineer, finance IT manager, tech support phone jockey, and pizza maker. He currently leads several tech communities and serves as a board advisor for the Value Stream Management Consortium, and as co-chair for the Value Stream Management Interoperability technical committee.

Al Shalloway is the CEO of Success Engineering and is renowned for developing FLEX (FLow for Enterprise Transformation) which is the basis for PMI's Disciplined Agile Value Stream Consultant workshop. He has since created the Amplio system which is getting recognition as a leading Lean-Agile approach. Holding master's degrees from MIT and Emory in EE and computer science and mathematics, he's an international speaker, former SPC Trainer, and SAFe® contributor. He is also the co-author of 7 books, spanning Design Patterns to Agile at Scale. Al is an influential figure in Lean, SAFe®, Kanban, Scrum, Design Patterns, and ATDD. Al empowers clients to implement Agile practices at scale and trains internal change agents for efficient team development.

Table of Contents

2

Solving Complex Business Problems with Agility 25

3

Establishing Lean Flows to Improve Productivity 49

5

Introducing the VSM Implementation Roadmap 113

6

Navigating Value Stream Optimization 135

7

Connecting the Value Stream Network 163

Part 3: Achieving Lean-Agile and VSM Mastery: For Product-Oriented Business Transformations

8

Implementing the Basic Lean-Agile Solution Team (BLAST) 191

Part 4: Driving Sustainable Transformation: Strategies to Achieve Lean-Agile Mastery

10

11

Preface

"*The Lean-Agile Way: Unleashing Enterprise Potential with Value Stream Management*" emerged from the collaborative efforts of lead author Cecil 'Gary' Rupp and esteemed colleagues Richard Knaster, Steve Pereira, and Al Shalloway. Together, they aimed to provide a comprehensive guide on modern Lean-Agile and value stream management practices tailored for IT specialists, business professionals, and domain experts across diverse industries and organizations.

Their journey began when Packt Publishing approached Gary to write a new book on modern Lean-Agile practices. Gary was drawn to this topic because of his long-term interest in it, which was fueled by his past practitioner and consulting experiences. Additionally, recent training engagements, including the delivery of an extensive online course to 600 IT specialists for a multinational client, reinforced his enthusiasm for exploring this area. Gary then approached his three colleagues to join him.

The collaborative effort of the authoring team ensures a rich and diverse perspective throughout this book, enriching the discourse and broadening its scope and relevance. It's worth noting that the authors are not academics in the formal sense; rather, they are professionals who work closely with their clients in real-world scenarios, tackling challenges head-on to facilitate effective work processes.

The primary objective of this book is to introduce the integration of Lean and Agile principles and practices, recognizing the evolution of Lean from manufacturing industries and Agile from the software industry. Lean principles focus on eliminating waste and streamlining processes to deliver value more efficiently with higher quality. At the same time, Agile methodologies prioritize iterative development and constant feedback to enhance responsiveness to customer needs.

The integration of Lean and Agile concepts, often referred to as '*Lean-Agile*,' leverages the strengths of both approaches. It ensures high-quality, efficient deliveries and the ability to adapt to evolving market dynamics, thereby driving sustained competitive advantage.

At its core lies the fundamental premise that organizations must embrace Lean-Agile principles and practices holistically across the enterprise. This involves optimizing productivity, throughput, and efficiency while remaining sufficiently flexible to adapt to changing business requirements, market dynamics, and customer needs.

Central to this approach is the concept of value stream management (VSM), advocated by the authors for driving continuous improvements across organizational value streams. Value streams organize the end-to-end business processes within organizations, serving as a more effective framework for delivering value to customers. The VSM concept helps organizations break down the cross-functional and departmental barriers that often impede efficient deliveries. By focusing on product-oriented activities and processes, value streams emphasize the importance of delivering value through the development and delivery of customer-centric products and services.

Aligned with their belief that methods must precede tools, the authors present a nine-step VSM methodology designed to assist organizations in identifying and prioritizing value stream improvements efficiently. At the core of this methodology lies value stream mapping, a critical technique for visualizing and analyzing business processes to pinpoint opportunities for enhancing efficiency and reducing waste.

In this book, the authors introduce advanced concepts focused on evaluating value stream improvements across a spectrum, ranging from early-stage development to maturity, characterized by standardized activities, high throughput, quality, and efficient flows. Additionally, they present the Basic Lean-Agile Solutions Teams (BLAST) framework, designed to integrate the work of multiple teams collaboratively using both Lean flow and Agile iterative and incremental development practices. This book also introduces the Business Agility System for the Enterprise (BASE) concepts, which integrates work across an enterprise to produce customer-centric increments of new product-oriented value continuously and on cadence.

In an era dominated by digital technologies, effective information use has revolutionized organizational competitiveness. The authors introduce the Business-Role-Information-Action (BRIA) process as a means to find the information needed to make informed and timely decisions. Beyond theory, BRIA offers practical strategies for harnessing digital advancements to improve business processes, systems, products, and services.

This book is structured into four parts, progressing systematically from foundational concepts to advanced strategies for organizational transformation. Each section offers actionable insights and guidance to facilitate seamless adoption and sustained practice. However, those who are time-limited and need to cut to the chase should read *Part 4* (*Chapters 10, 11, and 12*) first, as these summary-level chapters discuss data and information management, Lean-Agile and VSM implementation, and cross-cutting themes.

As you embark on this learning journey, bear in mind the significance of collaboration and collective wisdom in driving meaningful change. The authors' goal is not only to disseminate information but also to empower individuals and organizations to embrace Lean-Agile principles with confidence and competence.

While intentionally remaining neutral among the plethora of methodologies and frameworks promoting Lean-Agile and Value Stream Management concepts, the authors focus on advocating foundational principles and practices essential for driving enterprise change toward continuous, customer-centric, and value-based improvements.

Most importantly, the methods, tools, and frameworks presented in this book are designed to simplify and sustain Lean-Agile adoptions, even within organizations already invested in other Lean-Agile frameworks. The authors cut through the clutter, distilling concepts for practical implementation and enduring success.

You are invited to join the authors on this odyssey of discovery—a journey towards Lean-Agile mastery and value stream management, where the quest for excellence and innovation knows no bounds. Welcome to *The Lean-Agile Way: Unleashing Enterprise Potential with Value Stream Management.*

Who this book is for

This book is for business and technology professionals striving to optimize value delivery while minimizing costs. Whether you're a VSM manager, a member of a product delivery team, a DevOps engineer, or an IT specialist, this book offers proven methods for effectively identifying and implementing improvement opportunities. Product owners looking to prioritize backlog items and corporate executives aiming to demonstrate positive returns on information technology investments will also find this book helpful.

Get in touch

Feedback from our readers is always welcome.

General feedback: If you have questions about any aspect of this book, email us at `customercare@packtpub.com` and mention the book title in the subject of your message.

Errata: Although we have taken every care to ensure the accuracy of our content, mistakes do happen. If you have found a mistake in this book, we would be grateful if you would report this to us. Please visit `www.packtpub.com/support/errata` and fill in the form.

Piracy: If you come across any illegal copies of our works in any form on the internet, we would be grateful if you would provide us with the location address or website name. Please contact us at `copyright@packtpub.com` with a link to the material.

If you are interested in becoming an author: If there is a topic that you have expertise in and you are interested in either writing or contributing to a book, please visit `authors.packtpub.com`.

Share Your Thoughts

Once you've read *The Lean-Agile Way*, we'd love to hear your thoughts! Scan the QR code below to go straight to the Amazon review page for this book and share your feedback.

`https://packt.link/r/1835461875`

Your review is important to us and the tech community and will help us make sure we're delivering excellent quality content.

Download a free PDF copy of this book

Thanks for purchasing this book!

Do you like to read on the go but are unable to carry your print books everywhere?

Is your eBook purchase not compatible with the device of your choice?

Don't worry, now with every Packt book you get a DRM-free PDF version of that book at no cost.

Read anywhere, any place, on any device. Search, copy, and paste code from your favorite technical books directly into your application.

The perks don't stop there, you can get exclusive access to discounts, newsletters, and great free content in your inbox daily

Follow these simple steps to get the benefits:

1. Scan the QR code or visit the link below

`https://packt.link/free-ebook/978-1-83546-187-7`

2. Submit your proof of purchase
3. That's it! We'll send your free PDF and other benefits to your email directly

Part 1: Building on Lean-Agile Foundations: Mastering the Basics

In *Part I* of this book, we delve into the challenges of competing in the **digital age**. Today's business and technology professionals must navigate increasingly complex environments while continuously delivering value to customers and the business to remain relevant.

In response to rapidly shifting market dynamics and internal organizational challenges, professionals must actively engage in continuous learning, process optimization, and teamwork to achieve superior outcomes. This journey isn't just about survival; it's about taking the lead, fostering innovation, and setting new benchmarks in a competitive arena.

In this section, we explain why mastering the concepts behind Lean and Agile principles and practices is necessary to improve an organization's ability to efficiently deliver customer-centric value and enhance business processes and products through digital solutions.

We then take a deeper dive into the basics of Lean and Agile practices. In *Chapter 2*, you'll learn how Agile-based practices leverage an iterative and incremental development approach to address complex business problems, support strategic and tactical planning, and continuously deliver new value through processes, business systems, artifacts, products, and services.

In *Chapter 3*, you learn how Lean practices help optimize productivity, efficiency, and quality, and accelerate your ability to deliver customer-centric value. Embracing these Lean-Agile principles can help propel you to the forefront of the digital revolution.

By absorbing the insights in the following chapters, you'll elevate your professional skills and competencies, positioning yourself as a true leader at the forefront of change:

- *Chapter 1, Navigating Lean-Agile Transformations*
- *Chapter 2, Solving Complex Business Problems with Agility*
- *Chapter 3, Establishing Lean Flows to Improve Productivity*

1
Navigating Lean-Agile Transformations

"The man who grasps principles can successfully select his own methods. The man who tries methods, ignoring principles, is sure to have trouble."

- Harrington Emerson

Imagine a world where companies invest millions in business transformations and digital solutions but still struggle to meet customer demands and enhance products. This unfortunate reality is all too common today. Welcome to this book, where we'll uncover the secrets of mastering Lean and Agile practices to improve the ability to efficiently deliver customer-centric value while enhancing business processes and products through digital solutions.

Lean principles boost productivity and efficiency, while **Agile** methodologies help manage change, solve problems, plan, and drive product development. This chapter explores why Lean and Agile are crucial complements for delivering high-value products and services. We'll also emphasize the pivotal role of **Value Stream Management** (**VSM**) in delivering value from the customers' perspectives.

Lean and Agile are not limited to software development. Organizations can apply Lean-Agile concepts to optimize business processes, product development life cycles, and flow across value streams of all types. Similarly, digital enhancements can improve business processes, product features, functions, and value stream flows. By mastering these concepts, you'll navigate transformative practices and witness their impact in real-world scenarios.

The following topics will be covered in this chapter:

- Charting the digital frontier
- Exploring Lean principles
- Embracing Agile methodologies
- Combining Lean with Agile
- Unlocking value with VSM
- Leveraging IT for Lean-Agile transformation

Charting the digital frontier

Part 1 of this book introduces the contemporary business landscape that requires the attention of all companies, government agencies, and non-profit organizations. Our global economy is undergoing rapid and disruptive change driven by digital technologies and digitally enhanced products. This section briefly introduces the concepts behind Lean, Agile, and VSM practices in a digital context.

Understanding the digital economy's landscape

The concept of the digital economy is more than just a trend. It's a new business paradigm. The term *digital economy* came into use in the 1990s and was the subject of Don Tapscott's 1995 book, *The Digital Economy: Promise and Peril in the Age of Networked Intelligence.*[1] As digital computing technologies and the internet have evolved, they've significantly transformed how businesses operate, particularly in eBusiness and eCommerce. Today, the lines between digital and traditional economies are increasingly blurred, making it challenging to distinguish between the two.

The digital economy is built on countless daily online exchanges. These exchanges involve diverse participants – from individuals with disparate roles and responsibilities to various entities, such as companies, government agencies, schools, and charitable organizations. Their interactions extend across numerous digital platforms, encompassing everything from large-scale servers to personal devices such as laptops, smartphones, and wearable technology.

Disruptive technology has broad implications. Players such as **Airbnb**, **Amazon**, and **Uber** do more than challenge the norm; they have redefined people's responsibilities, requisite skills, knowledge, and job opportunities. Navigating this enormous change demands more than tech comprehension – it requires a digital-first mindset. Those leveraging these connections will be able to compete as data-driven relationships between businesses and customers become the norm.

Embracing Lean-Agile and VSM in the digital economy

Lean-Agile principles present a robust structure for staying agile and adaptable to relentless change while remaining productive and efficient. These principles underpin businesses' ability to swiftly adapt, refine operations, and consistently offer value in a digital world marked by rapid shifts.

VSM complements Lean and Agile, providing a holistic viewpoint to identify, assess, and enhance value flow from end to end.

Pairing Lean, Agile, and VSM practices is the secret sauce for surviving and excelling in the digital economy. These methods are more than survival tools; they're the scaffolding upon which sustainable, competitive, and ever-evolving businesses can be built.

Let's begin our exploration with an introduction to Lean Thinking.

Exploring the hallmarks of Lean Thinking

The goal of Lean is to maximize customer value, quality, and efficiency by minimizing waste and non-value-adding costs while optimizing delivery speed and throughput. The elimination of waste is the hallmark of Lean principles, as depicted in *Figure 1.1*:

Figure 1.1 – Classic eight wastes of Lean

The essence of Lean is simple: organizations should refrain from investing in endeavors that produce excess work, features, or capabilities that customers neither desire nor find valuable. Failing to do so might drive external or internal customers to seek alternative products or services. The complexity lies in determining what customers need and the level of quality they anticipate while eliminating any elements that fail to align with their objectives. Lean practitioners refer to these excesses as **waste**.

A Lean enterprise's imperative is continuously maximizing customer value at the lowest possible cost by minimizing waste. The objective is not to reduce staff numbers to achieve these goals, but rather to optimize workforce utilization. The focus is on avoiding and eliminating existing wasteful activities and processes, streamlining workflows, and ensuring that resources are allocated effectively to enhance productivity and deliver superior value to customers.

Figure 1.2 illustrates four focus areas and the 14 elements of Lean Thinking as illustrated in *Figure 1.2*.

Key elements of Lean thinking			
Foundational principles	**Streamlined flows**	**Customer value**	**Optimized flows**
Continuous improvement (Kaizen)	Waste reduction (Muda)	Customer-centricity	Eliminating unnecessary constraints
Quality improvement	Value stream mapping	Productivity	Pull-oriented systems
Employee involvement	Standardized work	Efficiency	
Respect for people	Visual management	Cost reduction	

Figure 1.2 – Key elements of Lean Thinking

Foundational principles

The foundational principles focus area centers on the fostering a culture of perpetual enhancement through practices such as continuous improvement (**Kaizen**) and quality improvement, alongside promoting active employee involvement and cultivating respect for people.

Streamlining flows

The streamlined flows focus area emphasizes optimization of processes by targeting waste reduction (**Muda**) and employing tools such as VSM and value stream mapping to identify and eliminate inefficiencies. Additionally, Lean advocates for standardization of work procedures and utilizes visual management techniques to enhance clarity and efficiency across operations.

Customer value

The customer value focus area revolves around aligning organizational efforts with customer needs to enhance their overall satisfaction and loyalty. This involves optimizing productivity, efficiency, and cost-reduction strategies to deliver products and services that maximize customer value.

Optimized flows

The optimized flow focus area advocates implementing pull-oriented production control systems, starting new work based on upstream demand signals, thus minimizing waste, and enhancing responsiveness to customer needs.

Having established the key elements of Lean thinking, we will now explore why they are so critical.

Prioritizing Lean methodologies – redefining operational excellence

Too often, in less disciplined organizations, we fall into a trap where everything becomes a priority, which leads to conflict, constant firefighting, and employee burnout. However, Lean organizations cut through all that clutter by constantly evaluating changes that have the greatest impact on adding value to their customers. Through the elimination of constraints and waste and leveraging the resources available, Lean organizations maintain a focus on what truly matters, which sustains competitive advantage and avoids all the issues associated with making everything a priority.

In Lean organizations, operational excellence is not just a goal, but a guiding principle ingrained in every aspect of the organization. Unlike traditional management structures, where inefficiencies may be tolerated or overlooked, Lean organizations prioritize continuous improvement, waste reduction, and customer value creation as core tenets of their operations. By systematically adopting Lean practices and principles, these organizations achieve streamlined processes, empowered employees, and a culture of relentless innovation. From the Agile teams or shop floor to the boardroom, Lean organizations differentiate themselves by their unwavering commitment to efficiency, quality, and customer satisfaction.

This is a book on the integration of Lean and Agile practices. So, now that we have a high-level understanding of the fundamental goals and elements of the Lean enterprise, let's explore Agile principles and practices to see how they contrast with Lean.

Embracing Agile methodologies

While Lean principles focus on enhancing efficiency and productivity, Agile practices serve as an effective approach to develop new solutions and address business challenges. Agile prioritizes enhancing business agility, enabling organizations to embrace changes to retain value and competitiveness.

Agile introduces methods and tools that facilitate proactive change, foster creativity, and promote innovation, allowing you to tackle complex problems. Unlike Lean's continuous flow philosophy, Agile advocates an *iterative and incremental* timeboxed approach empowering teams to create new value in rapid development cycles that align work with customers' evolving needs and the dynamic business landscape.

This book provides actionable insights into how Agile's iterative development and incremental delivery mindset can accelerate problem-solving and innovation, benefiting your professional career by honing essential skills. Let's commence by grasping the core Agile concepts that will empower your professional journey.

Understanding the origins of Agile

To comprehend Agile methodologies, it's essential to understand their origins. While Lean principles originated in auto manufacturing, particularly at Toyota, Agile emerged from the software industry. This stark contrast sheds light on their unique approaches to achieving efficiency and delivering value.

Lean principles trace their lineage to post-World War II Japan, where Toyota grappled with limited resources and the aftermath of a global conflict. To thrive under these constraints, Toyota developed Lean practices, focusing on optimizing processes and conserving resources to deliver maximum value with minimal waste, laying the foundation for efficient production systems.

In contrast, Agile methodologies originated in the dynamic realm of software development. Engineers and developers faced a fundamental problem – traditional linear-sequential and plan-driven project management approaches couldn't cope with the unpredictability of software projects. Agile introduced an iterative development paradigm with rapid deliveries, encouraging small, valuable increments of a product to address evolving requirements and ensure customer satisfaction and product excellence.

Expanding Agile – beyond software development

While Agile's origins may be in software, its principles have proven highly adaptable and beneficial across various industries and business domains. Agile's iterative and incremental development approach has found application in sectors ranging from healthcare and manufacturing to marketing and education, offering opportunities for teams to excel.

Therefore, organizations seeking sustainable competitive advantage should recognize that the Agile mindset extends beyond software development, enhancing teamwork and driving continuous improvement across all business domains. This evolution of Agile from a specialized software development approach to a versatile problem-solving and innovation methodology underscores its enduring relevance and impact. It equips teams with a valuable skill set to remain competitive and drive success.

With this understanding, let's now explore how the Agile workflow differs from the pull-oriented concepts of Lean.

Iterating to deliver incremental value

Agile methodologies prioritize iterative value creation, avoiding upfront requirement predictions that often quickly become irrelevant and a costly form of waste. Instead, they advocate continuous development of small, valuable product increments with active customer and stakeholder involvement, promoting flexibility, adaptability, and responsiveness. This approach contrasts with Lean's pull-oriented approach, which focus on streamlining processes and minimizing waste through continuous flow. Agile engages in timeboxed iterations, typically lasting 1 to 4 weeks, where work is pulled from a product backlog based on priorities and readiness, enabling focused development efforts. Unlike Lean's continuous flow, Agile ensures a collaborative yet structured environment by assigning work based on individual capacity and skills. Some Agile teams integrate Lean elements such as Kanban to further optimize workflows, highlighting the flexibility of both methodologies.

Understanding these foundational concepts and Agile's historical context prepares you to explore its practices and applications effectively. Next, we'll discuss the importance of organizing work across multiple small teams.

Harnessing the power of small, collaborative teams

Agile methodologies strongly advocate using small teams, typically composed of three to seven members, with a maximum limit of 9. This emphasis on small teams extends across various business domains, including the organization of value streams, for several reasons.

Firstly, small teams have a clearer focus on their goals and a stronger sense of purpose, enabling them to effectively align their work toward shared common objectives. Small teams are renowned for their agility and making decisions swiftly and operating efficiently, thus adapting to changes in the market or evolving customer needs.

Additionally, small teams foster better communication among members, leading to open, transparent, and effective lines of communication. They tend to have more engaged employees who take the initiative and drive innovation. Collaboration and mutual support are facilitated within small teams, with members trusting each other readily and assisting one another when needed.

Moreover, small teams can specialize in certain areas while ensuring they remain self-contained with all required skills in-house. This enhances accountability as everyone's contributions are visible, leaving no room for favoritism or bureaucratic hurdles. If you need more people, add more small teams and teach them how to synchronize and integrate their work. We'll discuss this topic in more detail in *Chapter 8, Implementing Basic Lean-Agile Solutions Teams (BLAST).*

We've completed our brief introduction to Lean and Agile concepts as separate strategies for productivity improvements and organizational agility. In the next section, we'll start to bring them together as complementary practices.

Combining Lean with Agile

As you explore the intricacies of Lean and Agile in this book, you'll come to appreciate that each methodology brings a distinct set of principles, practices, and advantages to the table. Across industries, Lean's strength lies in its ability to reduce waste and optimize processes. Conversely, Agile applies an iterative development and incremental delivery process that emphasizes adaptability, flexibility, and customer-centricity.

But here's where it becomes interesting. The true magic unfolds when you bring these two approaches together, as described in the next section.

Living in a Lean-Agile house

So far, we have explored Lean and Agile principles and practices in isolation. Now, it's time to bring them together. To do that, we need to grasp the characteristics that define a Lean-Agile enterprise.

To kick off our introduction, we'll explore our **House of Lean-Agile**, as depicted in *Figure 1.3*. This figure depicts an evolved rendition of the traditional **House of Lean** .

Figure 1.3 – The House of Lean-Agile

This contemporary adaptation expands upon the foundational principles beyond their Lean origins, providing a visual representation of Lean-Agile management within organizations.

Originating from Toyota and integral to its ascent as a global automotive leader, the *House of Lean* initially symbolized a steadfast commitment to refining operational processes for optimal efficiency and effectiveness. Our updated model, the *House of Lean-Agile*, retains this dedication while integrating Agile methodologies, emphasizing iterative changes that incrementally deliver new value to our customers.

Let's consider each aspect of the House of Lean-Agile.

Establishing a strong foundation

The foundation of our Lean-Agile house represents the key enablers for business success. This includes the following:

- **Lifelong learning**: Crucial for staying competitive, lifelong learning in a Lean-Agile house prioritizes continuous development for individuals and the organization. By dedicating resources to learning, teams can adapt to market demands, acquire new skills, and drive innovation.
- **Building quality in**: Quality is central in Lean-Agile houses, with a relentless focus on delivering excellence in products and services. Embedding quality into every development aspect minimizes errors or defects, enhances satisfaction, and builds a reputation for reliability.
- **Adapt and evolve**: Essential for survival in a rapidly changing landscape, Lean-Agile houses embrace adaptation and evolution. By monitoring trends, responding to feedback, and innovating, organizations stay ahead and remain resilient.
- **Minimize waste and constraints**: Lean-Agile teams identify and eliminate waste to boost efficiency and productivity. Streamlining processes, reducing complexity, and optimizing resources deliver value to customers quicker, improve quality, and cut costs.
- **Five principles of Lean**: Offering an optimization framework, Lean principles guide process improvement and waste elimination. The five principles are considered a recipe for improving workplace efficiency and include:

    I. Defining value

    II. Mapping the value stream

    III. Creating flow

    IV. Establishing a pull system

    V. Pursuing perfection

- **Agile Manifesto**: Marking a seismic shift in software development, the Agile Manifesto promoted flexibility, collaboration, and customer-centricity. In Lean-Agile houses, it serves as a guiding philosophy for iterative development, adaptive planning, and problem-solving, extending its applicability beyond software to any domain requiring agility and innovation.

Next, we'll look at each of the three pillars supporting our Lean-Agile house.

Supporting pillars in our Lean-Agile house

While the foundation provides the strength to uphold our Lean-Agile house, we require a framework to bolster the functionality of our organization. Our Lean-Agile house consists of three primary pillars for this purpose.

Pillar 1 – respect for people

In the Lean-Agile enterprise, respecting people is more than a lofty ideal; it is a pivotal force propelling organizations toward excellence. Respect for individuals and teams is critical because if they are unhappy, they may disengage, leave, or even sabotage the organization's efforts. This fact underscores the significance of cultivating a culture of respect and recognition within Lean-Agile environments to ensure sustained productivity and success.

Fostering a work environment that values and respects every individual's contribution is key to cultural change. It focuses on creating a positive, safe, and performance-driven culture where trust and respect form the foundation.

The following three areas are fundamental in demonstrating respect for people within the Lean-Agile organization:

- **Understand and respect others**: Both Lean and Agile stress the importance of understanding and respecting others while fostering collaborative environments. Embracing diverse skills enriches teams, while detractors undermine value and hinder performance. Lean-Agile prioritizes lifelong learning, quality, and waste reduction for competitiveness, guided by continuous improvement and customer-centricity principles.
- **Develop people**: In Lean and Agile, developing people fosters continuous improvement and adaptability. Empowering individuals enhances problem-solving, innovation, and value delivery, enabling swift responses to change and success in dynamic environments. Individuals take responsibility for their development, encouraged by principles of continuous learning and personal growth, aligning with Agile's collaborative, iterative nature.
- **Foster trust and employee engagement**: Trust and engagement are crucial in Lean-Agile, facilitating teamwork and innovation. Effective collaboration and change acceptance enhance productivity and satisfaction, while engaged employees drive organizational goals and continuous improvement. This culture of empowerment, central to Lean-Agile, enables self-organized teams to deliver high value to customers.

In conclusion, it should be evident that the value of respect extends beyond mere courtesy. It serves as a strategic core value in Lean-Agile organizations, cultivating an environment where continuous improvement and collaboration are encouraged and expected. Embracing respect as a core value is essential for any organization aspiring to thrive in today's fast-paced, ever-changing world.

Pillar 2 – optimize flow

Efficient flow is essential for any Lean-Agile organization striving to deliver value to its customers effectively and continuously. In this subsection, we'll explore the three key strategies for optimizing flow within the organization. By organizing around value, ensuring uninterrupted flow, and decentralizing execution, organizations can streamline their processes, reduce waste, and enhance overall efficiency.

- **Organize around value**: Organizing operations around value entails aligning production resources according to value streams, mapping out workflows, and identifying areas for improvement to streamline processes and enhance efficiency
- **Make value flow without interruption**: Adopting pull-oriented production control systems prevents excess work and bottlenecks while identifying and eliminating constraints ensures a steady flow of value by removing obstacles and avoiding unnecessary work-in-progress
- **Decentralize execution**: Decentralizing decision-making empowers teams to respond swiftly to customer needs and market changes, fostering agility and adaptability to maintain an efficient flow of value

In conclusion, optimizing flow is integral to the Lean-Agile organization's ability to deliver value to customers efficiently and continuously. By organizing around value, ensuring uninterrupted flow, and decentralizing execution, organizations can streamline their processes, reduce waste, and enhance overall efficiency. Embracing these principles allows organizations to adapt and thrive in today's dynamic and competitive business environment.

Pillar 3 – continuously improve (Kaizen)

At the heart of Lean-Agile philosophy lies the commitment to continuous improvement, known as **Kaizen**. This section explores the principles of ongoing, iterative, and incremental development, which are central to driving organizational growth and success. By embracing the concepts of *"Go and see"* (**Gemba**), iteratively improving, and enhancing productivity while reducing costs, organizations can continuously evolve and adapt to meet the ever-changing needs of customers and markets.

- **Go and see (Gemba)**: Gemba, or "Go and see," underscores the importance of firsthand observation in understanding the work environment, identifying inefficiencies, and fostering collaboration with frontline workers to optimize workflows and enhance productivity
- **Iterative and incremental improvements**: Lean-Agile philosophy embraces iterative improvement, encouraging small, incremental changes based on feedback and experimentation to adapt quickly to changing requirements and drive continuous innovation and value delivery
- **Improve productivity and reduce cost**: Lean-Agile organizations prioritize improving productivity and efficiency through process optimization, waste elimination, and non-value-adding cost reduction measures, enabling accelerated delivery of high-quality products and services while maximizing resource allocation and maintaining competitiveness

In conclusion, the commitment to continuous improvement, embodied by the principles of "Go and see" (Gemba), iterative improvement, and productivity enhancement through waste elimination, lies at the heart of the Lean-Agile philosophy. By embracing these principles, organizations can evolve and adapt to meet the ever-changing needs of customers and markets, driving sustainable growth and success in today's dynamic business environment.

Finding shelter in our Lean-Agile goals

The roof of the Lean-Agile house embodies the core goal of organizations adopting Lean-Agile practices: maximizing customer value, ensuring high-quality products and services, minimizing waste and non-value-adding costs, and optimizing speed and feedback:

- Organizations prioritize value creation by understanding customer needs, refining offerings, and delivering exceptional customer experiences to enhance customer loyalty and market competitiveness
- Quality is paramount, encompassing reliability, performance, and customer satisfaction, fostering trust and differentiation from competitors
- Minimizing waste and costs through streamlined operations and resource allocation enhances efficiency and innovation, sustaining competitiveness
- Speed and feedback optimization enable organizations to deliver value swiftly, adapt to market changes, and maintain a competitive edge

In summary, the Lean-Agile house's roof represents organizations' overarching goals, driving sustainable growth and customer satisfaction. These objectives lay the foundation for subsequent Lean practices and align closely with Agile values, which we'll explore further in the next chapter.

In the next section, we'll explore the business and product improvement principles upon which the House of Lean-Agile is built.

Synthesizing modern management principles

In exploration of modern leadership principles, the authors of this book humbly recognize that these ideas were not born of our own invention. Instead, they draw inspiration from the wisdom and innovations of esteemed predecessors. This list, while not exhaustive, provides examples of the following Lean-Agile leadership principles:

- **Agile and Lean influence**: Inspired by Agile and Lean philosophies, we embrace adaptability, collaboration, transparency, and continuous improvement. These principles reflect Agile and Lean mindsets, prioritizing response to change, valuing individuals, optimizing value flow, and fostering a culture of learning and efficiency.

- **Team of Teams approach**: General Stanley McChrystal's Team of Teams approach to work emphasizes decentralization and empowerment, aligning with our mission-driven autonomy principle. This approach empowers teams with clear missions and decision-making authority, fostering collaboration and responsiveness organization-wide.[2]
- **Flow economics**: Don Reinertsen's flow economics and batch size reduction insights resonate with our focus on optimizing value flow and embracing complexity. By prioritizing flow efficiency and economic trade-offs, leaders can enhance organizational competitiveness.[3]
- **Flow Framework**: Mik Kersten's Flow Framework guides the management of flow amidst digital disruption, shifting from project-oriented to product-centric views. By applying this framework, leaders navigate digital challenges, optimizing value flow in their organizations.[4]
- **Leader-Leader model**: David Marquet transformed a demoralized crew into an empowered, motivated fighting force. He replaced the military's traditional "leader-follower" structure with a "leader-leader" model that gave crew members autonomy over their work. The crew learned to think and act proactively, determining what was needed and the best way to do it rather than waiting for detailed directions.[5]
- **Knowledge creation**: Ikujiro Nonaka's focus on knowledge creation aligns with our shared vision principle. By fostering openness and knowledge sharing, leaders enable innovation and adaptation within their organizations.[6]
- **System management**: W. Edwards Deming's emphasis on active system management aligns with our adaptive empowerment principle. Leaders empower teams while guiding the overall system, promoting proactive problem-solving and continuous improvement.[7]
- **Embracing complexity**: This principle acknowledges the complexity of modern challenges, resonating with insights from thought leaders. Leaders encourage creative problem-solving, avoiding oversimplified solutions.

In summary, these Lean-Agile leadership principles offer a comprehensive approach that embodies the core philosophies of Agile and Lean, enriched by the insights of leadership pioneers. By implementing these principles, leaders can adeptly navigate the complexities of today's business landscape, empower their teams, and foster continuous improvement. This positions their organizations for success in an interconnected and rapidly changing world. Our Lean-Agile Leadership principles reflect the collaborative evolution of leadership thinking, shaped by the contributions of great minds and a shared pursuit of excellence.

Integrated practices for enhanced effectiveness

This subsection briefly introduces the importance of combining Lean and Agile, highlighting the intrinsic synergy that exists between these practices. While each methodology is robust in its own right, its integration elevates organizational effectiveness and responsiveness to new heights. It's not about replacing one with the other; it's about harnessing the strengths of both to create a harmonious and highly efficient culture within your organization.

Introducing the BLAST and BASE frameworks for Lean-Agile transformation

Elevating your understanding of how to integrate Lean and Agile practices at both the team of teams and enterprise levels, we'll introduce two key strategies later in this book: BLAST and BASE.

Chapter 8, Implementing Basic Lean-Agile Solutions Teams (BLAST), describes a framework designed to help organizations coordinate the activities of multiple teams involved in product or service delivery, planning, or working on resolving a complex business problem.

These teams may employ both Lean or Agile practices as the situation demands, but the real essence of the BLAST framework lies in establishing a collaborative structure between multiple teams. Here, teams learn to work together seamlessly, driving continuous improvements to enhance the value generated through the organization's products, services, and business systems.

Chapter 9, Defining a Business Agility System for the Enterprise (BASE), is a conceptual model and pattern language that integrates Lean and Agile practices at the enterprise level, enabling organizations to integrate, coordinate, and synchronize work across the entire enterprise. By embracing BASE, businesses can foster continuous improvements across product life-cycles, delivering customer-centric solutions with agility and innovation.

BASE doesn't add new roles or responsibilities. Instead, it provides a framework to align product development, delivery, and support activities to meet your customers' needs. The goal is to simplify, creating a product life cycle model that largely maintains the organization's existing roles and functions. However, the BASE framework integrates Lean and Agile principles to consistently deliver new value in a predictable pattern repeatably.

Since we've introduced the terms *framework* and *pattern languages*, let's define them in the context of Lean-Agile principles and practices.

Defining a Lean-Agile framework

A Lean-Agile framework provides a structured and comprehensive set of guidelines, principles, and practices that provide a foundation for organizing work, decision-making, and processes within an organization. It typically offers a high-level structure that helps define roles, responsibilities, and the flow of work.

For example, Lean-Agile frameworks, such as the **Scaled Agile Framework** (**SAFe**), **Disciplined Agile** (**DA**), **Scrum@Scale** (**S@S**), **NEXUS**, or **Large-Scale Scrum** (**LeSS**), offer a structured approach to scaling Agile practices across larger enterprises. Like BASE and BLAST, these frameworks establish a common language and a structured approach for teams to work together cohesively while adhering to Lean and Agile principles.

However, BASE and BLAST differ in their ability to align the work of multiple Lean and Agile teams to continuously deliver new increments of value following your organization's unique business practices, roles, responsibilities, domains of knowledge, and terms.

Defining a Lean-Agile pattern language

In our Lean-Agile methodology, a pattern language offers a carefully selected collection of proven practices to tackle recurring challenges within specific contexts. It provides adaptable patterns, each containing practices aimed at addressing identified problems and leveraging associated benefits.

These context-specific patterns can be tailored to meet project, team, or organizational needs while maintaining alignment with Lean and Agile principles.

For example, BASE and BLAST provide structured approaches to delivering value increments through products and services, following a cadence of minimum valuable increments (MVIs) and minimum valuable releases (MVRs). These approaches can be tailored by organizations to fit their unique industry and business requirements.

In summary, while Lean-Agile frameworks offer top-down organization and scalability, pattern languages provide bottom-up flexibility and context-aware solutions. Both are invaluable in Lean-Agile, with frameworks offering structure and guidance and pattern languages providing adaptability.

Now, let's shift our focus to prioritizing improvement activities. Organizations must strategically allocate their limited resources to activities with the highest impact, a topic we'll explore in the next subsection.

Avoiding local optimization with Value Stream Management (VSM)

VSM offers a strategic approach that avoids localized improvements by providing a comprehensive view of your organization's product delivery process. The issue with focusing on localized solutions is that they may not address the organization's actual constraints and can have minimal impact. By identifying and prioritizing enhancement opportunities across all areas, you can avoid the common pitfalls of local optimization and significantly increase the value delivered to customers.

VSM provides a powerful framework for examining every aspect of the product life cycle, from concept to delivery. It aligns with the BASE model principles, enabling thorough workflow examination, bottleneck identification, and value creation assessment. Implementing VSM fosters cross-functional collaboration and informed decision-making, paving the way for meaningful improvements.

Before we get into the mechanics of implementing BASE (in *Chapter 9*), *Chapter 4*, *Driving Improvements with Value Stream Management (VSM)*, will delve into practical implementation strategies for VSM. You'll receive a step-by-step guide to leveraging this methodology effectively, including techniques for identifying value streams, mapping them, and pinpointing areas for improvement. By that chapter's end, you'll possess the tools and knowledge necessary for informed decision-making that optimizes your organization's capacity to deliver value.

Now that we understand the importance of integrating Lean and Agile principles for customer-oriented value improvements, let's explore the cadence of deliveries.

Creating a cadence of continuous value delivery

In *Chapter 9, Defining a Business Agility System for the Enterprise (BASE)*, we'll learn how to implement a cadence to ensure the regular delivery of new increments of value through products and services. These increments, known as **minimum valuable increments** (**MVIs**), may contain improvements that enhance organizational flow or address critical business problems, minimizing waste.

Product enhancements and other business-oriented deliverables can be packaged and deployed within a single MVI, or multiple concurrent MVIs may be in flight - deployed as MVRs, each addressing different product and business needs. This flexibility distinguishes the **BASE framework**, which allows standalone MVIs to be released independently of others.

The concept of MVIs came about as an expansion on the ideas of 'minimum marketable product,' a term coined by Mark Denne and Jane Cleland-Huang in their 2003 book Software by Numbers. The word *Valuable* is used instead of *marketable* since not all increments are marketed – many are used internally – and it applies equally to businesses and government organizations.

In the BASE conceptual model MVIs encompass a range of deliverables, including products, enhancements, and improvements to business functions and value streams. Each MVI requires a product owner or value manager to assess and guide release priorities based on value considerations, gathering input from various stakeholders.

In the next section, in *Part 2* of this book, we'll explore how VSM provides the methods and tools necessary for making value-based determinations.

Unlocking value with Value Stream Management (VSM)

In this section, we'll briefly introduce the concepts behind VSM, a Lean-oriented practice that stands as a cornerstone in facilitating continuous and highly impactful improvements to enhance customer-centric value deliveries across your organization.

The evolving nature of VSM

A modern-day definition of VSM, as highlighted in a Forbes Innovation article by Flint Brenton, describes it as an Agile business practice aimed at evaluating the worth of software development and delivery endeavors and resources.[8] It's important to recognize that VSM has been a key part of value stream improvement since the early 2000s, originating in non-IT domains. In this book, you will learn how to apply VSM methods and tools to enhance software development and also to optimize any value stream within your organization.

Describing the VSM methodology

The concepts behind modern VSM practices originally evolved to support other domains than software. For example, you can find books on how to apply VSM as a method to assess value stream improvement opportunities in supply chain management, manufacturing, health care, administration and to create Lean office environments.

In *Chapter 4, Driving Improvements with Value Stream Management (VSM),* we'll introduce a common set of VSM steps to identify and prioritize your value stream improvement opportunities. These steps are depicted in *Figure 1.4*:

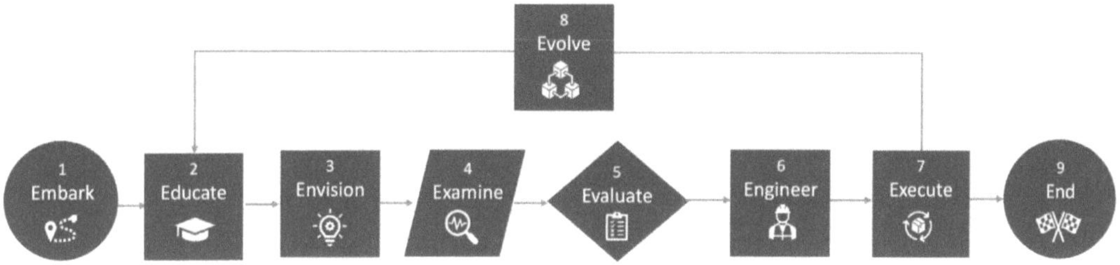

Figure 1.4 – Nine-step VSM methodology

These nine steps can be applied in any value stream assessment, regardless of the type of business domain, industry, government, or non-profit environment. The VSM process is genuinely universal.

So, whether you are in IT or any other business domain, you can apply these steps. In the next subsection that follows, you will find out where in this book you can learn more about the versatility of VSM.

Unveiling the versatility of VSM

The versatility of VSM extends beyond software development or IT, offering valuable support for enhancing value streams in various organizations. Understanding VSM practices is crucial for assessing high-impact improvement opportunities and aligning IT with broader organizational enhancements.

In *Chapter 3, Establishing Lean Flows to Improve Productivity*, you'll explore Lean-oriented production control systems, waste reduction, and constraint management strategies to improve flow across the organization's value streams. Additionally, *Chapter 3* highlights the significance of selecting appropriate metrics within integrated Lean-Agile practices. These insights pave the way for *Part 2, Attending to our Value Steams,* and specifically to *Chapter 4, Driving Improvements with Value Stream Management (VSM),* which delves into evaluating value stream improvements and their impact on customers and businesses, equipping you with practical skills for professional growth.

While *Chapter 4* provides us with a basic understanding of foundational VSM concepts, there is so much more to learn. For example, in *Chapter 6, Navigating Value Stream Optimization,* we'll learn the importance of shifting our mindsets from Projects to Products, and how to harness digital enhancements to support our business transformations. And, in *Chapter 7, Connecting the Value Stream Network,* we'll explore their role in optimizing value delivery capabilities within organizations. Through topics like mapping customer journeys and refining operations, *Chapter 7* demonstrates how aligning value stream networks enhances overall organizational efficiency and effectiveness.

Now that you understand the breath and scope of VSM, let's talk about some of its core principles.

Enhancing professional expertise with VSM

Acquiring knowledge about VSM enhances your professional toolkit, encompassing skills such as creating value stream maps, utilizing metrics for value assessments and productivity improvements, and establishing dedicated VSM improvement teams.

VSM is pivotal for identifying inefficiencies and improvement opportunities within organizational value streams. By visually mapping value stream flows, VSM methods and tools help identify bottlenecks and areas misaligned with customer-centric goals. In addition to visualization, key metrics such as cycle time, lead time, throughput, work in progress (WIP), changeover time, and defect rate are essential for prioritizing improvement opportunities.

Finally, forming skilled and impartial VSM teams is crucial for driving continuous enhancements across value streams, and maximizing improvement impact.

These teams serve as change catalysts, guiding organizations toward increased customer-centricity and value delivery. Moreover, they are the key to sustaining organizational transformations.

Leveraging IT for Lean-Agile transformation

Leveraging IT is crucial in driving Lean-Agile improvements across the organization. Digital enhancements play a pivotal role in enhancing business processes, products, and services. By focusing on IT, organizations can become leaner, improving productivity and efficiencies throughout their operations.

Additionally, the IT organization supports business agility by providing the necessary information to adapt and evolve rapidly, supporting emergent business focuses, changing market dynamics, and evolving customer needs. In essence, IT acts as a catalyst for organizational transformation, enabling businesses to stay competitive and responsive in today's dynamic marketplace.

But how do we determine the specific information required and its sources, as well as where to place our IT investment priorities? We'll cover that topic in *Chapter 5, Introducing the VSM Implementation Roadmap*. But let's start with a quick introduction in the next subsection.

Investing in IT value stream improvements

Investing in IT value stream improvements is crucial given the significant impact of digital enhancements on products, services, and critical business processes. To enhance productivity and efficiency within IT value streams, it's essential to invest in appropriate tooling and skills.

In Lean, VSM has long been recognized as a proven method for identifying and prioritizing value stream improvement investments. Now, the IT community has embraced these concepts to drive enhancements across their DevOps-based software delivery pipelines.

Modern IT VSM methods and tools provide a strategic framework for optimizing value stream processes, IT infrastructure, tooling, and software products. *Chapter 5, Introducing the VSM Implementation Roadmap*, delves into the **Value Stream Management Consortium's** (**VSMC's**) role in this effort, and its VSM implementation Roadmap, which is pivotal in advancing Lean-Agile and VSM concepts within the DevOps community.

DevOps emphasizes Lean-oriented flow strategies, improving value delivery by facilitating collaborations and integrating the work of development and operations teams. For a deeper understanding, Gary Rupp's book *Driving DevOps with Value Stream Management* further explores DevOps' significance, highlighting its reliance on Lean principles.[9]

With modern VSM tools, DevOps-based software delivery pipelines are enhanced, offering visibility to identify bottlenecks and enhance collaboration. This enhanced visibility, combined with analytics capabilities, helps the IT department drive value across the organization, by aligning *their activities to support* other value stream improvement initiatives.

Evaluating information requirements and flows

We now understand how DevOps pipelines with integrated VSM tools can help derive productivity and efficiency improvements in IT and provide visibility to align their work with the organization's priorities. However, to further that goal, we must also be able to understand how to improve decision making in a Lean-Agile enterprise. *Chapter 10, Enhancing Decision Making in the Lean Agile Organization*, provides guidance on how to evaluate the questions and information that have the most impact on driving business value. The core focus of this chapter is on teaching the BRIA process (short for Business, Role, Information, Action), a business intelligence framework that empowers you to define essential information needs. BRIA assists individuals at all levels of an organization in evaluating essential questions to determine the necessary data for creating informed decisions and taking appropriate actions.

This wraps up *Chapter 1, Navigating Lean-Agile Transformations*. By reading this chapter, you've gained valuable insight into what lies ahead in this book. We genuinely hope you'll find this book both engaging and valuable as you embark on your professional learning journey.

Summary

In this chapter, we delved into the foundational principles of Lean, Agile, and VSM. We explored their collective strength in enhancing product development, managing transformative changes, and driving continuous improvements, especially in a digitally evolving landscape. Through these lenses, we unveiled how Lean amplifies productivity, Agile aids in navigating complex challenges, and VSM provides a structured method for pinpointing and addressing pivotal improvement opportunities, ensuring that all endeavors are constantly aligned with customer perspectives.

As we advance to *Chapter 2, Solving Complex Business Problems with Agility*, we will dive deeper into Agile's organizational role in responding to change. We'll explore the intricacies of frameworks such as Scrum and emphasize the importance of inter-team collaboration across value streams. This upcoming chapter promises insights into achieving harmony among teams throughout product life cycles for optimal results.

Questions

This section is offered for those who want to evaluate comprehension and retention of the information provided in this chapter. There are 9 questions. The answers are provided in the subsection that follows. Recalling the exact verbiage across this book is not important. Instead, it's more important to recall the concepts and their applications.

Let's start:

1. Choose at least two of the four hallmarks of Lean

- Foundational lean principles
- Streamlining operations
- Delivering customer value
- Optimizing resources

2. True or false: Do Lean and Agile practices share common objectives?
3. What is another word that describes the iterative and incremental delivery process of mainstream Agile frameworks, such as Scrum and BLAST?
4. What is the Basic Lean-Agile Solutions Team (BLAST)?
5. What is the Business Agility System for the Enterprise (BASE)?
6. How does this book compare the relative strengths of Agile and Lean practices?
7. Identify the nine VSM steps used to identify and prioritize your value stream improvement opportunities.
8. Where did the value steam mapping concepts evolve, and what were they originally called?
9. Why is the BRIA concept so important?

Answers

1. Two hallmarks are Lean are: Foundational lean principles and Delivering customer value.
2. True: Lean and Agile practices share many common objectives, such as delivering customer-centric value, continuous improvements, making information visible, responsiveness, and respect for people.

3. Timeboxed is another word that describes the iterative and incremental delivery process of mainstream Agile frameworks, such as Scrum and BLAST.
4. A Basic Lean-Agile Solutions Team (BLAST) is a framework and pattern language that's designed to help organizations orchestrate the activities of multiple teams involved in product delivery.
5. Business Agility System for the Enterprise (BASE) is a conceptual model and pattern language that's designed to help organizations orchestrate the activities of multiple teams involved in product delivery.
6. This book compares the relative strengths of Agile and Lean practices as follows:

   A. Lean's strength lies in its ability to reduce waste, optimize processes, and drive efficiency across various industries.

   B. Agile applies an iterative development and incremental delivery process that emphasizes activities of multiple teams involved in product delivery.

7. The following nine VSM steps are used to identify and prioritize value stream improvement opportunities:

   1. Embark
   2. Educate
   3. Envision
   4. Examine
   5. Evaluate
   6. Engineer
   7. Execute
   8. Evolve
   9. End

8. VSM concepts originated from Lean manufacturing and were originally referred to as "*Material and Information Flow Mapping*" at Toyota, where the methods were initially conceived.
9. BRIA is a business intelligence framework that empowers you to define essential information needs. Its important because it helps people at all levels within an organization evaluate the questions they must be able to answer at a moment's notice, what information they need to answer those questions, what decisions they will need to make, and finally, what actions they should logically take.

Further Reading

1. Tapscott, D. (1995). The Digital Economy: Promise and Peril In The Age of Networked Intelligence (1st ed.). McGraw Hill.
2. McChrystal, G. S. (2015). Team of Teams: New Rules of Engagement for a Complex World. Portfolio.
3. Reinertsen, D. G. (2009). The Principles of Product Development Flow: Second Generation Lean Product Development. Celeritas Publishing.
4. Kersten, M. (2018). Project to Product: How to Survive and Thrive in the Age of Digital Disruption with the Flow Framework. IT Revolution Press.
5. Marquet, L. D. (2013). Turn the Ship Around!: A True Story of Turning Followers into Leaders. Portfolio.
6. Nonaka, I., & Takeuchi, H. (1995). The Knowledge-Creating Company: How Japanese Companies Create the Dynamics of Innovation. Oxford University Press.
7. Deming, W. E. (2000). Out of the Crisis. MIT Press.
8. Brenton, F. (2019, July 8). What Is Value Stream Management? A Primer For Enterprise Leadership. Forbes Innovation Article. Retrieved from `https://www.forbes.com/sites/forbestechcouncil/2019/07/08/what-is-value-stream-management-a-primer-for-enterprise-leadership/?sh=417c93d27b67`
9. Rupp, C. G. (2022). Driving DevOps with Value Stream Management. Packt Publishing Ltd.
10. Denne, M., & Cleland-Huang, J. (2003). Software by Numbers: Low-Risk, High-Return Development. Pearson. Upper Saddle River, NJ.

2

Solving Complex Business Problems with Agility

"Agility is the ability to adapt and respond to change … agile organizations view change as an opportunity, not a threat."

– Jim Highsmith

In today's fast-paced business world, understanding and mastering agility is not just a competitive edge – it's a necessity. You and the teams you support face an array of complex business problems. Traditional business management methods often don't measure up, driving the need for more Agile and collaborative approaches. This chapter delves into the essence of agility, highlighting its foundational principles and illustrating its pivotal role in resolving intricate business challenges.

This chapter introduces the core concepts behind organizational agility, the mechanics behind Agile methodologies, the importance of implementing smaller teams, and essential insights on managing collaboration across diverse teams. By this chapter's conclusion, your understanding will go beyond theoretical concepts, and you'll be armed with the knowledge to champion agility and collaboration in your professional endeavors.

In the broader context of your professional career and the ever evolving business landscape, agility is fundamental to modern success. Embracing these concepts will elevate your professional development and empower you and your teams to pioneer innovation, foster adaptability, and adeptly navigate the complexities of today's digital and business environments.

This chapter covers the following topics:

- Embodying organizational agility
- Embracing Agile frameworks for collaboration
- Amplifying team efficacy with Scrum
- Facilitating effective collaboration through Scrum collaboration
- Embracing the **Team-of-Teams** (**ToT**) approach

Technical requirements

Scrum is the reference Agile framework for the practices taught in this chapter. Though not necessary, having a basic understanding of Agile practices and frameworks, such as Scrum, will help you understand the information provided. For additional learning, we recommend Cecil Rupp's book *Scaling Scrum Across Modern Enterprises: Implement Scrum and Lean-Agile Techniques Across Complex Products, Portfolios, and Programs in Large Organizations.*[12]

Embodying organizational agility

In an era where rapid change and unpredictability dominate the business landscape, organizations are compelled to adapt and evolve swiftly. Embodying organizational agility is no longer just a competitive advantage – it's a fundamental requirement for survival and sustained success. As we delve into this section, we'll explore what it truly means for an organization to be Agile, its benefits, and its transformative impact on every facet of a business.

Understanding the foundations of business agility

At its core, agility is built on a framework of principles, practices, and behaviors that equip organizations to maneuver effectively through complex environments. It's not merely about reacting quickly but understanding and anticipating market dynamics to make informed decisions.

Central to this adaptive prowess is the embrace of fault-tolerant experimentation. This practice urges organizations to encourage innovation through trial and error, understanding that occasional missteps can offer critical insights, but minimizing risks through small and frequent change iterations. The freedom to test, learn, and iterate becomes a driving force behind true agility.

Beyond the buzzword, agility is a structured approach that relies on clear communication, collaboration, continuous learning, and adaptability. This chapter will explore the foundational elements that make up organizational agility, enabling businesses to navigate with foresight and fluidity in an ever-changing landscape.

Applying Agile principles

Principles are fundamental truths or beliefs. However, Agile principles go beyond mere suggestions. To act on them, we need to establish a new mindset emphasizing customer collaboration, a willingness to respond to change, and a focus on delivering real value quickly.

Business agility is grounded in principles that enable organizations to respond rapidly and efficiently to changes in their external environment. Here are some fundamental principles that support business agility:

- **Customer-centricity**: Prioritize customer needs and feedback, ensuring products and services are continually aligned with their changing demands.

- **Adaptability**: Cultivate a willingness and capability to change direction quickly in response to new information or changing circumstances.
- **Continuous improvement**: Always look for ways to enhance processes, products, and services through iterative feedback loops.
- **Empowerment**: Trust and empower teams and individuals to make decisions while fostering a sense of ownership and accountability.
- **Collaboration**: Promote cross-functional teamwork and open communication to ensure alignment and collective problem-solving.
- **Simplicity**: Keep processes as simple as possible, but not too simple, removing unnecessary bureaucracy and complexity.
- **Value-driven decision-making**: Focus on activities that deliver the most significant value to the organization and its customers.
- **Transparency**: Maintain open communication channels and provide visibility into processes, decisions, and performance metrics.
- **Quick feedback loops**: Implement practices to quickly obtain feedback on products, services, and processes to make rapid adjustments.
- **Innovation and experimentation**: Encourage a culture of innovation where intelligent risks are taken, and learnings from failures are embraced.
- **Learning mindset**: Invest in continuous learning and development, staying updated with technical capabilities, market trends and evolving customer needs.
- **Resilience**: Develop the capability to overcome setbacks and adapt to new challenges or changes in the business environment.

By instilling these principles within your team and across your organization, you can pave the way for an adaptive and responsive business that remains attuned to market demands.

As you progress through this chapter, you will learn how to translate Agile principles into strategic advantages. By recognizing how agility strengthens a company's position in the market, you will be equipped to shape decisions that enhance competitiveness.

Responding with agility

At its core, Agile methodologies emphasize responsiveness. They ensure organizations remain nimble, adjusting swiftly to market dynamics, business strategies, and new opportunities. The essence of Agile is its iterative and incremental approach, allowing for rapid evolution in response to continuous customer demands, competition, and market influences.

We'll explore what it means to be responsive over the following subsections.

Supporting Lean practices

Agility and Lean thinking go hand-in-hand. Lean focuses on removing inefficiencies and optimizing productivity. Later, you will learn that Value Stream Management (VSM) is a Lean approach to assess and prioritize the potential impact of proposed changes.

However, identifying and eliminating waste is just the start. Once Lean sets the direction by highlighting inefficiencies, it's often Agile teams that step in with their adaptive, iterative methods to design and implement solutions that genuinely realize Lean's objectives.

Let's take a closer look at how Agile teams can support Lean improvement objectives:

- **Delivering customer-centric value**: Agile teams refine and adapt solutions to ensure they continuously align with evolving customer desires, emphasizing constant stakeholder feedback
- **Eliminating waste**: While Lean identifies waste, Agile teams design adaptive solutions to bridge gaps, enhancing productivity and eliminating inefficiencies in every iteration
- **Streamlining workflows**: Agile teams further the Lean initiative by making workflows more efficient, leveraging collaboration and iterative feedback to refine processes continuously
- **Aligning production and demand**: While Lean sets the balance, Agile teams ensure that solutions are flexibly tailored to meet changing market demands and shifts in priorities
- **Reducing work in process (WIP)**: Agile teams address excessive WIP, focusing on prioritized tasks and breaking projects into sprints for aligned value delivery

In essence, while Lean Flow improvement opportunities help guide the work, by highlighting areas for waste and constraint elimination, it's the Agile teams, with their flexible and collaborative approach, that bring these strategies to fruition. They are the problem solvers, the innovators, and the builders that turn Lean objectives into actionable results.

Leaving the comfort of tradition

This section discusses the traditional approach to managing projects, often called the Waterfall approach. You may already know this information, so feel free to skip this section. But, if you are unfamiliar with traditional project management practices, this information is vital to grasp how Agile practices differ. Moreover, there are still many areas where the Waterfall approach is better suited to managing large or complex projects where evolutionary change is not feasible.

The so-called Waterfall model is at the heart of the traditional approach to development. Characterized by its sequential and plan-driven workflow, this model has been a mainstay in various industries, especially those where precision, predictability, and stability are paramount and possible.

In other words, the Waterfall model still works well when the underlying activities of a product lifecycle are well understood, have little variability, and can be planned upfront. For example, the Waterfall model's linear-sequential and plan-driven approach to project management works well in large and complex construction activities where the design, development, testing, and deployment processes are well understood and not likely to change significantly.

So, let's take a quick look at the fundamental characteristics that define the traditional project management approach.

Key features of the Waterfall model

Here are some of the key features of the Waterfall model:

- **Contractual constraints**: Projects initiated under this model are tightly bound by predefined constraints, encompassing scope, budget, schedule, benefits, quality, and risks. Often, these specifics are carefully detailed in formal charters or contract agreements.
- **Linear-sequential workflows**: One phase follows the completion of another, ensuring a systematic, step-by-step progression.
- **Plan-centric**: A significant emphasis is placed on planning, often before any learning has occurred, with little room for mid-course adjustments.
- **Formalized change management**: Since the goal is to plan in advance, changes are not typically welcomed, and significant changes may not be feasible - such as adding a new floor to a building under construction. Yes, it's possible, but usually not practical.
- **Overly-detailed documentation**: Detailed documentation is not just encouraged but is often deemed necessary, providing a comprehensive record of every stage.
- **Heavyweight processes**: The development model is predicated on robust, often cumbersome processes with stringent guidelines and standards.

Strengths of the Waterfall model

These are some of the strengths of the Waterfall model:

- **Well-defined projects**: The model thrives in scenarios where there's clarity in requirements and processes. Therefore, when a customer's needs, architectural considerations, designs, and methods are well-defined and not anticipated to undergo significant transformations, the Waterfall model is an excellent fit. For example, its often appropriate for constructing ships, buildings, utilities, and large infrastructural projects.

Limitations of the Waterfall model

Some limitations of the Waterfall model that Agile practices aim to address are:

- **Inflexibility to change**: Waterfall's linear approach makes it difficult to incorporate changes once the project is underway, unlike Agile's IID approach

- **Delayed feedback and testing**: Software testing in Waterfall occurs after all development is completed, leading to late discovery of issues, whereas Agile emphasizes continuous testing
- **Longer time to market**: Waterfall's phase-based structure often results in slower product delivery, in contrast to Agile's quicker iterative releases of incremental value
- **Limited customer engagement**: Customer involvement in Waterfall is minimal after the requirements stage, unlike Agile's regular customer collaboration
- **Resource inefficiencies**: Waterfall can lead to delays while waiting for other phases, whereas Agile and Lean ensure continuous customer engagement and better resource use

In rapidly changing industries, where business requirements, market prospects, and customer needs constantly evolve, the Waterfall model often struggles to keep pace. Its rigidity often clashes with the demands of dynamic environments. In such cases, a development model that embraces change is essential for evolving business systems and processes.

Important note

Our intent in highlighting the limitations of the Waterfall model is not to disparage its efficacy. Instead, it emphasizes that while it has its place, modern business challenges often necessitate a more adaptable approach.

The following sections will explore Agile practices, highlighting how they more effectively address these dynamic needs.

Evolving to agility

The shortcomings of the traditional Waterfall model, especially in dynamic business environments, led to the rise of "lightweight" development methodologies. These methods originated in the software industry, defined by software engineers dissatisfied with Waterfall's rigidity. These engineers, constantly under pressure for failing to meet frequently shifting requirements and wrestling with unrealistic deadlines, envisioned an alternative approach to development that was more accommodating and responsive.

A list of the better-known lightweight software development approaches is shown in *Figure 2.1*:

Lightweight Software Methodologies			
Extreme Programming	Scrum	Adaptive Software Development	Feature-Driven Development (FDD)
Iconix	Crystal	Dynamic Systems Development method (DSDM)	Pragmatic Programming

Figure 2.1 – Lightweight software development methodologies

Although each lightweight method is unique, they share the following attributes:

- **Small teams**: These methods advocate for teams that are autonomous, self-directed, and complete with the diverse skill sets essential to carry out their assigned tasks
- **Iterative development cycles**: A foundational tenet, these development and delivery cycles are typically brief, spanning one to four weeks
- **Incremental enhancements**: Rather than attempting a 'Big Bang' delivery, the focus shifts to breaking work down and implementing new capabilities, features, and functions incrementally with each new iteration
- **Product focus**: Moving away from the short-lived nature of projects, the emphasis in Agile is on continuous enhancement and support for software products throughout their economically viable life cycle
- **Customer-centricity**: Responsiveness to customers' needs and priorities, plus a commitment to aligning each increment with customer feedback, is a hallmark of Agile-based practices
- **Change embracement**: Change isn't merely tolerated; it's embraced, ensuring adaptability remains at the heart of the development process

> **Important note**
>
> It's crucial to underscore that while these methodologies were considered "lightweight," it isn't a commentary on their robustness or effectiveness. Instead, it's an acknowledgment of their simplified processes that enables teams to pivot in the face of evolving requirements effortlessly.

Now that you understand how Agile has advanced beyond the Waterfall model for most software development projects, let's quickly discuss one area where there is still some debate regarding the best approach: **Commercial Off-The-Shelf (COTS)** software.

Managing COTS implementations: Agile versus Big-Bang

Many business and IT executives believe that enterprise-class Commercial Off-The-Shelf (COTS) software cannot be effectively deployed using Agile's iterative and incremental development practices, as they require the entire solution to be fully operational from the start. Consequently, they may view Waterfall or Big-Bang approaches as more suitable for delivering a complete business solution all at once.

While we understand these concerns, we believe that Waterfall or Big-Bang (i.e., all at once) approaches may not necessarily offer a significant advantage. For instance, if your organization already has well-defined competitive processes, compliance controls, and financial and reporting requirements, replicating these within a new system may prove more complex and challenging than anticipated.

COTS software provides economic benefits by reducing development time and costs through pre-built, tested solutions. However, achieving a true competitive advantage often requires more than what comes out of the box. Implementing COTS typically involves substantial customization, integration, and data migration to align with specific business needs. The greater the divergence between your business processes, information requirements, and reporting needs compared to the capabilities of the COTS software, the more customization will be required.

Addressing compliance issues

Compliance is a critical concern for many organizations, encompassing areas such as regulatory, financial, operational, legal, and corporate requirements. For instance, public companies must adhere to **Sarbanes-Oxley** (**SOX**) requirements, which mandate the implementation of primary and secondary controls to mitigate risks. Since there is no standard set of SOX controls—varying by company size, industry, and risk types—organizations must tailor their approaches accordingly. SOX also mandates annual reporting to demonstrate accurate and secure financial reporting, driving customization requirements for Commercial Off-The-Shelf (COTS) implementations.

When addressing compliance, both Agile and Big-Bang approaches offer distinct pros and cons:

- **Agile**: Provides flexibility and continuous feedback, which is beneficial for adapting to evolving compliance requirements. However, Agile may struggle with the rigorous documentation and comprehensive controls required by strict regulations like SOX. Additionally, rolling out customized processes, controls, and reports can be time-consuming and complex.
- **Big-Bang**: Ensures a comprehensive implementation of business process customizations, data management, reporting, and compliance controls, which can streamline meeting both business and regulatory requirements. However, this approach involves higher risks and longer development cycles, potentially complicating audits and increasing the likelihood of significant issues. The extended timeline and accumulated costs can delay deployment and heighten the risk of discovering problems late in the process.

In the end, neither Waterfall nor Big-Bang approaches will deliver a complete working solution faster. However, Waterfall and Big-Bang approaches carry greater risks and potential delays due to the late discovery of issues, bugs, and defects. Therefore, we recommend using Agile practices, which support incremental roll-outs of new functionality throughout the development life cycle, offering ongoing improvements and adaptability. Even if your release deployment needs to be delayed incorporating necessary business processes and controls, you will know that you have a more robust solution to deploy when it is ready.

Now that we understand the early foundations upon which Agile values and principles are built, let's look at how the business development landscape has shifted.

Transitioning to product-oriented thinking

Agile methods signify more than just a tweak in development practices; they represent a holistic change in how businesses approach product and service delivery. They move away from managing projects to focusing on value delivery across the economic lifecycles of our products and services.

Let's look a little more closely at how these concepts play out.

In the rapidly evolving digital landscape, the outdated approach of organizing projects, with their finite timelines and clear endpoints, is no longer feasible for businesses aiming for sustainability and continuous innovation.

In his seminal work *Project to Product*, Mik Kersten underscores the necessity to pivot from project-centric mindsets to product-oriented thinking.[3] Unlike projects, which often prioritize short- term goals and tend to operate in silos, a product-centric approach is holistic, emphasizing enduring value delivery and iterative refinement. Organizations can better align their IT endeavors with business outcomes by focusing on products and fostering a more integrated, responsive, and adaptive IT ecosystem.

This transition promotes a culture where teams are invested in the long-term success and evolution of what they build rather than just ushering a project to its conclusion and moving on. This shift is not just a change in terminology. It represents a profound transformation in organizational culture, strategy, and execution, making businesses more agile and resilient in the face of technological disruption.

We must note that Kersten's book emphasizes process efficiency and flow, which are lean concepts. However, Agile prioritizes adaptability and customer-centric iteration, and both development approaches are essential for modern product development.

Let's look at how a product-oriented philosophy plays out in Agile.

- **Iterative and incremental development**: This approach embraces cyclical development processes, rolling out new product and service functionality across a series of iterative increments.
- **Rapid value delivery**: Due to its iterative nature, Agile ensures that new value reaches customers faster, enhancing responsiveness and adaptability.
- **Rethinking Waterfall**: Agile doesn't completely discard the steps of the traditional Waterfall model but re-imagines it. By incorporating Waterfall's life cycle steps into repeating plan-do-check-adjust (PDCA) cycles, Agile transforms the traditional single-pass flow into frequent, iterative and incremental development cycles.

> **Important note**
> The essence of Agile is adaptability. It allows organizations to remain attuned to shifting needs and priorities, ensuring they're not just reacting to change requests but proactively steering their development processes to address customer needs and priorities.

Now that we have defined the characteristics and principles of agility, let's look at an event that brought Agile to the forefront of software development practices - The Manifesto for Agile Software Development, and the Agile methodology that became the de facto standard at the small team level, Scrum.

Embracing Agile frameworks for collaboration

In this section, we will revisit the event that brought Agile into the mainstream - "*The Manifesto for Agile Software Development*" - and the leading lightweight software development methodology that followed: the Scrum framework. We'll start by revisiting the Agile Manifesto to understand its role in shaping modern agile thinking.

Rediscovering the Agile Manifesto

In Utah's snowy peaks of the Wasatch Mountains, a landmark event transpired between February 11 to 13, 2001, at The Lodge at Snowbird ski resort. Seventeen renowned thought leaders from various corners of the software development industry convened. Their goal? To bridge their methodologies and discover a unified approach to software development. From this summit, the Manifesto for Agile Software Development was born. And it has become the defining description of what it means to be an Agile software development organization.

The manifesto (source: `https://agilemanifesto.org/`) reads the following. We are uncovering better ways of developing software by doing it and helping others do it. Through this work we have come to value:

- Individuals and interactions over processes and tools
- Working software over comprehensive documentation
- Customer collaboration over contract negotiation
- Responding to change over following a plan

"While we acknowledge the value of the components on the right, we believe those on the left hold greater significance."

The manifesto also outlines the Principles behind the Agile Manifesto. But since we provided a modern list of Agile principles earlier in this chapter, we won't list the 12 principles here. If you want to learn more, you can find them here: `https://agilemanifesto.org/principles.html`.

> **Important note**
>
> This manifesto was more than a statement. It provided the collective wisdom of pioneers who sought to break free from the shackles of conventional, documentation-heavy software development processes. It marked the genesis of an approach rooted in collaboration, adaptability, and delivering tangible value.

So, time moves on, and as it does, people inevitably learn from their experiences and question what has become dogma. That statement is undoubtedly true for the Agile Manifesto. While still quoted often, some detractors feel we need to refine the original thinking. In the next section, you'll discover some critiques and new thinking about what agility means today.

Moving beyond the Agile Manifesto

The Agile Manifesto has been the foundation of the Agile movement, driving change in software development and project management. Over two decades later, the world of technology has evolved drastically, and so have the contexts in which Agile practices are applied. This has led to debates and discussions about the current relevance of the values and principles laid out in the manifesto. So, let's explore some of the current thinking and the evolution of the Agile movement.

Expanding Agile's horizons

Initially designed for software development, Agile methodologies have expanded into other business domains, and even hardware development. With this expansion, there's been a realization that some principles of the Agile Manifesto, while universal in spirit, may require rethinking to fit contexts outside of software development. For instance, the focus on working software as the primary measure of success needs to be translated differently in non-software domains.

This issue is a primary driver for our developing the BASE conceptual model and pattern language, which we'll introduce in *Chapter 9, Defining a Business Agility System for the Enterprise (BASE).*

Harmonizing continuous delivery with Agile

The Agile Manifesto has always emphasized customer collaboration and the ability to adapt to change. These are human-driven endeavors. However, with the exponential growth in technology and user expectations, there's been an undeniable push for continuous delivery and streamlined operations through advanced tooling, integrations, and automation.

This modern demand for seamless software delivery has drastically reshaped our understanding of agility. Continuous integration and continuous delivery (CI/CD) pipelines, augmented by DevOps practices and tooling, introduce frequent integration of work, streamlined information flows, and a heavy reliance on automation.

This modern approach speeds up software development work and requires a shift in mindset. Being Agile is no longer just about iterative cycles and feedback loops; it now entails a deep integration of these cycles into continuous delivery processes, ensuring that agility permeates every stage of the software development lifecycle.

The manifestation of this shift is evident in the rise of DevOps and VSM. These modern paradigms champion holistic value delivery and challenge the traditional boundaries of siloed iterative development.

Merging the cadence of Agile iterations with the consistency of continuous delivery presents a dynamic blend, redefining how businesses approach product development.

We'll discuss methods to integrate Lean and Agile cadences later in this book, starting with *Chapter 8, Implementing Basic Lean-Agile Solutions Teams (BLAST)*. For now, it's important to understand that we can have more than one team working in collaboration across a product life cycle. This emphasis on product development has profoundly influenced the essence of operating as a value-centric Agile business, distinct from managing constraint-based projects.

Expanding digital horizons

In the section on transitioning to product-oriented thinking, we discussed the importance of emphasizing products over projects. However, the topic extends beyond just managing software delivery products.

As we transition from a project-centric to a product-centric mindset, we must recognize that products include all types of products and services, many of which are integrated as solutions. The *Internet of Things (IoT)* is a good example. Additionally, we need to be aware that software products can support value stream improvements for the organization, whether internally and externally facing. Today, everything from tangible products to processes and services can be enhanced through digital tools.

In *Chapter 4, Driving Improvements with Value Stream Management (VSM)*, we'll underscore the importance of a comprehensive organizational improvement strategy, one that goes beyond just software. You'll also learn how to make product-oriented, value-based improvement assessments.

Given the constraints on resources, it's imperative to strategize where we can maximize returns on our investments. It may not always be linked to software. Yet, software and digital solutions can often be catalysts for transforming a process or enhancing a tangible product or service.

Given that all organizations have limited resources, we must evaluate where we get the biggest bang for our investments, which might not be software-related. Still, in many cases, software and digital services can facilitate a change in a process and a physical product or service. The generic VSM methods and tools we'll introduce in *Chapter 4* and the business intelligence strategy you'll learn about in *Chapter 10, Enhancing Decision-Making in the Lean-Agile Enterprise*, will help you make those types of business assessments and investment decisions.

Embracing the rise of business agility

Agile transformation has moved beyond IT departments. Organizations now see agility as a business-wide competency. This has led to discussions on whether the Agile Manifesto's values sufficiently address broader organizational concerns, such as strategy, governance, and culture. Business agility encompasses a more holistic view, considering market adaptability, organizational flexibility, and cultural agility. While the Agile Manifesto provides a strong foundation, some argue it may not be comprehensive for this broader scope.

Revisiting the role of individuals

The Agile Manifesto values "*individuals and interactions over processes and tools.*" However, with the rise of digital tools and platforms that facilitate Agile practices (such as Jira, Trello, or Slack), there's an ongoing debate about the balance between human interactions and the role of tools in enhancing collaboration. While tools help us visualize and streamline processes, the essence of Agile remains in human cooperation. Finding the right balance is an ongoing challenge.

Adapting to globalization with a distributed team

The manifesto emphasizes face-to-face communication. However, the global nature of today's businesses often means distributed teams working across time zones. The COVID-19 pandemic further amplified remote working. This has led to questions about how the manifesto's principles apply in such distributed, remote settings. Effective agility in this new context requires a mix of digital tools, revised communication strategies, and trust-building.

In summary, while the Agile Manifesto remains a foundational document, the evolution of the Agile movement requires continuous reflection and adaptation. The principles laid out in the manifesto provide a compass, but the journey of agility is dynamic, shaped by the changing landscapes of technology, business, and global contexts.

At this point, you should have a relatively comprehensive understanding of what it means to achieve business agility, both past and present. Now, let's discuss the leading Agile framework, Scrum, and how it supports business agility.

> **Important note**
>
> This chapter uses Scrum as its reference Agile framework for individual team environments. We will also introduce team-of-teams (ToT) concepts for more extensive development and problem-solving requirements that require multiple teams to collaborate and integrate their work.

Charting Scrum's ascendancy in Agile practices

The Scrum framework stands out among the various lightweight software development methodologies, emerging as the predominant approach for small teams. For example, the *16th Annual State Of Agile Report* (2022) by Digital.ai underscores its popularity. The report notes that "*Scrum continues to lead, increasing from 58% in the 14*th *survey to 87% in the current survey.*" The Scaled Agile Framework® (SAFe®) remains the most popular choice for enterprises, yet only 26% of respondents reported using it, which is a decline of over 50% compared to the previous year. However, the survey's scaling agility question changed which might account for the majority of this decline.

The official Scrum Guide (`https://scrumguides.org/`) defines Scrum as "*a lightweight framework that assists individuals, teams, and organizations in deriving value through adaptive solutions for intricate challenges.*"

Scrum retains its leadership role for small teams because of its simplicity, flexibility, and proven success in promoting collaboration and adaptability in diverse project environments. Its iterative approach and emphasis on continuous feedback make it highly effective in delivering valuable products or solutions to complex problems quickly and responsively.

As we progress through this chapter, we'll review how Scrum works. For now, it will be helpful to know that Scrum implements an iterative and incremental model of Agile via Sprints. Every Sprint, or development iteration, commences with a working hypothesis that can be tested. As the Sprint progresses, teams adjust incrementally, drawing from their observations and experiments.

We'll take a quick look at the Scrum events that guide the flow of work across a Sprint, as shown in *Figure 2.2*, in the following subsection.

Understanding the Scrum Sprint cycle

The following diagram details the Scrum events that guide its workflow:

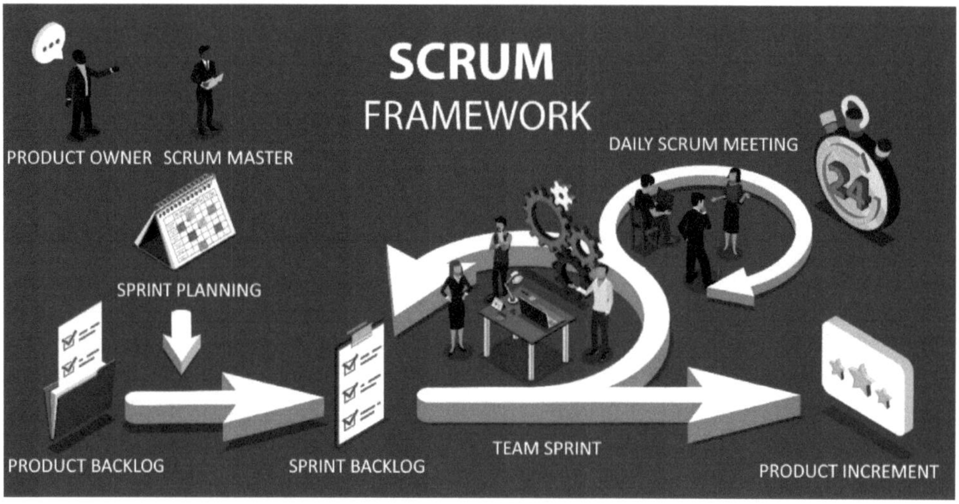

Figure 2.2 – Scrum framework

Work starts with creating the **Product Backlog**, which is managed by the **Product Owner**, and incorporating input from various stakeholders, including the **Scrum Team** and customers. During **Product Backlog Refinement**, the Scrum Team clarifies the backlog items and their priorities. The Sprint begins with **Sprint Planning**, where the team selects the highest-priority work items from the Product Backlog, creating the **Sprint Backlog**. Sprints are **time-boxed** development cycles, which means the durations are fixed, regardless of whether the Scrum Team meets its Sprint Goal objectives.

Developers pull items from the Sprint Backlog based on their capacity. Ideally, any team member can handle any job, but specialization is sometimes required. The Daily Scrum is a daily, time-boxed 15-minute meeting to inspect progress toward the Sprint Goal and adapt the Sprint Backlog as necessary, adjusting the upcoming planned work as needed. The entire Scrum Team is responsible for creating a valuable, useful, and potentially releasable *Increment* every Sprint. Each iteration concludes with two events: the Sprint Review, where the increment is inspected, and the Sprint Retrospective, which allows the team to reflect on how to improve quality and effectiveness. The Scrum Master is accountable for the team's effectiveness, helping it improve its practices and communication and removing barriers.

Now that we've introduced the basics of Scrum, let's review why it works.

Applying Scrum's foundational principles

These are the two primary concepts that underpin Scrum:

- **Empiricism**: Scrum operates on the principle that knowledge is derived from practical experiences and iterative experimentation, making decisions based on observations.
- **Lean Thinking**: The Scrum Guide acknowledges the influence of Lean Thinking on Scrum, although it does not explicitly specify fundamental Lean principles, such as eliminating waste or improving value flow. However, Scrum shares several Lean concepts, such as focusing on adding value from the customers' perspectives, delivering in short cycles, providing immediate feedback, respecting people, and improving continuously.

To optimize value delivery, combining Scrum with Lean's comprehensive concepts is essential. To accomplish this objective, the BASE and BLAST frameworks integrates the work of multiple Lean-Agile teams to support product and value stream improvements, streamlining work, material, and information flows, recognizing and mitigating constraints, centering work around specific products and services, and eliminating wasteful processes.

Adapting to Scrum's deliberate flexibility

Scrum's founders, Ken Schwaber and Jeff Sutherland, quickly point out that Scrum is an intentionally incomplete framework. Rather than prescribing a specific way of working or limiting the types of work it can be applied to, Scrum remains generically designed, offering broad applicability across various domains. In other words, Scrum provides a foundational framework to improve agility, whether the challenge lies in business, science, or technical problem-solving.

Scrum's flexibility offers the following benefits:

- **Widescale applicability**: Scrum's versatile nature ensures that it is suitable for diverse problems or business domains, granting teams the flexibility to address various challenges.
- **Freedom of methodology**: Development teams are granted autonomy within the Scrum framework. They have the skills and knowledge necessary for their tasks and can choose the best methods and tools that align with their unique work requirements.
- **Framework adherence**: While Scrum grants autonomy, it also emphasizes discipline. Every Scrum Team operates within the boundaries set by the framework. These guidelines serve as beacons, guiding Scrum team interactions and ensuring harmonious relationships.

In essence, Scrum provides a flexible yet structured environment, striking a balance between freedom of operation and the consistency of a framework. Note that a small team delivering the work is at the heart of every Sprint iteration. We'll talk about that next.

Amplifying team efficacy with Scrum

Whether you're a newcomer or a seasoned professional, understanding the dynamics of small teams can redefine how you approach work. Their inherent strengths foster clear communication, trust, and swift decision-making, all of which are crucial tools in today's business world. The Scrum framework capitalizes on these strengths, introducing roles and artifacts that seamlessly fit into your work patterns.

In this section, you'll discover how embracing the advantages of small teams can boost your career, enhancing adaptability, collaboration, and tangible results.

Mastering the art of small teams

When empowered and autonomous, small teams can act as potent problem-solving engines. Their limited size allows for nimbleness, a close-knit understanding among members, and a conducive environment for creativity and innovation.

Typically, an ideal small team in Scrum consists of fewer than 10 members. This size strikes a balance between diverse skills and manageable communication channels. Within such a group, every individual's voice can be heard, leading to richer brainstorming and collaborative decision-making.

Small teams are better suited to address the intricate challenges with innovation and adaptability. In the following subsection, we'll talk about how they foster an environment of collaboration and innovation.

Fostering a culture of collaboration and innovation

Fostering an Agile culture is vital. By promoting an environment where everyone feels invested in the outcome, where innovation is rewarded, and where collaboration is second nature, teams become more than the sum of their parts. They evolve into cohesive units that drive solutions with unparalleled dedication.

Managing Agile-based teams requires a different approach to the traditionally hierarchical and department structure. Moreover, the need to achieve greater agility forces us to evolve our managerial and leadership strategies to foster a robust culture emphasizing collective responsibility, out-of-the-box thinking, and seamless collaboration. And everyone's roles and responsibilities must change. Fortunately, Scrum provides some guidance in this area.

Defining team roles and responsibilities

In Scrum, the emphasis isn't placed on rigidly defined roles and responsibilities but rather on clear accountabilities. The Scrum Team consists of the following three defined accountabilities:

- **Developers**: Developers execute tasks to achieve Sprint Goals, creating usable Increments of value-based deliveries during each Sprint. They bring a diverse skill set tailored to their specific domain, ensuring the team remains a self-sufficient unit.

- **Product Owner**: Bridging the business and its consumers, the Product Owner collaborates with stakeholders to maximize the value of the product resulting from the work of the Scrum Team.
- **Scrum Master**: The Scrum Master is the cohesive force for the team, accountable for the Scrum Team's effectiveness. They address roadblocks provide guidance on Scrum, and ensure the team remains focused by guarding against external disruptions during a Sprint.

The three roles in Scrum are minimally defined to ensure clarity of responsibilities and promote efficient communication within the team. The same simplicity carries over to other defined Scrum concepts, such as its artifacts, as described earlier.

This completes our section on leveraging small teams as problem-solving engines. Now, we will move on to the importance of collaboration.

Facilitating effective collaboration through Scrum

In the dynamic ecosystem of the modern professional world, collaboration and adaptability are not just admirable skills; they are necessities. This isn't just about getting along with colleagues; it's about orchestrating multiple teams with expertise and objectives, into a cohesive unit that consistently delivers value.

Furthermore, the principles and events of Scrum provide a roadmap to enhancing these collaborative efforts. By understanding and applying the empirical pillars of Scrum – *Transparency*, *Inspection*, and *Adaptation* – and acquainting yourself with its events, you'll foster better teamwork, streamline processes, anticipate challenges, and swiftly adapt to change.

Next, we'll discuss the broader collaboration challenges and then present Scrum as a potential solution.

Encouraging cross-team collaborations

Large organizations are often involved in numerous projects spanning diverse value streams and requiring support from multiple teams. While each team might have its area of responsibility or specialty, the overarching objective is best achieved through effective collaboration between these units. Such cross-team interactions don't merely facilitate operations; they are pivotal in enhancing the organization's agility.

Grasping the intricacies of cross-team interdependencies is essential for business agility. It requires a strategic approach to synchronize diverse workflows, integrate tasks, and manage dependencies.

Later in this chapter, we will discuss Scrum-of-Scrum (SoS) and Team-of-Team (ToT) structures to support multiple streams of work. They offer a structured yet flexible framework to bolster this collaborative approach and harmonious synchronization across multiple teams. As we progress, we will elaborate on these concepts, providing insights into holistic team integrations.

However, first things first: the next two subsections delve into the foundational principles of Scrum's empiricism and its five events. As you familiarize yourself with these concepts, consider their relevance and applicability in cross-team collaborations. Employed sensibly, these tools and techniques can be significant assets in your pursuit of organizational agility and professional growth.

Exploring the three pillars of Scrum's empiricism

Embracing the nuances of Scrum requires a deep dive into its foundational tenets. In this subsection, we'll be dissecting the empirical backbone of Scrum: the three indispensable pillars that hold the house of Scrum up – *Transparency*, *Inspection*, and *Adaption*:

- **Transparency**: Transparency demands complete clarity on the team's strategies, goals, and results. By utilizing tools such as JIRA and visual charts, every process step is clear to both the team and stakeholders, ensuring decisions are based on Scrum's actual state.
- **Inspection**: Inspection involves consistent and detailed assessments of the team's progress toward Sprint objectives. Through Scrum's structured events, deviations are swiftly identified, aligning outcomes with aspirations.
- **Adaptation**: Should the results fall short of expectations, immediate corrective actions are vital. Scrum teams are committed to continuous adaptation, adjusting promptly as insights from inspections emerge.

By understanding how these three pillars work together, you'll be better equipped to implement Scrum events effectively, enhancing not just project outcomes but also team dynamics. So, let's move on to see how these principles interplay, guiding teams to make informed decisions, enabling continuous growth, and supporting proactive adaptations across the five Scrum events.

Embracing the team of teams (TOT) approach

In today's business landscape, singular teams, regardless of their proficiency, often find themselves challenged by intricate problems that necessitate a broader, collective approach. This section highlights the importance of collaboration, from recognizing the limits of individual teams to strategically coordinating multiple units. In scrum parlance, these integrated team concepts are known as Scrum-of-Scrums (SoS).

SoS is a concept that naturally evolved from the Scrum framework as organizations tried to scale their Agile practices to larger groups or teams. The origin of SoS is not attributed to a single individual but emerged as a way for multiple Scrum teams to coordinate and communicate effectively. In this book, we'll use a more general term, team-of-teams (ToT).

The ToT approach has been popularized in the Scaled Agile Framework® as an Agile Release Train (ART), the description of which is beyond the scope of this book. However, for those who want to dive deeper, check out SAFe® Distilled by Richard Knaster and Dean Leffingwell.[5]

By exploring the ToT concept and insights from leaders such as General Stanley McChrystal, our objective is to equip you with the understanding required to manage and lead in large and complex environments. This knowledge serves as a foundation for enhancing enterprise agility, fostering inter-team synergy, and ensuring cohesive, value-driven outcomes.

No matter how efficient a team is, there are boundaries to what it can achieve alone, especially when dealing with large-scale complexities. Recognizing this limitation is the first step to creating a holistic, collaborative approach.

When facing large-scale complexities, you will learn to recognize the limitations of relying solely on individual teams and understand the necessity of extensive collaboration across multiple teams to address these multifaceted challenges.

Orchestrating the combined efforts of multiple teams requires skill. It's not about micro-management but harmonizing. Regular cadence and synchronization, shared tools, and platforms, along with fostering a culture of open communication, ensure that the multiple cogs of this vast machine are aligned.

Lastly, you will enhance the ToT's capability to steer collaborative endeavors, synchronize efforts, ensure harmony across teams, and direct the collective toward continuous value delivery.

In managing all the activities across a product's life cycle, except for the very smallest of companies, one Agile team cannot do it all. This is where the concept of a ToT becomes invaluable. It's not just a scaling-up of resources; it's about scaling collaboration, synchronization, and the shared ownership of outcomes.

- **Integrated Workflow**: A team-of-teams approach promotes interconnected value delivery, where each team's output feeds into another, ensuring collaborative rather than just sequential integration for success.
- **Managing dependencies**: Multi-team environments come with dependencies. Recognizing and addressing them proactively is critical. This approach provides an overarching perspective to anticipate and handle dependencies, preventing misalignments and delays.
- **Synchronized delivery**: More than individual milestones, a cohesive final product requires teams to align efforts. Scaled Scrum frameworks such as the **SoS**, SAFe® **Large Scale Scrum** (**LeSS**), and **NEXUS** facilitate this alignment, ensuring a unified solution that fulfills overarching objectives.
- **Promoting collaboration**: The ToT mindset goes beyond task integration; it instills a sense of shared purpose, mutual respect, and collective drive, solidifying teams as parts of a cohesive whole.

In conclusion, as organizations strive to tackle more significant challenges and cater to diverse customer needs, the ToT concept becomes more than just a logistical necessity; it's a strategic imperative. By fostering integrated workflows, addressing dependencies, synchronizing efforts, and nurturing a collaborative spirit, organizations can harness the collective strength of their teams, turning intricate challenges into groundbreaking solutions.

Adopting insights from the ToT philosophy

The ToT approach is fundamental when dealing with Agile scaling frameworks such as the Scaled Agile Framework (SAFe®), LeSS, SoS, and others. These frameworks specifically address the challenges of scaling Agile across large enterprises with multiple teams working on interconnected components of a larger product or service.

The developers of these competing frameworks actively seek to differentiate their approaches from a value-added perspective. Still, we can find some common ground among them. Here are some examples:

- **Adapting to complexity**: This involves highlighting that in complex environments, hierarchical structures and traditional management methodologies fall short. ToT concepts provide a structure that's both flexible and integrated, allowing for faster decision-making in rapidly changing scenarios.
- **Shared mission**: This is a crucial principle where everyone understands the mission and has access to the information they need to execute it. In the context of Agile teams, this means every team understands the broader product vision and how their work supports the larger and holistic vision.
- **Empowered execution**: Individual teams have autonomy and are empowered to make decisions. They're not just following a set of predefined tasks but are dynamically adapting to the situation on the ground.
- **ToT Liaisons:** Introduce ToT liaison roles to improve communication and manage challenges and dependencies across teams.

These four guides help synchronize, coordinate, and integrate the work of multiple small teams, while also extending Agile principles and practices to a multi-team environment.

It is beyond the scope of this book to evaluate these disparate approaches and frameworks for scaled Agile practices. However, for those who want to take a deeper dive, check out Cecil Rupp's book, *Scaling Scrum Across Modern Enterprises* .[2]

Summary

In this chapter, *Solving Complex Business Problems with Agility*, we explored the transformative power of agility in addressing intricate business challenges. We examined the essence of organizational agility, its dynamic response to evolving circumstances, and its relationship with Lean practices to enhance efficiency. The Agile Manifesto provided foundational values shaping Agile's trajectory, while the Scrum framework highlighted its strengths in iterative project management, emphasizing the use of small teams as problem-solving engines and the importance of transparency and continuous feedback.

Collaboration was a key theme, underscoring the value of large-scale efforts in distributed environments, with insights from the ToT philosophy. These lessons equip you to harness agility for solving business problems, while offering a comprehensive understanding of Agile and Scrum methodologies. Looking ahead to *Chapter 3, Establishing Lean Flows to Improve Productivity*, we will delve into Lean-oriented practices, Agile methods tailored to organizational contexts, and metrics tracking business outcomes. Join us to continue learning how to be both lean and agile.

Questions

Answer the following questions to test your knowledge of this chapter:

1. How many of the core principles of Agile can you recall?
2. List how Agile teams can support Lean-oriented organizations.
3. What are the two primary concepts underpinning Scrum?
4. What are the three defining Scrum team accountabilities?
5. What are the three artifacts of Scrum?
6. True or false: Scrum's founders, Ken Schwaber and Jeff Sutherland, are quick to point out that Scrum is an intentionally incomplete framework.
7. What are the three pillars of Scrum's empiricism?
8. What are the five essential events of Scrum?
9. Why is the concept of ToT so important in Agile-based practices?
10. What are some of the commonalities across competing scaled Agile frameworks?

Answers

1. The core principles of Agile include customer-centricity, adaptability, continuous improvement, empowerment, collaboration, simplicity, value-driven decision-making, transparency, quick feedback loops, innovation and experimentation, learning mindset, and resilience.
2. Agile teams can support Lean organizations by:
   - **Delivering customer-centric value**: Agile teams refine and adapt solutions to ensure they continuously align with evolving customer desires, emphasizing constant stakeholder feedback
   - **Eliminating waste**: When Lean identifies waste, Agile teams design adaptive solutions to bridge gaps, enhancing productivity and eliminating inefficiencies in every iteration.
   - **Streamlining workflows**: Agile teams further the Lean initiative by making workflows more efficient, leveraging collaboration and iterative feedback to refine processes continuously.
   - **Aligning production and demand**: While Lean sets the balance, Agile teams ensure that solutions are flexibly tailored to meet changing market demands and shifts in priorities.
   - **Reducing WIP**: Agile teams counteract excessive WIP highlighted by Lean, focusing on prioritized tasks and breaking projects into sprints for aligned tangible value delivery.

3. The two primary concepts underpinning Scrum are:

   - **Empiricism**: Scrum operates on the principle that knowledge is derived from practical experiences and iterative experimentation, making decisions based on observations throughout each Sprint
   - **Lean Thinking**: While Scrum enhances agility and expedites delivery, it does not inherently encompass the complete breadth of Lean's value-stream principles

4. The three defining Scrum team accountabilities are:

   - **Developers**: Developers execute tasks to achieve Sprint Goals, bringing a diverse skill set tailored to their specific domain, ensuring the team remains a self-sufficient unit
   - **Product Owner**: Bridging the business and its consumers, the Product Owner collaborates with stakeholders to define requirements, ensuring consistent delivery of customer-focused value efficiently
   - **Scrum Master**: The Scrum Master is the cohesive force for the team, addressing roadblocks and ensuring the team remains focused by guarding against external disruptions during a Sprint

5. The three primary Scrum artifacts are:

   - **Product Backlog**: A dynamic and prioritized list detailing all work required for a product, service, or other deliverables and managed by the Product Owner
   - **Sprint Backlog**: A subset of the Product Backlog that comprises tasks handpicked by the developers for the upcoming Sprint
   - **Increment**: Represents tangible progress toward completing the Sprint Goal, which, in turn, represents a usable segment that contributes toward achieving the overarching Product Goal

6. True. Scrum's founders, Ken Schwaber and Jeff Sutherland are quick to point out that Scrum is an intentionally incomplete framework. Developers are free to use whatever skills, method and tools they require within their domain of expertise.
7. The three pillars of Scrum's empiricism are:

   - **Transparency**: Transparency demands complete clarity on the team's strategies, goals, and results
   - **Inspection**: Inspection involves consistent and detailed assessments of the team's progress toward Sprint objectives
   - **Adaptation**: Should the results fall short of expectations, immediate corrective actions are vital

8. The five essential events of Scrum are:

    - **Sprints**: Sprints are time-boxed iterative development cycles that last between 1 to 4 weeks. They establish a consistent rhythm or cadence for the team's workflow.
    - **Sprint planning**: As the kickoff to every Sprint, the Scrum team collaboratively defines the Sprint's goals, ensuring they have a comprehensive understanding of the objectives. They also map out the specific tasks and assignments to realize Sprint's vision and definition of done.
    - **Daily Scrum**: The Daily Scrum is a 15-minute huddle where team members update one another on their progress over the past day, share plans for the next 24 hours, and highlight any impediments.
    - **Retrospectives**: This reflective event occurs at Sprint's culmination, offering teams a forum to dissect their processes and methods.
    - **Reviews**: Showcasing the fruits of the team's labor from the concluded Sprint. Stakeholders, including customers and end-users, provide feedback, enabling the team to gauge the success of their efforts and gather insights for further enhancements.

Further Reading

1. Cecil 'Gary' Rupp, 2021. Driving DevOps with Value Stream Management: Improve IT value stream delivery with a proven VSM methodology to compete in the digital economy. PACKT Publishing, Birmingham, UK.
2. Cecil Rupp, 2020. Scaling Scrum Across Modern Enterprises: Implement Scrum and Lean-Agile techniques across complex products, portfolios, and programs in large organizations. PACKT Publishing, Birmingham, UK
3. Kersten, M. (2018). Project to product: How to survive and thrive in the age of digital disruption with the flow framework. IT Revolution Press.
4. Rupp, C., & Beal, H. (2021). Driving DevOps with Value Stream Management: Improve IT value stream delivery with a proven VSM methodology to compete in the digital economy. Packt Publishing.
5. Knaster, Richard, and Dean Leffingwell. SAFe® 5.0 Distilled: Achieving Business Agility with the Scaled Agile Framework®. Addison-Wesley Professional, 2020.

3

Establishing Lean Flows to Improve Productivity

"Flow is the movement and delivery of customer value through a process. In knowledge work, our whole reason for existence is to deliver value to the customer. Therefore, it stands to reason that our whole process should be oriented around optimizing flow."

– Daniel Vacanti in Actionable Agile Metrics for Predictability

In today's market, 55% of shoppers prioritize quality and product value, yet ultimately base their purchase decisions on finding a good deal. For instance, 75% of Baby Boomers, 71% of Gen X, 68% of Gen Z, and 67% of Millennials prioritize price over quality and value (First Insight, 2022). Consequently, businesses must recalibrate their product delivery strategies to compete on price, features, and quality. This chapter explains how organizations can meet this challenge by harnessing the power of Lean principles.

Lean principles offer a practical solution to help organizations compete in a market where customers prioritize affordability above all else. This chapter introduces Lean principles, basic practices, implementation strategies, and key terms, including value streams, constraints, pull systems, waste, and metrics. We'll delve into how Lean enhances efficiency by optimizing processes, eliminating constraints, and streamlining value delivery. You will learn that efficiency encompasses more than waste elimination; it also entails maximizing value delivery speed and cost-effectiveness.

We'll cover the following topics in this chapter:

- Unlocking Lean efficiency
- Identifying wasteful constraints
- Streamlining value delivery
- Installing Lean strategies for a competitive edge
- Driving continuous improvement

Technical requirements

Having a foundational awareness of Lean principles and practices is nice to have but not necessary. Those who want to dive more deeply into the topics of Lean Thinking can find more information in Cecil Rupp's[12] and Al Shalloway's books, listed in the *Further reading* section at the end of this chapter.

Unlocking Lean efficiency

In today's rapidly evolving business landscape, efficiency isn't just a buzzword – it's the lifeblood of successful organizations. With competitors always a step away and customers demanding more for less, the pressure is intense. This section is not about painting a dire picture; it's about illuminating the pathway forward with Lean efficiency. By the end of this section, you will have grasped foundational Lean practices that focus on delivering unmatched value through meticulously streamlined operations.

As we begin this discussion, looking at Lean concepts through the lens of systems thinking and in the context of improving flows is helpful. For example, look at *Figure 3.1* and ask yourself which workflow represents the leanest workflow:

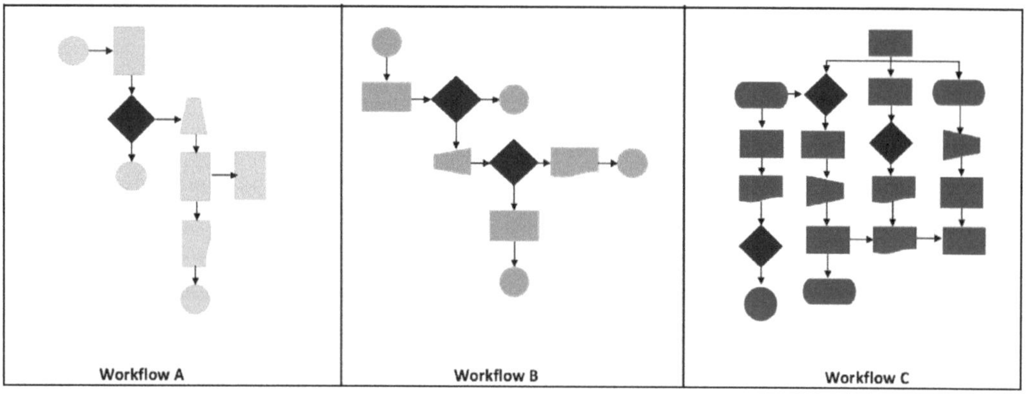

Figure 3.1 – Workflow comparisons

Workflow A has five activities and one decision point. **Workflow B** also has five activities but two decision points. Finally, **Workflow C** has 15 activities and three decision points. At first glance, it is logical to assume that **Workflow A** offers the leanest set of activity flows. By the end of this chapter, you will realize the answer is not always so simple. But, for now, assuming all three produce the same product or service, we'll go with **Workflow A** as it has the fewest activities and decision points.

With this most basic concept of Lean Flows in place, let's move on to discuss why companies need to be Lean and not just Agile. Harmonizing agility and Lean – dual pillars for optimal efficiency

In today's competitive landscape, it's not enough for organizations to be Agile; they must also embrace the Lean mindset. The core philosophy behind Lean is starting every endeavor with the customer's perspective, aiming to deliver unparalleled value through the products and services offered. Companies with a genuine Lean orientation don't stop striving for improvement. Instead, they are on a perpetual journey of exploration, continuously experimenting with new ways to refine their operations. The end goal? Delivering maximum value by eliminating waste.

The concept of Lean value streams captures this intent beautifully. It outlines a complete, value- focused sequence of activities that starts with an idea or a customer request and ends with delivering that value. However, Lean philosophy is not just about processes; it's about a holistic approach to business. By continuously evaluating and improving the **Five Ms**: **Manpower**, **Material**, **Machines**, **Methods**, and **Money**, Lean practitioners can coordinate these elements to achieve the best results for both the customer and the business. Simply put, Lean is about doing more and better with less.

Figure 3.2 illustrates the five principles of lean thinking, which originated from the **Toyota Production System** (**TPS**). The aim of these principles is optimize the flow of products and services through entire value streams and to continuously improve.

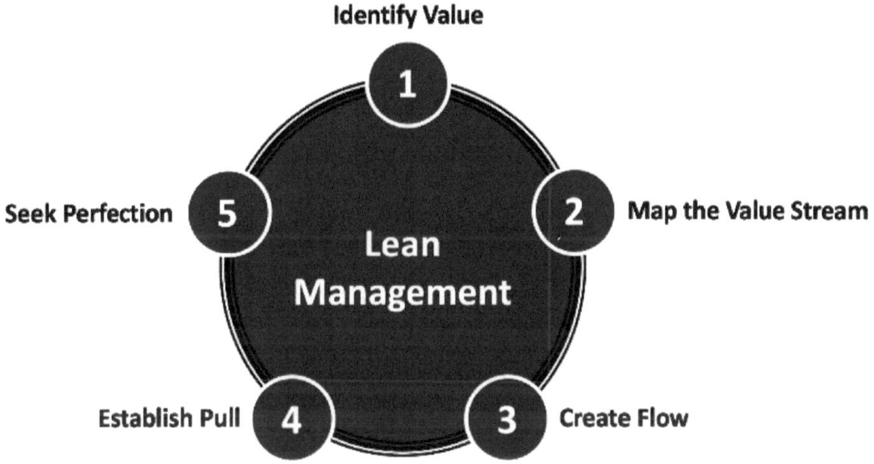

Figure 3.2 – Lean management

These principles were later articulated and popularized in the Western world by James P. Womack, Daniel T. Jones, and Daniel Roos in their 1990 book, "The Machine That Changed the World," and further elaborated in their 1996 book, "Lean Thinking." These lean thinking principles have been widely adopted beyond manufacturing and applied to software and hardware across various industries and business domains to improve efficiency and effectiveness.

The first principle is to identify opportunities to improve value using our customers' perspectives as a North Star to guide our decision-making. Next, we map the value streams and their activities that deliver value. As we map our current state and explore options for improvement, our focus is always on minimizing waste and improving the flow of work, materials, information, and people to deliver value most efficiently and rapidly. Lean implements pull control systems, such as Kanban, to reduce the potential for excess inventory, bottlenecks, and delays. Finally, Lean organizations always seek perfection, never letting up on their efforts to improve. Those who do this well have a distinct and continuing competitive advantage over those who do not.

Orchestrating value streams

The very essence of value streams lies in their ability to represent the complete, end-to-end series of processes and activities crucial to converting an initial concept or customer request into delivered value. This continuous sequence transcends traditional departmental barriers and integrates cross-functional efforts. Ironically, while many companies adhere to hierarchical organizational structures for administrative purposes, the real challenge is ensuring these hierarchies do not inadvertently create silos for solution development.

Organizational silos, often found in traditional bureaucratic systems, obstruct the free flow of value. Therefore, executives must recognize these divides and proactively bridge them. They should fine-tune both controls and incentives to eliminate barriers, positioning people and resources to enhance value stream flows at a detailed, product-line level.

Figure 3.3 shows a Lean production flow on the left and a traditional hierarchical organizational structure on the right:

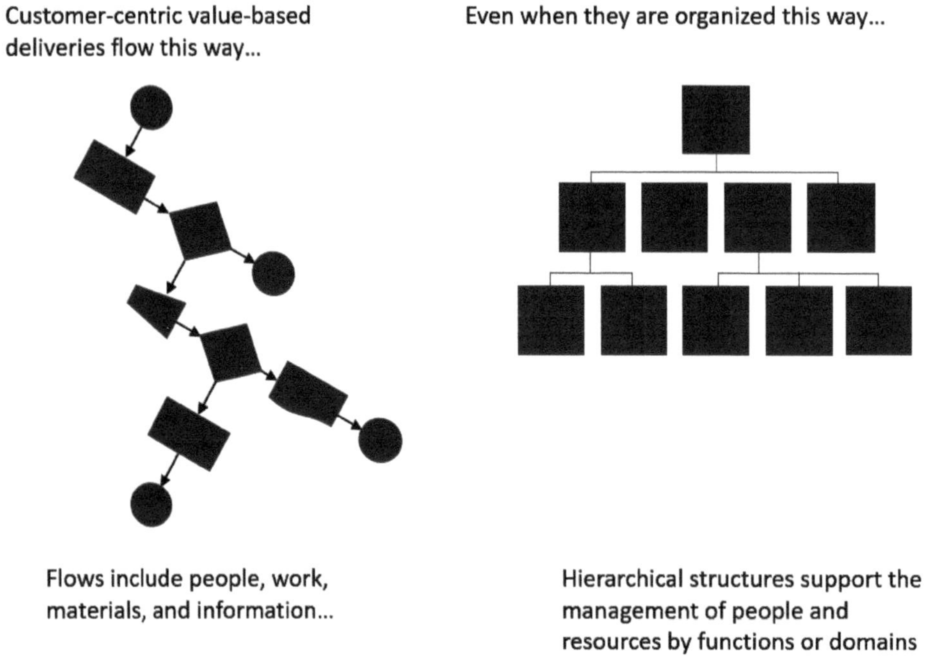

Figure 3.3 – Lean flows within hierarchical organizations

Classically, companies often attempt to manage business flows within a department and use cross-functional processes and business systems to manage work, information, and material flows. The problem with this approach is that the organization stays with a siloed approach to business management. A more effective approach is to identify and focus solely on value-adding activities, unconstrained by departmental boundaries or divisions. This is the essence of the concept of value stream flows, as illustrated in the Lean flows diagram on the left side of *Figure 3.3*.

It's not necessary to turn an organization upside down to implement Lean-oriented value streams. However, it is easier to manage people across value streams where value-delivery work is being performed. We will revisit this topic repeatedly throughout the book. For now, it's essential to understand that organizations can still maintain a traditional hierarchical management structure, even as they have value streams operating both within and across the various departments.

An example of this approach is seen in **Toyota**, the birthplace of Lean principles. While Toyota employs a distinct hierarchical structure, which encompasses global corporate offices cascading down to geographic and then product line divisions, the core intent remains the same: decentralized decision-making. This decentralization tailors decision-making to address local product and regional nuances more effectively. Yet, in daily operations, the spotlight remains on managing work as continuously refined value delivery streams. Remember, the path to enhancing these streams requires consideration of the Five M's - Man, Machine, Material, Method, and Metrics.

Next, we'll touch on the philosophy governing Lean principles and practices.

Understanding the Lean philosophy

At its heart, Lean isn't just a methodology – it's a philosophy. Originating from the Japanese manufacturing industry, particularly Toyota, Lean has transcended its roots to become a universally applicable approach for enhancing efficiency across various industries and business domains. Central to this philosophy is the relentless pursuit of delivering the most value with the least amount of waste. Everything that doesn't add value, from a customer's perspective, is seen as waste and is, therefore, a candidate for elimination. We'll get into the details on the types of waste in the next section, *Identifying waste and constraints*. But first, let's find out what we mean by the term **value**.

Delivering value – the core of Lean

Before diving deep into efficiency, let's understand the Lean-oriented concept of value. In Lean terms, value is anything the customer is willing to pay for. For example, it could be the features and quality of a product, the responsiveness of a service, or the user-friendliness of software.

Now, reflect on this: How many of our daily operations genuinely contribute to this perceived value? You might realize that numerous processes, while integral from an organizational standpoint, don't directly enhance customer value. On the other hand, many existing functions are necessary, but they could still benefit from Lean's efficiency-driven lens to eliminate wasteful elements within them. So, let's talk about that in the following sub-sections.

Creating operational efficiency – the Lean way

Lean's magic lies in its ability to identify and minimize waste, allowing operations to flow more smoothly. Waste, in Lean terms, is classified into eight types: **defects**, **overproduction**, **waiting**, **non-utilized talent**, **transportation**, **excess inventory**, **motion**, and **extra-processing**. By recognizing and addressing these wastes, businesses can significantly amplify their operational efficiency.

For instance, consider a simple process such as document approval in a corporate setting. Traditional methods might involve multiple handoffs, manual signatures, and prolonged waiting times. By applying Lean principles, we might shift to digital approvals, streamline the number of approvers, or even question the necessity of certain approval stages. The result? Quicker approvals, less waiting time, reduced motion waste, and, most importantly, accelerated value delivery.

Again, we'll get into the details of identifying and eliminating waste in the next section. But we have a couple of other issues to address first, starting with what it means to meet our customers' needs.

Meeting customer needs effectively

In the opening statistics, at the beginning of this chapter, we noted that a significant majority of shoppers, from Baby Boomers to Gen Z, prioritize price over quality and value. It's a clear signal that, while quality is indispensable, efficiency (which often translates to cost-effectiveness) cannot be overlooked. Efficient operations, shaped by Lean practices, can lead to reduced costs, which, in turn, might allow businesses to offer competitive prices without compromising quality.

Remember, customers today have an abundance of choices. If they can get the same quality of product or service at a reduced price (thanks to operational efficiencies), they'll likely choose the more cost-effective option. Moreover, operational efficiency also means faster delivery times, quicker responses, and more timely innovations – all crucial in meeting and exceeding customer expectations.

Lean-oriented efficiency does not happen by accident. It takes constant diligence and effort across the organization to identify, prioritize, and execute strategies to eliminate waste. This is the human element of Lean.

Valuing the human element

While tools, techniques, and methodologies form a significant part of Lean practices, the human element is paramount. It's the people on the ground – the ones involved in the daily grind – who often first spot inefficiencies. Lean empowers these individuals to voice their observations and even champion change. By fostering an environment where every team member is a potential efficiency enhancer, organizations can tap into a vast reservoir of on-ground insights.

Furthermore, operational efficiency isn't a one-time milestone; it's a continuous journey. The market, customer preferences, and technologies are perpetually in flux. What's efficient today might become a bottleneck tomorrow. Hence, the real skill isn't just in implementing Lean practices but in perpetuating a Lean mindset – an ethos of continuous improvement and relentless pursuit of adding value.

This completes our discussion on what it means to unlock lean efficiencies. Before we move on to learning how to identify waste, let's summarize what we've learned so far.

Embracing operational transformation

Lean efficiency is not about doing more with less but about doing what's right for the customer and the organization. It's about a strategic alignment of processes to ensure that every step, every action, and every decision inches the business closer to its goals. By understanding and implementing the principles discussed, you're setting the stage for an operational transformation – one where value isn't just delivered but is amplified at every turn.

Now, we'll move on to learn about the different forms of waste that hinder our ability to deliver maximum value to our customers.

Identifying waste and constraints

Success in the business – whether commercial, government, or non-profit – is not just determined by how well you can add value but also by how proficiently you can prevent value leakage. Inefficiencies, if left unchecked, can erode an organization's competitive edge, resulting in wasted resources, missed opportunities, and diminished profitability. In this section, we will delve into the art and science of pinpointing wasteful constraints and effectively weeding them out, empowering you to champion operational excellence in your professional journey.

Viewing the spectrum of waste

Waste can manifest in obvious forms, such as a defect in a manufactured product, or more subtle ways, such as an unnecessary approval step in a process flow. To holistically address inefficiencies, you must first be adept at identifying waste in all its forms. The general categories for Lean-oriented waste are listed in *Figure 3.4*, for both traditional and software categories:

Traditional Value Stream Wastes	Software Delivery Wastes
Defects	Defects
Extra-processing	Relearning (and unnecessary work)
Inventory	Partially done work (excess WIP)
Motion	Context switching
Overproduction	Extra (or unneeded) features
Transportation	Handoffs
Underutilized talent	Underutilized human talent
Waiting	Delays

Figure 3.4 – Types of waste

As noted previously and shown in the *Traditional Value Stream Wastes* column of *Figure 3.4*, Lean practices have historically delineated eight primary forms of waste. Let's look at these in more detail:

1. **Defects**: Defects and poor quality lead to rework and corrections, consuming valuable resources and potentially damaging customer trust.
2. **Overproduction**: Producing more than is required can tie up resources and capital, resulting in unnecessary storage, increased costs, and potential obsolescence.
3. **Waiting**: Delay time between processes indicates inefficiencies and can increase the overall production timeline. Waiting can be an indicator of upstream bottlenecks, insufficient supplies, dependencies, too much work in process (WIP), lack of automated processes and more.
4. **Non-utilized talent**: Failing to use the skills and knowledge of employees leads to overlooked innovations and ideas, underutilized skills and expertise, and diminished learning opportunities and productivity.
5. **Transportation**: Unnecessary movement of products or materials adds costs and can increase the risk of damage or loss.
6. **Inventory excess**: Holding excessive inventory ties up capital, consumes space, and can lead to spoilage or obsolescence, all of which add to our costs.
7. **Motion Waste**: Redundant or unnecessary motions by workers can lead to inefficiencies and increase the risk of injury.
8. **Extra-processing**: Adding more steps than required to a process or over-engineering a product can consume resources without adding value to the end customer.

While these classifications sprouted from manufacturing, their essence is universally relevant. Whether you're in software development, financial services, or healthcare, these waste categories can provide a structured lens to evaluate processes and identify inefficiencies. Still, it is often valuable to tweak the list of wastes to reflect the variances across domains of work, as we have done in the following subsection for software-oriented waste.

Tweaking elements of waste by domain

We've touched upon the traditional eight types of waste that are applicable across various industries. However, fine-tuning them to specific contexts can enhance their relevance. For instance, in a digital service firm, "inventory excess" might pertain to unused software licenses , incurring needless expenses. Similarly, "motion waste' could be reflected in frequent handoffs during a project, leading to delays and possible communication breakdowns.

So, let's see how the concept of Lean-oriented waste translates into software development:

1. **Defects**: In the software realm, defects lead to buggy applications, diminished user experience, and increased maintenance efforts.

2. **Relearning (also unnecessary work)**: Redoing tasks or revisiting solved problems due to poor knowledge retention or documentation wastes time and delays progress.
3. **Partially done work (excess WIP)**: Having excessive WIP can obscure the project's actual state, reduce agility, and delay the realization of value.
4. **Context switching**: Constantly shifting focus between tasks or projects reduces efficiency, forces relearning, and can lead to increased errors or missed details.
5. **Extra/unneeded features**: Developing unnecessary features consumes resources, complicates the user experience, and can make the product overly complex and challenging to use, all of which are non-value-added from our customers' perspectives.
6. **Handoffs**: Passing work between teams or individuals can lead to communication breakdowns, potential bottlenecks and delays, and a dilution of responsibility.
7. **Underutilized human talent**: Not harnessing the full potential of software professionals can lead to missed innovative solutions and decreased morale.
8. **Delays**: Waiting for decisions, feedback, or dependencies can hinder progress, delay releases, and frustrate teams.

By classifying and understanding these waste forms, you will equip yourself to effectively spot and address inefficiencies across various product lines and service offerings. But now, we need to move on and discuss perhaps the most critical issue, which is constraints.

Constraints – the silent value blockers

While waste can be seen as actions or steps that add no value, constraints are barriers that actively hinder value delivery. A constraint could result from excessive cycle times or setup times creating a bottleneck in a manufacturing line, a software server that can't handle required transaction volumes, or even an organizational policy that impedes rapid decision-making.

Recognizing these constraints is paramount. The **Theory of Constraints** (**ToC**), a management paradigm developed by Eliyahu Moshe Goldratt – outlined in his book The Goal, posits that in any complex system, there's often one major limiting factor that defines the system's capacity.[3] Let's look at *Figure 3.5* to see the value of identifying our constraints:

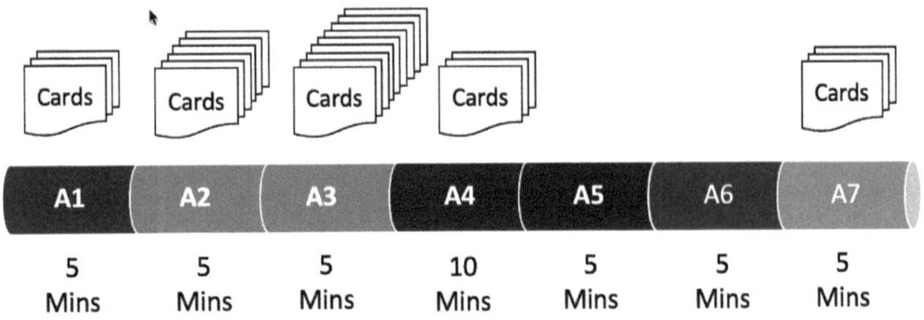

Figure 3.5 – ToC example

Figure 3.5 depicts a value stream comprising seven activities, each taking 5 minutes, with one exception: a central activity (**A4**) that requires 10 minutes. This lengthier activity creates a bottleneck, causing a backlog of work in the steps leading up to it. Meanwhile, subsequent activities lack work, awaiting input from the bottlenecked step.

At this point, we may not know why it takes 10 minutes to complete activity 4. For example, it could be the result of a lengthy setup, the work duration, an inspection process, or waiting on information, materials, or resources causing the delays. However, by identifying and addressing this constraint, we can significantly elevate the system's performance.

Eliminating constraints is pivotal for optimizing workflow and maximizing value. By prioritizing waste removal based on constraints, organizations can address the most impactful bottlenecks first, ensuring smoother processes and heightened efficiency.

In your professional journey, understanding the concept of constraints is invaluable. Not only does it allow you to enhance operational flow in your respective domain, but it also positions you as a strategic thinker capable of holistic problem-solving.

Mapping a value stream

In the previous subsection, *Figure 3.5* provided a very simple graphical representation of a value steam flow. Usually, our real-life value streams are much more complex, plus we need to capture more information on materials and information flows.

Figure 3.6, or the enlarged version in *Appendix A: Machine Shop Value Stream Example*, shows a value stream map for a manufacturing line. Since it's not the focus of this book to teach value stream mapping practices, we will not spend time here going through this map. Instead, we'll spend our time going through the mapping process.

However, for those who want to take a detailed dive into the mechanics of value stream mapping, Author Cecil Rupp goes into this topic extensively in his previous book, *Driving DevOps with Value Stream Management.* [4] The *Further reading* section also includes references to several well-known books on this topic. [5,6,7,8,9,10]

In *Figure 3.6*, text readability is not critical; the diagram is meant to provide an graphical depiction of flows across of a automotive manufacturing line:

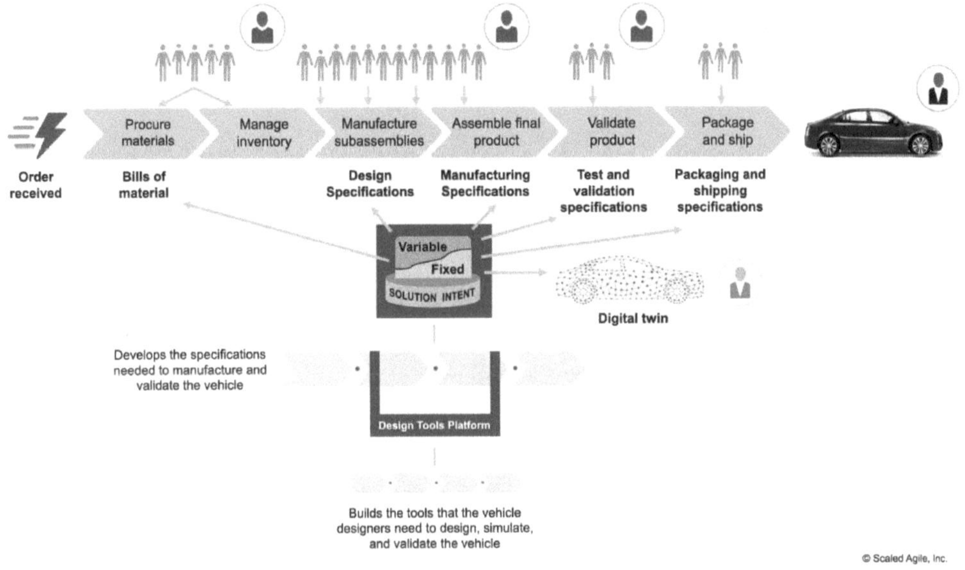

Figure 3.6 – Manufacturing value stream map example

Value stream mapping is a visual tool originating from Lean manufacturing that is used to analyze and design the flow of materials and information required to bring a product or service to a consumer. The goal is to identify waste and areas of improvement within processes.

Figure 3.7 provides a quick overview of the work involved in mapping a value stream:

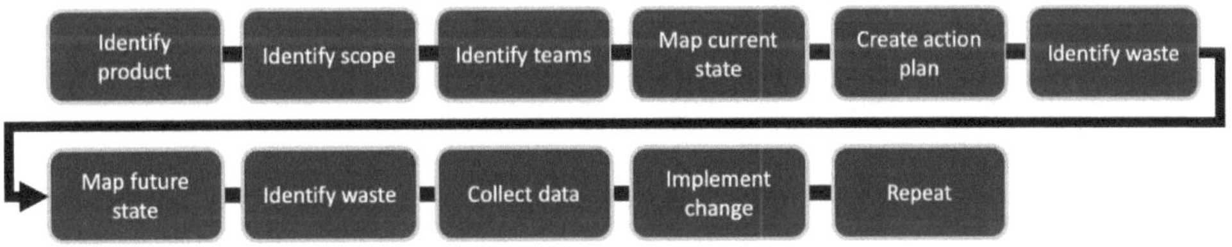

Figure 3.7 – Value stream mapping and improvement process

Here is a concise summary of the mapping process, consistent with Lean practices:

1. **Identify the product/service**: Begin by choosing a product or service to map. This should be something that is critical to your business, or a process that is known to have issues or inefficiencies.

2. **Define the scope and boundaries**: Clearly define the start and end points of the process you are mapping. This might be from the moment an order is placed until its delivery or from raw material to finished product.
3. **Gather a cross-functional team**: Assemble a team with representatives from each function involved in the value stream. This will provide multiple perspectives and a holistic understanding of the process.
4. **Map the current state**: Start by mapping the current state of the process as it operates, not as you think it operates. Document the steps, flows, and information necessary to deliver the product or service. This typically includes the actions, inventory, waiting times, and information flows that occur as a product or service moves through the process.
5. **Collect data**: For each step, gather data such as cycle time, wait time, defect rates, inventory levels, and any other metrics that indicate how the process is performing. This quantitative data is crucial for identifying bottlenecks and waste.
6. **Identify waste**: Within the map, distinguish between steps that add value from the customer's perspective and those that do not (waste). Non-value-added steps are targets for improvement.
7. **Map the future state**: Using the current state map and the collected data, design a future state map that shows how the process should operate after the waste has been removed or reduced. Focus on creating a flow that delivers value as efficiently as possible, minimizing wait times and reducing non-value-added steps.
8. **Create an action plan**: Develop a plan to transition from the current state to the future state. This includes assigning tasks, setting deadlines, and determining the resources needed to implement changes.
9. **Implement changes**: Execute the action plan, make the necessary changes to the process, and ensure that all team members are trained in the new process.
10. **Review and continuously improve**: After implementing changes, monitor the process to ensure that improvements are sustained. Regularly revisit the value stream map to identify further areas for improvement. Repeat the process for the next value stream.

In *Chapter 4, Driving Improvements with Value Stream Management (VSM)*, we'll dive a bit more deeply into the approach to identify and prioritize the most impactful improvement opportunities.

By visually laying out all the steps in a process and linking them to the flow of information and materials, value stream mapping allows you to see the sources of waste and any inefficiencies. With this insight, teams can collaborate on a targeted approach to creating more value for the customer with less work, which is the essence of Lean.

Amplifying IT's impact – driving operational efficiency and strategic value

Why is all of this vital to your professional career in IT? In today's landscape, where margins are slim and competitors are relentless, achieving operational efficiency is essential. By adeptly identifying and reducing inefficiencies, you enhance the organization's capacity to deliver value both swiftly and economically. Being in IT, you're positioned uniquely to champion and implement digital improvements across products, services, processes, and value streams.

The benefits extend directly to the bottom line. Minimizing waste translates to conserving resources by not spending them on activities that don't add value. By addressing bottlenecks, you ensure timely and effective product or service delivery, meeting market demands head-on. Such expertise doesn't just boost profitability; it heightens customer satisfaction and elevates the brand's stature.

Moreover, organizations today are on the lookout for professionals who don't just execute tasks but think critically about enhancing value delivery. By mastering the skills of waste identification and constraint recognition, you position yourself as an invaluable asset, capable of driving strategic improvements and fostering a culture of continuous enhancement.

Prioritizing efficiency – the Lean imperative for organizational success

Inefficiencies, whether from waste or constraints, are a common challenge for organizations. Yet, they can be addressed and mitigated. With the Lean principles and practices detailed in this section, organizations can systematically address these inefficiencies, ensuring a smoother flow of value. As the business landscape grows more competitive, the ability to harness efficiency becomes crucial. It allows organizations not only to deliver value effectively but also to maintain profitability. By adopting Lean, organizations are investing in their sustained success and reinforcing their commitment to operational excellence.

This completes our section on identifying waste and constraints. In the next section, we'll focus on the approach to streamlining value stream flows.

Streamlining value delivery

Throughout this book, we note that in today's fast-paced business environment, timely and cost-effective value delivery is paramount. This section delves into the approach to refining value stream flows. It provides insights on aligning processes and techniques to balance time and cost, ensuring that organizations are adeptly positioned to meet, if not surpass, market demands.

Classifying value streams

At the heart of any organization is its commitment to delivering value, and value streams serve as the primary conduits for this delivery. These are end-to-end sequences where work, materials, and information synergize, moving smoothly to offer customer-centric value via products, services, or other tangible results.

> **Value streams**
>
> A value stream is the series of steps and activities that an organization employs to design, develop, and deliver products or services to its customers. Value streams chart the flow of materials and information from the very start, often from a supplier or raw material, all the way through to the delivery of the end product to the customer.

Historically, pioneers in the software industry, such as James Martin in his seminal work *The Great Transition*, cataloged numerous distinct value stream types by business processes prevalent in commercial entities.[11] However, contemporary business transformation experts have simplified the classification of value stream types into two or three broad categories – **operational**, **development**, and **support**:

1. **Operational value streams**: These types of value streams deliver direct value to external customers. Whether it's through tangible products, services, or specific results, operational streams encompass myriad functions, from order taking, processing, and fulfillment to manufacturing, and post-sales customer support, and more.
2. **Development value streams**: These streams focus on problem-solving and value creation to define, design, test, and evolve new solutions. These types of value streams create products and services for both internal and external customers This category of value streams includes product management, R&D, and IT services. For those in the IT sector, **continuous integration/continuous delivery** (**CI/CD**) and DevSecOps pipelines live within development value streams.
3. **Support value streams**: While they might not be direct contributors to customer value, support streams are the unsung heroes that provide essential support to the core value streams within an organization. The steps and activities in support value streams enable operational and development value streams to function efficiently and effectively, although they do not directly contribute to products or services delivered to customers. These streams encompass various internal functions such as human resources, finance, IT, procurement, legal services and supply change management.

Various thought leaders and organizations interpret these value stream categories slightly differently. For instance, SAFe pinpoints operational and development streams, while PMI extends this to include support value streams. Similarly, experts such as Martin and Osterling distinguish between core value streams, which directly add customer value, and supporting ones, which are necessary for the primary value streams to function effectively and efficiently.

You now know what value streams are. So, now, we can start looking at how to improve them, starting with the balancing act between speed of delivery, quality, and costs.

Balancing speed and cost

Every organization faces a crucial balancing act: how to deliver products or services rapidly without compromising on quality or escalating costs. This becomes even more vital when we factor in the ever-evolving customer expectations and the pressure to innovate consistently. Speed without accuracy can lead to errors, rework, and a tarnished brand image. Conversely, a meticulous approach that's time-consuming can result in missed market opportunities and reduced competitiveness.

Mastering this balance begins with understanding and optimizing the processes that underpin value creation and delivery. Consider, for instance, the business domain of software development. Rapid application development techniques prioritize speed but can sometimes lead to post- deployment issues if we haven't fully considered critical requirements, architecture, and usability concerns. In contrast, traditional Waterfall models might ensure a thorough product planning effort. Still, they could delay time-to-market and not provide sufficient flexibility to address changes brought on by ever-evolving customer, business, and market requirements.

The key is to find a middle ground by employing hybrid approaches and continuously refining methodologies to enhance speed while keeping costs in check. For example, in a Lean-Agile enterprise, value streams help ensure predictable and efficient outputs, while Agile-based teams evaluate and implement the most value-adding improvements.

Lean-Agile organizations seek a balance between efficiency and change. Such optimization requires a keen understanding of the industry, the ability to forecast market demands, and achieving proficiency in leveraging tools and technologies to aid in efficient delivery. We must make sure that the changes we are working on have the most significant potential impact in terms of delivering more value at the lowest practical cost.

Agile practices are not limited to helping evolve our products. We also must consider how best to improve our value stream activities and cross-functional business processes that deliver value and support the business. Those improvements have the most impact on the speed and cost of delivery. So, we need Agile teams to also work on those types of issues. Moreover, in the following subsection, you will find that it often means we focus Agile business teams on fixing inefficiencies.

Enhancing efficiency by minimizing inefficiencies

This might sound intuitive, but the journey to greater productivity often begins by recognizing and rectifying inefficiencies. It's akin to paving a smoother road to ensure faster travel. By eliminating bumps (inefficiencies) in your processes, you ensure a swifter, less costly value delivery.

Here, again, assessing the location of our constraints is the critical indicator of where our inefficiencies lie. Inefficiencies can manifest in various forms: redundant processes, outdated technologies, communication barriers, or even a lack of skillset alignment. Recognizing these pain points is the first step to improving our business value-adding work and information flows.

Another way that Lean practices create efficiency is by eliminating the delays in the steps on the value stream. These are often due to multitasking, which causes extra work to be created. Though we might like to think otherwise, humans are only able to process one thought or one series of actions at a time.

The bottom line is that by improving flow and waste, we become more efficient. Subsequently, applying Lean principles, automating repetitive tasks, refining communication channels, and ensuring continuous upskilling can drastically minimize these inefficiencies, paving the way for streamlined value delivery.

Before we leave this section, let's take a quick look at how your professional focus on assessing and eliminating inefficiencies can positively impact your professional career.

Carving a niche in the professional world

As your career progresses your ability to ensure swift, cost-effective value delivery can set you apart. Organizations may leap ahead through technical and product innovations. But they thrive when they have efficient operations that help maintain their competitive edge. By mastering techniques to optimize processes and minimize inefficiencies, you're not just contributing to the immediate project or product but influencing a culture of operational excellence.

Professionals who are adept at such optimization often find themselves in strategic roles, driving organizational policies and spearheading innovation. It's a skill set that resonates with leadership, investors, and customers alike. In a world where every second counts and every penny is scrutinized, proficiency in streamlining value delivery can be your ticket to professional recognition and organizational success.

The pursuit of streamlining value delivery is relentless. Market dynamics shift, technologies evolve, and customer preferences change. Amidst this flux, your ability to consistently deliver value efficiently can be the anchor. As you navigate your career, remember that every process can be refined, every methodology can be optimized, and every inefficiency can be minimized.

This completes our discussion on streamlining value delivery. This section has armed you with the insights and tools to make that happen. Embrace them, refine them, and apply them. The result? An enhanced professional profile and an organization that stands resilient, efficient, and profitable in the face of ever-mounting challenges.

In the next section, we'll introduce Lean strategies that help drive and sustain a competitive edge in your industry.

Installing Lean strategies for a competitive edge

In a dynamic global marketplace, the aim isn't just to survive but to thrive and lead. The fact is, if we don't set the pace, we won't survive for long or, at best, survive as a niche player.

Operational efficiency is a cornerstone for organizations and professionals striving for this goal. In the context of business competitiveness, efficiency is more than just reducing excess; it's about consistently delivering value promptly. Lean strategies offer a framework to achieve this, helping businesses remain competitive and adaptive.

Prioritizing value flows

In a Lean-Agile paradigm, the focus shifts to ensuring the optimization of value delivered through our products and services, as defined by our customers. This optimization extends throughout their economic lifecycles, transcending the conventional, often fragmented, project-based approach. Instead of fits and starts common in project-centric processes, Lean-Agile emphasizes a continuous flow, seamlessly integrating operations, development, and supporting value streams.

In the previous section, *Streamlining value delivery*, and specifically within the *Classifying value streams* subsection, we introduced three standard value stream types: operational, development, and support. We are going add a fourth value stream type, called **'product'**. After all, both Lean and Agile emphasize that everything we do, indeed our very livelihoods, depend on us meeting our customers' needs via our products and services.

To get a clearer picture of this, let's take a look at *Figure 3.8*:

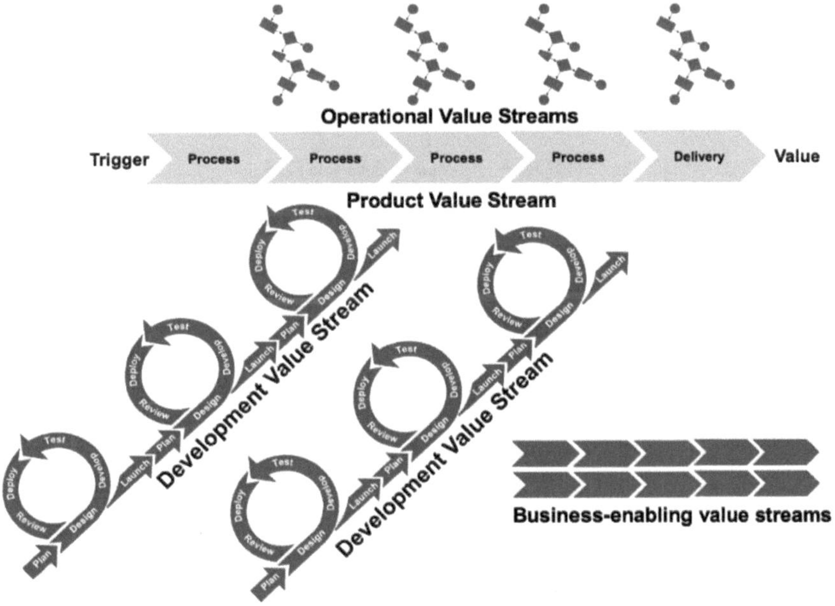

Figure 3.8 – End-to-end customer value stream flows

Figure 3.8 illustrates a product value stream that defines the end-to-end flow of work required to take a concept and incrementally deliver new value. Feeding the product value stream are any number of operational and development value streams. Business enabling value streams (often called support value streams) are not connected to the product value stream. However, they are needed to sustain the business (e.g., HR, Legal, Finance, Marketing).

So, why did we add the product value stream? Well, the classic definition of a value stream is an end-to-end set of activities from concept through delivery that collaboratively transforms inputs into outputs, ultimately providing value to the customer. That's a mouthful, but basically, it implies that a value stream encompasses virtually everything a company does to deliver value to its customers through its products and services.

However, the problem with that definition is that it doesn't make it easy to break work down into bite-size chunks that make sense in terms of how we need to run our businesses. To overcome this problem, various thought leaders began to organize value streams around operations, development, and support (business-enabling) functions. But, in doing so, we've lost the notion that everything we do must support the customers who fund our work. Again, they are the reason our organizations can exist.

In a large, multi-billion-dollar organization, there are hundreds, if not thousands, of potential value streams. However, the number of revenue generating value streams is limited to the primary products and services they offer to their customers.

In the following subsection, we'll take a closer look at many of the critical activities necessary to deliver value to our customers, from concept through delivery. Specifically, we will explore why there are so many potential value streams and how to organize them.

Demystifying organizational value streams

First, all organizations are driven to support a specific market, types of customer, and their needs. Organizational focus and alignment are critical to success and require a broad spectrum of work to deliver new increments of customer-centric value constantly.

Looking across an iterative product life cycle, we start with activities to define corporate, customer, product, and portfolio investment strategies. Other activities are needed to conduct market and product research. We often need to develop partnerships and supply chains to support our manufacturing, delivery, and support services. We require activities to promote and sell our products. Plus, we have activities to design, develop, test, and deploy our new or enhanced products and services. We have other activities to support the continuous production of our goods and services. And we still are not done because we need other activities to manage fulfillment and provide customer support.

Finally, it's essential to know that customer facing value streams must also support product evolutions across multiple development lifecycles. So, all of the activities noted in the previous paragraph are iterative to deliver new value incrementally. But hold on to that thought for now. We'll come back to it in *Chapter 9, Defining a Business Agility System for the Enterprise (BASE)*.

For now, let's et's look closer at this paradigm shift that has permeated virtually every industry.

The Lean paradigm – where efficiency meets value

Historically, Lean was rooted in manufacturing, aiming to reduce waste and streamline operations. Over time, its principles have permeated diverse sectors, from aerospace, banking and financial services, construction, consumer electronics, education, food and beverage, healthcare, information technology, pharmaceuticals, the public sector and government, and retail.

At its core, Lean is more than just a methodology; it's a mindset centered on value delivery. By eliminating non-value-adding processes (or waste) and focusing on what genuinely adds value from a customer's perspective, Lean ensures that every organizational effort amplifies customer satisfaction.

For instance, in an IT services company, if client feedback reveals that system stability and security are their top priorities over the latest innovative features, a Lean-oriented approach would prioritize efforts on rigorous testing and robust security protocols, which might require new tools, test scripts, and automation. This ensures the delivery of a product that aligns with the client's primary needs, reducing potential system vulnerabilities and costly post-launch fixes.

With this paradigm shift comes a competitive advantage. Let's see why.

Crafting competitive advantages with Lean

Competition in business isn't just about who offers a particular service or product; it's about who offers it best, quickest, and in alignment with customer expectations. Leveraging Lean methodologies can be your cornerstone for achieving this competitive advantage through these four areas:

1. **Customer-centricity**: By focusing on value from a customer's vantage point, Lean ensures organizations stay attuned to changing market demands, swiftly adapting and delivering what the customer genuinely wants.
2. **Optimized operations**: Lean encourages streamlined operations, reducing cycle times, and ensuring swifter market responsiveness. In sectors such as retail or tech, this can mean the difference between market leadership and obsolescence.
3. **Cost-efficiency**: By eliminating wasteful processes, Lean not only ensures time efficiencies but also drives cost savings. These savings can be strategically reinvested for innovation or passed on to customers, further enhancing competitiveness.
4. **Catalyst for innovation**: Lean isn't just about doing things right; it's about doing the right things. By freeing up resources from non-value-adding tasks, organizations can invest more in R&D, driving innovation and staying ahead of market curves.

Lean isn't just an operational tool; it's a strategic asset. By understanding and absorbing how Lean methodologies bolster competitive advantage, you can position yourself as an invaluable asset to your organization.

In roles ranging from operational management to strategic planning, the ability to deploy Lean-driven solutions that exceed customer expectations can set you apart. Imagine leading a project that not only meets its targets but does so ahead of time, on budget, and with innovations that the market hasn't even articulated yet. That's the prowess Lean brings to the table.

Furthermore, as businesses globally embrace the Lean mindset, professionals fluent in its principles and applications will find themselves in demand, transitioning from mere role occupants to strategic influencers. The beauty of Lean is that its principles are universal. Whether you're in healthcare, finance, tech, or manufacturing, Lean's focus on efficient value delivery remains a constant competitive differentiator.

Paving the way for market leadership

This concludes our discussion on Lean strategies for a competitive edge. We have learned that, in today's age, the market leaders of tomorrow are being defined by their ability to deliver unmatched value efficiently today. Lean strategies offer the blueprint to achieve this. By aligning organizational processes with customer value, optimizing operations, and continuously innovating, Lean ensures that businesses aren't just running the race but leading it.

As professionals, embracing Lean's tenets equips you with a potent combination of strategic foresight and operational excellence. It's a toolkit that ensures you not only contribute to your organization's competitive prowess but also carve a niche for yourself in a marketplace that values efficiency, innovation, and value above all.

Now, let's move on to discuss how Lean drives continuous improvement.

Driving continuous improvement – fostering sustained enhancements through Lean principles

In the ever-evolving business landscape, staying competitive requires more than just one-time process optimization. While the tactical approach of Agile retrospectives emphasizes quick, Sprint-specific improvements, Lean offers a broader, strategic perspective. Lean principles prioritize the most impactful improvements, irrespective of their associated time, cost, or effort. Therefore, Lean improvement initiatives may require approvals through the organization's portfolio management process.

This contrasts with Agile's emphasis on what can be immediately achieved by a team or team of teams within the constraints of an upcoming sprint. The unsaid part is that Agile teams are, therefore, limited in scope on the changes they can make.

However, to thrive amidst shifting market dynamics, consumer preferences, and technological advancements, organizations and professionals must understand and harness the depth of Lean's commitment to make the most impactful improvements.

An unwavering focus on impactful Lean improvements

Lean isn't a mere one-off intervention but a sustained pursuit of operational excellence. Central to Lean is the unyielding drive to eliminate waste and relentlessly focus on those improvements that promise the most significant impact. By targeting efficiency enhancements, cost reductions, and swift deliveries, Lean ensures that organizations continuously move towards an optimal state of operation.

The previous statement does not imply that Lean practitioners cannot make relatively low-cost and rapid improvements. Take manufacturing as an illustrative example. They continually monitor their production processes, identify bottlenecks, and apply corrective measures. So, instead of simply completing a batch and moving on, there would be analysis, feedback, and adjustments to ensure maximum efficiency and value in each production cycle.

But often, the most impactful changes require time, budget, and resources outside the limits of the value stream team authorities. In those cases, we rely on VSM methods to identify, prioritize, and seek budget approvals for a proposed change initiative. We will discuss this topic at length in *Chapter 4, Driving Improvements with Value Stream Management (VSM).*

Regardless of scope, the objective is to refine processes, systems, equipment, and tooling perpetually, ensuring products are of the highest quality, produced efficiently, and delivered promptly in response to market demand. Moreover, if designed and implemented correctly, those types of improvements almost always drive down our costs.

Still, it's people who will drive these efforts, and that type of dedication and mindset requires a change in culture.

Cultivating a culture of continuous improvement

While Lean tools and techniques are vital, the real magic unfolds when an organization's culture embraces continuous improvement. Here's how professionals foster such a culture:

- **Promote open communication**: Encourage teams to voice their observations, challenges, and suggestions. An environment where feedback is welcomed becomes a fertile ground for generating improvement ideas.
- **Celebrate small wins**: Recognize and reward even minor enhancements. This not only boosts morale but also reinforces the belief that every improvement, no matter how small, contributes to the bigger picture.
- **Invest in training**: Equip teams with the latest Lean techniques and tools. The more adept they are, the better they can identify opportunities for enhancement.
- **Embedded review mechanisms**: Periodic reviews ensure that the drive for improvement remains on track. These sessions should focus on assessing past actions, analyzing their outcomes, and charting the path forward. Value stream management is the right approach to ensure these reviews become mainstream.

- **Lead by example**: Leaders should not just endorse but embody the continuous improvement ethos. When team members see their leaders actively engaged in the process, they, too, are inspired to participate wholeheartedly.

So, now that you know Lean-based continuous improvements require a cultural change, how can you help make that happen? That is the topic of the following subsection.

Charting the course to sustained efficiency and profitability

For professionals, understanding and championing continuous improvement is not just a process enhancement strategy; it's a career enhancement tool. As you lead and contribute to initiatives that streamline operations, reduce waste, and elevate value delivery, you position yourself as a valuable human resource within the organization. More so, you align yourself with the organizational goals of delivering customer value efficiently while bolstering profitability.

Imagine the pride in seeing a process you refined to result in a 10% reduction in production costs or a tweak you proposed measurably enhances product quality and customer satisfaction. These aren't just operational victories; they are career milestones that showcase your value to the organization.

Moreover, in a world where businesses are constantly in the race to outdo competitors, being the torchbearer of continuous improvement ensures your organization remains a step ahead. Today's efficiency metrics become tomorrow's baselines. By continually raising the bar, you ensure that your organization doesn't just match industry standards but sets them.

Championing the transformative power of continuous improvement

This marks the end of this chapter on Establishing Lean Flows to Improve Productivity. You have learned that continuous improvement isn't just a Lean principle; it's a business imperative and a professional mantra. In an ever-changing market, resting on past achievements is not just stagnation; it's regression. The future belongs to those who iterate, innovate, and improve relentlessly. As professionals, embedding this ethos not only drives organizational excellence but also paves the way for personal success. Embrace the iterative pulse of Lean, foster a culture of constant enhancement, and witness the transformative power of continuous improvement in action.

Summary

In this chapter, you delved into the heart of Lean methodologies and their transformative power. Recognizing that a majority of consumers, spanning diverse generations, prioritize cost savings even when valuing quality, it becomes imperative for organizations to strike that delicate balance between quality and efficient delivery. You learned that the Lean approach is a potent tool in achieving this, shedding light on how to eliminate waste and constraints meticulously, ensuring products reach customers efficiently, cost-effectively, and without compromising on value.

These lessons hold paramount significance, especially in a competitive marketplace where customer preferences oscillate between quality and cost efficiency. Harnessing the power of Lean doesn't just bolster an organization's bottom line; it places you at the vanguard of industry leaders who understand and cater to nuanced customer needs. Armed with the strategies and insights from this chapter, you're poised to transform operational processes, ensuring that value delivery is not just a process, but an art form perfected over time.

We'll now move on to *Chapter 4, Driving Improvements with Value Stream Management*. In this chapter, you will learn how VSM as a methodology is applied to continuously drive the most impactful organizational improvements. For commercial enterprises, this means improving efficiency, quality, and customer alignment to achieve a competitive advantage. In non-profits and government agencies, the goals are similar, but the desired business outcomes focus on lowering costs for recipients of social and quality of life benefits and citizen services.

Questions

Answer the following questions to test your knowledge of this chapter:

1. What are the five Ms, and why do we care about them?
2. What are the eight types of waste identified in traditional Lean management practices?
3. True or false: Can the traditional Lean waste categories work in other industries besides manufacturing?
4. Why is it important to identify the constraints in our production systems?
5. What are the three most common classification types for value streams?
6. List some of the industries where Lean practices have proven their value.
7. What is the classic definition of value streams, and what is the issue we need to be concerned about when applying that definition?
8. What are the four areas we need to pay attention to drive competitive advantage?
9. How does the focus on continuous improvements differ between Lean and agile practices?
10. Who is responsible for cultivating a culture of continuous improvement?

Answers

1. The Five M's are Man, Machine, Materials, Methods, and Metrics, which provide the path to enhancing value streams
2. The eight types of waste are: Defects, Over production, Waiting, Unused talent, Transportation, Inventory, Motion and Extra-processing.

3. True. The traditional Lean waste categories, originally developed for manufacturing, can be effectively applied to other industries. These categories help identify and eliminate inefficiencies in various types of processes.
4. It's important to identify constraints in production systems to: maximize throughput, optimize resource utilization, improve process flow, focus improvement efforts, enhance quality, increase customer satisfaction, reduce cost and improve strategic planning.
5. The three most common types of value streams are: operational, development and support.
6. Some of the industries where Lean practices have proven their value are manufacturing, and software development.
7. The classic definition of a value stream is an end-to-end set of activities from concept through delivery that collaboratively transforms inputs into outputs, ultimately providing value to the customer. The problem with this definition is that it doesn't make it easy to break work down into bite-size chunks that make sense in terms of how we need to run our businesses. To overcome this problem, various thought leaders began to organize value streams around operations, development, and support functions. But, in doing so, we've lost the notion that everything we do is to support our paying customers.
8. The four areas for achieving competitive advantage with Lean are customer-centricity, optimized operations, cost-efficiency, and as a catalyst for innovation.

Further reading

1. Cecil 'Gary' Rupp, 2021. Driving DevOps with Value Stream Management: Improve IT value stream delivery with a proven VSM methodology to compete in the digital economy. PACKT Publishing, Birmingham, UK.
2. Cecil Rupp, 2020. Scaling Scrum Across Modern Enterprises: Implement Scrum and Lean-Agile techniques across complex products, portfolios, and programs in large organizations. PACKT Publishing, Birmingham, UK
3. Eliyahu Goldratt, 1984, 1986, 1992, 2004, 2014. The Goal: A Process of Ongoing Improvement. North River Press. Great Barrington, MA USA.
4. Cecil 'Gary' Rupp, 2021. Driving DevOps with Value Stream Management: Improve IT value stream delivery with a proven VSM methodology to compete in the digital economy. PACKT Publishing, Birmingham, UK.
5. Martin, K., & Osterling, M. (2013). Value Stream Mapping: How to visualize work and align leadership for organizational transformation (1st ed.). McGraw Hill Education.
6. Rother, M., & Shook, J. (2003). Learning to See: Value-stream mapping to create value and eliminate muda (1st ed.). The Lean Enterprise Institute.
7. Brunt, D., & Lovejoy, M. (2010). Seeing the Whole Value Stream (2nd ed.). Lean Enterprise Institute.

8. Tapping, D., & Schuker, T. (2001). Value Stream Management (T. Luyster, Trans.) (1st ed.). Productivity Press, NY.
9. Tapping, D. (2003). Value Stream Mapping for the Lean Office: Eight steps to planning, mapping, and sustaining Lean improvements in administrative areas (T. Schuker, Trans.) (1st ed.). Productivity Press, NY.
10. Tapping, D., Kozlowski, S., Archbold, L., & Sperl, T. (2008). Value Stream Management for Lean Healthcare (1st ed.). MCS Media, Inc., Chelsea, MI.
11. James Martin, 1995. The Great Transition. Using the Seven Disciplines of Enterprise Engineering to Align People, Technology, and Strategy. American Management Association (AMA). New Youk, NY.

Part 2: Attending to our Value Streams: Prioritize Improvements by their Value-Added Impact

Part 2 unveils essential insights and practical strategies to elevate your understanding and implementation of Lean-Agile principles with the following chapters:

- *Chapter 4, Driving Improvements with Value Stream Management*, describes its significance in today's competitive business landscape. It positions VSM as a continuous journey towards organizational excellence. By embracing VSM, organizations can systematically enhance processes and outcomes, fostering a culture of perpetual improvement essential for navigating the complexities of the modern business world.
- *Chapter 5, Introducing the VSM Implementation Roadmap*, explores the practical approach provided by the Value Stream Management Consortium (VSMC) through its Implementation Roadmap. By mastering this roadmap, you will gain the tools and knowledge to initiate transformative change, ensuring competitiveness and agility in today's dynamic marketplace.
- *Chapter 6, Navigating Value Stream Optimization*, introduces interconnected networks, essential for optimizing the flow of value within organizations. It underscores the importance of shifting from project to product thinking and leveraging digital enhancements to remain competitive. By understanding and refining value stream networks, organizations can enhance productivity, efficiency, and adaptability to meet customer's evolving needs.

- *Chapter 7, Connecting the Value Stream Network*, explores the concept of value stream networks as a holistic approach to capturing and analyzing the movement of work within an organization. The chapter delves into organizing value streams within a network, understanding customer journeys as external touchpoints, and mapping the value stream network. By emphasizing a shift from project-oriented thinking to a lifecycle-oriented, product-centric perspective, you gain insights into optimizing value-based flows and enhancing business outcomes through seamless coordination and alignment across organizational operations.

In these four chapters, you'll learn practical strategies, insights, and tools to navigate the nuances of Lean-Agile principles, empowering you to drive meaningful change within your organization. Whether you're a young professional seeking to refine your skills or an experienced executive striving for a competitive edge, *Part 2* book offers invaluable guidance on your journey toward Lean-Agile Mastery.

4

Driving Improvements with Value Stream Management

"Perfection is not attainable, but if we chase perfection, we can catch excellence." – Vince Lombardi, one of the greatest American football coaches

In an era where business efficiency and value creation are not just goals but survival strategies in the global competitive landscape, understanding and implementing **value stream management** (**VSM**) is essential. When your organization embraces VSM, a continuous transformation journey will drive your organization closer to the ever-elusive goal of perfection. The significance of VSM in fostering ongoing personal and organizational growth is immense, regardless of your role.

But why is this relentless pursuit important? Without the iterative, adaptive approach of VSM, organizations risk stagnation and decline. Ignoring the principles of continuous improvement and strategic prioritization can lead to inefficiency, misallocated resources, employee burnout, and, ultimately, a reduction in quality and customer satisfaction. Embracing VSM as a continuous evolutionary path ensures that every step taken leads to greater value, efficiency, quality, and customer alignment.

This chapter serves as a practical guide for embarking on a VSM transformation journey. Before delving into the details, addressing some potential misconceptions is essential. VSM isn't a novel concept nor merely a set of tools. Initially developed by Lean practitioners, VSM is a methodology that employs value stream mapping concepts, analytics, and **Kaizen** (change for the better) planning. VSM's goal is to identify and prioritize improvement opportunities, ultimately delivering maximum value to customers with the highest possible quality in the shortest sustainable lead time..

Embracing this continuous improvement process can distinguish you as a leader and innovator, propelling you toward operational excellence, increased profits, and enhanced customer satisfaction.

The topics covered in this chapter include the following:

- Laying the groundwork for value stream mastery
- Defining the VSM process using the E9 methodology
- Adopting a VSM platform

Laying the groundwork for value stream mastery

In this chapter, we will introduce you to VSM principles and practices, which serve as a foundation for Lean-Agile improvements. VSM is a powerful methodology that extends beyond software product development and delivery activities; its principles and practices are universally applicable to any workstream or process.

Moreover, VSM plays a crucial role in aligning investments in software delivery capabilities with other corporate change initiatives, ensuring that priorities are aligned with corporate objectives and customer needs. We'll explore how VSM serves as a continuous and less stressful business transformation strategy, discussing its purpose and goals.

VSM enables organizations to refine processes and adopt a Lean approach to eliminate inefficiencies such as constraints, delays, and waste, boosting value creation and competitiveness. Beyond the private sector, government agencies and not-for-profit organizations are challenged by the same forces of change that drive their commercial counterparts to accelerate their Lean-Agile transformations. The need for business (or mission) agility and the impact of digital disruption, globalization, ever-increasing cyber threats, aging legacy systems, and increasing dependency on technology are just a few of the factors equally concerning for government agencies and private industries.

At its core, VSM continually assesses value stream performance, prioritizing impactful enhancements to expedite customer-centric deliveries, enhance quality, and reduce costs. Our **nine-step VSM methodology** operationalizes this approach, fostering continuous business evolution and sustaining competitive advantage. Our unique approach to VSM incorporates Agile principles and practices to improve organizational flexibility, as discussed in the following subsection.

Adopting Lean-Agile concepts

VSM, grounded in Lean principles, is a proven method for driving productivity through value stream mapping and Kaizen planning techniques, fostering relentless value-based improvements. Agile principles enhance VSM, expanding its effectiveness with cross-functional teams, collaboration, and accountability, as well as its iterative development and incremental delivery approaches.

In practice, VSM strategically refines processes to maximize value delivery and minimize waste, ensuring organizations maintain a customer-centric focus throughout the product life cycle. Additionally, VSM tools provide clear process snapshots, enhancing clarity and enabling real-time analytics.

Waste elimination is central to VSM, improving efficiency and enhancing workflow, quality, and cost-effectiveness. Additionally, addressing constraints that impede flow accelerates product deliveries and removes waste.

Guiding strategic decision-making, VSM places customer needs at the forefront. Aligned with customer requirements, VSM enhances net promoter scores, reflecting its commitment to customer centricity. Emphasizing continuous improvement, VSM advocates ongoing evaluation, fostering agility in response to evolving business requirements, market dynamics, and customer needs. Ultimately, VSM embodies a value-driven mindset that shapes organizational approaches for sustained success.

Understanding the taxonomy of value streams

Organizing work across value streams is essential for developing product-centric workflows. **Value Streams** focus on streamlined operations, throughput maximization, constraint avoidance, and waste elimination. **Processes** within value streams, such as product development, order entry, and sales, convert input into value-added output. **Activities** aggregate information for performance reporting, while **Tasks** define work and deliverables. *Figure 4.1* illustrates the work taxonomy of value streams, which is vital for targeted improvements and enhanced efficiency.

Figure 4.1 – Value stream work taxonomy

This taxonomy is fundamental for value stream analysis and optimization. **Processes** outline value creation flow, while **Activities** aid monitoring and decision-making. Mapping processes and activities identify inefficiencies, ensuring each step adds value. Establishing standard work practices at the **Task** level maintains consistent performance and quality. This understanding enables targeted improvements, enhancing efficiency and effectiveness.

Now that you understand the foundational VSM groundwork, we will explore the strategic significance of VSM principles in driving organizational excellence and value delivery in the following subsection.

Applying VSM principles

VSM offers deeper insights into the flows across interconnected value streams. Through a systematic approach, it pinpoints, prioritizes, and addresses the most consequential improvement opportunities, ensuring a comprehensive strategy for optimal value delivery.

The emphasis on maximizing value extends beyond the efficiency of isolated processes or value streams; it's also about identifying and addressing flow constraints potentially hindering value delivery throughout a product's life cycle.

> **The primary purpose of value streams**
> Author Richard Knaster states, "*While value streams are critical aspects of Lean methods, it's a common misconception that improved efficiency is their primary objective. That's not surprising because eliminating waste is one of the most often discussed aspects of Lean. However, nothing could be further from the truth. Every value stream's goal is to deliver the maximum value to the customer with the highest possible quality and delight in the shortest sustainable lead-time.*"[1]

Drawing from the foundational insights of Lean and Agile, the following set of guiding principles helps drive business outcomes in any value-driven organization:

- **Holistic system optimization**: Using systems thinking, end-to-end processes and activities are frequently assessed to create, improve, and deliver new customer value via products and services.
- **Customer-centricity**: Customers are the ultimate deciders of value for the solutions created and maintained by a portfolio's value streams. Champion initiatives that align with the customer's desires, needs, and priorities. Make customer experience a top priority throughout an organization's actions and attitude.
- **Value stream insight**: Map the end-to-end customer journey, revealing constraints and waste throughout the organization. Customer journey maps enhance understanding, improve user experiences, align teams, inform decisions, increase satisfaction, identify opportunities, optimize resources, and boost retention by proactively addressing issues.
- **Demand-driven**: Fine-tune your organizational processes to quickly respond to customer demand, optimize inventory, and deliver high-quality value.
- **Flow optimization**: Concentrate on streamlining value delivery, tackling bottlenecks, delays, and excess **work in process** (**WIP**) to minimize costly constraints and accelerate throughput.

- **Waste elimination**: Learn to see and address inefficiencies, both obvious and hidden, to cultivate a lean, value-driven environment.
- **Pursue perfection**: Embrace the thinking of relentless improvement, advancing toward optimal operations with retrospectives each iteration and inspect and adapt events for Agile teams of teams.
- **Organizational alignment**: Foster respect and unity of purpose across all levels of the organization, ensuring a collective commitment to excellence in value delivery.

While these principles are foundational to VSM, their real power surfaces when implemented strategically to improve value delivery and time-to-market. However, we risk inefficient use of time and resources if we do not consider improvement opportunities in context with their overarching impact on the entire delivery system. In other words, we must avoid costly and ineffective *local optimizations* by employing systems thinking.

In the sections that follow, we'll explore the challenges of local optimization—acting without systems thinking and its effects.

Optimizing value flow with VSM

VSM is a comprehensive method designed to enhance value-based organizational flows by identifying and prioritizing improvements, eliminating waste, and overcoming constraints. Its core objective is to expedite customer value delivery by systematically addressing inefficiencies, improving quality, accelerating delivery, and reducing costs. This transformative approach relies on metrics and measures to gauge progress, foster continuous improvement, and enable data driven decision-making and bottleneck identification.

Before introducing our nine-step VSM methodology, we must first understand how to apply systems thinking to avoid local optimizations.

Avoiding the pitfalls of local optimization

Local optimization occurs when organizations prioritize individual improvement opportunities without considering the broader system. It often arises from undisciplined practices, where all items are treated equally in resource allocation, or when executives allow individuals to dictate priorities without a **systems thinking** approach. Local optimization overlooks waste and constraints from a customer-oriented and value-added perspective, leading to unintended negative consequences on overall performance. In contrast, a systems thinking approach aims to optimize the system by understanding its interconnected parts and feedback loops.

Unfortunately, organizations often narrow their focus to improving individual departments or value stream activities, which may not yield significant improvements in the broader delivery process. For instance, a process improvement targeting increased throughput in a specific activity or equipment may not be beneficial if it's not a constraint in our system. In such cases, resources are wasted, bottlenecks form, and excess WIP accumulates, hampering overall flow across the value stream. VSM practitioners emphasize a holistic evaluation of business processes to ensure alignment with customer aspirations and to avoid misdirected efforts.

Mapping the customer value stream, especially in siloed organizations, helps identify crucial streams for delivering value and reducing organizational waste. VSM emphasizes making organizational goals visible as value streams to foster alignment and reduce coordination costs. Now, let's explore the E9 VSM methodology.

Defining the VSM process using the E9 methodology

VSM offers a holistic method to visualize operations and enhance value delivery, prioritizing optimization of entire value streams to focus on customer value consistently. *Figure 4.2* illustrates the **E9 VSM process**, providing a comprehensive approach to continuous value stream improvement.

While E9 is presented linearly, the method operates like a network of activities occurring in parallel with feedback and iteration among steps. Additionally, an **End** state activity considers the eventual retirement of a product and the importance of life cycle management planning.

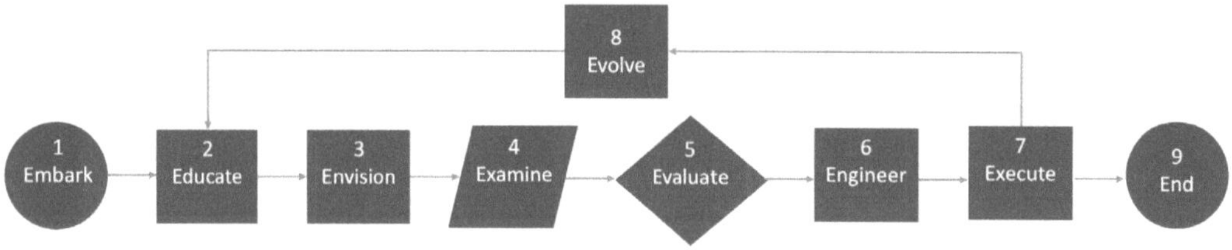

Figure 4.2 – E9 VSM process

E9 is a mnemonic for the nine steps of our VSM improvement method: **Embark, Educate**, **Envision**, **Examine**, **Evaluate**, **Engineer**, **Execute**, **Evolve**, and **End**. Let's look more closely at these nine VSM steps and their significance in contemporary business practices.

1. **Embark**: Begin the VSM journey with commitment and clarity.
2. **Educate**: Coach teams on Lean-Agile and VSM principles.
3. **Envision**: Define the future state vision in alignment with strategic goals.
4. **Examine**: Map current state value stream processes and metrics.
5. **Evaluate**: Diagnose processes to identify inefficiencies and waste.
6. **Engineer**: Strategize and develop Kaizen plan for the desired improvements.
7. **Execute**: Follow the Kaizen Plan to implement the agreed changes
8. **Evolve**: Iterate to refine processes and sustain improvements.
9. **End**: Implement effective end-of-life support procedures for products or services.

The E9 VSM method, while adapted to specific situations, has demonstrated its efficacy across various sectors, including manufacturing, healthcare, sales, services, technology, and lean office settings, bolstering their global competitiveness since the early 2000s. Notable examples include the series of books on VSM by Don Tapping et al. [5,6,7]

In an era of digital innovation, the imperative to leverage technology for improving products, services, and processes cannot be overstated.

With this groundwork laid, let's explore the significance of value stream optimization.

1. Embark – beginning the journey

Figure 4.3, Embark, is the first phase of the E9 VSM method and initiates the journey with a clear commitment and purpose. It begins with securing leadership support and assembling the VSM team.

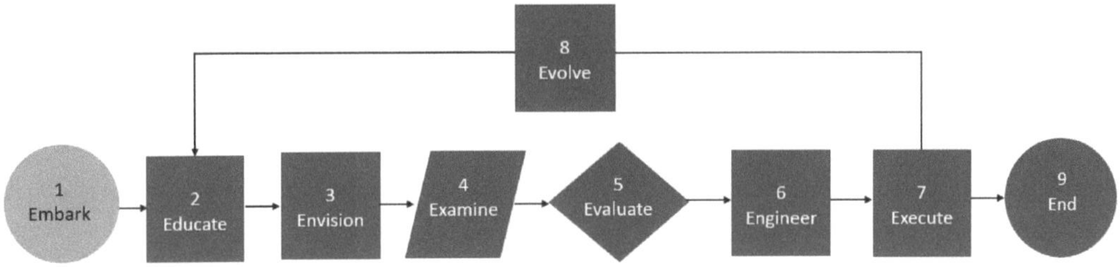

Figure 4.3 – Embark: beginning the journey

The start of a VSM initiative is not simply an icon representing a point in time on a VSM engagement roadmap. Instead, Embark represents a collection of activities necessary to identify the goals and objectives that justify the time and resources expended on the effort, securing executive sponsorship, and identifying the VSM team that will guide the effort. These activities are described in the following subsections.

Identifying the business justifications for VSM

Implementing a VSM initiative can bring significant benefits to organizations. However, securing executive sponsorship and funding requires a well-constructed and defensible business case. While we can't provide a specific business justification tailored to your organization, we have compiled a table of business reasons in *Figure 4.4* to support a VSM initiative. It outlines why executives should consider sponsoring and funding it.

Business reasons for supporting VSM		
Adaptability	Data-driven decision-making	Innovation
Competitive advantage	Employee engagement	Resource optimization
Compliance and regulation	Enhanced efficiency and productivity	Risk mitigation
Cost reduction	Faster time to market	Strategic alignment
Customer satisfaction	Improved quality	Sustainability

Figure 4.4 – Table of business reasons to support a VSM initiative

Demonstrating a strong **return on investment** (**ROI**) and alignment with strategic priorities enhances the chance of securing executive sponsorship and funding. You can start small and get started quicker if you take an incremental funding strategy, validate the benefits, and then move on to the next highest priority area. Keep the initial ask of executives small, build confidence and trust, and scale as needed, when appropriate. As Agile practitioners know, the best path forward is one of iterative and incremental change rather than a big-bang approach.

Now that we've briefly explored the benefits of initiating a VSM program, let's move on to securing leadership support and sponsorship for your initiative.

Establishing leadership support and sponsorship

To convince executives to fund a VSM initiative, you will need to identify someone at the executive level to sponsor and fund the initiative. It is usually necessary to gather supporting data, compile and present case studies, develop an implementation plan, and specify key areas for improvement.

VSM offers a strategic approach to managing change across organizations. Although Lean and Agile practitioners both champion continuous improvement, realizing this vision requires support, active engagement, and funding from senior executives. Convincing these leaders to invest in improvement requires a structured approach and a compelling argument for the initiative's benefits.

In the following subsections, we'll explore strategies for gaining executive and stakeholder support.

Aligning with strategic and operational objectives

To gain the interest of executives, it's best to align your VSM initiatives with the organization's strategic objectives, as depicted in *Figure 4.5*.

Figure 4.5 – Gaining executive sponsorship

Discuss how VSM can be a driving force behind achieving their critical goals. Executives are more likely to support initiatives that directly contribute to the bottom line. Also, identify the key stakeholders in your organization who influence the approval and support of your VSM initiatives. These individuals may include senior executives, department heads, influential managers, and other internal or external stakeholders.

Communicating potential benefits and gaining support

Prepare a persuasive pitch outlining VSM's potential impact, customized to your organization's needs, as discussed earlier. Employ data, metrics, and real-world case studies to demonstrate how VSM can bring about transformative change. Address the fundamental question executives are apt to pose: "What financial benefits does it offer us?"

Provide estimates of cost savings, revenue growth, or other financial benefits resulting from successful implementation. Executives are more inclined to support initiatives with a tangible ROI. However, when building your case, always be mindful of local optimizations, as they may prevent you from realizing your ROI.

Engage in focused discussions with key stakeholders to address their questions and concerns. Adapt your message to align with their needs, demonstrating a deep understanding of their concerns to strengthen your case.

Finally, internal advocates or champions who can promote the VSM initiative to executives should be identified. These champions, influential figures within the organization, passionately believe in the benefits of VSM. Their trust and commitment can make a significant difference in gaining support for the initiative.

Building trust and commitment

To secure sponsorship for a VSM initiative, involve peers in decision-making regarding people and resources, schedules, and scope. Share customer success stories from organizations that have benefited from VSM. The **Value Stream Management Consortium** (**VSMC**) has many resources your stakeholders and sponsors can read to gain additional information and trust.

Proposing a pilot program can effectively demonstrate the initiative's effectiveness and alleviate concerns. Persistence and proactive risk management further garner executive support and funding. We can build upon these successes by starting VSM projects with a relatively small scope but high reward, targeting the organization's early adopters. Eventually, as the benefits become evident and the processes become ingrained, even the laggards will come along and support future VSM programs. Ultimately, VSM becomes a way of life and an integral part of the organization's culture.

After gaining funding from your organization, it's time to establish the VSM team to lead the effort described in the following subsections.

Identifying the VSM team

The composition of a VSM team can vary depending on factors such as organization size, industry, and objectives. However, specific key roles and characteristics are generally valuable for a successful VSM initiative:

- **Executive sponsor**: A senior leader who champions the VSM initiative, secures resources, and ensures alignment with strategic goals
- **VSM leader/manager**: Oversees the entire initiative, possessing expertise in Lean-Agile practices and business process improvement
- **Value stream architect**: Designs and aligns business strategy, processes, and capabilities to achieve objectives, interfacing between business and IT stakeholders
- **Process owners**: Manage specific value stream processes, implement changes, monitor performance, and recognize their role within a complex business system that requires collaboration to achieve shared goals
- **Data analysts**: Gather, analyze, and interpret data related to the value stream's performance, providing insights for improvement
- **Cross-functional team members**: Bring diverse expertise to address inefficiencies within the value stream

- **Lean-Agile coach**: Guides the team in applying Lean and Agile principles effectively
- **Change management specialist**: Manages resistance to change and ensures the adoption of new processes
- **Communication specialist**: Facilitates effective communication among stakeholders

Not every organization can afford dedicated individuals for each role, so team members often take on multiple responsibilities. Additionally, the size and makeup of the VSM team can evolve as the initiative progresses across different product lines or value streams. Evolving the team requires considering specific industries, their unique requirements, and challenges. For example, expertise in production processes, supply chain management, robotics, automation, and quality control are essential in manufacturing.

After gaining sponsorship, funding, and establishing teams, our VSM methodology progresses to education, communications, and change management—vital for overcoming resistance to change, described in the following subsection.

2. Educate – Training, communicating, and managing change for success

In *VSM Step 2, Figure 4.6 - Educate*, we address crucial components essential for the success of your VSM initiative. Comprehensive training in Lean-Agile and VSM principles is imperative to prepare individuals for the upcoming changes.

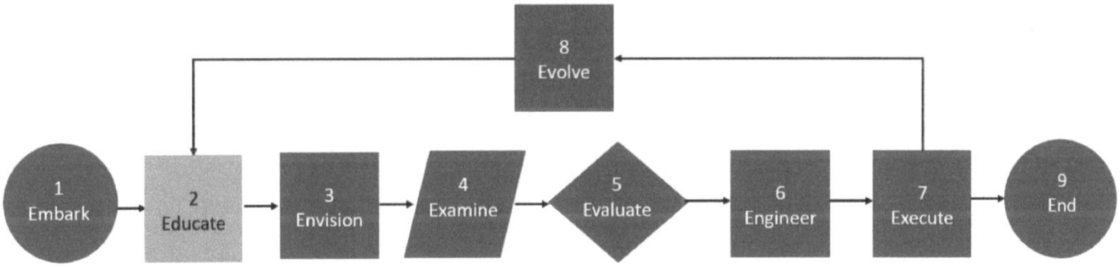

Figure 4.6 - Educate: Training, communicating, and managing change for success

However, education alone is insufficient. Effective communication is equally vital to convey the reasons behind the changes and their benefits, addressing stakeholders' concerns or fears. Additionally, change management practices are significant in managing resistance and ensuring a smoother transition as the organization embraces VSM.

Educating teams on Lean-Agile and VSM principles

Educating teams on Lean-Agile and VSM principles is vital for success, fostering alignment and understanding across the organization. Start by introducing Lean-Agile's key concepts, such as continuous improvement and customer-centricity. Similarly, familiarize teams with VSM's principles, emphasizing end-to-end value stream enhancement.

As shown in *Figure 4.7*, business training sessions can be informal. Smaller training sessions are often preferable and more effective in engaging participants and maintaining interest.

Figure 4.7 – Business training session

These training sessions provide a common language and mindset and foster collaboration across functional boundaries. Let's explore the scope of this training, beginning with Lean-Agile principles.

Teaching Lean-Agile principles and practices

Teaching Lean-Agile principles is essential for a successful VSM journey. Lean-Agile methodologies prioritize adaptability, efficiency, and customer focus, promoting continuous improvement by reducing waste and delivering value promptly.

Chapter 8, Implementing Basic Lean-Agile Solutions Teams (BLASTs), will describe how teams often switch between business-as-usual work and problem-solving activities. In other words, we'll explore in depth how team members seamlessly transition between Lean and Agile modes of working.

But let's quickly introduce the concepts here. Lean principles, including customer value, value stream mapping, and continuous improvement, are essential to sustain the efficient delivery of customer value through our products and services. In Agile, the focus is on work item refinement, iterative planning, and incremental development cycles (also known as **timeboxed development cycles**). These practices foster collaboration and innovation, making organizations more responsive to customer needs. By understanding these principles, teams can effectively embrace VSM concepts and practices.

Teaching VSM concepts

Teaching VSM concepts is essential for organizations aiming to enhance their end-to-end customer value streams. As a core component of Lean-Agile methodologies, VSM focuses on efficiently delivering customer value. Corporate training should prioritize comprehensive education on the nine-step VSM methodology, covering its nuances.

While VSM builds upon foundational Lean concepts, training must extend beyond that. It should begin by defining the purpose of each VSM step and emphasize the importance of determining the idealized customer value stream as the organization's guiding principle for performance improvements.

Training should focus on value stream mapping across the entire customer value stream to ensure a holistic approach and prevent local optimizations. Through gap analysis, participants can identify and prioritize impactful improvements, ranging from low-resource to higher-cost initiatives that require proposal submission and approval.

Ultimately, VSM training aims to equip teams with the knowledge and skills to effectively apply VSM principles, driving meaningful improvements in organizational value streams.

Coaching strategies

Training and coaching are essential to a successful VSM initiative, ensuring that VSM teams acquire the necessary skills and knowledge. Corporate VSM training programs should include immersive workshops, support for certifications, and hands-on experiential learning. These methods enable teams to deeply understand VSM principles and practices, enhancing their ability to visualize, analyze, and improve value streams.

However, knowledge alone isn't sufficient; application is key. Coaching plays a vital role in this regard. Business coaching requires proficiency in active listening, empathy, and providing constructive feedback.

Effective questioning techniques encourage critical thinking and self-discovery among those coached. Coaches also guide individuals in creating actionable plans and hold them accountable for implementing desired changes. By continually refining coaching skills and fostering a collaborative atmosphere, coaches facilitate self-awareness, personal growth, and improved performance in a business setting. Training and coaching are crucial for instilling VSM practices within an organization and driving meaningful change and improvement.

Communicating for change

When implementing any program, project, or VSM initiative, it's vital to have a well-defined communication strategy in place. This strategy ensures that everyone involved, from employees to stakeholders, is fully informed and prepared for the changes ahead. To tailor your communication strategy effectively, consider the unique needs of your initiative and adapt accordingly. Remember, it's often easier to refine an existing plan than to start from scratch.

Let's take a quick look at the scope of work involved in supporting the communications strategy.

1. **Define clear objectives**: Establish specific goals for your communication strategy.
2. **Identify stakeholders**: Recognize all parties with an interest in your communication efforts.
3. **Segment your audience**: Divide your target audience into distinct groups based on relevant criteria to tailor your communication effectively.
4. **Develop key messages**: Craft concise, impactful messages that align with and support your objectives.
5. **Choose communication channels**: Select the most effective platforms and mediums to reach your audience.
6. **Create a communication plan**: Structure a comprehensive strategy outlining tasks, timelines, and responsibilities.
7. **Provide regular updates**: Keep stakeholders informed with timely progress reports.
8. **Address concerns and questions**: Have a bias for quick action. Respond promptly and transparently to inquiries and issues.
9. **Encourage feedback**: Solicit input from stakeholders to improve communication effectiveness.
10. **Train communication champions**: Empower individuals to advocate for and effectively convey your messages.
11. **Evaluate and adjust**: Assess the performance of your communication strategy and make necessary modifications.
12. **Celebrate milestones**: Celebrating small wins boosts team morale and motivation. Recognize achievements publicly, fostering appreciation, engagement, and productivity.
13. **Use multiple channels**: Experiment with various communication methods, such as email, social media, short videos, newsletters, and in-person meetings, to effectively reach and engage a broader audience.
14. **Continuously improve**: Adapt and refine your approach based on feedback to ensure clarity, engagement, and alignment with organizational goals.

Figure 4.8 summarizes the elements of a communications strategy to develop a comprehensive communication plan.

Communicating Strategy	
Defining clear objectives	Addressing concerns and questions
Identifying stakeholders	Encouraging feedback
Segmenting your audience	Training communication champions
Developing key messages	Evaluating and adjusting
Choosing communication channels	Celebrating milestones
Creating a communication plan	Using multiple channels
Providing regular updates	Continuously improving

Figure 4.8 – Communications strategy

By following these steps, you can ensure that your communication efforts effectively convey the importance of the upcoming changes and engage your stakeholders throughout the process.

Now that we've covered the essentials of effective communication, let's shift our focus to change management strategies. Change management is crucial for navigating the complexities of transformational efforts and maximizing the chances of achieving your desired outcomes.

Implementing change management strategies and best practices

Change management is crucial for guiding organizations through transitions while minimizing disruption and resistance. Its goals include addressing concerns, maximizing adoption, reducing disruption, ensuring consistency, and optimizing benefits realization.

Here's how to achieve these goals effectively:

- **Addressing concerns**: Identify and swiftly address employee concerns to minimize resistance and foster a supportive environment for change
- **Maximizing adoption**: Ensure employees understand the reasons for change and actively participate in its implementation, fostering ownership and commitment
- **Reducing disruption**: Carefully plan and sequence changes to minimize disruption to ongoing operations and workflows

- **Ensuring consistency**: Maintain consistency in communication and messaging to ensure all employees receive accurate and timely information about the change
- **Optimizing benefits realization**: Focus on realizing the intended benefits of change quickly and effectively to achieve organizational objectives

Despite well-structured communication and change management strategies, resistance to change may persist. Proactive steps, including identifying sources of resistance and engaging with resistant individuals or groups, are essential to address concerns and foster alignment with proposed changes.

Now, let's dive into the practical process of managing change within our VSM initiative.

Managing change

Understanding key frameworks for change management is crucial for navigating organizational transitions effectively. Two fundamental proven change models are the following:

- **John Kotter's eight-step process**: Creating urgency is a critical first step to initiate change. Additional steps outlined in his seminal book Leading Change include building coalitions and vision, removing obstacles, creating short-term wins, building on the change, and anchoring the change in the new structure.[2] This eight-step process calls for patience, especially in the first critical steps to achieve high engagement from leaders.
- **Hiatt's ADKAR process**: The Prosci ADKAR five-step model by Jeff Hiatt advocates **Awareness**, **Desire**, **Knowledge**, **Ability**, and **Reinforcement** (**ADKAR**) through phases, preparation, design, implementation, and sustainability.

These two change management frameworks provide a structured approach for ensuring smooth transitions and maximizing the likelihood of successful outcomes. *Chapter 11, Implementing Strategies for Organizational Transformation,* will discuss these two change management processes in further detail. Understanding them will serve as a foundation for effective VSM change management initiatives.

The following subsection will cover stakeholder engagement, a critical component of successful change management in VSM initiatives.

Engaging stakeholders in the VSM initiative

Stakeholder engagement is crucial for the success of any VSM initiative. Stakeholders include employees, customers, suppliers, and others impacted by the initiative. To engage stakeholders effectively, you need to do the following:

- Identify and map key stakeholders, considering their interests and potential contributions
- Tailor communication to address the specific needs and priorities of each stakeholder group
- Involve stakeholders early in planning and decision-making stages to foster ownership and commitment

- Provide regular updates on progress, encourage feedback, and address concerns openly
- Incorporate stakeholders' input into change assessments for more effective solutions

Successful stakeholder engagement builds strong relationships, ensures alignment with initiative goals, and facilitates achieving desired outcomes. Next, we'll explore the Envision step in the VSM process.

3. Envision – designing the ideal future state

Traditional VSM methodologies often advocate creating a current-state value stream map before envisioning a future state. However, this approach can inadvertently reinforce existing inefficiencies. Instead, we propose envisioning the end-to-end activities required to deliver a product or service to customers and support it across its life cycle. By doing this, the focus is on identifying the most efficient and effective delivery path possible, minimizing constraints and waste. This step is shown in *Figure 4.9*.

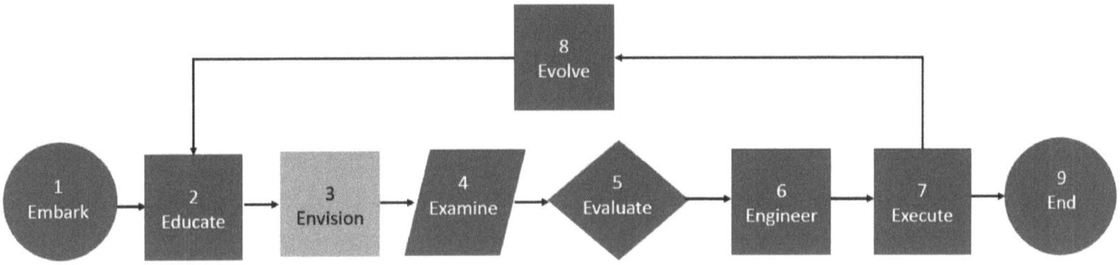

Figure 4.9 - Envision: designing the ideal future state

During this phase, avoid getting bogged down in detailed value stream mapping and performance metrics. The goal is to create an idealized value stream map free from unnecessary complexities and inefficiencies.

By prioritizing simplicity and efficiency from the outset, we can better identify opportunities for improvement and streamline the value delivery process, resulting in an idealized value stream map.

Defining the idealized customer value stream

Defining the **idealized customer value stream** sets the compass for transformation. Start by envisioning the perfect value stream—free of constraints and waste. Engage your team and stakeholders to imagine the optimal customer experience and how processes can deliver it consistently. Focusing on high-level ideals motivates your team and provides clear direction for the improvement initiative.

Setting strategic goals and alignment

Strategic goals act as a North Star for transformative change. So, after crafting the idealized value stream, aligning it with strategic objectives is the next step. Identify organizational goals, from enhancing efficiency to expanding market reach, and connect them with components of the ideal value stream. This alignment ties your VSM initiative to the bigger picture, driving success and transformation.

Creating a vision and mission for the value stream

Vision and mission statements are essential for strategic planning. Working with executive sponsors, define a concise mission statement outlining specific objectives and methods for value stream optimization. Then, craft a vision statement that delves into the broader purpose of the VSM initiative, aligning it with the organization's mission and values. These statements inspire teams and provide a shared sense of purpose.

Establishing metrics and success criteria

Measuring progress is integral to VSM. Establish metrics and success criteria as benchmarks after defining and aligning the ideal value stream with strategic goals. Identify **key performance indicators (KPIs)** tied to strategic objectives, such as lead time, cycle time, and customer satisfaction. Regularly review these KPIs to track progress and identify areas for improvement.

We can identify improvement opportunities and streamline the value delivery process by prioritizing simplicity and efficiency. This approach yields an idealized value stream map, laying the groundwork for transformation.

Hands-on knowledge of value stream mapping techniques is useful but not necessary to analyze the current and future states of the organization's value streams and delivery capabilities. However, the overview we provided in Step 2 should give you the foundational knowledge to help you understand the key concepts. For those who want to understand the detailed mechanics of value stream mapping, author Cecil Rupp extensively discusses this topic in his previous book, Driving DevOps with Value Stream Management.[3] Author Steve Pereira also guides readers through the practice in detail in his book Flow Engineering. The *Further reading* section also references several well-known books on this topic. [4,5,6,7,8,9]

4. Examine – assessing the current state and identifying inefficiencies

After designing the ideal state, the next step, *Examine* - identified in *Figure 4.10*, involves examining the current situation and thoroughly analyzing existing processes and metrics. Through this work, we can diagnose inefficiencies and waste, paving the way for strategic improvements.

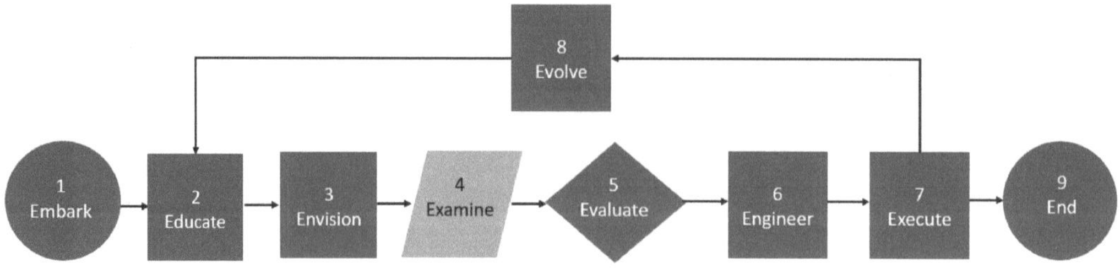

Figure 4.10 - Examine: assessing the current state and identifying inefficiencies

This phase evaluates your organization's current processes and metrics. Contrasting this information with your idealized value stream helps uncover opportunities for improvement and visualize how enhancements will impact value stream flows.

Here, you'll discover the significance of current state mapping and explore tools and techniques for mapping value streams. Additionally, we cover methods for gathering process data and metrics to understand your organization's workflow.

We will discuss conducting root cause analysis to uncover underlying issues and strategies for prioritizing areas for improvement. The following section provides the knowledge and tools to rigorously assess your organization's current state, setting the stage for meaningful VSM enhancements.

Examining current state processes and metrics

The value stream mapping process traditionally involves several key steps, depicted in *Figure 4.11*, which guide the examination and evaluation of value streams.

Value Stream Mapping Process			
1	Identify a value stream to improve	6	Identify steps in the current value stream flow
2	Identify value stream sponsors	7	Collect active and wait time metrics for each step
3	Identify a small team to map the value stream	8	Collect metrics on complete and accurate (the % of work that the downstream step can complete without returning it to the prior step)
4	Agree on logistics (times and places to meet)	9	Calculate flow efficiency (total time spent on value-added work/total flow time)
5	Agree on value stream boundaries, from start (request) to end (value delivery)	10	Identify bottlenecks and constraints, perform root-cause analysis, and prioritize areas for improvement

Figure 4.11 - Evaluate: assessing inefficiencies and waste with value stream mapping

Value stream mapping is a lean improvement technique for management that defines and illustrates the interconnected processes that bring a product or service from request to customer value delivery.

Understanding how value streams create value for software development can be complex. The inefficiencies are not as highly visible as the ones you might see at a lean manufacturing plant. For example, a catwalk above the factory floor lets you observe the manufacturing value stream to see if the 'line' is slowing or grinding to a halt.

Value stream mapping is the equivalent of the catwalk for digital and knowledge-work-oriented value streams, although it is also useful for showing flow efficiency metrics in any type of value stream. It allows you to see the entire value flow and identify bottlenecks and delays. Nevertheless, inefficiencies have the same effects: increased waste and costs, decreased productivity, overburdened workers, uncertainties, and lower quality.

Mapping the value stream begins from product or service consumption and moves upstream, including supplier processes and material flows. Key activities supporting the customer experience are confirmed, while unnecessary ones are eliminated. Performance metrics are gathered for each process to establish baselines, and identify waste such as overproduction and defects are identified.

Following this, processes are analyzed to identify bottlenecks and inefficiencies and develop improvement plans. A future state map is created to outline optimized processes. Implementation plans are formulated, support is obtained, and changes are executed. Continuous monitoring ensures performance aligns with expectations, with further improvement opportunities identified.

These steps provide a comprehensive assessment, laying the foundation for meaningful enhancements in VSM. They are commonly employed among Lean practitioners to bridge the gap between the current state and a desired future state. Notably, the value stream mapping process starts from delivery and moves upstream, a practice we will explore in the following subsection to understand its rationale.

Exploring reverse value stream mapping – starting with the customer and working backward

Commencing the value stream mapping journey with the end—the customer—may appear unconventional yet it is strategically sound. By mapping value streams, starting from the customer's perspective, you can identify steps that add value and those that don't. Moreover, this practice keeps the focus on defining the outputs that each preceding (upstream) step must deliver to support the current activity under investigation. This customer-centric approach ensures that value stream improvements directly benefit end users.

As we trace backward (upstream) through the value stream, scrutinizing each process, we naturally uncover inefficiencies and waste. This critical examination of activities allows us to refine processes akin to fine-tuning a high-performance engine.

Moreover, this reverse approach to value stream mapping fosters a culture of continuous improvement, a cornerstone of Lean-Agile principles. By constantly seeking enhancements, we maintain an efficient, streamlined value stream that consistently delivers exceptional customer value.

While unconventional, reverse value stream mapping ensures efficiency, quality, and better collaboration by considering both the product and customer delivery flows.

5. Evaluate – assessing inefficiencies and waste

As we progress through the generic VSM methodology, we arrive at *VSM Step 5, Evaluate*, highlighted in *Figure 4.12*. This critical phase is pivotal in optimizing the value stream, aiming for enhanced efficiency, quality, and customer satisfaction.

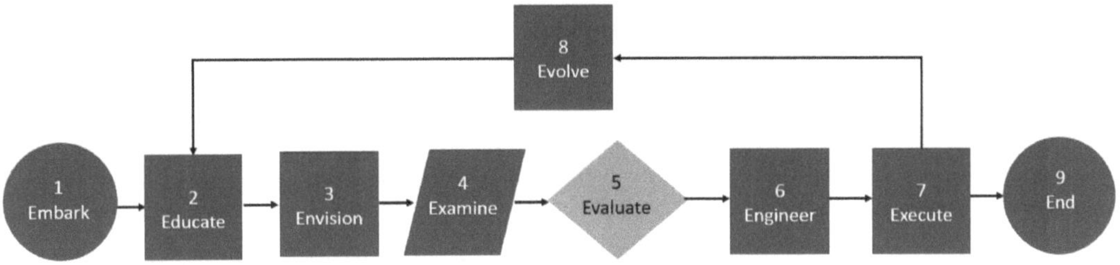

Figure 4.12 - Evaluate: assessing inefficiencies and waste

Assessing current state maps for inefficiencies

Before embarking on improvement initiatives, it's essential to grasp the existing processes thoroughly. Current state maps visually represent the value creation process across the value stream targeted for improvement. During this evaluation phase, we closely examine these maps.

This evaluation involves meticulously scrutinizing each step, input, and output within the value stream. Working backward, we question the necessity of each task, aiming to identify potential inefficiencies and waste.

For instance, we analyze whether preceding tasks are delivering requisite inputs or causing bottlenecks. We investigate potential excess or shortage of work and assess the quality of materials and information provided.

This detailed evaluation unveils the root causes of inefficiencies and waste within the value stream, laying the groundwork for targeted improvement initiatives. Such inefficiencies may manifest as unnecessary steps, delays, redundancies, and overproduction.

Identifying bottlenecks and constraints

As you learned in *Chapter 3, Establishing Lean Flows to Improve Productivity*, the concept of waste in Lean encompasses eight categories of non-value-adding work. These traditional waste categories are **Transportation**, **Inventory**, **Motion**, **Waiting**, **Overproduction**, **Overprocessing**, **Defects**, and **Underutilized Talent**. We often find our bottlenecks and constraints originate from these eight waste categories. These bottlenecks impede workflow, causing delays, clutter, and increased costs.

Value stream mapping aims to uncover these bottlenecks and constraints, disrupting the smooth workflows. Identifying and resolving them becomes crucial to prioritize improvement efforts. Pinpointing specific process points where work accumulates enables focused attention on alleviating these bottlenecks, ensuring a balanced workflow.

Performing root cause analysis

Root cause analysis offers problem-solving tools used to identify the actual causes of a problem rather than just fixing the surface-level symptoms. There is usually more than one cause of a problem, but the key is to avoid assumptions and logic traps, tracing the chain of causality from the effect to a root cause connected to the original problem.

The **five whys** is a proven problem-solving technique used to explore cause-and-effect relationships. Toyota developed and refined this process as a critical component of its problem-solving training. Taiichi Ohno, recognized as the father of the **Toyota Production System** (**TPS**), explains the five whys technique in his book, *Toyota Production System: Beyond Large-Scale Production*. He says, "*By repeating why five times, the nature of the problem, as well as its solution, becomes clear.*" *Figure 4.13* shows how this technique uncovers a problem's root cause.

The problem: The marketing campaign failed to meet its *new customer* sign-up target	
Why?	The engagement rate on the campaign's advertisements was lower than anticipated.
Why?	The content of the advertisements did not resonate well with the target audience.
Why?	The marketing team had inadequate insights into the preferences and needs of the target audience.
Why?	The market research was outdated and did not accurately reflect current trends and customer sentiments.
Why?	The team relied on secondary research from the previous year without conducting new primary research to validate and update their understanding.

Figure 4.13 – Five whys problem-solving for the failed marketing campaign

The five whys process typically involves the following steps:

1. **Identify the problem**: Clearly define the undesired outcome to address.
2. **Ask, "Why?"**: Question why the problem occurred and note the first answer.
3. **Repeat**: Continuously ask "Why?" for each answer received, leading to more specific causes.
4. **Reach the root cause**: Ideally, uncover the root cause or causes after asking why five times.
5. **Develop solutions**: Brainstorm and implement solutions to eliminate or mitigate the identified root causes.

Other root cause analysis techniques, such as the **Fishbone diagram** (Ishikawa or cause-and-effect diagram), **Failure Mode and Effects Analysis** (**FMEA**), and the **Pareto analysis**, are commonly used in different situations and industries. The choice of technique depends on the complexity of the problem and the specific context in which it occurs.

Prioritizing areas for improvement

Not all inefficiencies and bottlenecks within the value stream have equal impact. Hence, the final step of the evaluation phase is prioritizing improvement areas. Considering factors such as severity, overall effect on the value stream, and resource requirements, we can develop a structured plan for addressing these inefficiencies. Recall that, as a general rule, we attack constraints first. But excessive cost and quality issues can also dictate higher priorities. Prioritization ensures that efforts and resources are directed where they will have the most significant positive impact.

In conclusion, the *Evaluate* phase is crucial for initiating meaningful improvements. By meticulously examining current state maps, identifying bottlenecks, performing root cause analysis, and prioritizing areas for enhancement, organizations can establish a foundation for a streamlined and optimized value stream that efficiently delivers value to customers.

We are now ready to proceed to *Step 6, Engineer*, where we will focus on the strategic and tactical aspects of improvement and where planning and optimization take center stage.

6. Engineer – strategies and planning improvements

Having navigated through the initial phases of our VSM methodology, where we have identified our areas for the most impactful improvements, we now transition from planning to action.

This subsection will examine the essential aspects of engineering strategies and plans for improving your organization's value stream. The process involves a systematic approach to identify, plan, and implement changes that enhance efficiency, reduce waste, and, ultimately, deliver more value to customers. The position of the Engineer step is highlighted in *Figure 4.14*.

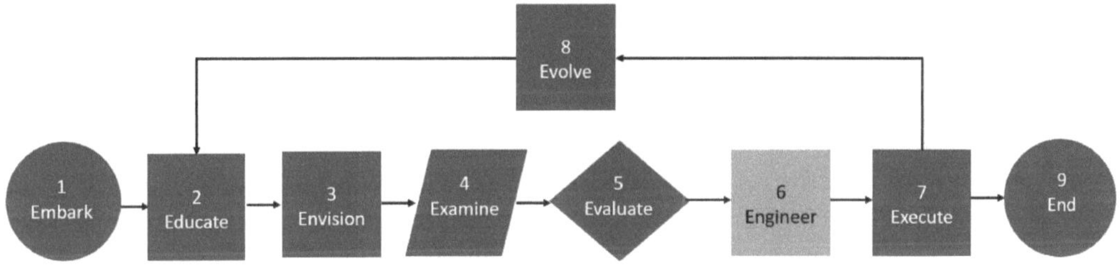

Figure 4.14 - Engineer: strategies and planning improvements

Given that VSM initiatives may uncover complex and potentially costly change opportunities navigating the company's decision-making and funding processes is essential. Lean Kaizen planning (or road mapping) and forecasting are needed to justify investments, which must demonstrate a pragmatic ROI within a predefined timeframe.

In other words, designing superior products and processes alone won't suffice if we fail to capture the market's attention and needs within the critical window of opportunity. If we miss this window, our competitors will step in to fill the void, and our efforts will be in vain.

Developing strategies and plans for desired improvements

Developing strategies and plans for improvements is essential for successful value stream optimization. This phase lays the groundwork for impactful transformations by identifying improvement areas, defining clear objectives, and establishing a precise direction. A well-structured plan guides your organization through the optimization journey and ensures the achievement of improvement goals. To navigate this process effectively, we've outlined suggested elements for your VSM change plan, as shown in *Figure 4.15*.

VSM change plan elements	
Objective Definition	Risk Assessment and Contingency Plans
Current State Analysis	Communication and Stakeholder Engagement
Future State Vision	Budget and Resource Allocation
Improvement Opportunities	Timeline and Milestones
Action Plans	Change Management Strategy
Key Performance Indicators (KPIs)	Continuous Improvement Framework
Objective Definition	Risk Assessment and Contingency Plans

Figure 4.15 – VSM change plan elements

To evaluate the effectiveness and alignment of these planning elements with our goals, we adopt the **SMART** approach, as explored in the following subsection.

Setting improvement objectives

Setting improvement objectives is the foundation of any value stream improvement effort. These objectives should be **SMART**, an acronym for **specific**, **measurable**, **achievable**, **relevant**, and **time-bound**. *Figure 4.16* details each improvement objective within the SMART acronym. A well-stated problem is essential to gaining a shared understanding of what needs to be achieved and serves as a benchmark to measure progress and success.

SMART Objectives		
S	Specific	Objectives should be clear, unambiguous, precise and focused on a particular outcome.
M	Measurable	Goals should be quantifiable, allowing progress to be tracked and evaluated using concrete criteria.
A	Achievable	Objectives should be realistic and attainable, ensuring they can be reached with available people and resources.
R	Relevant	Goals should be directly related to the broader objectives and mission of the organization, contributing to its overall success.
T	Time-bound	Objectives should have a defined timeframe, providing a sense of urgency and a target date for completion.

Figure 4.16 – SMART improvement objectives

The VSM improvement plan should go beyond a text-based narrative, as it will be difficult for your reviewers to fully grasp how the proposed changes will affect the overall flows across your customer value streams. So, just as we did when documenting how work flows in our current value stream, we need to create a future state value stream map to show how work, information, and materials will flow in the new environment.

Developing a future state value stream map

Developing a future state value stream map is crucial for visualizing the path to improvement. This map represents the ideal state of your value stream after implementing improvements. It serves as a blueprint for your improvement efforts.

A future state value stream map differs from the previously discussed idealized value stream map. While the idealized map sets a target for improvement, the future state map focuses on what's achievable within time and resource constraints. It specifies work, information, material flows, and projected improvement measures resulting from completed changes.

The good news is that a future state value stream map closely resembles the current state map. Since we've already covered the topic of value stream mapping in *Chapter 3, Establishing Lean Flows to Improve Productivity*, we won't revisit the process in this chapter.

Identifying potential improvements and solutions

Identifying potential improvements and solutions involves a creative process of analyzing the current state of your value stream. Techniques such as value stream mapping and root cause analysis help uncover optimization opportunities while brainstorming sessions and team collaboration generate innovative solutions for identified issues.

However, we often face financial and resource constraints when implementing all identified improvements, particularly in larger value streams. Therefore, it's crucial to assess the impact of the proposed changes on our ability to deliver value to customers profitably. The **Theory of Constraints** helps prioritize opportunities by focusing on anything disrupting workflow, especially those hindering us from achieving our **TAKT** time—a customer-centric metric representing the pace that meets customer demand given available capacity.

Tooling, equipment, materials, training, and information access improvements can reduce costs, enhance quality, and improve customer satisfaction. Balancing these factors maximizes value delivery through our products and services.

Given a choice between fixing constraints or eliminating costly waste with a set budget, how would you decide? In his book *Principles of Product Development Flow*, Don Reinertsen describes an economic model for prioritizing jobs called **Weighted Shortest Job First** (**WSJF**). [10]

Determining improvement priorities using WSJF

WSJF has been popularized in Lean-Agile frameworks such as the **Scaled Agile Framework (SAFe®)** to determine priorities. Applying WSJF ensures funding is allocated to deliver the most value in the shortest duration, providing the best economic return.

WSJF is estimated as the *relative* **cost of delay (CoD)** divided by the relative job duration. Using a modified Fibonacci sequence for the relative numbers (1,2,3,5,8,13,20) instead of money simplifies the calculation and avoids a false sense of accuracy. Most Agile practitioners know how to use relative estimation, which is another benefit. Job size offers a good proxy for the duration since it can be hard to determine how long an improvement item or feature will take to implement.

The CoD represents the money lost by delaying or not doing a job for a specific time. CoD consists of three parameters: user-business value, time criticality, and risk reduction/opportunity enablement. Dividing the CoD by the job size yields the WSJF. Jobs with the highest WSJF are the most important ones to do. WSJF conveniently ignores sunk costs, a fundamental principle of Lean economics.

Figure 4.17 provides a table and guidelines for calculating WSJF.

ID	Proposed Improvements	+ User-business value	+ Time criticality	+ RR/OE Value	= CoD	÷ Duration (Job Size)	= WSJF
1	Implement a Kanban board	1	3	5	9	1	9.0
2	System for tracking dependencies	3	1	8	12	2	6.0
3	Shorten iteration duration	8	5	1	14	5	2.8
4	Automate testing	13	8	13	34	13	2.62
5	Automate builds	8	3	8	19	8	2.38

Guidelines:

- Use the modified Fibonacci scale for each cell: 1,2,3,5,8,13,20.
- Do one column at a time. Put a "1" in each column with the *lowest* relative value. Each column must have at least one "1." More than one cell can have the same number.
- The COD and WSJF columns are calculated as shown. The highest priority is the highest WSJF score.

Figure 4.17 – Table for determining priorities using WSJF

In the following subsection, we'll outline the typical components of a Kaizen (change) plan.

Planning continuous improvements

Implementing a Kanban system that tracks the proposed improvements with the highest WSJF is a good practice. **Kaizen** is a Japanese term that roughly translates to change for the better, underscoring a culture of continuous improvement.

A Kaizen plan, central to the philosophy of continuous improvement, should contain the following key components to ensure structured, actionable progress toward steady incremental enhancements:

- **Objective**: Clearly define specific, measurable goals for process improvement, waste reduction, and productivity enhancements
- **Scope and timeline**: Detail the initiative's scope, covering relevant processes or areas, and establish a realistic implementation timeline considering the project's complexity
- **Team composition**: Form a cross-functional team representing all relevant departments involved in the improvement processes
- **Current state analysis**: Conduct a thorough analysis, including data collection, workflow mapping, and identifying bottlenecks or inefficiencies
- **Root cause analysis**: Using techniques such as the five whys or fishbone diagrams to identify root causes is crucial for developing effective solutions
- **Solution development and planning**: Brainstorm and select solutions, developing an action plan with assigned responsibilities and resources
- **Budgeting and approvals**: Establish a clear budget and approval process, aligning with organizational fiscal strategies and securing approvals from key stakeholders
- **Implementation and monitoring**: Execute the action plan, closely monitoring adherence to the timeline and solution effectiveness
- **Review and standardization**: Evaluate outcomes against objectives, standardize successful practices, and document lessons learned for future reference
- **Continuous improvement cycle**: Establish a cycle for regular process review and identification of further enhancements for implementation

A well-structured Kaizen plan nurtures a culture of continuous enhancement, driving long-term operational excellence.

When approaching continuous improvement, it's important to distinguish between Scrum **retrospective** practices and Kaizen plans. Scrum focuses on small, rapid, incremental changes during sprint retrospectives, while Kaizen planning excels in scaling larger, more complex changes for teams of agile teams. Kaizen planning offers a comprehensive evaluation and structured approval process, aligning well with **Lean Portfolio Management** (**LPM**) strategies to prioritize and execute large-scale investments.

Once the roadmap is set, we transition into *Step 7, Execute*, where the Kaizen plans are implemented, marking the tangible realization of our vision for an optimized value stream. Let's delve into these critical stages, where transformation shifts from ideation to implementation, driving real and impactful change across the value streams.

7. Execute – implementing changes and adjusting

All our work so far is meaningless if we don't successfully execute the plans we've developed. This is where action speaks louder than words. Here, we explore the practical steps in implementing changes within your organization, ensuring that your improvement initiatives align with your goals and drive positive outcomes. Shown in *Figure 4.18*, here we Execute our plan to bring it to reality.

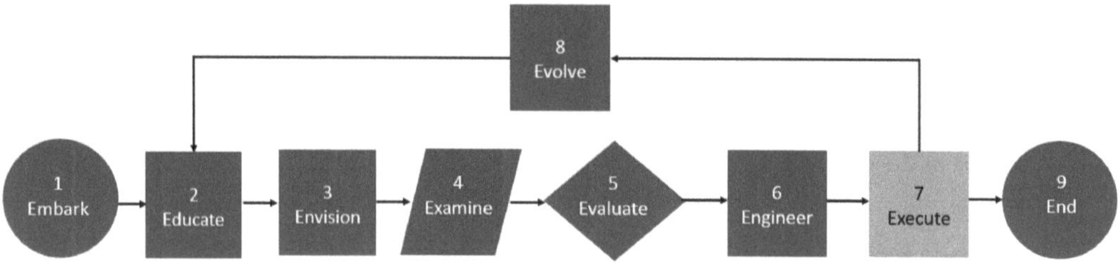

Figure 4.18 - Execute: implementing changes and adjusting

Not everything will work according to our plans. So, we emphasize the importance of adaptability, enabling you to adjust your plan as needed to ensure the successful execution of your improvement initiatives. This section equips you with the knowledge and tools to engineer and execute value stream improvements that drive your organization toward enhanced efficiency and value delivery.

Implementing changes and the improvement plan

Your well-crafted improvement plan serves as your roadmap, outlining the path to your organization's enhanced efficiency and value delivery. Effective implementation starts with a detailed understanding of your plan. Ensure your team comprehends the objectives, milestones, and specific actions required. While leveraging Agile's self-organizing and cross-functional concepts, the VSM team self-assigns their work. However, the VSM team lead, typically in the Value Manager role, should regularly review the plan to ensure alignment and encourage adjustments as necessary.

Monitoring progress and performance

Monitoring progress and performance is crucial to keeping improvement initiatives on course. Your plan should include documented goals in the form of metrics and KPIs that align with your objectives. Regularly measure progress against these metrics. Transparent reporting and communication of progress can keep stakeholders engaged and informed, fostering a culture of accountability and continuous improvement.

Handling resistance to change

Thoughtfully managing change is required, given the scope and potential impacts of improvements on how the organization operates and how people work. Resistance to change is natural but can be addressed effectively. Listen to concerns, empathize, communicate the rationale behind changes, and create a safe space for open dialogue. By acknowledging and addressing resistance, you can steer toward success better.

Navigating the Agile transition

Navigating the complexities of an Agile transition involves more than simply choosing a methodology; it requires careful consideration of several critical aspects that are frequently overlooked or poorly implemented. These include the following:

- **Rate of adoption:** Assess the extent of change you introduce at once. An overwhelming rate can hinder the transition process.
- **Depth of adoption**: Determine the depth to which you integrate Lean-Agile practices. Surface-level adoption may not yield the desired transformation.
- **Scope of adoption**: Evaluate the breadth of Lean-Agile practices and principles you apply. Covering a broad scope without prioritization can dilute the focus and impact.
- **Fit for purpose**: Tailor the Lean-Agile approach to align with the team's skills and organizational culture. A one-size-fits-all method often fails to resonate.
- **Support for new adopters**: Provide comprehensive support materials to facilitate the learning curve for individuals new to Lean and Agile practices.

Failure to address these aspects adequately can lead to resistance, decreased effectiveness, and a greater need for motivation to achieve success.

Adjusting the Kaizen plan as needed

The Greek philosopher Heraclitus said, "Change is the only constant in life." Despite good planning, unexpected challenges will likely occur. Consequently, having a bias for action and adjusting your plan is crucial, as flexibility is essential. Continuously review your initiatives, gather feedback, and incorporate lessons learned to ensure steady progress toward your goals.

As we work our way through the execution phase, our value stream improvement visions takes form. We propel our organization toward greater efficiency and value delivery by implementing our plan, monitoring progress, addressing resistance, and remaining adaptable.

Remember, execution is the bridge that transforms strategy into tangible results. Nevertheless, our business world will continue to evolve. In the next section, we'll explore the iterative process of continuously refining our value stream activities.

8. Evolve – evolving through refinement of value stream activities

In the *Evolve* phase (*Figure 4.19*), we focus on regularly evaluating and refining value streams to maintain efficiency and effectiveness. This section discusses sustaining improvements and ensuring alignment with evolving organizational goals.

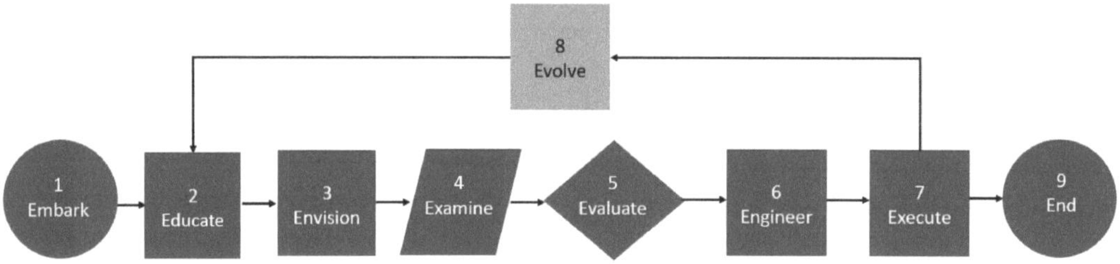

Figure 4.19 - Evolve: evolving through refinement of value stream activities

Continuously evaluating the value stream

Continuous evaluation is essential for the evolution of processes within the value stream. It involves regular assessment of each component's contribution to overall goals and identifying bottlenecks or waste that may have emerged over time. Organizations can proactively adjust by leveraging real-time data analytics and performance metrics to prevent minor issues from escalating into significant problems.

Modern VSM platforms supporting software development life cycles have embraced this concept. Once connected, these platforms provide end-to-end and real-time visibility, metrics, and analytics spanning all activities and tools supporting the development, testing, delivery, and support of the organization's software applications.

This proactive approach ensures that value streams maintain efficiency and effectiveness over time while remaining aligned with the organization's evolving goals. We must continually explore strategies to remain Agile in adapting to shifting business landscapes and changing customer expectations, all while optimizing efficiency and value delivery.

Gathering feedback from stakeholders

If digital tooling is involved, all value stream improvement initiatives require feedback from team members, stakeholders, and customers. Feedback from customers and employees who engage with the daily processes should guide process improvement.

Structured feedback mechanisms, such as surveys, focus groups, and feedback loops, can provide invaluable insights into the efficiency and effectiveness of the value streams. This information is critical for identifying areas that require attention and can also highlight opportunities for innovation. But none of it matters if we don't also analyze the data and act.

Iteratively improving processes

The core of process evolution lies in iteration, implementing incremental changes over continuous cycles that drive significant enhancements over time. While some improvements may demand substantial resources, organizations often have opportunities to make smaller, more manageable changes. These can be swiftly evaluated and implemented, fostering a culture of rapid adaptation and efficiency. However, always be mindful to manage flows through pull-oriented control systems, such as Kanban, lest you create bottlenecks and other forms of waste.

It is important to recall our previous discussion on local optimization. Also, if a proposed change takes time, resources, and funding beyond the team's authority, it should be considered by the enterprise's portfolio management function.

In Agile practices at the team level, iterative cycles and incremental improvements are distinct yet complementary. Iterative cycles involve regular repetition of a development process, allowing quick responsiveness to change. Incremental improvements are tangible advancements made at the end of each iteration, gradually building the complete product.

Although our focus has been on VSM initiatives, the concepts of iterative and incremental development from Agile methodologies are crucial in the Evolve step, ensuring ongoing improvements for sustaining our business's competitiveness and adaptability.

Sustaining improvements over time

Sustainability ensures that improvements endure, preventing the business from deteriorating amidst changing market dynamics and customer preferences. Establishing a culture of continuous improvement empowers every team member to identify and implement enhancements to their work processes.

Standardizing successful improvements and integrating them into the typical workflow ensures their incorporation into the organizational fabric, enhancing long-term efficiency and value delivery. Standardization is a fundamental concept in Lean, and without mechanisms to support these standards, improvements may rapidly degrade while individuals revert to old habits or less efficient practices.

In conclusion, the Evolve step in VSM fosters a culture of continuous improvement within the organization. Its systematic approach of regular evaluation, feedback, iteration, and sustaining improvements ensures that value streams remain resilient, responsive, and strategically aligned. This evolutionary process enables organizations to stay agile and competitive in delivering customer value.

Next, we will delve into *VSM Step 9, End*, focusing on a product or service's retirement or **end-of-life**.

9. End – retiring a product

We've reached the final stage of our VSM methodology. As depicted in *Figure 4.20*, here, our focus shifts to the critical aspect of concluding a product's life cycle, a phase as crucial as any other and demanding careful attention.

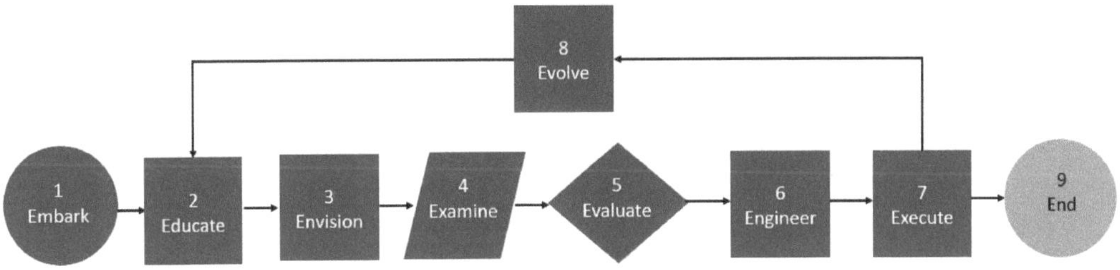

Figure 4.20 - End: retiring a product

In this section, we will guide you through the primary steps of recognizing when a product or service has reached its end-of-life (EOL), planning for the conclusion of its value stream, managing the retirement of products and services, and ensuring customer satisfaction. This section aims to help you navigate this phase strategically, balancing operational considerations with customer-centric practices.

Recognizing when a product or service has reached its EOL

Identifying when a product or service has reached its EOL is vital for effective VSM. This awareness hinges on declining sales, rising maintenance costs, market shifts, technology obsolescence, and other sustainability factors. Proactively identifying these factors enables strategic planning for product phase-out rather than reactive responses to market pressures.

A balanced approach is essential for monitoring and interpreting these signals effectively, as in this example:

- **Analyzing quantitative data**: Regular assessment of sales figures, profit margins, maintenance costs, technical debt, and customer satisfaction through data analytics reveals declining trends and increased costs, signaling the EOL of a product
- **Observing market evolution**: Tracking industry trends, technological advancements, and competitor actions often provides good insight into market shifts that could render a product obsolete
- **Gathering and analyzing customer feedback**: Collecting feedback through customer surveys, focus groups, and social media helps identify satisfaction and usability issues, offering objective data into declining sales or customer retention challenges
- **Competitive analysis**: Regularly reviewing competitors' offerings and strategies provides perspective on your product's market position and reveals whether continued investment in your product is warranted

These strategies underscore the comprehensive nature of Lean-Agile and VSM practices, highlighting the need for organization-wide involvement. They emphasize that managing value streams requires diligent oversight from inception to EOL, without shortcuts in effectively managing each stage.

Planning for the conclusion of the value stream

Once the EOL of a product is acknowledged, the next step is to plan for the orderly retirement of its value stream. This decommissioning involves several activities:

- **Discuss the proposal to EOL with stakeholders**: Retiring a product is a strategic decision that may affect many other departments, including sales, marketing, legal, finance, customer success, and human resources. It should involve key stakeholders of your organization, particularly your executive staff and, in some cases, the board of directors, partners, and key customers.

- **Develop an EOL product roadmap**: You can create a roadmap to strategically think through and map out your plan for taking your product through the EOL process, including a plan for a replacement product or service. Don't forget to address data security, environmental, and other disposal issues associated with eliminating old products.
- **Getting approval for your EOL plan**: Once you've built a business case based on evidence, you can take your data-supported proposal to sunset your product to your executive stakeholders.
- **Communicate your EOL plan**: Discuss how the product's end-of-life will affect sales and marketing materials and customer presentations, and help these groups identify alternative solutions to steer prospects toward in the future.
- **Reallocate people and resources**: Now that you have a plan to sunset your product or service, you can start preparing how to redeploy the people, resources, and budget that has been freed up. Handled properly, you'll find you have extra capacity to make newer products or services more successful.
- **Documenting lessons learned and best practices**: The final phase of a product's life cycle (EOL) presents a valuable opportunity for reflection and learning. This retrospective typically involves documenting lessons learned and best practices, getting input from cross-functional teams across the enterprise, conducting retrospectives, and turning the documentation into a dynamic knowledge base to share across the organization and incorporate into future endeavors.

Adopting a VSM platform

A **VSM platform** (**VSMP**) is essential for optimizing end-to-end software product deliveries and improving business outcomes and IT operations. In DevOps environments, a VSMP supports process integration and automation while providing analytics for data-driven decision-making. It helps enable a customer-centric approach, prioritizing features that improve the customer experience while fostering team alignment and collaboration.

While traditional VSM methods involved manual mapping of current and future state activities, modern VSMP software has revolutionized the process by enabling real-time monitoring, particularly in DevOps-based software delivery pipelines. These solutions leverage graphical representations, data analytics, and artificial intelligence to enhance decision-making and effectiveness.

Organizations may need to adapt existing tools, systems, and applications to effectively capture, visualize, and analyze value stream flows. Integration of technology enhances VSMP's effectiveness, providing powerful tools for optimization.

VSMPs connect to your existing software development, testing, and support tools and import data from all phases of software product delivery, from concept to value delivery. They help software engineering leaders identify and quantify opportunities to improve software product performance by optimizing cost, operating models, technology, and processes. Modern VSMPs use **artificial intelligence** (**AI**) and **machine learning** (**ML**) powered analytics, providing automated insights to identify constraints, diagnose bottlenecks, and improve flow.

The primary components of a VSMP include the following:

- **Visualization and mapping**: Visualize and map value streams to clearly understand workflow
- **Analytics and reporting**: Collect and analyze data for insights into performance and generate customizable reports
- **Integration and collaboration**: Seamlessly connect with other tools and systems to enable data and workflow synchronization and facilitate team collaboration
- **Workflow automation**: Streamline processes by automating tasks and improving efficiency
- **Continuous improvement**: Implement feedback mechanisms for ongoing improvement
- **Customization and flexibility**: Adapt to unique organizational needs and changing requirements

In the next chapter, you'll build on the foundation by mastering the VSM implementation roadmap. You'll understand how VSM, when applied consistently and strategically, becomes an integral part of your organization's DNA, fostering a culture of perpetual improvement. You'll learn how to identify and prioritize value streams, envision ideal states, and execute effective strategies within a framework that evolves and adapts over time. By embracing the continuous improvement of VSM, you'll position yourself and your organization to excel in today's dynamic business environment, setting you apart as a leader and innovator in the pursuit of operational excellence.

Summary

In this chapter, you've learned that VSM isn't just a Lean improvement methodology. It's a continuous transformation journey that drives your organization toward operational perfection. The significance of VSM in fostering personal and organizational growth is immense, making it crucial for professionals at all levels. It's a journey of informed decision-making that improves processes and outcomes, involving every team member in the quest for continuous improvement and excellence.

These lessons are important because organizations risk stagnation and decline without the iterative and adaptive approach of VSM. Ignoring continuous improvement principles and strategic prioritization can lead to inefficiency, misallocated resources, employee burnout, and declining quality and customer satisfaction. Embracing VSM as a continuous transformational path ensures that every step taken leads to greater efficiency, quality, and alignment with customer needs.

Next up is *Chapter 5, Introducing the VSM Implementation Roadmap*. This chapter covers the Value Stream Management Consortium's approach to implementing value stream management practices. While this chapter covered the Lean VSM model, the VSMC promotes VSM methods and tools tailored for Lean-Agile enterprises and their software deliveries.

Questions

This section is offered for those who want to evaluate comprehension and retention of the information provided in this chapter. There are 10 questions. The answers are provided in the next subsection. Recalling the exact phrasing of the original content is not important. Instead, it's more important to recall the concepts and their applications.

1. What are the primary objectives of VSM as outlined in the foundational principles?
2. How does VSM differ from traditional Lean practices in its approach to improving organizational processes?
3. What is the primary goal of defining an idealized customer value stream in a VSM initiative?
4. Why is establishing metrics and success criteria crucial in a VSM initiative?
5. Why is it important to start value stream mapping from the point of product or service delivery to the customer?
6. How does prioritizing areas for improvement benefit a VSM initiative?
7. Why is adaptability key in the execution phase of a VSM initiative?
8. How does addressing resistance to change impact the successful execution of VSM improvements?
9. Why is continuous evaluation crucial in the Evolve step of VSM?
10. What is the importance of documenting lessons learned and best practices at the end of a product's life cycle?

Answers

1. The primary objectives of Value Stream Management (VSM) include optimizing the end-to-end flow of value throughout an organization, eliminating waste, overcoming productivity, eliminating constraints, as well as expediting the delivery of value to customers by addressing inefficiencies, improving quality, accelerating delivery, and reducing costs.
2. Value Stream Management differs from traditional Lean practices in its approach to improving organizational processes by adopting a holistic view that emphasizes the entire customer journey, ensuring every operational facet is aligned to support customers effectively and prevent the risk of local optimization, integrating Lean and Agile principles to drive profound organizational enhancements.
3. The primary goal of defining an idealized customer value stream in a VSM initiative is to envision the cleanest path to delivery possible, setting a visionary benchmark that aims for a flow with no constraints or waste that customers won't value
4. Establishing metrics and success criteria is crucial in a VSM initiative because they act as benchmarks for progress, helping to measure the impact of VSM efforts against strategic objectives and ensuring continuous improvement toward achieving the ideal state of the value stream.

5. Its important to start value stream mapping from the point of product or service delivery to the customer because every step in the value stream revolves around meeting and exceeding customer requirements and expectations, focusing on optimizing customer satisfaction.
6. Prioritizing areas for improvement benefits a VSM initiative by ensuring that efforts and resources are allocated where they will have the most significant positive impact, making the improvement process more efficient and effective.
7. Adaptability is key in the execution phase of a VSM initiative because unforeseen challenges can arise, requiring adjustments to the plan to maintain progress toward goals in a dynamic environment.
8. Addressing resistance to change is crucial for successful execution because it involves listening to concerns, communicating benefits, and supporting individuals in adapting to new processes, thus navigating through resistance smoothly.
9. Continuous evaluation is crucial in the Evolve step of VSM because it allows for regular assessment of the value stream's contribution to goals, identification of emerging inefficiencies or waste, and alignment with evolving organizational objectives.
10. Documenting lessons learned and best practices at the end of a product's life cycle is important because it provides valuable insights for future projects, helping to avoid past mistakes and replicate successes, fostering continuous improvement and innovation within the organization.

Further reading

1. Knaster, Richard. Value Stream Management for the Digital Age, 2021.
2. Kotter, J. P. (2012). Leading Change. Boston: Harvard Business Review Press
3. Cecil 'Gary' Rupp, 2021. Driving DevOps with Value Stream Management: Improve IT value stream delivery with a proven VSM methodology to compete in the digital economy. PACKT Publishing, Birmingham, UK.
4. Martin, K., & Osterling, M. (2013). Value Stream Mapping: How to visualize work and align leadership for organizational transformation (1st ed.). McGraw Hill Education.
5. Rother, M., & Shook, J. (2003). Learning to See: Value-stream mapping to create value and eliminate muda (1st ed.). The Lean Enterprise Institute.
6. Brunt, D., & Lovejoy, M. (2010). Seeing the Whole Value Stream (2nd ed.). Lean Enterprise Institute.
7. Tapping, D., & Schuker, T. (2001). Value Stream Management (T. Luyster, Trans.) (1st ed.). Productivity Press, NY.
8. Tapping, D. (2003). Value Stream Mapping for the Lean Office: Eight steps to planning, mapping, and sustaining Lean improvements in administrative areas (T. Schuker, Trans.) (1st ed.). Productivity Press, NY.
9. Tapping, D., Kozlowski, S., Archbold, L., & Sperl, T. (2008). Value Stream Management for Lean Healthcare (1st ed.). MCS Media, Inc., Chelsea, MI.
10. Reinertsen, D. G. (2009). The Principles of Product Development Flow. Celeritas Publishing

5

Introducing the VSM Implementation Roadmap

Adopting Value Stream Management is not just a step, but a journey towards continuous improvement to create an ever-evolving insights-driven culture.

– Adapted from the VSM Consortium

Previously, in *Chapter 4*, we introduced VSM as a methodology for prioritizing opportunities using a Lean approach. This chapter explores the **VSM Implementation Roadmap** from the **Value Stream Management Consortium** (**VSMC**)[1]. The VSMC promotes value stream methods and tools for Lean-Agile enterprises, particularly in organizations heavily invested in digital technologies. They facilitate optimizing strategic investments and end-to-end operations, avoiding siloed decision-making. This road map enables the widespread deployment of the VSM methodology throughout your organization, leveraging both Lean and Agile concepts while aligning the technology departments to support the organization's value stream improvement activities.

The VSM Implementation Roadmap comprises the following steps: **start**, **assess**, **vision**, **identify**, **organize**, **map**, **connect**, **inspect**, and **adapt**. It combines Lean and Agile practices, aligned with the fundamental principles of our book — *The Lean-Agile Way*.

The VSM implementation roadmap goes across industry boundaries, ensuring holistic, end-to- end value stream assessments essential for achieving significant flow improvements and avoiding **local optimizations**, common when systems thinking is ignored.

Mastery of the VSM implementation roadmap enables your organization to optimize value streams systematically, understand their complexities, and implement transformative change within your enterprise.

The following topics are covered in this chapter:

- Introducing the VSM implementation roadmap
- Exploring the nine steps of the VSM implementation roadmap
- Comparing the VSM methodology and VSM implementation roadmap

Unveiling the VSM implementation roadmap

Before explaining the purpose and the essential steps of the VSM implementation roadmap, it's helpful to understand VSM's history, which has paved the way for this modern approach to implementation.

Learning from history

The concept of value streams has a substantial historical background, with numerous contributors influencing its development. While we have come a long way, this history remains relevant as it helps us understand the necessity of today's VSM implementation roadmap. So, before we go on, let's take a look at some of the most impactful historical events in the evolution of Lean thinking and practices.

- **Toyota's early use**: Toyota is credited with the early implementation of value stream concepts, using visual displays of production processes, known as **material and information flow diagrams**. However, controversy exists about when these concepts and tools were initially used at Toyota (Baudin 2013).[2]
- **Womack and Jones**: James Womack and Daniel Jones introduced the term "value stream" in the '*From Lean Production to the Lean Enterprise*' Harvard Business Review article.[3] It emphasized that value streams define the Lean enterprise and encompass all activities needed to deliver maximum customer value.
- **James Martin's insight**: James Martin, a highly respected figure in the computer industry, defined value streams in the context of a holistic practice he called '*Enterprise Engineering*' (Martin 1994).[4] Martin advocated against automating poorly designed business processes mapped to hierarchical management structures, which invariably cause siloes and inefficiencies across functional and organizational workstreams.
- **Emergence of VSM books**: In the early 2000s, books on VSM began to appear, with '*Value Stream Management: Strategy and Excellence in the Supply Chain*' (Hines et al. 2000) as one of the earliest.[5] This book described VSM as practices that enhance customer experiences and listed seven value stream mapping tools.
- **Refining versus mapping**: Subsequent books, including '*Learning to See*' by Mike Rother and John Shook and '*Seeing the Whole Value Stream*' by David Brunt, Jim Womack, Dan Jones, and Matthew Lovejoy, played a significant role in refining value stream mapping techniques. [6,7] These publications began incorporating Lean metrics to facilitate the discovery of constraints and waste affecting an organization's end-to-end value stream flows.
- **VSM as a methodology**: Books by Don Tapping and his co-authors further refined VSM as a methodology for continuous improvement using Lean principles and value stream mapping.[8]
- **Widespread adoption**: Over time, the application of value stream improvement concepts expanded to various industries. Karen Martin and Mike Osterling's book, 'Value Stream Mapping: How to Visualize Work and Align Leadership for Organizational Transformation' (Martin, Osterling 2013) significantly popularized these ideas.[9]

- **Scope and internal value streams**: Martin and Osterling further emphasized setting boundaries and limitations in value stream mapping to enable organizations to stay focused and promoted the idea of support-oriented value streams to map processes for internal activities such as HR, IT, Finance, and Sales.

Several other important contributors have or are continuing to evolve modern VSM practices. However, this historical perspective offers a sufficient background to understand why modern VSM practices must incorporate Lean-Agile concepts and the primary reason for creating the VSM Implementation Roadmap. Also, the Scaled Agile Framework has been a significant contributor to popularizing value stream concepts outside of the manufacturing domain and within agile frameworks.

Examining the need for a VSM roadmap

What we have learned so far is that value streams embody a Lean concept that has evolved to address issues associated with the conventional practice of managing business processes within isolated silos designed to accommodate hierarchical organizational structures. Too often, these hierarchies have resulted in gross inefficiencies, political infighting for people, funding, and other resources, lack of focus on customer-centricity, and an inability to evaluate investments holistically, let alone from a customer-centric point of view.

In contrast, value streams are centered on comprehending how organizations generate value from their customers' perspectives, transcending organizational boundaries and self-interests. In essence, value streams define a seamless flow of work, materials, information, and resources that efficiently deliver value without being confined by organizational boundaries. The aim of value streams is to eliminate waste and constraints that often lead to product delays, increased costs, and decreased quality.

In *Chapter 4*, we explored how VSM emerged as a methodology designed to assist organizations in assessing their most critical improvements to value flow. As a methodology, VSM follows this generalized pattern:

- Teaching Lean-Agile concepts
- Identifying and prioritizing value streams
- Defining an idealized value state for benchmarking
- Utilizing current state value stream mapping through Gemba walks to uncover waste and constraints
- Visualizing proposed value stream improvements through future state value streams
- Developing Kaizen improvement plans that document recommended changes, including assessments of the current state , desired future state, gap analysis, ROI justifications, prioritization, and alternative recommendations.
- Executing the Kaizen plan to achieve defined goals and metrics
- Establishing a culture of continuous improvement and transformation

- Stopping the continuous improvement process for a product or service when it reaches the end of its economically viable life cycle

This comprehensive approach ensures that organizations identify improvement opportunities and execute and sustain these improvements as an integral part of their transformative business culture. However, with the advent of Agile methodologies, it becomes essential to rethink how the VSM methodology should integrate Lean and Agile practices. That is the subject of the following section.

Exploring the VSM Implementation Roadmap

Embracing the Lean-Agile mindset, the VSMC's approach to VSM is designed to enhance value delivery through continuous improvement and customer focus.

Figure 5.1 illustrates the VSM implementation roadmap, which is a series of high-level steps guiding an organization adopting VSM ways of working. Each step establishes a foundation for the next, contributing to the evolution of an organization that practices VSM-led approaches, continually optimizing the customer experience, and illustrates the VSMC implementation roadmap, which is integral to the VSM methodology. While identifying and prioritizing continuous improvement, the VSM roadmap integrates **inspect** and **adapt** concepts from Agile. Inspecting and adapting enables continuous progress review and adaptation strategies based on new learning and market shifts. Each step of the roadmap brings us toward excellence in customer value delivery and satisfaction. It consists of the following steps:

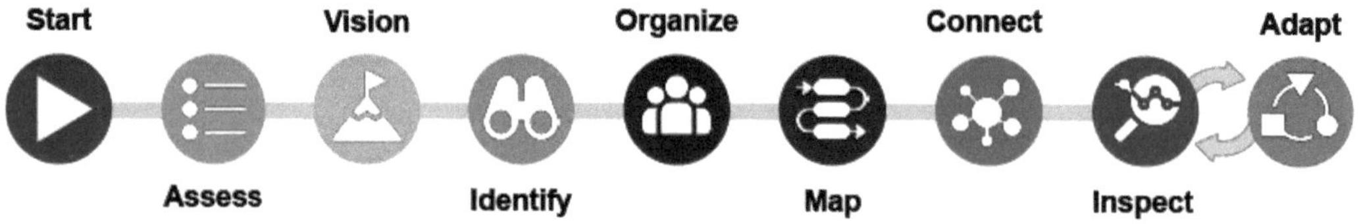

Figure 5.1 – VSM Implementation Roadmap graphic

Although the roadmap presents the implementation steps as a linear flow, in reality, each step may occur iteratively based on feedback and learning. The list that follows identifies the purpose of each step.

1. **Start**: Initiate VSM by setting the step for change and commitment, aligning the mission with Lean-Agile principles.
2. **Assess**: Evaluate the current operational landscape (culture, capability, and context), baseline current performance, and establish a business case for improvement.
3. **Vision**: A compelling vision for the future inspires and motivates people to act, establishing a clear and strategic direction for value creation and visualizing the outcomes that will drive success.
4. **Identify**: Select a value stream to improve. Focus on customer value to identify the organization's value streams. This can be challenging for project-centric organizations, as long-lived products, unlike short-lived projects, reveal value streams, with anything delivering a product or service constituting a value stream.

The first value stream to target for improvement is often the one that lies at the intersection of four criteria: strong leadership support, highly visible value stream, existing Agile teams, and a significant challenge or opportunity.

5. **Organize**: Systematically organize people, resources, and workflows around a product or service to optimize the flow of value for a product or service across functional departments, and the entire system.
6. **Map**: Assemble the VSM team, to identify and understand the current steps and activities involved in delivering value to the customer. Mapping helps identify bottlenecks, delays, and areas for improvement in the value stream.
7. **Connect**: Integrate and connect people, processes, and tools within value streams that foster communication and teamwork. When work items can be traced throughout the entire value stream, delays, rework, and waste become visible. These insights drive improvements, and feedback informs decision-making.
8. **Inspect**: Monitor performance by analyzing data, setting improvement goals, defining critical metrics, and leveraging automated data collection systems for accurate tracking. Continuous inspection, management, and improvement of flow and value realization are feasible only by making data and insights available from the digital value stream.
9. **Adapt**: Once you have data and insights to inform action, it's time to implement changes. Encourage continuous, iterative refinements to adapt to change and proactively strive for excellence.

By adhering to its structured approach, the VSMC roadmap streamlines operations and persistently aligns them with the overarching goal of delivering superior value to our customers. Each step offers a commitment to the Lean-Agile mindset, ensuring enterprises stay Agile, responsive, and customer-centric in our journey toward operational excellence.

We will further explore each roadmap step.

Implementing Value Stream Management

According to the VSMC, implementing VSM goes beyond operational improvements. It embodies efficiency, responsiveness, and strategic foresight. Consequently, this perspective is foundational for appreciating the nuances of their VSM implementation roadmap. The following sections provide a detailed overview of the nine roadmap steps.

1. Start – initiating value stream management

Your VSM implementation journey begins with your current state, regardless of the maturity of your digital processes. At the core of each business are value streams and networks of value streams designed to fulfill customer needs or serve citizens (in government contexts). Organizations continuously innovate, develop, and deliver products or services regardless of their profit orientation.

Whenever there is a spark of innovation or a proposed change, it goes through design, development, and delivery before the customer can realize its value. Many organizations have long since adopted Agile methodologies, DevOps practices, or Lean principles. Others might be navigating through structural changes such as reorganizations, mergers, or acquisitions. These factors do not prevent enterprises from adopting and driving the use of VSM methodologies and tools. Instead they strengthen the business case for change. However, leaders must be wary of the fatigue that comes with constant change. Clearly articulate the purpose and vision of the VSM implementation and help knowledge workers understand how their work contributes to the organization's overall goals and objectives. A good purpose offers the why behind the change and motivates people to come along on the journey and to be actively engaged in its success.

The typical obstacles to adopting VSM are the absence of senior leadership endorsement and limited resources. Forward-thinking individuals should proceed with the intent to course-correct rather than wait for permission, bringing leaders along in the process. Proactive individuals recognize that perceived resource limitations are often alleviated when inefficiencies are eliminated, unlocking capacity within the system. Still, this proactive stance does not abdicate executives from their duties in transforming the organization.

Jumping in front of a parade does not make you a leader. True leadership involves more than just being at the forefront. It requires vision, empathy, and the ability to inspire and guide others toward a common goal. A true leader listens, collaborates, and leads by example rather than merely seeking the spotlight.

Leaders earn the credibility and authority to steer the company forward through a hands-on approach and intimate knowledge of the organization's inner workings. This involvement goes beyond leading change to being an integral part of the transformation, ensuring that the implementation of VSM is a shared journey.

While emphasizing the importance of leadership involvement, we do not advocate for a scenario where leaders direct all tasks or make every decision single-handedly. Such centralization can lead to detrimental outcomes, including decision-making bottlenecks, uninformed choices, and biases that contradict the actual dynamics of the organization.

Effective leaders understand the value of delegation and place trust in their teams to handle the tactical, day-to-day decisions. Handing off decision-making is easier when the organization makes visible activities and critical metrics that define progress against goals and plans. This approach empowers employees, fosters a culture of accountability, and ensures that the organization's direction is shaped by diverse insights and expertise, leading to a more robust and resilient VSM implementation.

The "**Start**" step of the VSM Implementation Roadmap involves the following primary activities, as shown in *Figure 5.2*:

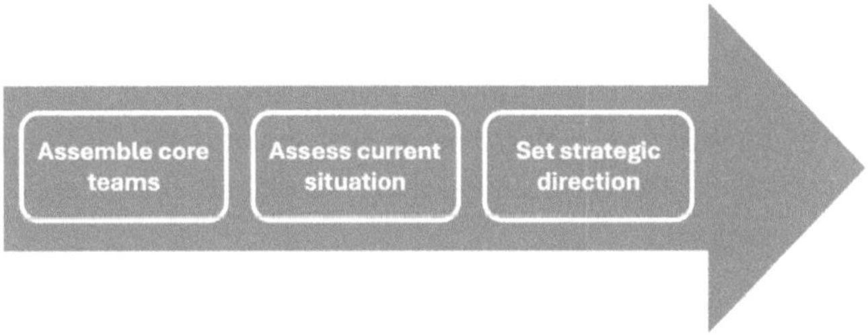

Figure 5.2 – VSM starting activities

These key activities lay the foundation and set the direction for effective VSM implementation:

- **Assemble core teams**: Creating a foundational team for VSM should bring together individuals with a wide range of expertise. Two types of teams are recommended:
  - **VSM SME team** – A small, specialized group of VSM **subject matter experts** (**SMEs**) who facilitate, educate, and mentor throughout the organization's various VSM initiatives. They are responsible for driving the VSM methodology and overseeing the implementation of VSMC roadmap activities.
  - **Value stream improvements team** (**VSIT**) – This team has individuals actively involved in enhancing the targeted value streams. They possess critical domain knowledge and play a vital role in implementing the concepts later outlined in *Chapter 9, Defining a Business Agility System for the Enterprise* (*BASE*), including establishing a rhythm to support the objectives of the **minimum valuable increment** (**MVI**). The composition of the VSIT is dynamic and may vary with each MVI.
- **Assess the current situation**: This step requires an initial assessment of the current landscape. Immediate executive support is ideal, but if that's not available, the goal is to generate momentum and gather the support and resources needed for the VSM journey.
- **Set strategic direction**: The focus here is to outline the strategic goals and objectives of the VSM initiative. This means considering how it supports the company's broader strategic goals, enhances customer value, improves operational efficiency, and boosts overall business performance.

These three '**start**' activities offer several benefits to organizations. First, they establish the core resources necessary to kickstart a successful VSM initiative by forming specialized teams. Secondly, they provide a rapid assessment of the organization's current status, bridging the gap between its existing state and the strategic goals required to achieve the broader business strategies. Another benefit it provides is the alignment and direction needed to enable decentralized decision-making and execution, tapping into the collective intelligence of teams.

With these three critical activities completed, the VSM and VSIT teams embark upon the second VSM step, '**assess**.'

2. Assess – evaluating and baselining current performance

Assess, the second step in the VSM implementation roadmap, builds upon the '**start**' step, and involves a comprehensive evaluation of existing VSM capabilities to establish baseline performance metrics and identify areas for improvement.

The VSMC developed a VSM assessment that is aligned with the implementation roadmap steps. It is designed to baseline the current state and for ongoing reassessment during your VSM implementation journey. This assessment phase emerged from collaborative efforts within the VSMC, underscoring the importance of benchmarking the current state at the beginning of the VSM journey and maintaining continuous progress monitoring.

The VSMC's assessment tool utilizes a **Likert** scale questionnaire, as shown in *Figure 5.3*, prompting respondents to rate their current state on a scale ranging from **Strongly agree** to **Strongly disagree** and **Not applicable**.

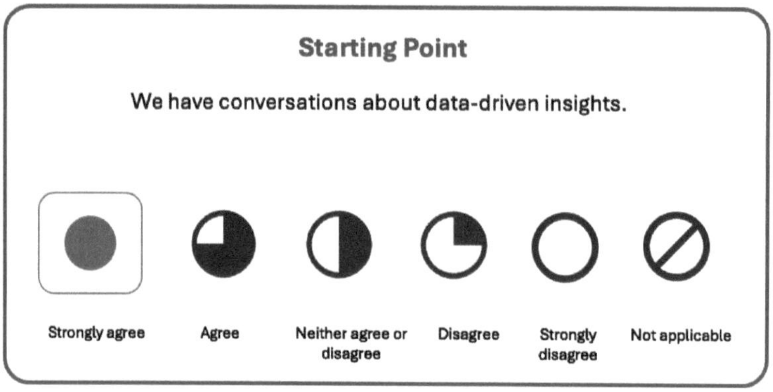

Figure 5.3 – Likert scale assessment

Tailored for use by consultants and enterprise practitioners, this assessment tool is valuable for identifying focus areas, establishing a baseline for future measurement, and comparing performance against industry benchmarks.

Available online as a self-service tool, the assessment invites teams to respond to standardized questions – **VSM Assessment** (`vsmconsortium.org/vsm-assessment`). This tool aids in internal benchmarking and allows for a comparison with other teams and organizations. It starts with evaluating the organization's vision and leadership support – key drivers of successful VSM adoption.

By leveraging this tool, teams can systematically uncover strengths and weaknesses in their approach, providing a clear, quantifiable measure of their VSM journey and identifying a path forward to elevate their value stream practices to world-class standards.

Having completed the thorough '**assess**' phase, where current processes are evaluated, we now transition to the '**vision**' step. Here, we shift our focus from understanding the current state of our value stream to defining our desired future state vision.

3. Vision – creating a unified vision and goals

In the **vision** step, organizations must define and articulate a long-term vision and objectives that guide their transformation journey. This vision must be well understood and broadly shared across the organization, becoming the new norm. Put simply, this is the way we do things around here. It's not merely about fighting through existing systems, but evolving the organizational mindset and instilling new habits. *Figure 5.4* depicts the essential elements of the vision step:

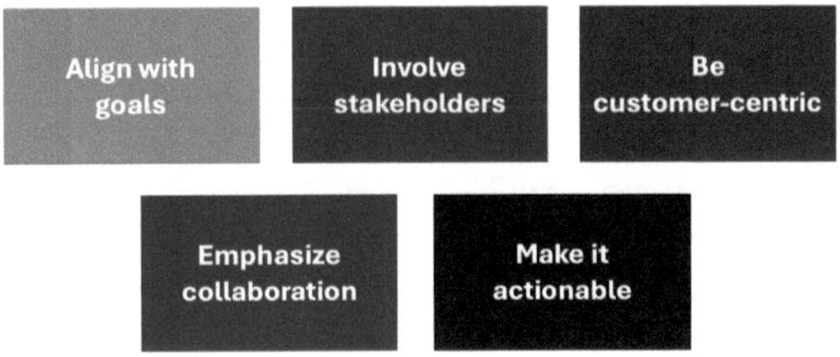

Figure 5.4 – Developing a shared vision

The vision reinforces an organization's dedication to defining the seamless flow of valuable customer outcomes. It is a process where the organization envisions a future free from waste and unnecessary constraints, gains a deep understanding of customer experiences, and promptly acts on them, with each insight driving tangible improvements.

The goals associated with this vision are inherently united with enhancing organizational effectiveness, especially critical in the **digital for-profit sphere**. These goals encompass high responsiveness to customer needs, transparency of work in process, empowering value stream autonomy, and achieving a competitive edge in the market. Measured improvement forms the foundation for these objectives, enabling tracking and optimizing delivery speed, customer impact, cost efficiency, and market leadership.

The goals of the vision step are designed to elevate organizational effectiveness by emphasizing agility, transparency, and adaptability to market dynamics. The objective is to promptly address customer needs, ensure clear and effective processes, and enable value streams to directly influence financial success. Goals must be aspirational and measurable using leading indicators. The SMART criteria discussed in *Chapter 4* offer a structured approach for tracking business objectives and metrics.

Leading indicators enable tracking an organization's proficiency in enacting changes swiftly, efficiently meeting customer demands, managing costs effectively, and sustaining competitive advantage within its market.

Executive leaders must embrace their role of setting the strategic course and empowering teams with strategic insight to actively engage in the transformation. It is a collaborative effort where goals are set, such as improving customer experience, reducing process waste, shortening feedback loops, and aligning with financial models. In *Chapter 9, Defining a Business Agility System for the Enterprise (BASE)*, we'll discuss the use of OKRs (Objectives and Key Results) to help executives set clear expectations.

Each objective is associated with quantifiable outcomes such as increased customer engagement, faster delivery of value, improved decision-making, and positive financial returns. By breaking down the vision into measurable targets, teams can pursue incremental progress, making the vision a tangible and achievable reality.

Having a clear vision lays the groundwork for transforming aspirations into measurable outcomes, propelling the organization forward on its VSM journey with a shared direction.

4. Identify – surfacing value streams

The goal of the **identify** step is to define and describe the value streams within an organization. Seeing value streams in a landscape often dominated by hierarchal organizational structures and project-based thinking can present challenges. Unlike projects, which are temporary and finite, value streams represent the life cycle of a product or service, from inception to delivery and beyond. They are the sequences of activities required to transform an idea into a valuable outcome for the customer.

To illustrate, in the context of an e-commerce system for selling products, core value streams include the activities most critical to the mission of the organization, while supportive value streams include the platforms and CI/CD pipelines facilitating core value stream activities. We go further into classification methods for types of streams in *Part 3*.

The identification process involves recognizing various products, services, platforms, and their respective internal or external customers. Each value stream has a starting point where an idea is generated and an endpoint where value is delivered to the customer. It is essential to map these value streams, understand where they intersect and support one another, and identify dependencies.

The goal is to take incremental steps toward improvement. Organizations can systematically unravel the complexities of their value streams by beginning with small-scale experiments and learning from them. The primary focus is on identifying and naming value-adding steps, identifying the customers they serve, and mapping out the entire journey from start to finish. Adopting this approach allows even the most intricate systems to be effectively navigated and optimized over time.

You may notice that the VSM implementation roadmap has Lean and Agile elements. In this context, we utilize the **iterative and incremental development** process from Agile to identify opportunities for Lean-oriented improvements within the organization. During the '**inspect**' and '**adapt**' phases, we'll revisit the concepts of iteration and incremental improvement. However, we still have more ground to cover as we move on to the next step – '**organize**.'

5. Organize – streamlining cross-functional collaboration

The **organize** step acknowledges the shift from traditional siloed structures to a more integrated approach where technology teams are intrinsically aligned with the business. The evolution from DevOps to a broader inclusion of departments such as Finance, HR, Sales, Marketing, Product Management, and **Governance, Risk and Compliance** (GRC) highlights this shift.

The problems inherent in silos are significant. Handoffs between teams present risks of errors, delays, or lost opportunities. Moreover, organizational layers and disconnects can lead to misalignment with business intentions, resulting in slower delivery and reduced customer satisfaction.

Therefore, core value streams must be seen as spanning the entire journey from concept to customer realization without artificially separating business and technology. Certain roles, such as portfolio managers, may not be dedicated to single value streams due to their overarching nature. Similarly, specialized roles such as release and cloud engineers may operate across multiple streams, possibly within a platform or enabling teams.

Many people, both internal and external to the organization, may care about the products and services we deliver. However, the ultimate stakeholder is the customer, and value streams should operate autonomously to serve them.

Although roles are situated at specific points within the value chain, all roles should focus on the flow and realization of value within their respective streams rather than their mere contribution to the process.

The following considerations are vital to the 'organize' step:

- **Identification of VSM and cross-functional teams**: Recognize the necessary roles and form teams that can operate across functional boundaries to improve the value stream
- **Definition of roles and responsibilities**: Delineate what each team and its members are accountable for, ensuring that every role is geared toward enhancing the value provided to the customer
- **Communication**: Establish robust communication that facilitates seamless interaction and information sharing across all teams
- **Training and support**: Provide comprehensive training and resources to teams, enabling them to fulfill their VSM roles effectively
- **Monitoring and adjustment**: Continuously monitor the performance of the value stream, ready to adjust team organization and dynamics to ensure optimal functioning and value delivery

By embracing these principles, organizations can create a cohesive environment that promotes efficiency, alignment, and customer-centricity, moving away from siloed operations toward a fully integrated digital value stream.

We are poised to move forward with the VSM teams in place to facilitate training, coaching, and mentoring of the cross-functional VSIT teams assembled. *Step 6*, '**map**,' will examine the value stream mapping process, which equips teams to pinpoint areas for enhancement.

6. Map – visualizing process efficiency and opportunities

Building a value stream **map** is a key step that offers a structured approach to analyzing and improving the flow of value. The process typically consists of the following steps:

- **Assemble your mapping team**: This initial step involves gathering a cross-functional team whose members were identified earlier during the Organize step. This team will work collaboratively to create the value stream map, bringing together their diverse expertise and perspectives.
- **Define the scope**: The scope of the mapping exercise must be clearly defined, establishing the boundaries of the value stream to be mapped. This includes setting the starting and ending points, typically from the initial customer request to the final product delivery.
- **Create the current state map**: Working backward from value delivery to the initial customer request, the team visually represents the value stream's current state, composed of each distinct process in the flow. This map serves as a baseline for identifying waste, bottlenecks, and areas for potential improvement.
- **Gather process data**: In this phase, the team collects relevant data for each process within the value stream. Important metrics include cycle times, value-added time to the initial customer request, work in process, wait times, and other metrics to understand the flow and delays.
- **Analyze the map**: The final step thoroughly analyzes the current state map. Team members are encouraged to share insights and perspectives on potential changes or optimizations. This collaborative review is designed to generate a shared understanding of the value stream and foster consensus on the next steps for improvement.

Through these steps, the mapping process captures the current state of the value stream and serves as a springboard for continuous improvement. By involving a cross-functional team, the mapping exercise ensures consideration of all perspectives, leading to a more comprehensive and effective approach to improvement.

The VSMC's approach to value stream mapping is consistent with modern Lean practices, as shown in *Figure 5.5*:

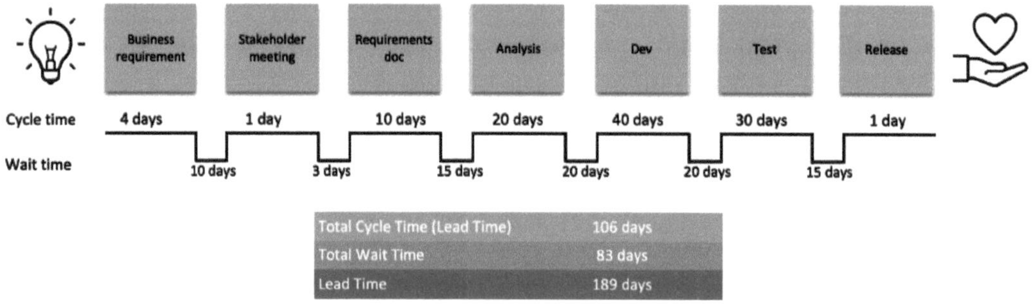

Figure 5.5 – Sample value stream map

After mapping the value stream, we'll discuss the next phase, '**connect**.' That is where we integrate people, processes, and tools within our value streams, enhancing effective communication, enabling collaboration, and anchoring decisions from data-driven insights.

7. Connect – orchestrating people, processes, and tools

Given our imperative to compete in the digital era, **connect** is pivotal for integrating the DevOps toolchain into the value stream. The toolchain spans the entire life cycle of an idea, beginning with portfolio management and progressing through the product backlog, **continuous integration/continuous deployment** (**CI/CD**), release and environment management, and finally, the service desk. This comprehensive suite of tools is integral for tracking an idea from its origin to the realized value as perceived by the customer, allowing for a deep analysis of the customer experience.

Modern DevOps, CI/CD, and VSM tooling and platforms can be expensive. However, definable benefits can be substantial, as shown in *Figure 5.6*:

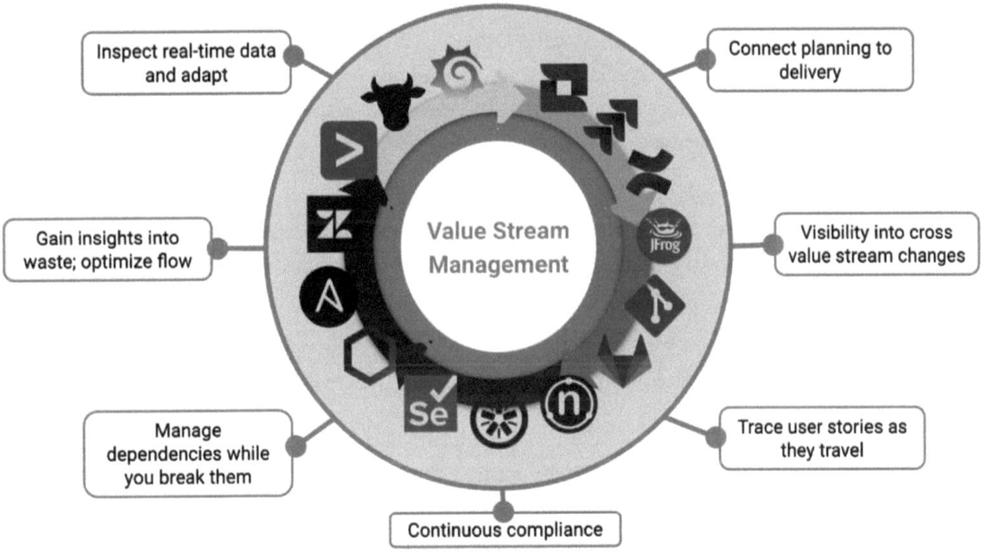

Figure 5.6 – Capabilities delivered via VSM tool and platform connections

The '**connect**' activities are designed to create a seamless and efficient workflow by integrating communication, technology, and feedback. Modern VSM tools and platforms provide the integration, visualization, and analysis capabilities to support the connect phase.

The following provides a brief overview of the connect activities:

- **Define communication protocols**: This activity involves establishing clear guidelines on how team members exchange information, ensuring that communication is consistent and effective across all value stream levels.

- **Integrate technology and tools**: This step combines various technology solutions and tools into a cohesive system that supports the value stream, enhancing the team's ability to work cohesively and efficiently.
- **Automate data collection**: This activity aims to reduce manual effort, minimize errors, and provide a consistent and reliable data flow for analysis and decision-making.
- **Enable real-time visibility**: This involves setting up systems that provide immediate insight into the value stream's performance, allowing for prompt identification of issues and opportunities for improvement.
- **Establish feedback loops**: Creating feedback loops supports continuous learning and improvement, enabling the value stream to adapt and evolve based on the insights gathered from the team's experiences and the data collected.

Each of these activities plays a vital role in connecting the various elements of the digital value stream, ensuring that the process is as efficient and responsive as possible.

Tracing work items throughout the entire value stream is a powerful capability provided by the tools shown in *Figure 5.6*. They illuminate delays, rework, and any waste that occurs along the way. The insights gathered can inform improvements by making these elements visible, while the feedback drives informed decision-making.

In summary, connecting people, processes, and tools creates a cohesive, transparent workflow where every action and outcome can be traced back to its source. It ensures the team is aligned, learning from real-time data, and continuously adapting to optimize the value stream. This connection phase is not just a step but an ongoing practice that underpins a culture of efficiency and continuous improvement.

8. Inspect – using the Plan Do Study Act (PDSA) cycle to improve value streams

Value streams originated with Lean, but W. Edwards Deming's Plan Do Study Act (PDSA) guidance provided a significant foundation. So, it shouldn't be surprising that we recommend using the **PDSA cycle** he popularized to improve our understanding of value streams.

PDSA goes beyond simple "inspect and adapt." It uses evidence-based decision-making, which avoids speculation in favor of empiricism while using validated theory. This process takes us ahead of preconceived notions found in traditional methods.

- **Plan**: Before we do something, we need a hypothesis and a plan. The timeframe for planning can vary from minutes to days. The plan sets an expectation of what we think will happen. This tests our understanding of the situation and how well it works. It provides a baseline to see how well we understood the current situation.

- **Do**: This is where we execute the plan's activities. However, if evidence proves things are not going as expected, we refine the plan to reflect on our new understanding of the situation. The Deming PDSA cycle applies continuous learning for a planned timebox.
- **Study**: We use fast feedback to determine whether what is happening (or "Do") matches what we expected (our "Plan"). This feedback loop can be continuous or conducted at the end of the planned increment. Looking at the disparity between plan and do, we can pivot and challenge our understanding. In other words, we study to ensure we are building the right product in the right way while making sure we are also thinking correctly.

  This process is called **double-loop learning**. **Single-loop learning** is about getting better at what you are doing. Double loop learning challenges the "what you are doing" to see whether there is a better way to work and whether what you're working on is correct. Any process that doesn't allow you to change its practices effectively limits double-loop learning.

  Triple-loop learning is about learning how to learn. Triple-loop learning teaches us how to challenge our assumptions. The article on double-loop learning by Chris Argyris at `https://infed.org/mobi/chris-argyris-theories-of-action-double-loop-learning-and-organizational-learning/` offers greater detail on this topic.
- **Act:** After the "Study" phase, our focus turns to producing what we are building by following our plan while improving our understanding of the model we used to develop the plan.

The VSMC advocates for inspecting value along two principal dimensions:

- **Flow**: Ensuring the work travels smoothly from conception to delivery, representing a consistent delivery of value to customers
- **Value**: Actualization of the desired business outcomes, where customers experience the intended value

These dimensions help the organization assess the health of the value stream and the customer experience to assess efficiency and effectiveness.

The '**inspect**' phase allows us to focus on analyzing and enhancing the performance of value streams. This involves a series of strategic actions aimed at understanding and improving the various facets of the value stream processes. Here are the key activities that drive this phase:

- **Define relevant metrics**: Define essential performance indicators for your value streams, such as lead time, cycle time, throughput, ongoing work, and defect rates.
- **Leverage automated data collection**: Use real-time data from DevOps tools to analyze performance and understand the true progress of work. For example, developers mark work as '**Done**' in a Kanban system, but the completed work from the story may sit in another team's release queue for months. DevOps tools and data present a more accurate view, basing metrics on the end-to-end process.

- **Monitor performance**: Keep a constant watch on your value stream's performance by analyzing real-time data and insights from DevOps tools to prevent service disruptions. Teams must continuously monitor system attributes such as security, reliability, performance, scalability, and more.
- **Analyze the data**: Examine the data collected to assess how well your processes work and spot areas needing refinement, including business outcomes for products and services.
- **Set experimental improvement goals**: Craft targeted goals for experimental improvements to boost your value stream performance based on thorough data analysis.

Maintaining a smooth flow of work and achieving desired business outcomes necessitates a vigilant and proactive approach to management and refinement. The wealth of data and insights in the digital value stream provides the mechanisms that teams need to sustain a perpetual cycle of inspection and adaptation.

9. Adapt – communicate, scope, and plan interventions

The Adapt phase represents the culmination of the VSMC's VSM implementation roadmap, where insights and data converge to prompt actionable change. Here, the focus shifts to implementing and iterating on changes that emerge from the **Inspect** phase. This phase is characterized by seven key actions, each aimed at evolving and refining the value stream:

- **Embrace continuous improvement**: Commit to relentless improvement, always seeking ways to enhance the value stream
- **Eliminate waste**: Identify and remove inefficiencies to streamline processes and maximize value
- **Measure results and iterate**: Evaluate the outcomes of changes and make iterative adjustments to ensure continuous progress
- **Fine-tune processes**: Adjust and optimize existing procedures for greater effectiveness and efficiency
- **Automate workflows**: Implement automation to reduce manual effort and increase consistency and speed
- **Share good practices**: Cultivate and apply successful patterns and techniques across the enterprise's value streams.
- **Foster a culture of adaptation**: Nurture an environment where flexibility and change are embraced across the organization to drive improvement

These adapt activities are not isolated efforts. They represent a cohesive approach to adaptation that is integral to the VSM life cycle. The inspect and adapt steps are intrinsically connected, feeding into each other in a continuous loop that reflects the Agile principles of iterative and incremental development. Through this agile-based approach, collaborating teams ensure the value streams are optimized, resilient, and responsive to change.

The '**adapt**' stage is also about leveraging your value stream map as a communication tool to outline, scope, and coordinate the necessary changes. It is a strategic phase where you formulate and document hypotheses on the potential impact of changes and develop a clear, structured roadmap detailing immediate actions, next steps, and future considerations.

It is essential to acknowledge that each change in the value chain carries the potential for unintended consequences. A value stream does not operate in isolation; a systems-thinking approach is indispensable for a comprehensive understanding and effective management.

Figure 5.7 illustrates a structured approach to developing and refining hypotheses for adaptation, ensuring alignment with the intended vision while celebrating the milestones achieved along the way:

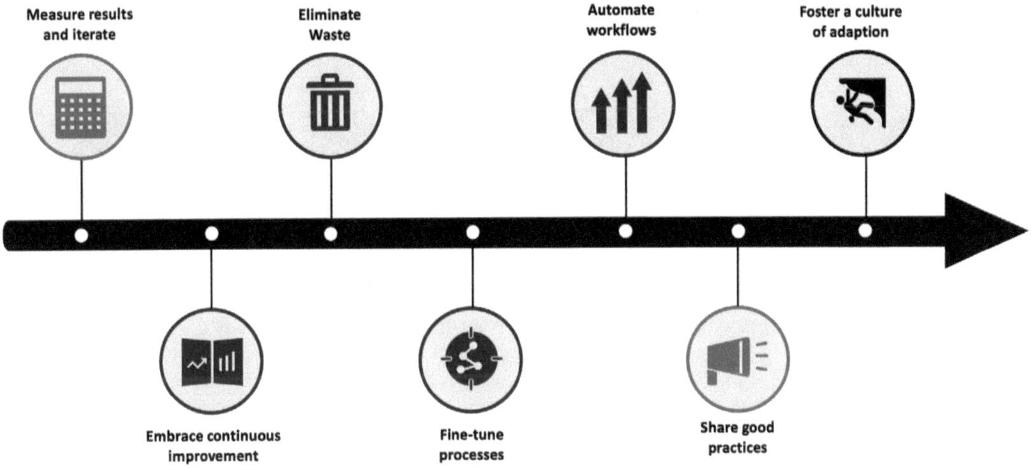

Figure 5.7 – The VSM adapt phase

As change occurs, the value stream map becomes a living document, highlighting enhancements and redefining the current state. This is where the iterative nature of Agile adaptation shines, providing continuous improvement and a perpetual cycle of development and enhancement.

In our digital era, the VSM inspect step helps VSIT teams find opportunities to use digital advancements to improve areas that challenge the organization's usual methods. Once insights and data are gathered, it is crucial to implement changes, which is the main focus of the VSM adapt step.

Value stream mapping can draw attention to improvements and redefine the current state. It is essential to recognize that once actions are taken, the map should evolve to avoid future misunderstandings and misalignment.

Comparing VSM methodology and the VSM implementation roadmap

At first glance, the E9 VSM methodology and the VSMC's implementation roadmap appear to have similar processes, goals, and objectives. They both have nine steps, and some have similar names. But their areas of focus differ. *Figure 5.8* and *Figure 5.9* compares the two and illustrates the critical differences we will explore in this section:

The VSM methodology has a history of over twenty years, and in our E9 VSM model, comprises a structured set of nine steps, as shown in *Figure 5.8*:

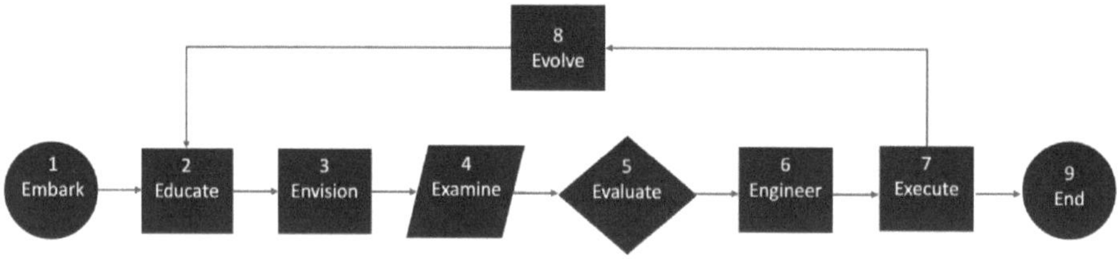

Figure 5.8 – The VSM methodology

The VSMC's implementation roadmap is almost three years old and coincidently comprises a distinct set of nine steps, as described in this chapter and shown in *Figure 5.9*:

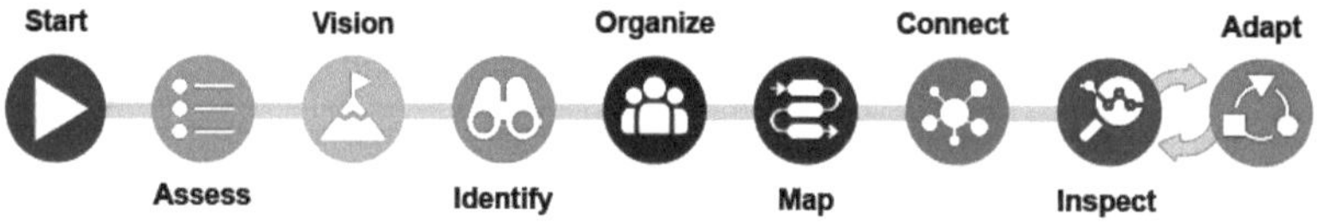

Figure 5.9 – VSMC implementation roadmap

While both roadmaps share similarities in processes, goals, and objectives, critical differences exist. The VSM Methodology is a proven Lean-oriented approach to drive improvements in productivity, efficiencies, and quality in any type of value stream. In contrast, the design of the VSMC implementation roadmap modernizes the VSM approach to support competitiveness and provide value-added services in the digital age. Moreover, the VSMC's roadmap instills Agile's iterative concepts for inspection and adaptation.

It is not a matter of choosing one approach over the other. Both serve the purpose of enhancing value streams, but they have distinct roles:

- The **VSM methodology** assists organizations in identifying and prioritizing value stream improvements that span organizational boundaries. Specifically, it enables collaborating teams to assess and evaluate cross-functional and cross- departmental change opportunities, ensuring that improvements deliver the most impactful customer-centric value with the available resources.

- The **VSM implementation roadmap** incorporates Agile's inspect and adapt steps to improve agility. This roadmap also aligns the activities of the IT organization, driving digital enhancements across the organization's products and processes. It focuses on creating IT infrastructure to support digital improvements and enhance competitiveness.

Together, these approaches complement each other, ensuring that the value stream improvement teams effectively address the broader organizational improvements and the IT-specific digital enhancements.

While IT organizations can improve their development and delivery services in isolation, they must align with the broader organization's improvement needs. The VSM roadmap assists in identifying areas where digital enhancements are vital, ensuring that IT effectively supports the organization's end-to-end value streams for core products and services.

Summary

In this chapter, you have gained insights into the VSMC implementation roadmap, a comprehensive approach that the VSMC presents for effectively implementing VSM principles and practices. This chapter offered a practical path to kickstart your organization's business transformation journey, whether you are a young professional developing future-ready skills or an executive striving for a competitive edge.

The lessons you have learned here are important because they equip you with the knowledge and tools needed for transformative change. The VSM implementation roadmap helps optimize value streams systematically, ensuring holistic assessments that lead to unparalleled improvements. It transcends industry boundaries and prevents the pitfall of "local optimizations."

In the next chapter, we will explore how to shift from managing projects to products while leveraging digital enhancements.

Questions

This section is offered for those readers who want to evaluate comprehension and retention of the information provided in this chapter. There are 10 questions. The answers are added in the following subsection. Recalling the exact verbiage of the original content is not essential. Instead, it is more important to recall the concepts and their applications.

1. What are the three crucial actions involved in the "**Start**" step of the VSMC Implementation Roadmap, and how do they contribute to the success of a VSM initiative?
2. How does the VSM Assessment tool contribute to the "assess" phase in the VSM Implementation Roadmap?
3. What is the primary objective of the "vision" stage in *VSM Step 3*, and how does it impact organizational transformation?

4. What distinguishes "core value streams" from "supportive value streams" in the context of *VSM Step 4*, "identify"?
5. What are the key considerations for effectively implementing *VSM Step 5*, "organize," to streamline cross-functional collaboration?
6. What are the five steps involved in the value stream mapping process according to the VSM Implementation Roadmap?
7. What are the primary activities involved in *VSM Step 7*, "connect," to orchestrate the integration of people, processes, and tools?
8. What are the three pillars of empiricism that underpin *VSM Step 8*, "inspect," and how do they contribute to enhancing value stream performance?
9. What are the seven key actions of the VSM "adapt" phase, aimed at refining the value stream?
10. What are the key differences between the traditional VSM methodology and the VSM Implementation Roadmap?

Answers

1. The three crucial actions involved in step 1, "**Start**" step are assembling core teams, assessing the current landscape, and setting strategic direction, which together establish foundational resources, provide a rapid organizational assessment, and align VSM initiatives with broader strategic goals.
2. The Comparative Agility VSM Assessment tool used in step 2, "**Assess**" facilitates a comprehensive evaluation of an organization's current VSM capabilities, enabling benchmarking, identifying improvement areas, and guiding teams toward optimizing their value stream practices.
3. The primary objective of step 3, "**Vision**" step is to define a long-term vision and objectives that evolve the organizational mindset, ingraining new habits and aligning with measurable goals to enhance effectiveness and competitive edge in the digital, for-profit sphere.
4. In the context of step 4, "**Identify**" Core value streams directly deliver an organization's core products and services, while supportive value streams enable and support these core functions, such as development platforms or customer relationship management systems.
5. Effective implementation of VSM step 5, "**Organize**" requires identifying VSM and cross-functional teams, defining roles and responsibilities, establishing communication pathways, providing training and support, and continuously monitoring and adjusting for optimal value stream functioning and delivery.
6. In step 6, "**Map**," the five steps involved in the value stream mapping process are assembling the mapping team, defining the scope, gathering process data, creating the current state map, and analyzing the map to identify improvement opportunities.

7. The primary activities of step 7, "**Connect**," include defining communication protocols, integrating technology and tools, automating data collection, enabling real-time visibility, and establishing feedback loops to create a seamless, efficient, and responsive digital value stream workflow.
8. The three pillars of empiricism in step 8, "**Inspect**" are transparency, inspection, and adaptation, contributing to value stream performance enhancement by promoting trust, encouraging continuous feedback, and guiding iterative improvements based on factual and evidence-based decision-making.
9. The seven key actions of step 9, "**Adapt**" are measuring results and iterating, embracing continuous improvement, eliminating waste, fine-tuning processes, automating workflows, sharing good practices, and fostering a culture of adaptation to evolve and refine the value stream.
10. The key differences between the VSM methodology and the VSMC's Implementation Roadmap are the modernized approach of the latter to enhance competitiveness in the digital age. The VSMC's roadmap incorporates Lean and Agile concepts, and focuses on IT infrastructure and digital enhancements. The VSM methodology remains valuable for broad, organizational improvements and cross-departmental changes.

Further reading

1. `https://www.vsmconsortium.org/`
2. Baudin, Michel. "Where do "Value Stream Maps" come from?" Michel Baudin's Blog. October 25, 2013. `https://michelbaudin.com/2013/10/25/where-do-value-stream-maps-come-from/`.
3. Womack, James P., and Daniel T. Jones. "From Lean Production to the Lean Enterprise." Harvard Business Review 72 (1994): 93-103.
4. Martin, James. 1995. The Great Transition: Using the Seven Disciplines of Enterprise Engineering to Align People, Technology, and Strategy. New York: Amacom.
5. Hines, Peter, Rich, N., Bicheno, J., Brunt, D., Taylor, D., Butterworth, C. and Sullivan, J. (2000). Value Stream Management: Strategy and Excellence in the Supply Chain. Financial Times/Prentice Hall.
6. Rother, Mike, and John Shook. 1999. Learning to See: Value-Stream Mapping to Create Value and Eliminate Muda. Lean Enterprise Institute.
7. Brunt, David, Matthew Lovejoy, Dan Jones, and Jim Womack. 2003. Seeing the Whole Value Stream. Lean Enterprise Institute.
8. Tapping, Don, Tom Luyster, and Tom Shuker. 2002. Value Stream Management: Eight Steps to Planning, Mapping, and Sustaining Lean Improvements. New York: Productivity.
9. Martin, Karen, and Mike Osterling. 2013. Value Stream Mapping: How to Visualize Work and Align Leadership for Organizational Transformation. New York: McGraw Hill.

6

Navigating Value Stream Optimization

The pessimist complains about the wind; the optimist expects it to change; the realist adjusts the sails.

- William Arthur Ward

In the fast-paced world of business management, one key element often separates successful leaders from the rest: the ability to navigate and optimize the flow of work and deliver value within an organization. For example, imagine your organization is like a well-designed ship with a motivated crew and you have a clear destination—delivering value to your customers. Everything seems perfect, but as we all know, the currents and winds of business are not always predictable.

This chapter will explore how to shift from managing projects to products while leveraging digital enhancements. Sticking with our previous nautical metaphor, we'll illustrate how navigating your value stream's path is like sailing through shifting winds and flows.

Value streams constantly change; nothing remains stagnant. However, two shifts remain constant in today's landscape to become a Lean enterprise:

1. **Shifting from projects to products**: To remain competitive and customer-centric, we must change our focus from managing short-term projects to continuously evolving our business processes, products, and services across their economically viable life cycles
2. **Harnessing digital enhancements**: Employing digital enhancements is key to effectively improving processes, products, and services

It's vital to introduce value stream operating models to build a solid foundation for adaptation, offering a holistic view of value creation and delivery across the organization. These new operating models integrate people, processes, information, and technology to optimize workflow. The shift from project to product and embracing customer-centricity enables sustainable value creation and delivery.

By understanding how optimizing value streams drives organizational transformation, you can improve solutions for customer needs, foster agility, and gain a competitive edge. You will be equipped with strategies for enhanced productivity, efficiency, adaptability, and value delivery.

The following topics are covered in this chapter:

- Shifting from projects to products
- Understanding value stream operating models
- Identifying and overcoming obstacles to streamlined workflows
- Balancing innovation and efficiency in value streams
- Optimizing value streams for enhanced performance

Shifting from projects to products

In the evolution of digital knowledge work, there's a pivotal shift from project-based to product-centric models, transforming how organizations deliver value and respond to market demands. Mik Kersten's book *Project to Product* drew significant attention to this change, offering a structured framework and practical guidance that solidified the concept.[1] Building upon discussions within the Agile and DevOps communities, Kersten's work reinforced the importance of product-centric thinking, which Agile methodologies and the DevOps movement had already laid out.

Traditionally, the project-centric paradigm, often associated with the **Waterfall development model**, emphasized discrete, temporary efforts with a specific scope, budget, and timeline. However, this model proved to be inefficient, unnecessarily delaying projects and allowing coding errors and defects to accumulate, making them increasingly difficult to resolve. Moreover, it often led to siloed efforts focused solely on predetermined deliverables and meeting project milestones rather than on addressing end user needs or fostering continuous improvement.

The modern transition to a product-centric approach represents a fundamental shift in strategy and execution in the digital landscape. Unlike projects, products are seen as living entities that evolve with customer needs and market trends. This shift aligns with Lean, Agile, and DevOps practices, emphasizing long-term value creation, cross-functional collaboration, and a relentless focus on customer experience and feedback loops.

This transition facilitates a more adaptable and responsive organizational culture, where teams are empowered to iterate and innovate rapidly. The product-centric model fosters a sense of ownership and accountability, as teams are continuously engaged with their product throughout its life cycle, leading to higher quality outcomes and greater alignment with business objectives.

Incorporating the product-oriented approach requires a fundamental shift in mindsets, processes, and management structures within organizations. It aligns more closely with the needs of digital knowledge work, where agility, responsiveness, and continuous improvement are key to sustaining a competitive advantage in a rapidly evolving digital marketplace.

Figure 6.1 contrasts the two models, project versus product, across various dimensions, highlighting the transition from a traditional, delivery-focused approach to a modern, customer-centric one. The product operating model's emphasis on continuous improvement, adaptability, and customer satisfaction represents a significant shift in how organizations approach digital knowledge work:

Operating Model	Project	Product
Primary goal	To complete the project as planned within constraints	To continuously deliver value to the customer and adapt to their changing needs
Focus	Delivering specific deliverables within a defined scope, budget, and time	Meeting the evolving needs of customers and the market
Measurement of success	Success is measured by adherence to budget, timelines, and scope	Success is measured by the product's impact on the market and user satisfaction
Team structure	Temporary teams are formed for the project and disbanded upon completion	Persistent cross-functional teams that adapt with the product
Lifecycle	Defined start and end dates; concludes upon project completion or delivery	Ongoing with no predefined end and focuses on continual improvement and iteration
Approach to change	Changes are managed through formal processes and may be resisted due to scope and budget constraints	Changes are expected and embraced as opportunities for improvement and adaptation

Figure 6.1 – Comparison of project and product operating models

In practice, the shift from project to product is rarely a binary switch and can happen at different times in various ways and extents. To better align with product-centric operating models and principles, it's helpful to consider differences in behavior and operating model across a spectrum as shown in *Figure 6.2*.

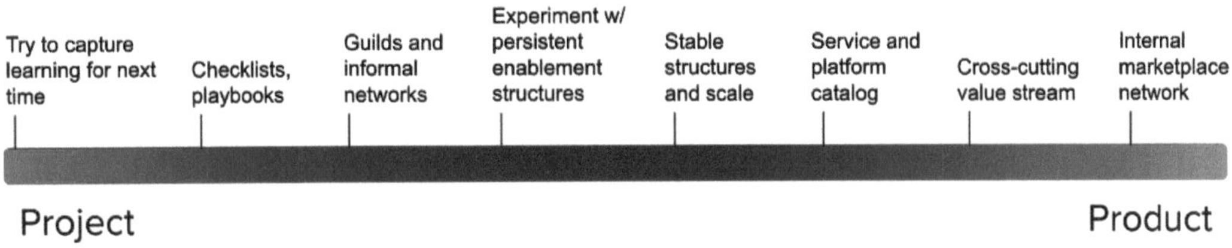

Figure 6.2 – The project to product spectrum

At one end of the spectrum, behaviors are aligned with traditional project management paradigms; at the other end, behaviors reflect a modern product-centric philosophy. This spectrum is best visualized as a gradient since organizations might find themselves at various points, transitioning from project to product-oriented behaviors as they adopt new practices and mindsets.

Evaluating project-centric behaviors

In project-centric environments, teams exhibit several distinct behaviors that shape their approach to work and collaboration:

- **Fixed scope emphasis**: Teams prioritize delivering specific outputs within predefined constraints, focusing heavily on adherence to the original plan, budget, and timeline.
- **Temporary teams**: People are allocated to projects and disbanded upon completion. From project-to-project, team composition frequently changes, leading to potential disruptions in knowledge continuity and team dynamics.
- **Change resistance**: Change is often seen as a threat to the project's scope, budgets, and timelines, leading to rigid change control processes that can slow adaptation.
- **Success metrics**: Success is measured by the project's adherence to predefined specifications, deadlines, and budget rather than long-term value or customer satisfaction.
- **Siloed workflows**: Work tends to occur in departmental or functional silos, with limited cross-functional collaboration, often resulting in hand-offs that can delay delivery and reduce efficiency.

Now that we've established a common understanding of project-centered behaviors, let's explore how these behaviors evolve as organizations transition toward product-centric development strategies.

Transitioning behaviors

As organizations transition toward product-centric development strategies, they exhibit transitional behaviors characterized by a shift toward balanced priorities, flexible team structures, openness to change, evolving success metrics, and integrated workflows. Let's explore these behaviors in more detail.

- **Balanced priorities**: Organizations begin to balance the need for delivering specific project outputs with understanding the broader impact on customer value and strategic goals.
- **Flexible team structures**: There's an increased emphasis on stable, cross-functional teams, though they may still be project-bound. Teams start to form around capabilities and products.
- **Openness to change**: Changes are managed more flexibly, with a growing understanding that adaptation can lead to better outcomes. Iterative methodologies such as Agile may facilitate this.
- **Evolving success metrics**: While traditional project metrics remain important, there's an increasing focus on measures such as customer feedback and market impact.
- **Integrated workflows**: Efforts to break down silos begin, with increased emphasis on collaboration across functions and stages of work.

As we progress through the transition from project-centric to product-centric behaviors, let's now explore the transformative shift toward product-centric approaches. Here, teams prioritize continuous value delivery, embrace change, and foster seamless collaboration.

Contrasting product-centric behaviors

As organizations transition to product-centric behaviors, they prioritize continuous value delivery, embrace change, and foster seamless collaboration. For example, they focus on enabling flow demanded by a continuous, holistic product focus as described below.

- **Customer and market focus**: Teams are primarily focused on delivering continuous value to customers and responding to market changes. The scope is flexible and evolves based on feedback and insights.
- **Persistent, cross-functional teams**: Teams are stable, long-term, and organized around products or services. They possess all the necessary skills to deliver value from end-to-end.
- **Embrace change**: Change is seen as an opportunity to learn and improve. Teams rapidly adapt based on real-world feedback, using method such as continuous delivery and deployment.
- **Value-based success metrics**: Success is measured by the product's impact on the market, customer satisfaction, and the ability to deliver business outcomes over the long term.
- **Seamless collaboration**: Workflows are highly integrated, with a strong emphasis on transparency, communication, and collaboration across all levels and functions within the organization.

Product-based organizations are in a constant state of evolution, moving from rigid, project structures and behaviors towards more dynamic, product-oriented models that prioritize agility, customer value, and sustainable growth.

Let's examine flow at different levels, macro and micro, to enable the greater emphasis on flow that continuous, holistic, product-focus demands.

Understanding flow at organizational and individual levels

In this subsection, we explore how identifying constraints within processes and employing principles such as the theory of constraints, Lean flow, and metrics can systematically address these challenges, leading to a more efficient and effective flow of work and value creation. Addressing these challenges helps us achieve more with fewer resources, maintain high-quality standards, deliver enhanced customer value, foster employee satisfaction, and accelerate deliveries.

As we explore the process of streamlining value streams, we must examine two distinct levels of flow: the **macro level**, encompassing the organization's collective workflow, and the **micro level**, focusing on individual employees' personal work experiences.

Let's take a closer look at these levels to gain a comprehensive understanding of how optimizing flow can lead to improved efficiency and satisfaction:

- **Macro level (collective flow)**: This perspective includes the entire organization's workflows, which ensures cohesion and efficiency. Like a relay race, these flows involve a synchronized, cross-organizational flow that allows work to progress rapidly and efficiently through the usual stages of planning, developing, testing, and deploying. This macro approach reflects how lean flow principles improve productivity and efficiency while leveraging Agile's iterative and incremental planning process, fostering adaptability and evolution across our value stream flows. The macro level effectively represents a view of our value stream flows.
- **Micro level (personal flow)**: On an individual level, flow relates to an employee's work experience. It involves uninterrupted time, deep and focused work without the risk of burnout, a dedication to one's area of expertise, and the need for acknowledgment. The personal flow is illustrated by the balance between challenge and skill, which is fundamental to achieving joy and satisfaction at work, as depicted in *Figure 6.3*.

Both the macro and micro levels of flow are critically interdependent. Enhancing flow within an organization should include efforts to do the following:

- Reduce delays
- Lower friction
- Increase engagement
- Boost performance

When seeking improvement, people often tend to concentrate on either the macro or micro aspects. However, both aspects must be considered simultaneously to establish high-performance systems. When addressing the macro level, measure the impact on the individual and vice versa.

As we explore optimizing value streams further, our next step is to identify obstacles to flow. These challenges obstruct work, create confusion, and reduce productivity. By identifying the most frequent types of flow interruptions, we can understand why unintentional value streams form. Recognizing and eliminating these obstacles is necessary because they persist when the flow isn't intentionally designed to avoid them.

Identifying obstacles to streamlined workflows

Making value flow without interruption is the first step to optimizing flow, as obstacles persist when workflows lack intentional design to address these problems. *Figure 6.3* depicts typical challenges, highlighting how they impede the efficient delivery of products and services:

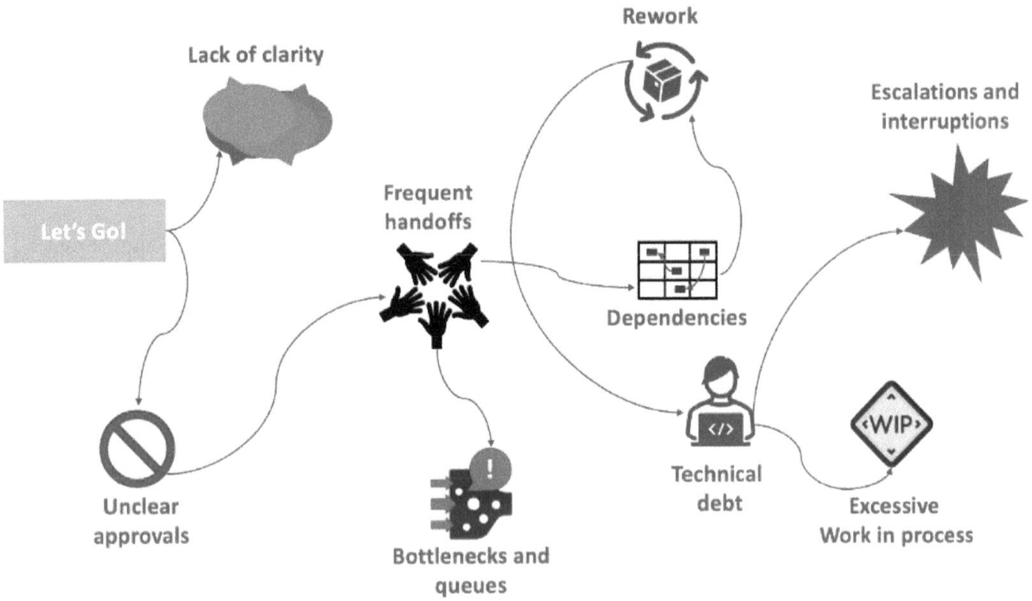

Figure 6.3 – The path to value often winds through a maze of challenges

The following is a list of typical impediments to flow:

- **Lack of clarity**: This causes confusion and misdirection, leading to wasted effort and resources, as team members may not understand the goals or processes.
- **Unclear approvals**: Unclear approvals cause delays and bottlenecks in a value stream, disrupting the smooth flow of processes.
- **Frequent handoffs**: This disrupts the flow by increasing the chances of miscommunication, delays, and errors. They can lead to inefficiencies and cause longer overall process time.
- **Bottlenecks and queues**: They slow progress as tasks get queued, waiting for previous activities to be completed, reducing overall efficiency and increasing lead times.
- **Dependencies**: You may encounter a situation where one team's work is blocked while another team's related work is completed. These handoffs typically occur when there is a gap in responsibility, knowledge, collaboration, and fast feedback.
- **Excessive work in process (WIP)**: Too much WIP causes priorities and resources to be shuffled, tasks to be frequently switched, and operating expenses to increase. It reduces productivity and throughput and increases wait times for new functionality.
- **Rework**: This is a waste of time and resources, as completed work needs to be done again due to errors or changes in requirements.

- **Technical debt**: The cost of deferring fixes or addressing identified issues, which leads to increased maintenance costs and reduced agility over time as accumulated shortcuts or incomplete solutions must be corrected later.
- **Escalations and interruptions**: These distract from planned work, often requiring immediate attention, disrupting workflow, and leading to project delays.

In the next subsection, we will explore how aligning work to value streams helps overcome these obstacles.

Seeing the organization in terms of flow

Eliminating the constraints imposed by traditional hierarchical structures improves productivity and efficiency, enabling a smoother flow of work across functional silos. Dr. Melvin Conway's article in Datamation, titled *'How Do Committees Invent?'*, discusses the relationship between organizational and technical design. His conclusion was that "*Organizations which design systems (in the broad sense used here) are constrained to produce designs which are copies of the communication structures of these organizations.*" [2] Simply put, the architecture of a system mirrors the communication structure of the organization that designed it.

What does Conway's law mean in practice? "*Suppose the technology department at ABC Insurance has three main workgroups: one focused on insurance claims, a second for underwriting, and a third for actuarial analysis. Conway's law predicts that your system design will mirror your organizational structure and communication pathways. In turn, there will be a separate software module for each of these three capabilities. Each will likely have a unique architecture, design, infrastructure, and systems integration protocols. The implications of team structure on architecture are often overlooked. The team's organizational design should align with the desired technical architecture, not the other way around.*"[3]

In traditional hierarchical and domain-based structures, work tends to align with these siloed teams and departments. It obstructs visibility into how value flows across the organization, making it challenging to see bottlenecks and inefficiencies. Furthermore, the additional cross-departmental and cross-functional processes required to overcome these silos create **excess processing waste**, which means doing more work or adding more components than necessary to meet customer requirements. *Figure 6.4* depicts traditional hierarchical organizational structures:

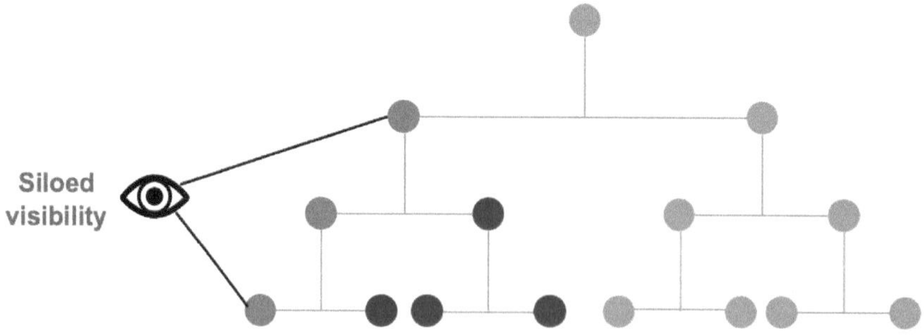

Figure 6.4 – Siloed organizational structures

Traditional organizational structures are typically function- or domain-based, resulting in siloed processes, hindering workflows, and adding complexity across functions and departmental operations. As a result, organizations often need additional processes and systems to facilitate inter-departmental workflows.

To break free from these traditional structures and embrace a value stream perspective, organizations can streamline their processes, enhance collaboration, and achieve greater efficiency. However, that means ignoring the dogma associated with the traditional hierarchical model as the only way to organize work. In many cases, aligning resources along your organization's product and service flows will make more sense, working backward from the customer outcomes you aim to deliver. We'll show an example of that in the context of a customer journey.

Instead of adhering to conventional structures, organizations must chart a definitive course toward value creation. This requires an examination of value stream flows that transcend departmental divisions. An organization's structural rigidity often hampers the fluidity necessary for seamless value delivery, as workflows are frequently hindered by compartmentalization and siloed practices. To address this issue, first conceptualize your value stream and then overlay it on top of the conventional hierarchical model.

In *Figure 6.5*, the highlighted line shows how value flows across a traditional hierarchy. As you can see, no single function or department can deliver a product or service independently:

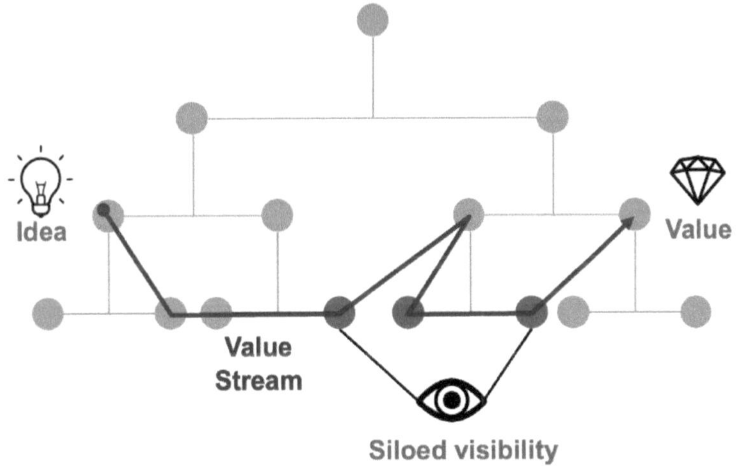

Figure 6.5 – Superimposed value stream flow

This figure illustrates the actual workflow across functional silos, such as product management, architecture, specialist teams, development, customer success, marketing, legal, and more.

When you map the workflow across your organization, you will find significant waste and inefficiencies. However, when we flatten this hierarchy and visualize the flow as a path from concept to value delivery, value flows smoothly without interruption.

Figure 6.6 highlights the importance of streamlining flows across business functions. After all, a straight line is always the shortest path to a destination:

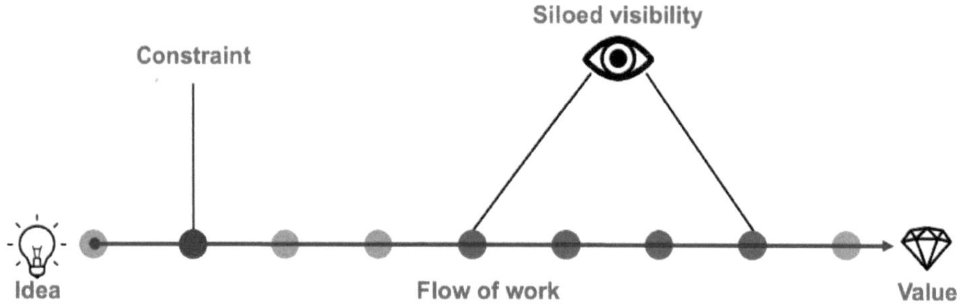

Figure 6.6 – Limited visibility allows constraints to remain hidden

In *Chapter 8, Implementing Basic Lean-Agile Solutions Teams (BLAST),* we delve into strategies to address the **fuzzy frontend**, where we must proactively build our product backlog in the face of insufficient information. Additionally, many of the downstream issues result from invisible upstream problems that are unaddressed. The efficiency of a value stream is not solely determined by its automation, integration, and synchronization downstream. Its effectiveness is also contingent on a steady influx of new work identified and refined adequately. Without this, our streamlined value streams can become underutilized.

Value streams – embracing continuous improvement in software delivery

In software development, adopting value-stream thinking and organization fosters continuous improvement. *Figure 6.7* illustrates an oversimplified value stream for delivering software from concept to support:

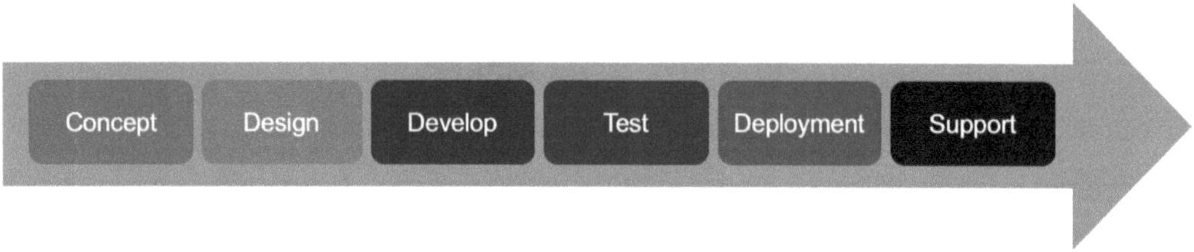

Figure 6.7 – Software development life cycle

The software development lifecycle shown in *Figure 6.7* is a simplified representation of the flow of work within a single value stream. The overarching objective of leveraging value streams is to achieve a comprehensive understanding and ultimate design of a discrete workflow delivering customer value. This perspective helps identify potential process bottlenecks at the system level, facilitating more informed decision-making, optimizing resources, and avoiding local- optimization. In *Chapter 7*, we'll go further to define the interconnected network of value streams at the organizational level.

By identifying and optimizing the flow of value, teams can address inefficiencies and prioritize customer satisfaction. This underscores the importance of value streams in elevating software delivery practices and preparing the groundwork for a deeper discussion on optimizing software development workflows for better outcomes.

Once you progress beyond the disruptive project model of pulling contributors together to work on a finite effort, improving performance becomes a regular and critical pursuit. Product and service delivery value streams provide an effective structure to leverage Lean–Agile practices to improve performance. Additionally, portfolios of products and services are delivered by a network of value streams that can be effectively mapped, measured, and intentionally designed for peak performance.

Investment in long-lived and evolving products and services demands the sustained measurement and refinement of performance through these value streams. It advocates for employing metrics that gauge efficiency, quality, and customer fulfillment to enable continuous improvement. This strategy is particularly pertinent amidst the shift from traditional project approaches to Lean product software development methods, which prioritize ongoing value delivery to customers over the completion of isolated projects.

Creating pathways to value – understanding and identifying value streams

Within an organization lies a complex network of value streams, each serving as a vital channel for delivering value to both internal and external customers. Recognizing these streams is crucial, yet it can be a complex task for organizations unfamiliar with the concept or evolving toward a value-oriented framework.

To demystify these streams, begin with the customer outcomes that signify success for the organization. A customer outcome, which goes beyond the general idea of customer satisfaction, identifies the exact value provided, such as a feature's utilization, new customer acquisition, or a completed sale.

Consider the sales process, an internal value stream that mirrors a customer's journey in evaluating their business or user needs, reviewing competitive offerings, and making informed purchasing decisions. This process experiences variable lead times, influenced by factors such as customer product reviews, competitive value analysis, and buying processes. While inherently operational, the sales-oriented value stream remains adaptable and open to improvement through Agile methodologies applied to organizational CRM tools, sales processes, pre-sales roles, availability of competitive and customer information, and product capabilities.

In the previous subsection, we emphasized the significance of superimposing a value stream across our organizational structures to better appreciate how work flows. But how do we define the value stream in the first place? Discovering a value stream involves a reverse journey from the customer outcome, inquiring about the processes and decisions that lead to the realization of that outcome. This backward journey often leads to the source of the process, which could be a customer request, a stakeholder's need, or an output from another value stream.

Initiating our value stream design by first defining what our customers want ensures that we stay aligned with their needs throughout the process. As we map the journey backward customer delivery upstream across our value stream flow to the initial order, we continuously inquire about the information and other product or service components that must be delivered at each stage of our value stream. This iterative approach guides us step by step, eventually leading us all the way back to the point of the initial customer order or request. It serves as a customer-centric foundation upon which we trigger our value stream flow.

In the process of optimizing our software delivery pipeline, we work our way backward through each phase of the **software development life cycle** (**SDLC**). Our goal is to ensure that each stage is seamlessly integrated and aligned with the principles of customer-centric value stream design. To achieve this, we incorporate the essential elements of value streams: people, process, information, and technology. As we navigate our way upstream from support all the way back to concept or the initial order/request—we will define the critical components that contribute to a robust and efficient software development process.

This backward exploration of value stream flows is not strictly applied to software delivery pipelines. All value steams need to be assessed in this manner to make informed improvements. Ideally, software delivery teams participate in these assessments to evaluate areas where software enhancements can improve the targeted value stream.

Once identified, value streams become concrete elements that an organization can optimize to improve value delivery. They are actionable avenues where businesses can exercise control to transform customer interactions into reliable, gratifying experiences that propel organizational success.

By mapping these streams, an organization not only gains insight into its operational status quo but also lays the groundwork for targeted enhancements that streamline the flow of value. Embracing this method promotes ongoing improvement to enhance each stream and amplify customer value.

Charting pathways to value – identifying value streams

Identifying value streams within an organization is like charting a course through a complex landscape. It begins with pinpointing the destination—what we refer to as the target outcome. This is the summit where value is perceived and realized by the customer. To reach this peak, one must consider the product or service being offered and the journey the customer undertakes to interact with this offering.

Figure 6.8 illustrates three potential starting points: target outcome, a specific product/service, or customer journey:

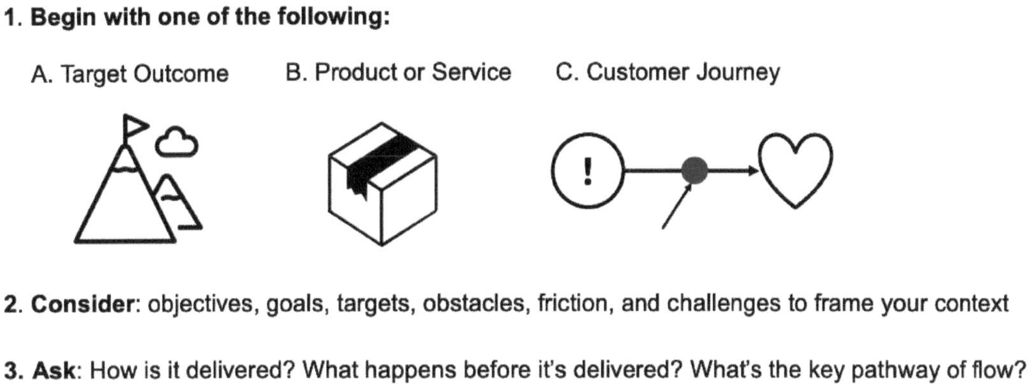

Figure 6.8 - Identifying value streams

To truly map out the value streams, we must delve into the questions that dissect the delivery mechanism of our products and services. It is essential to ask certain questions: how is value delivered? How do we measure it? What triggers the start of a new delivery? What are key value stream metrics? How do we gauge our successes after delivery? By answering these questions, the value streams begin to emerge, revealing not just the flow of value but also the obstacles, friction points, and challenges that may impede its progress.

Consideration of your objectives, goals, and targets frames the context for this exploration. The context is crucial—it gives perspective to the value stream, distinguishing it from mere processes by its purposeful orientation toward delivering outcomes.

Products and services act as vessels carrying value, and their selection can serve as an entry point in understanding the associated value streams. Whether one looks at a comprehensive product catalog or zeroes in on a specific offering, the objective remains to map the path back from the customer to the source of its creation.

The customer journey encompasses all interactions and experiences a customer encounters, from initial awareness to post-purchase interactions. Mapping this journey reveals touchpoints where the organization interacts with customers, influences their experience, and offers opportunities to enhance value delivery. By tracing these touchpoints backward, we unveil the underlying value streams.

When these elements—target outcomes, products and services, and the customer journey—are considered together, an even clearer picture begins to form. The streams become visible, flowing from the source of creation to the point of customer interaction. It is along these streams that we can navigate, optimize, and innovate to ensure that the journey to performance improvement is as smooth and as enriching as possible.

In the upcoming subsection, you will gain valuable insights into the essential roles and responsibilities involved in value stream mapping. Specifically, we will explore how each key player contributes to the success of the mapping effort in the context of a mobile application project, where their collective expertise is leveraged to optimize the value stream and enhance operational efficiency.

Mapping flow

Value stream mapping (VS mapping) is a strategic exercise in business process improvement that is crucial for visualizing the flow of materials and information and working on the creation and delivery of a product or service. The clarity of roles and responsibilities is essential for the success of VSM, as depicted in *Figure 6.9*, which outlines the key players in the VSM initiative for a mobile application project.

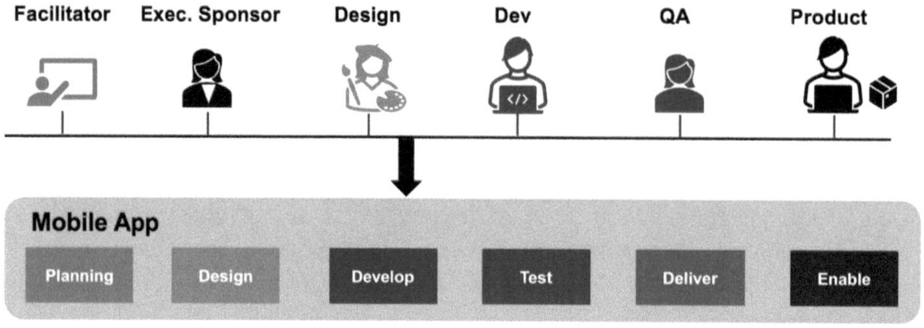

Figure 6.9 – Roles involved in value stream mapping

In the following list of VS mapping roles, we introduce the crucial participants in a VS mapping exercise. Each plays a distinct role in visualizing and improving the flow of materials, information, and work in the creation and delivery of products or services. These roles represent crucial contributors to any cross-functional, end-to-end effort to improve flow and value delivery:

- **VSM facilitator**: The facilitator is central to the VSM initiative and is responsible for guiding the team through the mapping process. This individual ensures that the mapping activities are conducted methodically, encourages participation, and ensures that all voices are heard and documented. The facilitator may be the value stream leader assigned to support the value stream or an external expert in lean-oriented VS mapping practices.
- **Executive sponsor**: The executive sponsor provides the VSM initiative with its directive and mandate. Their role is to secure resources, overcome organizational resistance, and empower the team with the authority needed to carry out the mapping and subsequent improvement initiatives.
- **Product owners, UI/UX designers, developers, quality assurance (QA), and testers**: These functional roles provide their perspective as contributors to qualify and quantify what is happening in the flow of work, how it performs, and where they see issues and opportunities.

Each step of the flow, starting from the final outcome and working backward to inception, is mapped, analyzed, and optimized to ensure that the value stream is as lean and efficient as possible, minimizing waste and maximizing value to the customer.

Through VSM, the collective expertise of these roles is leveraged to dissect and understand the end-to-end process, identify inefficiencies, and improve the flow of value. This collaborative effort is instrumental in creating a flow that not only meets customer expectations but also contributes to the organization's competitive edge and operational excellence.

Inspecting efficiency and effectiveness

When we map and inspect value streams, we must consider both value stream efficiency and effectiveness *as shown in Figure 6.10*. These results could encompass various aspects such as streamlined workflows, improved customer experience, value delivery, financial performance, and the impact on organizational outcomes.

	Efficiency	Effectiveness
Goal	Eliminate waste and constraints	Deliver the most amount of value and quality in the shortest sustainable lead time
Results	Streamlined workflows	Accelerated business outcomes
Measures	- Lean metrics - Flow metrics - DORA metrics - Quality metrics	- Customer satisfaction - Business performance metrics - Business OKRs and KPIs - Business competitive metrics

Figure 6.10 – Workflow versus value realization

On one side, we have **efficiency**, which focuses on the performance of internal processes. Outputs such as rate of flow, frequency of delivery, waste in the value stream, and types of work underway are critical indicators of a value stream's health. These metrics are essential for gauging how well the internal processes are functioning and how efficiently value is being delivered through the value stream.

Transitioning to **effectiveness**, the emphasis shifts to business outcomes, particularly in terms of customer experience. Here, outcomes are most important. For example: active usage of the platform's capabilities by customers, the rate at which new customers are acquired, direct customer feedback on their experiences, and the financial health of the value stream are all vital signs of how effectively the organization is delivering value to its customers and stakeholders.

It's important to maintain a balance between streamlined workflows and accelerated business outcomes. It's not enough to be efficient internally; an organization must also ensure that this efficiency translates into real-world effectiveness that customers can feel and appreciate. This balance is the cornerstone of a thriving value stream and, ultimately, a successful business.

Balancing innovation and efficiency in value streams

Figure 6.11 illustrates a crucial dimension for classifying and influencing organizational value streams: the balance between innovation and operational efficiency. It underscores the importance of recognizing where each value stream falls on the spectrum, from a focus on disruptive innovation to a commitment to stability and efficiency:

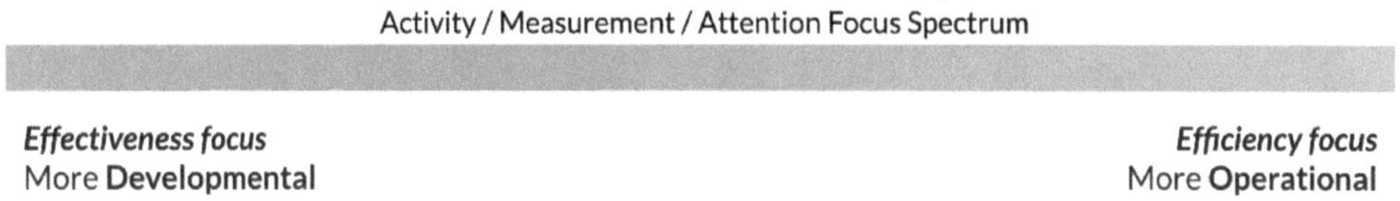

Figure 6.11 – The spectrum of performance focus

The drive for effectiveness and innovation

At one end of the spectrum, as shown on the left in *Figure 6.12*, we have value streams delivering products and services that are unique and novel and differentiate the organization's offerings from the competition. This is where innovation and disruption are born:

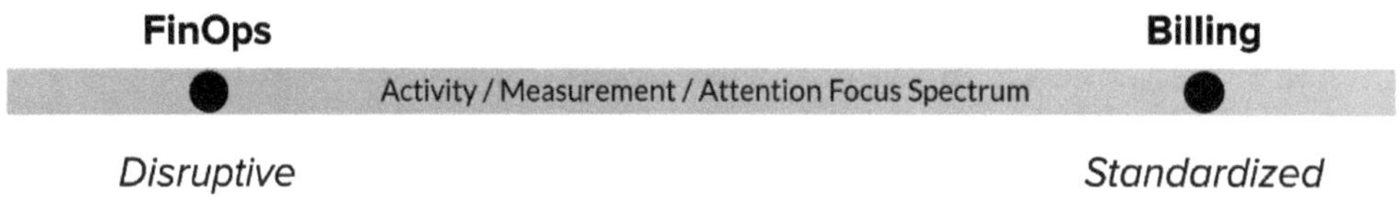

Figure 6.12 – Streams can be plotted to place them in relative context

These are areas where the organization is actively seeking to break new ground, often characterized by new capabilities, experimentation, and exploration of new practices. The emphasis here is on creating value through innovation and embracing change to stay ahead of market trends.

The drive for efficiency and stability

Conversely, on the opposite end, we find processes such as billing, infrastructure services, payroll, and human resources. These are established, highly commoditized practices that prioritize efficiency, stability, and predictability. In such domains, the goal is to refine and optimize, reducing variation and increasing margins through operational cost efficiencies. These value streams are mature, well-evolved areas where consistency and security are paramount, and the focus is on maximizing profitability through standardization. At the extreme, they may be so commoditized and standardized that they are most beneficial as an outsourced capability.

The dynamic nature of value streams

What's particularly noteworthy here is that value streams are not static. They can shift positions across this spectrum over time, either through deliberate strategic repositioning or as a response to evolving market and internal conditions. The recognition that value streams can transition between focusing on innovation and efficiency opens up possibilities for strategic management and intentional transformation.

Implications across organizational dimensions

This spectrum has far-reaching implications, affecting creativity, exploration, operational management, and resource allocation. It informs the approach to leadership, investment in technology, and process development. Understanding where a value stream sits on this continuum is critical for aligning organizational efforts with broader strategic objectives.

Contextualizing performance focus

In essence, this visualization is a strategic tool that helps leaders understand and direct the evolution of value streams within their organization. It provides insight into how to foster an environment where innovation can thrive without sacrificing the operational excellence necessary for long-term success.

Using FinOps and billing as representative points on this spectrum helps to contextualize the diverse nature of value streams. While FinOps may be situated toward the innovation end – continually adapting and evolving, billing would typically be found toward the operational efficiency end – emphasizing reliability and cost-effectiveness.

Using this spectrum, you can discuss what it might mean to shift a value stream further toward one end or another and what targets and behaviors might enable that. We'll discuss how targets, metrics, and measures drive this change in the following section. Moreover, in the following chapter, we'll show how this deep commitment to learning. Here, the work processes are more experimental, spectrum forms the backbone for mapping your organization as a network, as well as the strategic and tactical implications of your value stream network map.

Striking the balance – from learning to results in value streams

When exploring the strategic dynamics within an organization, one can consider a continuum that spans from the **flow of learning (Explore)** to the **flow of results (Exploit)**, as shown in *Figure 6.13*:

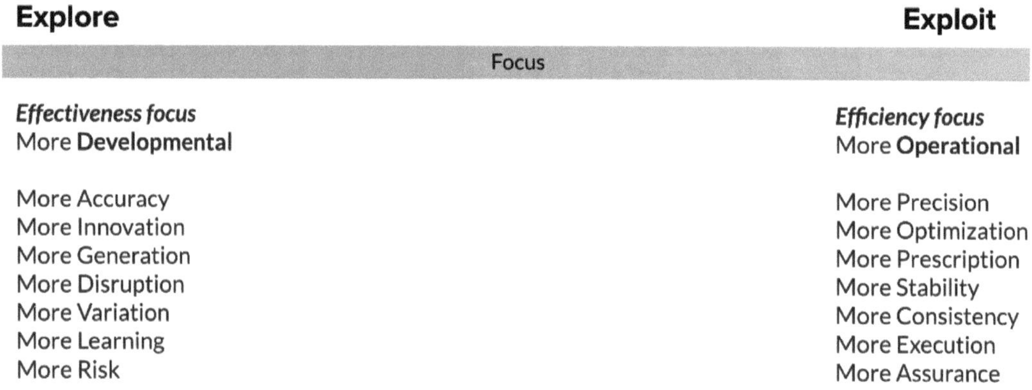

Figure 6.13 – Spanning the spectrum from the flow of learning to the flow of results

At the left end of this continuum lies the realm of innovation and effectiveness, characterized by a deep commitment to learning. Here, the work processes are more experimental, exploratory, and often disruptive. It's an environment where ideas are incubated and nurtured over time, and gaining acceptance for a groundbreaking innovation is considered a desirable outcome. The focus is on long-term value creation rather than immediate returns. This approach can be more time-consuming and less about immediate efficiency, but the potential for transformative outcomes can justify the investment in learning and experimentation.

To the right of the spectrum, the focus becomes efficiency and sustainable delivery—the flow of results. Here, the emphasis is on speed of delivery, predictability, and consistency. Value streams operating at this end often manage a backlog of mostly uniform tasks that need to be processed with high efficiency and effectiveness. The primary goal is to drive down costs and streamline processes to maximize output. Also, the ability to increase margins is more constrained, as there's a limit to how much one can optimize existing processes without introducing new innovations or disruptive methods.

Refining the process – questions for progress

Another critical point to consider is that *Figures 6.11* to *6.13* underscore a fundamental principle: the coordinates at which a stream is placed within this bi-dimensional framework directly result from what it does, prioritizes, and measures. However, these figures do not show how a stream might move after considering the results of priority and measurement. To shift a stream, the team adjusts its priorities and measurements. As a result, we can see not only the present flow of activities but also a future state flow by defining changes to targets that drive changes in behavior.

Paraphrasing the teachings of Eliyahu M. Goldratt, the author of *The Goal* and the developer of the **theory of constraints**, it can be said that "*the elements an organization chooses to measure will inevitably align with its achievements.*" He is also often quoted as saying, "*Show me how you'll measure me, and I'll show you how I'll behave.*" Said another way, your outcomes are a downstream effect of what you measure upstream. This is because the act of measurement does more than just record data—it focuses attention and resources, dictating what the organization will actually execute.

So, with this information, we can answer these questions on the value of metrics and measurements:

- Why do metrics and measurements matter?

  Understanding the influence of metrics and measurement on organizational positioning is not just an academic exercise; it is crucial to tangible progress in any business domain. It matters because the metrics we prioritize are the rudders steering our collective efforts. They shape our decision-making processes, influence our resource allocation, and ultimately define our success criteria.

- How do we release more often?

  To enhance the frequency of our releases, we should focus on the efficiency of our release mechanisms. By measuring the lead time and the proportion of automated processes versus manual interventions, we can identify bottlenecks. Tracking the influence of constraints and the handoffs between teams can reveal inefficiencies and areas ripe for innovation.

- How can we change the way we work?

  Effective alteration of our work methods requires a shift in what we measure. By setting new performance indicators, we influence behaviors and reshape the operational model. The focus of the team naturally shifts to align with these new metrics, driving them to adapt their approaches and innovate their practices.

- What if we want to change [variable]?

  If a change is desired in a specific area, noted as "[variable]" in the question, it is essential to start by identifying the relevant metrics that can trigger a change in that domain. Measure the current state, set a target for the desired state, and monitor progress against those metrics. This structured approach to change can catalyze a shift in behavior, workflows, and, ultimately, outcomes.

By revisiting what we measure, we do not just change numbers on a dashboard; we instigate a culture of transformation that permeates through the layers of our organizational practice, altering the way we operate, innovate, and grow. The act of measurement, therefore, is not just a reflective tool but a formative one—it shapes the path we take toward our aspirations.

Now let's move on to introduce five steps to optimize our value streams.

Optimizing value streams

The E9 VSM Methodology presented in *Chapter 4* offers a robust approach to conducting a VSM engagement. But for the purposes of this chapter, we can simplify it. For example, *Figure 6.14* presents a streamlined view of value stream management, encapsulating the essential steps for optimizing business processes:

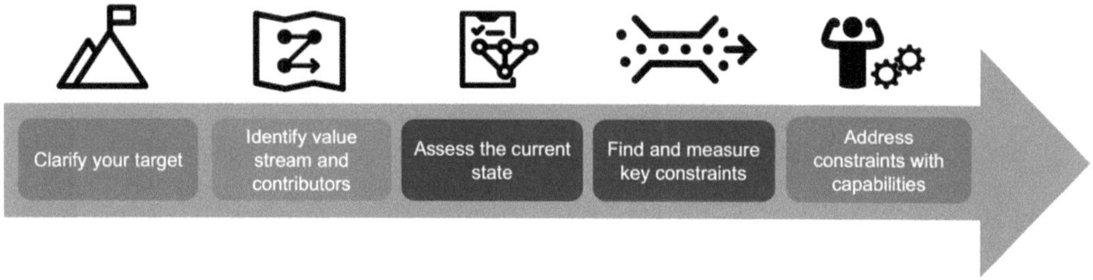

Figure 6.14 – The flow of value stream management

The objectives for each of the five key steps are:

- **Clarify your target**: Establish a clear goal that your value stream efforts aim to achieve. This will set the direction for all subsequent actions and decisions.
- **Identify stream and contributors**: Determine the specific value stream that aligns with your target and recognize the contributors who influence the flow of value.
- **Assess the current state**: Evaluate the present condition of your value stream to understand where you stand in relation to your target.
- **Find and measure key constraints**: Identify and quantify the bottlenecks that are hindering your value stream. Understanding these constraints is critical to prioritizing efforts for improvement.
- **Address constraints with capabilities**: Utilize available capabilities to resolve the constraints, thereby enhancing the performance and efficiency of your value stream.

This approach to value stream management facilitates a focused and effective strategy for process improvement, ensuring that efforts are aligned with desired outcomes. Still, we need to keep in mind why we are executing these five steps to streamline value deliveries.

Streamlining value delivery

Navigating through the intricacies of value stream management requires a focus on several pivotal elements that ensure a seamless and dynamic flow of value to the customer:

- **Delivery focus**: The core emphasis lies in the sustainable delivery of value. This involves a persistent commitment to not just planning or outlining the value streams but operationalizing and executing them efficiently.

- **Topology supporting value streams**: A well-defined team topology is the foundation of successful value streams. The interaction of multiple teams within a network facilitates a comprehensive, interconnected system that propels value delivery forward.
- **Set new targets**: Shifting the performance focus necessitates setting new targets and benchmarks. By altering what is measured and expected, behaviors and outcomes within the value stream are redirected toward the desired change.
- **Visualize flow across the organization**: It is crucial to understand and see the flow of value not just in isolated pockets but across the entire organizational structure. This broad perspective is essential for a holistic approach to value stream management, ensuring that all parts of the organization are aligned and contributing to the flow of value.

Now that we have explored various strategies for inspecting, refining, and optimizing value stream operations, we have one last dimension to define where our value streams sit within our organization - which is evolution.

Managing value stream evolution

In this section, we show how to chart the dynamics of value stream flows and explore strategies for optimizing their performance. By mapping value streams, organizations gain a clear understanding of their improvement opportunities.

Specifically, we continue to examine the two dimensions of customer proximity and operational focus. Through this two-dimensional network of value streams, we expose the complex interplay of organizational activities. This network view empowers leaders to pinpoint each value stream's position relative to its strategic importance and operational emphasis.

We also explore how value streams vary in their customer visibility and operational focus, from customer-centric, front-facing elements such as mobile banking to highly efficient yet less customer-visible processes such as billing. This mapping isn't just a static representation; it's a dynamic model that reflects the fluid nature of value streams.

Finally, we will examine how changes in one area can ripple through the network, influencing adjacent streams. Whether it's the introduction of innovative **financial operations** (**FinOps**), the automation of platforms, or the deliberate strategic repositioning of value streams, each connection represents a decision point where the balance between innovation and efficiency must be managed. Understanding these interconnected dynamics is crucial for strategic agility, aligning internal processes with organizational goals, and delivering value to both customers and the organization.

We'll start this section with a discussion on how value stream mapping helps organizations align customer-centric innovation with operational efficiency, guiding strategic decisions for a cohesive and efficient operation.

Synchronizing core and supportive workflows

In this subsection, we continue with our mobile app use case to demonstrate how external-facing core value stream processes can translate into supporting value streams for internal customers. Here, we will find that numerous support value streams can be created to assist the core, depending on activities that require operational or development-oriented support.

Figure 6.15 illustrates the interplay between core and supportive streams within our organizational workflow. It depicts the flow of work across standard development value stream processes. The dotted lines provide visibility to where efficiencies can be gained and where efforts may be diluted.

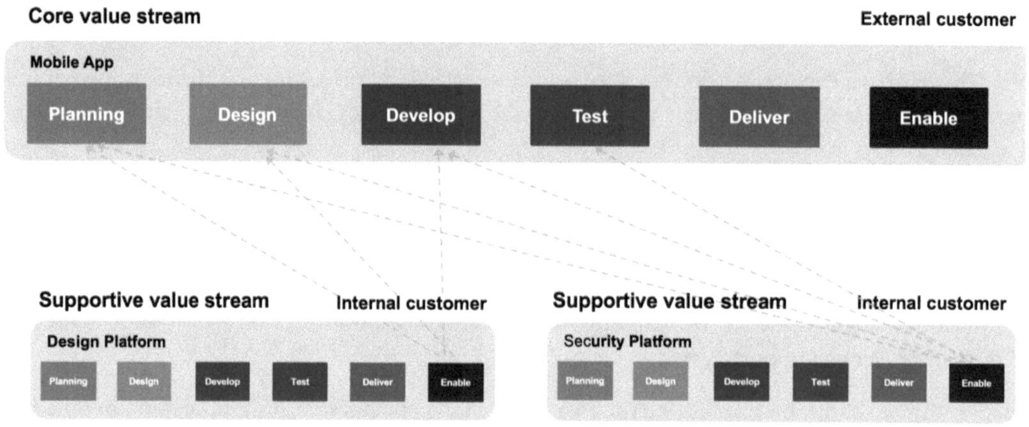

Figure 6.15 – Core and supportive streams

Core streams directly engage with external customers, delivering the final products or services that define our market presence. These streams are depicted through the mobile app process flow, which includes the **Planning**, **Design**, **Develop**, **Test**, **Deliver**, and **Enable** phases. The proximity of the core streams to the end users is a fundamental concept, as it indicates that the deliverables are closely aligned with the customers' needs and expectations.

In contrast, supportive streams function internally, providing essential capabilities that empower the core streams. These supportive streams, illustrated as **Design Platform** and **Security Platform**, undergo a similar process flow, ensuring that the capabilities they develop are robust and align with the overarching goals of the core streams. These platforms undergo their own **Planning** to **Enable** phases, ensuring a structured and thorough approach to internal service provision.

As another example, the design platform may offer tools and frameworks that enhance the **Develop** phase of the mobile app, while the security platform provides security protocols and infrastructure crucial for the mobile app's **Test** and **Deliver** stages. This symbiotic relationship is vital for internal customer satisfaction and for maintaining a seamless workflow.

The integration between core and supportive streams highlights the organizational focus on internal synergy, with the ultimate goal of achieving peak efficiency and effectiveness in delivering to external customers. By aligning internal capabilities with external demands, the organization ensures that both internal and external customer needs are met, fostering a robust, responsive, and Agile operational model.

In the next subsection, we step into a future era where the narrative of our workday shifts from reaction to creation. Lean–Agile teams evolve into ecosystems driven by autonomy, mastery, and purpose, with a heightened focus on continuous, customer-centric delivery.

Transitioning from functions to stream-aligned synergy

In this digital era, success transcends mere task completion; it is now measured by the value delivered. CI/CD and DevOps platforms empower teams and team members to become both Lean-Agile contributors and creators. As we move forward, our mission extends beyond software product development to crafting experiences for both customers and teams, seamlessly blending agility, innovation, and customer-centricity into our organizational DNA.

Empowering transformation: orchestrating change with platform teams

In this transformative journey from traditional IT functions to streamlined value streams, one of the key enablers of change has been the emergence of **platform teams**. These specialized teams represent a paradigm shift in how organizations approach software development. They act as architects of efficiency, weaving together the tools, services, and capabilities that empower development teams to navigate the turbulent seas of dependencies and inefficiencies.

Platform teams, in the context described, refer to specialized groups or teams within an organization that focus on developing and maintaining shared platforms, tools, and capabilities that enable other development teams to work more efficiently and effectively. These platform teams are responsible for creating a set of services and resources that streamline and simplify the development process for other value-stream teams across the organization.

> **Platform Teams:**
>
> Specialized groups within a software delivery organization that develop and maintain the underlying infrastructure, tools, and services that support and enable the efficient development, deployment, and operation of applications.

Key characteristics of platform teams include the following:

- **Self-service**: Platform teams offer self-service access to their tools and resources, allowing other teams to use them without extensive manual intervention or support
- **Tools and capabilities**: They provide a range of tools, libraries, and infrastructure components that help development teams automate tasks, adhere to best practices, and accelerate their development cycles

- **Responsiveness**: Platform teams are responsive to the needs of their internal customers (other development teams) and work closely with them to understand their requirements and pain points
- **Standardization**: They establish and maintain standardized practices and patterns across the organization, ensuring consistency and reducing complexity
- **Scalability**: Platform teams design their service delivery solutions to be scalable, accommodating the needs of various development teams and projects
- **Continuous improvement**: They continuously evolve and improve their offerings based on feedback and changing technology landscapes

In essence, platform teams act as enablers, providing the infrastructure and tools necessary for other teams to focus on their core objectives, such as developing software products, while minimizing common operational challenges and dependencies. This approach promotes agility, accelerates development, and enhances overall efficiency within the organization.

As Lean-Agile teams and individuals navigate their way through the currents of change, they bear witness to a profound transformation. This journey is characterized by a transition from a structure weighed down by dependencies to one that champions flow and autonomy. Let's look at the progression of this transformation.

Navigating dependencies with streamlining efforts

Improvement efforts often began with the installation of Agile software development teams using Scrum, often entangled in the web of complex subsystems. Their days were punctuated by the push and pull of interdependencies, where the quest for progress was met with the inertia of inefficiency.

This was an era of disruption, a time when progress stumbled over the hurdles of hierarchical constraints. Software development teams integrated tools and systems and process automation to address these issues across the enterprise and then found it useful to apply these same capabilities within their own IT domains.

Elevating teams with platform empowerment

Metaphorically, the winds of change brought forth the concept of platform teams, akin to architects laying down bridges over chasms of chaos. These platforms emerged as enablers of self-service, offering tools and capabilities that turned pipeline delivery obstacles into gateways. Stream-aligned teams, once hindered by the unpredictable tides of dependencies, now found themselves in a rhythm, a harmonious flow that resonated with continuous delivery.

> **Stream-Aligned Teams:**
> Cross-functional teams in software development organized around specific value streams or customer journeys, responsible for end-to-end delivery and continuous improvement of a particular aspect of the product or service, ensuring alignment with business goals and customer needs.

Figure 6.16 depicts our transition from isolated, function-based operations to cohesive, customer-centric value streams. It highlights the transformation from Agile team structures, which often operate across disparate systems, to stream-aligned teams. These stream-aligned teams work within standardized, self-service development environments that facilitate seamless integration with value streams.

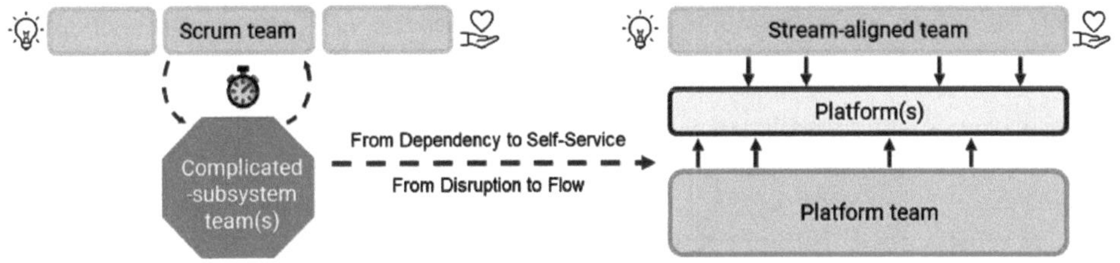

Figure 6.16 – Shifting from functions to streams

To better understand the structural evolution detailed in *Figure 6.16*, let's examine the distinct roles and relationships within this transformative team topology framework:

- **Scrum team**: Traditionally, Scrum teams are focused on specific functions or products, often working within silos. They manage complex subsystems, as indicated by their connection to complicated subsystem team(s), highlighting their role in handling intricate system details.
- **Complicated subsystem team(s)**: These teams are specialists in complex system components requiring in-depth knowledge and expertise. Their close association with the Scrum team suggests they offer specialized support, emphasizing the compartmentalized nature of traditional structures. Too often, they support many scrum teams and remain overloaded, interrupted, and distracted, which causes delays to flow.

> **Complicated Subsystem Teams:**
> Specialized teams in software development focused on complex, technical subsystems that require deep expertise, responsible for designing, maintaining, and optimizing intricate components or services that integrate with other parts of the system.

- **Stream-aligned team**: As the driving force behind the shift from *functions to streams* evolution, these teams align with end-to-end value streams, ensuring workflow contributes directly to customer value. They operate within a continuous delivery framework facilitated by self-service capabilities provided by supporting platforms. This loose coupling and on-demand enablement allow for a more continuous flow of work.
- **Platform team**: Tasked with the development and maintenance of platforms, this team supplies the stream-aligned teams with self-service tools. For example, develop and provide platforms to internal stream-aligned teams as a supplier to internal customers, aiming to provide a consistent and uninterrupted workflow, bridging gaps that could disrupt customer value delivery.

This section has highlighted a significant paradigm shift in software development, moving from the siloed approach of traditional Scrum teams requiring extreme coordination across tightly-coupled groups, to a more integrated and fluid value stream orientation. It illustrates the crucial role of platform teams and platforms in equipping stream-aligned teams to deliver continuous customer value, bypassing the intricate subsystems and dependencies that once hindered progress. This evolution signifies a transition from the fragmented functions of earlier frameworks to a unified, customer-focused model of value streams.

Continuing on from the stream-aligned paradigm, we now look deeper into how software organizations cultivate a continuous delivery environment focused on customer centric value.

Cultivating continuous delivery and customer centricity

In the pursuit of cultivating continuous delivery and customer centricity, we must shift our daily tasks from reactive responses to proactive creations. This transformation allows our teams to mature into dynamic ecosystems with a strong foundation of autonomy, mastery, and purpose. This evolution not only enhances our software delivery process but also reshapes our success criteria to align with the genuine value delivered to our customers.

With the stream-aligned platforms in place, our workday undergoes a profound shift, transitioning from a reactive stance to one rooted in proactive creation. Teams no longer function as mere groups of individuals but transform into thriving ecosystems guided by our foundational principles. Our focus sharpens, emphasizing not only the act of delivery but also the art of it—continuity, consistency, and a deep understanding of our customers' ever-evolving needs.

In this new era, the measure of success is no longer just the completion of tasks but the value delivered. The platforms underpinning our teams are not just tools; they are enablers of a vision where every team member becomes both a contributor and a creator, and every product is a testament to the organization's commitment to efficiency, stability, and customer satisfaction.

As we continue to realign, recalibrate, and reimagine our operational models, we're not just building products—we're crafting experiences, both for our customers and our teams. This is the new blueprint of our organizational DNA, one that weaves the fabric of agility with the threads of innovation and customer-centricity.

Summary

This chapter delved into the intricacies of defining and optimizing value streams within organizations, which are crucial for maintaining competitiveness and customer focus in a rapidly changing business environment. It emphasized two pivotal shifts necessary for today's businesses: transitioning from a project to product focus and leveraging digital technologies for process and product improvement. It introduced the concept of value stream operating models, providing a comprehensive view of value creation and delivery that integrates people, processes, information, and capabilities across the organization.

We covered the quest for organizational and individual flow, identifying obstacles to optimized workflows, and the importance of viewing the organization in terms of flow to foster efficiency and productivity. We addressed how traditional organizational structures, often siloed, can impede workflow, and we suggested a value stream perspective to enhance collaboration and efficiency. We explored the importance of mapping value streams for continuous improvement in software delivery, identifying and addressing inefficiencies and bottlenecks. We also discussed balancing innovation with efficiency, highlighting the need for organizations to navigate between these two priorities strategically.

In addition, this chapter presented strategies for optimizing value streams, including clarifying targets, identifying contributors, assessing current states, and finding and addressing key constraints, while leveraging capabilities to enhance value stream performance. In the next chapter, we'll explore the idea of mapping a Value Stream Network on a two-dimensional surface, which will provide us with a comprehensive understanding of the entire process in context with our customers journeys.

Questions

This section is offered for those readers who want to evaluate comprehension and retention of the information provided in this chapter. There are three questions. Recalling the exact verbiage of the original content is not important. Rather, it's more important to recall the concepts and their applications.

1. In the context of value stream mapping and analysis, how does aligning internal processes with the stages of the customer journey contribute to more effective customer engagement and product development?
2. What are the key roles in **value stream mapping** (**VSM**) for a mobile application project and how do they contribute to the overall success of the project?
3. What is the significance of balancing efficiency and effectiveness in value stream operations and how does this balance impact an organization's success?

Answers

1. In the context of value stream mapping and analysis, aligning internal processes with the customer journey is crucial for effective customer engagement and product development. This alignment ensures that each step of the customer experience, from initial curiosity to post-purchase review, is supported by corresponding internal value streams like marketing campaigns and product development. By mapping these value streams to the customer journey, organizations can effectively guide customers through each step, ensuring a seamless and engaging lifecycle.
2. In Value Stream Mapping for a mobile app project, key roles include the Facilitator, Executive Sponsor, Design, Development, Quality Assurance, and Product teams. The Facilitator guides the mapping process, ensuring participation. The Executive Sponsor provides resources and support. The Design team ensures user-focus and customer alignment, while the Development team builds the product. The QA team assesses quality at various stages. The Product team aligns the project with business goals.

3. The significance of balancing efficiency and effectiveness in value stream operations is crucial for translating internal proficiency into customer benefits. Efficiency optimizes internal processes, measured by workflow rate and delivery frequency, while effectiveness focuses on customer outcomes like platform usage, acquisition rates, and feedback. This balance ensures internal optimizations enhance customer experience, driving sustained success and competitive advantage.

Further reading

1. Kersten, M. (2018). Project to Product: How to Survive and Thrive in the Age of Digital Disruption with the Flow Framework. IT Revolution Press.
2. Conway, M. E. (1968). How do committees invent? Datamation, 14(4), 28–31.
3. Knaster, Richard. Value Stream Management for the Digital Age. 2021.

7
Connecting the Value Stream Network

"Success today is not about surviving change; it's about leading it." – Peter Drucker

Imagine your organization as a vast communications network, coordinating work, information, and resources from initial ideas to final outcomes, from requests to deliveries. As business and IT professionals, your success hinges on managing these complex flows efficiently to support customer journeys and drive business outcomes. How do you ensure that these processes run smoothly across your organization?

Managing these disparate pieces of work requires more than a single value stream—it demands coordinated efforts across streams aligned with customer needs.

Value Stream Networks (**VSNs**) are interconnected pathways within your organization that are strategically aligned to deliver holistic value. VSNs show how work items flow through multiple value streams while supporting a broader network that serves our business, stakeholders, and customer needs.

The seamless flow of work and information across this network maximizes the value delivered through products and services. However, these interconnections can introduce complexities, constraints, and potential waste that must be managed effectively. The network's ability to create value depends on maintaining reliable, scalable, and efficient operations.

Even if individual value streams are streamlined, their interconnected nature and constant evolution introduce complexities. This chapter presents strategies to manage these complexities.

A VSN can function to some degree without visualization and measurement. However, without a visual representation of the value stream network, the organization will struggle to improve workflows and risk local optimizations that may have detrimental side effects.

This chapter covers the following topics:

- Managing and optimizing value stream networks
- Visualizing organizational workflows
- Guiding value stream strategies and investments
- Evolving the value stream network

Managing and optimizing value stream networks

Value stream networks, as defined by Mik Kersten in his book *From Project to Products*, refer to a holistic approach that captures and analyzes the movement of work within an organization[1]. Value stream networks provide a holistic view of an organization by illustrating how people, processes, information, and technology integrate to optimize customer value delivery. This approach helps shift mindsets from project-based thinking to a product-centric and customer-focused perspective.

VSNs foster collaboration among teams and processes, ensuring efficient value delivery across the organization. At their core, they facilitate the progression of value from inception to delivery, encompassing interactions, handoffs, and dependencies among various teams. For instance, when you order a product online, multiple teams—from design and development to fulfillment and marketing—collaborate to ensure its successful delivery.

Dynamic and responsive, VSNs evolve continually in response to software updates, market shifts, and budget adjustments, requiring ongoing adaptation for sustained effectiveness. Drawing on principles akin to graph theory, which studies the connections (edges) between points (nodes) in a network, they navigate diverse pathways across teams, offering insights beyond traditional hierarchical organizational charts.

Understanding VSNs is essential for grasping the intricate network that drives organizational efficiency and value delivery. It transcends organizational charts, offering a deeper understanding of how ideas translate into tangible outcomes.

Integrating multiple value streams within VSNs serves several key objectives:

- **End-to-end visibility and coordination**: Organizations gain a holistic view of how work and information flow across different departments, functions, and processes, enhancing coordination toward common business objectives
- **Optimization of value delivery**: By identifying and eliminating inefficiencies, organizations optimize the speed and efficiency of value delivery to customers

- **Cross-functional collaboration**: VSNs promote collaboration among diverse teams, breaking down silos and improving problem-solving capabilities and innovation
- **Continuous improvement**: Supporting a culture of continuous improvement, organizations analyze processes, gather insights, and implement changes to enhance performance and adapt to market demands
- **Customer-centricity**: Integrating value streams helps organizations align activities with customer needs, enhancing satisfaction and loyalty

While often associated with Lean-Agile methodologies in software development, VSN principles apply broadly across various industries that employ Lean's value stream concepts:

- **Manufacturing**: Optimizing material flows and production processes
- **Healthcare**: Streamlining patient care and payer processes for better outcomes
- **Supply chain management**: Enhancing inventory management and responsiveness
- **Service industries**: Improving customer service processes and satisfaction
- **Government and non-profit sectors**: Enhancing service delivery and efficient resource allocation

In essence, value stream networks drive operational efficiency, promote collaboration, foster continuous improvement, and enhance customer-centricity across diverse sectors beyond software development.

Organizing value stream networks

In this subsection, we will look at how value stream networks are applied within an organization. Instead of visualizing our network as a shapeless web, we'll anchor it to one or more customer journeys, highlighting its proximity to the customer and depicting the focus of its activities to either development or operations. Additionally, we can simulate and hypothesize the effects of changes in measurement, operating model, and strategy for each stream, as well as the network.

Adopting a value stream network model for software delivery includes all the tasks that are necessary to produce software, as well as the integration of people, processes, information, and technology as enabling capabilities that support the software development lifecycle and across all value stream flows. This model covers the entire end-to-end process, from the initial idea or customer request through development, testing, deployment, and ongoing support.

But value stream networks are not just about connecting software development activities. As you navigate this chapter, you will discover the importance of connecting all value streams to support our customers' journeys. In turn, we align our software delivery streams to assist in the improvement of all operational, development, and support value streams. Value stream management provides the methods and tools we use to identify and prioritize our improvement activities.

Before diving into the network, let's review the value stream model as a reference for flow and value delivery. We'll begin with *Figure 7.1*, which depicts the value stream network visualized.

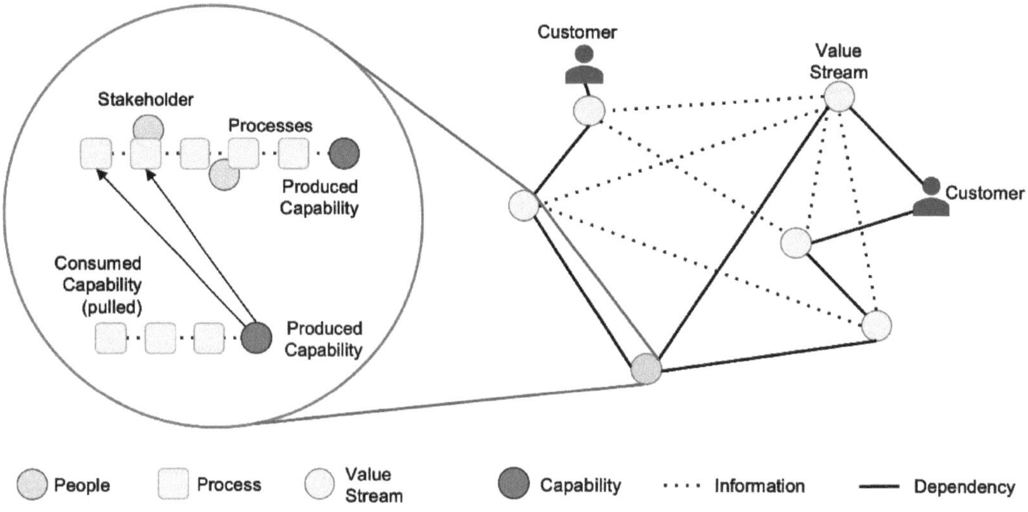

Figure 7.1 – The value stream network visualized

Value stream networks represent a transformative paradigm that transcends conventional organizational structures. For example, this holistic model integrates people, processes, information, and technologies that produce capabilities across an interconnected virtual organization to optimize holistic flow, as shown in this figure.

These networks provide a panoramic view of an organization's workflow, fostering continuous improvement and the seamless delivery of value to customers. By defining them, we're better able to plan, discuss, and diagnose opportunities for performance improvement. In the sections that follow, we'll delve further into the fundamental principles of Value Stream Networks and their application in contemporary software delivery processes.

Defining customer journeys

Customer journeys have become a popular method to consider value delivery from the customer's perspective and an invaluable reference for product management in recent decades. Customer journeys can be mapped, measured, and used to drive customer and outcome-centric conversations. They serve as an excellent reference point for technology leaders to engage business leaders on common ground. It's also a far more valuable context than mapping the network with a strictly internal or isolated scope.

The business exists to create value for customers, while the customer journey provides a common foundation for teams and organizations as they begin to embrace the concept of value streams. It offers an outside-in, customer-centric perspective and a visual tool for understanding value delivery from the customer (or business outcomes) backward to an idea or request.

It's crucial to recognize the distinction between customer journeys and a value stream. The customer journey, as depicted in *Figure 7.2*, is mostly beyond the organization's influence. It takes place at the borders of the organization, where customers interact with products and services. Its path is primarily determined by customers, which may limit the organization's ability to fully influence or optimize it.

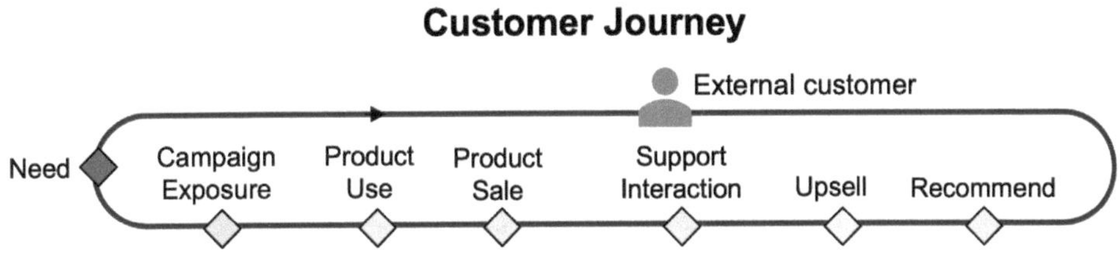

Figure 7.2 – An illustration of a typical customer journey

For example, consider two customers: one is referred to a product by a friend and buys it immediately. The other discovers our company's products or services through advertising, investigates alternatives, gets distracted by other needs, and only returns to purchase when timing, needs, and cost align. If these two scenarios were viewed through the lens of value streams, they would have dramatically different paths and attributes. Lead times for these scenarios would be significantly different. Furthermore, there are insufficient mechanisms for measuring work in process, value-added time, or percent complete and accurate for customer interactions. Customer journeys are typically measured by sentiment, probability of purchase, cost of acquisition, conversion rate, order size, and more.

In contrast, organizations have significant control over how their value stream operates. While they cannot dictate customer actions, they can implement standardization and automation to facilitate improved flow. Key metrics such as lead time, value-added time, throughput, quality, and work in process are essential. Organizations can guide work through a value stream much more effectively than they can direct a customer's journey.

The customer journey serves as a foundation for understanding value streams because without it, value streams have no clear direction or focus. They also have no clear connection to other streams in the network. With the customer journey anchoring flow, we can connect value streams to demonstrate how they motivate and support the customer journey at critical touchpoints.

For instance, a marketing campaign value stream aids in a customer's discovery and knowledge, potentially leading to a sale, while the sales and purchase processes—streamlined through easy-to-use systems such as checkouts or shopping carts—represent separate value streams that culminate in the purchase. This means that when we experience an issue with the customer journey, we can trace it directly to the contributing value streams. Now, let us discuss how we can visualize the proximity of our value stream to our customers.

Visualizing value stream proximity to customers

Figure 7.3 illustrates a fundamental aspect of value stream classification: the proximity of various streams to the customer. For instance, at the top of the chart are mobile applications, which directly reach and benefit external customers. At the lower end of the spectrum, billing is listed as a value stream primarily benefiting the organization by enabling mobile banking applications. You can also think of this spectrum as external to internal focus, where proximity to customers defines where streams are placed along this dimension.

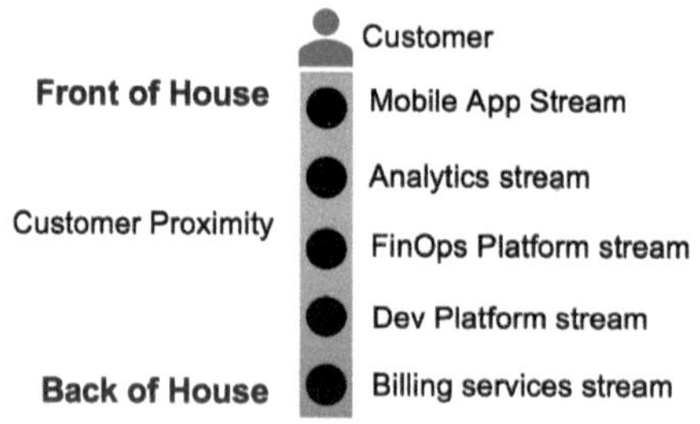

Figure 7.3 – Visualizing value stream proximity to customers

At the lower end of the spectrum lies a function such as billing—an internal process that is essential to the organization but invisible to the customer. These internal value streams are no less critical, as they support the external offerings. However, their purpose is more internally focused, dealing with operations that keep the organization running smoothly, such as reconciliation and procurement processes.

Displaying value streams as a spectrum provides clarity on where the end user's interactions and satisfaction are paramount, such as mobile banking applications, and those with an internal operational focus, such as billing, which ensure the efficiency and stability necessary to support customer-facing services.

Figure 7.4 shows how the network begins to appear in service of a customer journey:

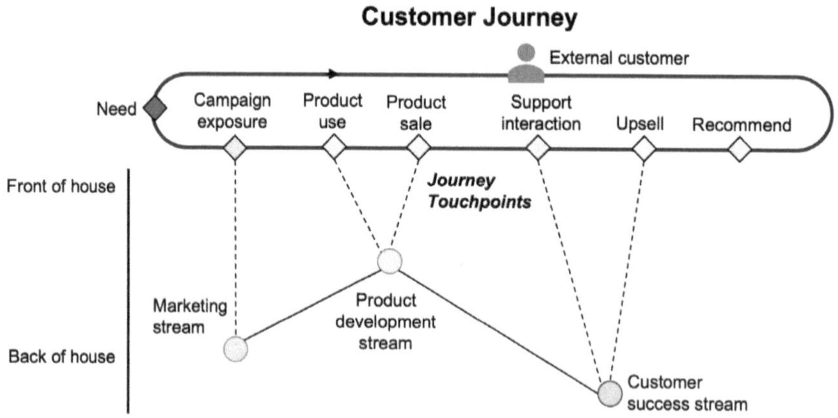

Figure 7.4 – Using the customer journey as an anchor

The product use phase is directly linked to a product development value stream. Afterward, the review and recommendation stages can be bolstered by additional supportive value streams. The primary value stream, product development, can be so influential that it propels customers through the entire journey. However, other supportive value streams play a vital role by facilitating each stage of the journey, making it smoother for customers to transition from one phase to the next.

As we explore the relationship between customer experience and value streams, the next section will delve into the concept of the customer journey. Understanding this dynamic framework is essential in using value streams to navigate and enhance the customer journey effectively.

In the following section, we will further explore the pressing challenges faced by organizations, emphasizing the need for a strategic approach to streamlining value stream networks.

Connecting value streams to customer journeys

The journey of a given customer is an individualized path that often eludes the direct control of an organization. It starts with an innate need or want, sparking curiosity that leads to the discovery of a product or service. As customers move through various stages such as sale, purchase, use, and review, they follow a course that is inherently personal and self-directed. The customer journey can be envisioned as a series of interconnected experiences, each potentially influenced by different value streams within the organization.

Figure 7.5 depicts an enterprise **Software as a Service** (**SaaS**) customer journey. It starts with campaign exposure to make customers aware of a product via marketing efforts, so that they then try the product in a limited capacity, choose to purchase it, and progress through the customer experience. The figure demonstrates how each stage of the customer journey is supported by value streams consisting of planning, designing, building, validating, and releasing activities to ensure a seamless and engaging customer experience.

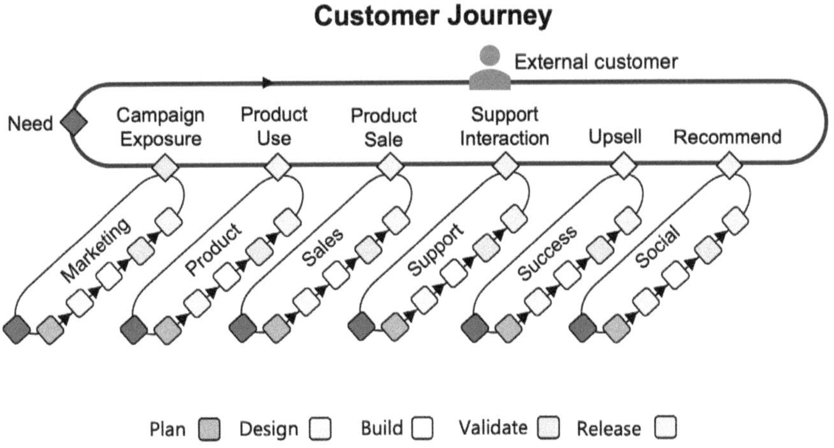

Figure 7.5 – Connecting value streams to the customer journey

The visualization of this journey lays the foundation for understanding how value streams operate and directly impact customer outcomes in a Lean-Agile organization. By orchestrating work across value streams, we create significant opportunities for refinement and optimization. Through standardization and automation, organizations can shape these value streams to effectively support the customer journey.

At the outset, a marketing campaign value stream plays a pivotal role in triggering the customer's journey from initial curiosity to product use, product sales, and support. By allowing the customer to trial a product or service, it sets the stage for a potential sale. The journey then transitions into more tactical value streams, such as the sales process, where streamlined systems such as intuitive checkouts or shopping carts facilitate the purchase phase.

The product development value stream becomes especially crucial as it aligns with the use phase of the customer journey. It is here that the quality and features of the product come to the forefront, influencing the customer's direct experience and satisfaction. Subsequent stages, such as review and recommendation, may be enhanced by other supportive value streams focused on customer engagement and loyalty.

Ultimately, while the primary value stream of product development enables the customer to complete their journey, the importance of the supporting value streams cannot be understated. They are the threads that weave through the customer's experiences, ensuring that each transition is seamless and each interaction is meaningful. Together, these value streams form a spectrum that not only defines but also enriches the customer's journey.

Harnessing flow within the value stream network

Value is not just an abstract concept; it is delivered tangibly as benefits through our products and services. Once it has been quantified or qualified, value can be delivered, and its creation and delivery are influenced by improving the supporting value streams. *Figure 7.6* graphically reveals the interconnected nature of value streams that underpin our business operations, from the operational level right through to customer delivery.

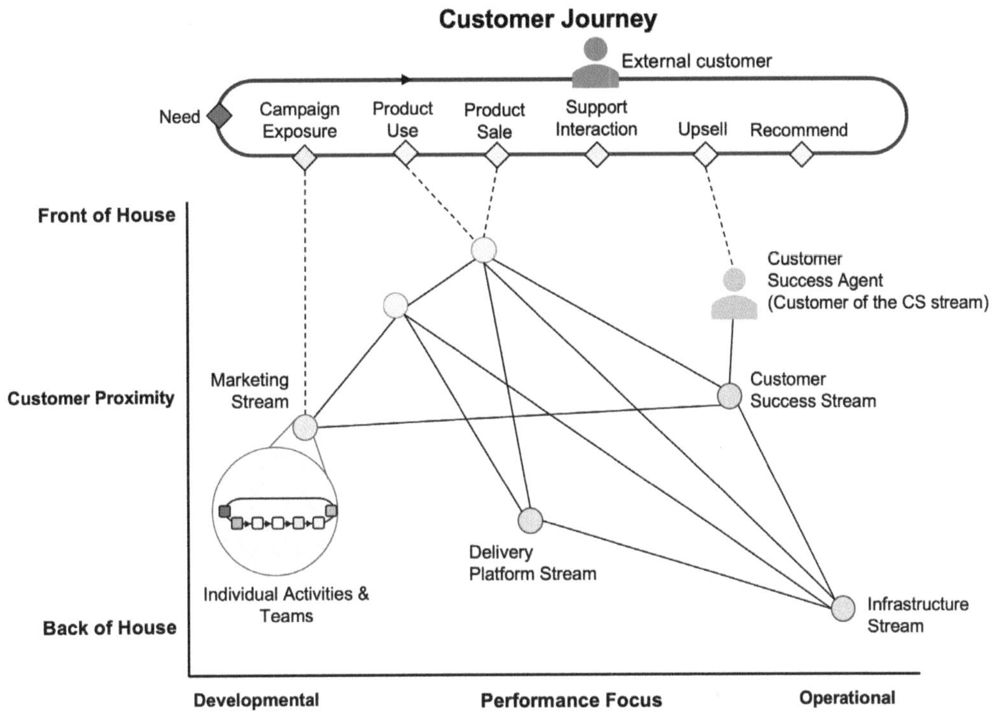

Figure 7.6 – Value stream network example

In this graphic, the Customer Success Agent plays a vital role in ensuring that customers can achieve their desired outcomes with a company's products or services. They provide onboarding support, ongoing assistance, and proactive engagement, building strong relationships, advocating for customer needs, and offering training to maximize product value. This person helps drive customer satisfaction, retention, and long-term success.

This visual representation illustrates how each value stream—whether its focus is operational or developmental—interacts and contributes to the overall value delivered to the customer. It's a network of value creation, where each flow of work, materials, information, and resources is orchestrated to support and enhance the others.

In *Figure 7.6*, we can see each interdependent value stream plotted based on its proximity to external customers (vertical axis) and its performance focus (horizontal axis). We can see the interdependence of streams either producing or consuming capabilities and services delivered by others. By zooming in on each stream, we can see the individual activities performed and teams involved in delivering a specific product, service, or capability. To anchor this holistic visualization of value creation and delivery, we can see every component connected to the customer journey.

Although it's possible to visualize an entire organization this way, there is diminishing value in including aspects that are unrelated to the current target objective, so it's important to map the network relative to what is currently most important. For example, if the goal is to increase the sales of a particular product, we can visualize the customer journey to increase sales and understand where that product connects to the journey. We can look upstream to the marketing streams enabling the journey, as well as further into the network where internal streams support the product's development and delivery.

Returning to *Figure 7.6*, we can see that there's currently insufficient investment in driving recommendations, which could have a major impact on sales. This figure serves as a practical model for understanding the flow of value throughout an organization. As we progress through this section, we will delve into how these value streams can be optimized and adapted based on current customer requirements. As we integrate the network view into our organizational strategy of VSM, we pave the way for a more profound application of flow principles at a larger scale and greater impact. This not only enhances specific aspects of organizational performance but also allows us to maintain a holistic view of flow across the organization.

In the subsection that follows, we will explore the pressing challenges faced by organizations, emphasizing the need for taking a strategic approach to streamlining value stream networks.

Addressing organizational challenges

Most organizations face the daunting task of improving efficiency and quality while managing a growing backlog of identified improvement opportunities. These challenges are interconnected and tackling them requires a strategic approach that hinges on optimizing operational flow.

In the following list, we will explore the work involved:

- **Achieving more with available resources**: Businesses need to achieve better outcomes with the resources they have as they scale and compete. This means streamlining processes, eliminating waste, and leveraging technology to enhance their ability to deliver the most value. Mapping the value stream network starting with customer outcomes, we can re-engineer flow to emphasize what is most critical to value creation and minimize non-value-added activity, problematic dependencies, and waste.
- **Elevating quality standards**: Quality cannot be compromised in the quest for efficiency. Organizations must find ways to enhance their quality control processes, such as building quality to ensure that the products or services delivered meet or exceed customer expectations. By mapping dependencies and the full flow of activities to outcomes across the organization, we can gain insight into which efforts will have the greatest impact on delivered quality. We can zoom in on details and zoom out to see interconnected impacts.

- **Enhancing value delivery**: The goal here is to provide more value to customers, which could be achieved through innovative solutions, better service, or more responsive support. Companies must continuously evolve to meet and anticipate customer needs. By incorporating the customer journey in our network map, we can gain the ability to more closely attribute efforts and investments to identify the greatest impacts on customer value, whether those be upstream or downstream, and at what proximity to the customer they are.
- **Fostering talent satisfaction**: Keeping employees happy is essential for maintaining a creative, innovative, and efficient workforce. This involves creating a work environment that supports and encourages employee growth and satisfaction. By providing a holistic representation of value creation and delivery across the organization, we can ensure that contributors can see how their work adds value, connect their efforts to business objectives, and understand their work in the context of customer outcomes.
- **Accelerating throughput**: The need for speed is ever-present. Organizations must refine their workflows to deliver products and services faster without sacrificing quality. Visualizing interdependent flows of work enables understanding why certain streams are under- or over-utilized, as well as where the constraints causing bottlenecks are. We can identify critical and centralized capabilities and ensure that they operate at optimal performance in the long term.

Implementing a methodical approach to tackling flow challenges is crucial. By identifying the constraints within processes and employing principles such as the **theory of constraints**, **Lean flow**, and **Lean metrics**, businesses can systematically address these issues to create a more efficient and effective flow of work that drives value creation and delivery. Putting this interconnected work in the context of value, customers, and business outcomes facilitates a greater focus on what matters to the organization and its long-term success.

Visualizing organizational workflow

Visualizing and plotting the organization at varied levels allows us to consider the organizational structure and flow of work from different perspectives. In this section, we will explore these relationships more thoroughly.

We will start by reviewing *Figure 7.7*, where we can see that value stream networks represent the macro view at the top, team topologies in the middle, and the organization's value chain capabilities at the bottom. *Team Topologies* is a framework that categorizes software delivery teams into four types: Stream-aligned, Enabling, Complicated-Subsystem, and Platform teams. This approach helps organizations structure their teams for optimal flow, clarity, and collaboration in delivering software solutions.

Figure 7.7 illustrates the organization's delivery structure, from the overarching end-to-end processes to the specific interconnection of value chain capabilities and components. This multi-layered approach helps clarify the varying scales of detail involved in a value stream network, allowing us to pick the right level of detail to match our objective and audience:

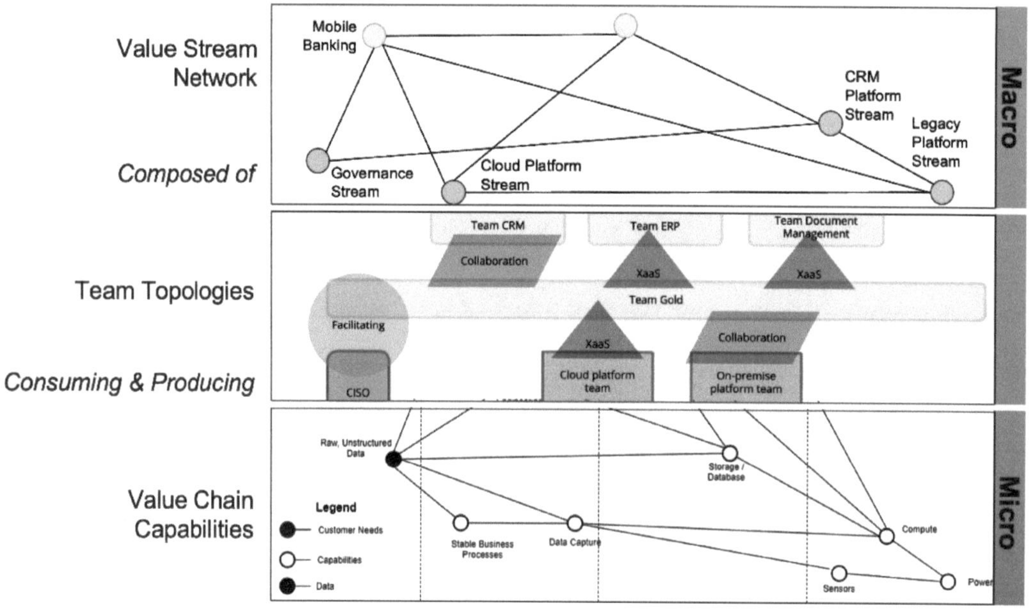

Figure 7.7 – Visualizing organizational flow

This visualization underscores the importance of recognizing the different layers within the organization's workflow. This multi-faceted approach is instrumental for leaders and teams to navigate and optimize the organization's value stream network effectively.

We'll delve deeper into this diagram in the subsections that follow.

Value stream network (top level)

At the top level, we can see the big picture of the value stream network, which encapsulates the *macro* perspective of how work is delivered within the organization. This is the broadest view, where the focus is on how value streams connect holistically from start to finish without delving into the details of individual components or technical dependencies.

Team topologies (middle level)

Moving to the middle level of the visualization, we encounter team topologies, a model that outlines how teams within the organization are structured and how they interact. This level zooms in from the end-to-end flow to show the topology of teams, such as **stream-aligned teams** working alongside **complicated-subsystem teams**, and supported by **platform teams** that provide foundational services.

Team topologies, as defined by Matthew Skelton and Manuel Pais in their 2019 book *Team Topologies: Organizing Business and Technology Teams for Fast Flow*, are concepts in organizational design and software delivery.[2] These topologies describe how teams are structured and interact within an organization to optimize workflow, reduce bottlenecks, and enhance collaboration. Skelton and Pais provide valuable insights into how various team types, such as stream-aligned teams, complicated-subsystem teams, and platform teams, can be organized to support an organization's goals and facilitate efficient value delivery.

Beyond mere structure, they define three interaction modes —**Collaboration**, **X-as-a-Service**, and **facilitation**—to make the connections between teams explicitly defined operating models.[3] In the context of VSM, an **operating model** can be thought of as a blueprint that outlines how an organization delivers value to its customers, manages its resources, and achieves its strategic goals.

By establishing clarity on how teams interact, we can avoid many of the pitfalls of siloed operations where handoffs (the baton) of the value stream "relay race" are dropped, delayed, or fumbled.

Value chain capabilities (bottom level)

At the bottom (or micro) level, the graphic delves into the specifics of the capabilities and components that compose and contribute to delivered value. This level of detail is where individual features and functions are identified and examined for their contribution to the customer journey, from the initial concept to the final delivery and support.

Guiding value stream strategy and investments

The **Wardley map** in *Figure 7.8* provides a visual tool that helps organizations understand their business environment and strategize accordingly. It helps us answer the question "Where should we invest?" and, to a lesser extent, "How can we deliver?"[4].

This map consists of two main components:

- **Value chain (y-axis)**: This shows the components needed to meet user needs, from visible user-facing components to hidden infrastructure. A component is any element or part of a system (or value chain) that contributes to delivering a product or service to the end user.
- **Evolution (x-axis)**: This indicates the stages of evolution of each component, ranging from genesis (novel and uncertain) to commodity (ubiquitous and well-defined). A value chain is the series of activities that comprise the life cycle of a product or service, from genesis through production to purchase by the end customer.

In our use case, we are evaluating whether we should invest in an AI-based imaging tool to improve our value stream.

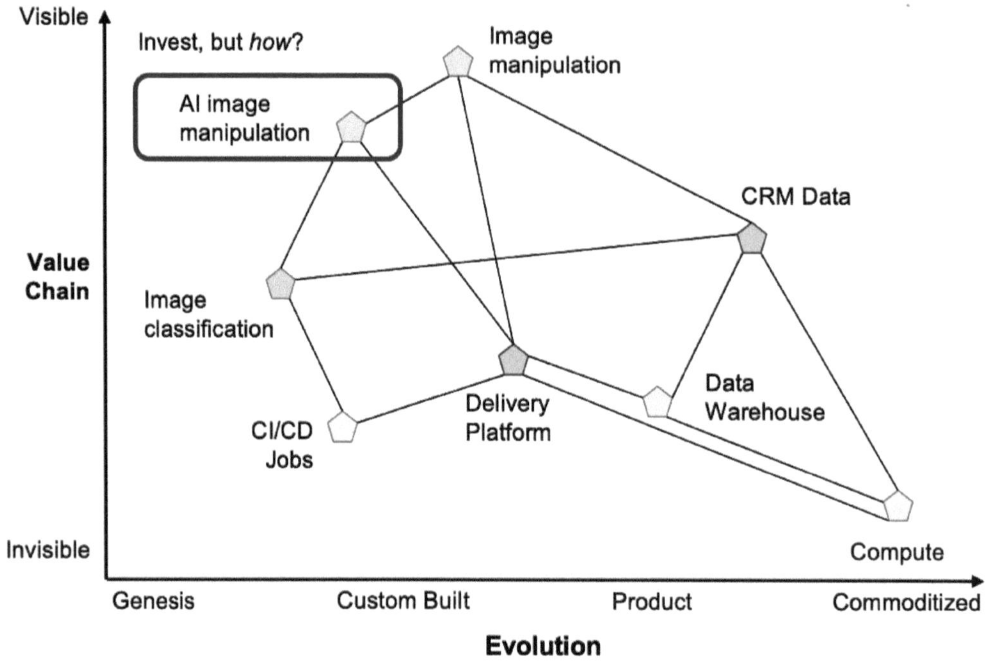

Figure 7.8 – Wardley helps answer where to invest and how to deliver

This map will help our organization answer strategic questions, such as the following:

- Which components should we focus on developing or outsourcing?
- Which components are mature and should be commoditized?
- Where should we invest in innovation?
- How can we anticipate changes in our competitive landscape?

By visualizing these elements and their relationships, organizations can make more informed decisions about resource allocation, innovation, and competitive positioning. It's a valuable tool for strategic planning, particularly in technology and business contexts.

By mapping the interconnected capabilities of an organization with customer needs, this framework provides a comprehensive overview that balances the importance of innovation with the inevitability of commoditization.

At the heart of our Wardley map are elements that are critical to supporting customer needs, such as online image manipulation and photo storage, plotted against the axes of value chain and evolution. The value chain axis illustrates whether the value is visible to customers, while the evolution axis shows the journey from unique genesis to standardized commodities.

Strategic investment decisions

As capabilities evolve toward commoditization, the organization must decide where to allocate resources to drive innovation and maintain competitiveness. Our map suggests strategic investment areas in **Artificial Intelligence** (**AI**) image manipulation, shown in the red rectangle, which highlights a potential point for enhancing the customer journey or improving efficiency and inertia in platform capabilities.

Wardley charts help identify potential investment opportunities by mapping key capabilities and activities along an evolution axis from an idea to a commodity product. Assess the maturity of each component against industry standards, engage stakeholders for insights, and regularly update positions to reflect changes in the industry, technology, and customer needs. This process provides a clear visual representation of your organization's capabilities, aiding in strategic planning and identifying areas for innovation and growth.

Orchestrating strategic architecture

The assembly of services such as compute or online storage is depicted not just in their relation to the customer but also in their architectural context by their interdependence with other capabilities and components. By mapping out these services, the organization can scrutinize its investment strategy, identifying both strengths and opportunities.

Aligning strategy and operations

Although a Wardley map is valuable for defining where to invest, it does not illustrate how capabilities are produced and consumed. The value stream network defines how each capability is produced and consumed by different value streams and identifies their intersection.

Figure 7.9 shows the integration of value stream and value chain visualizations to depict the what, why, and how of our value-based investments. These combined visualizations not only illustrate where our investments should be directed but also provide insight into their purpose and execution.

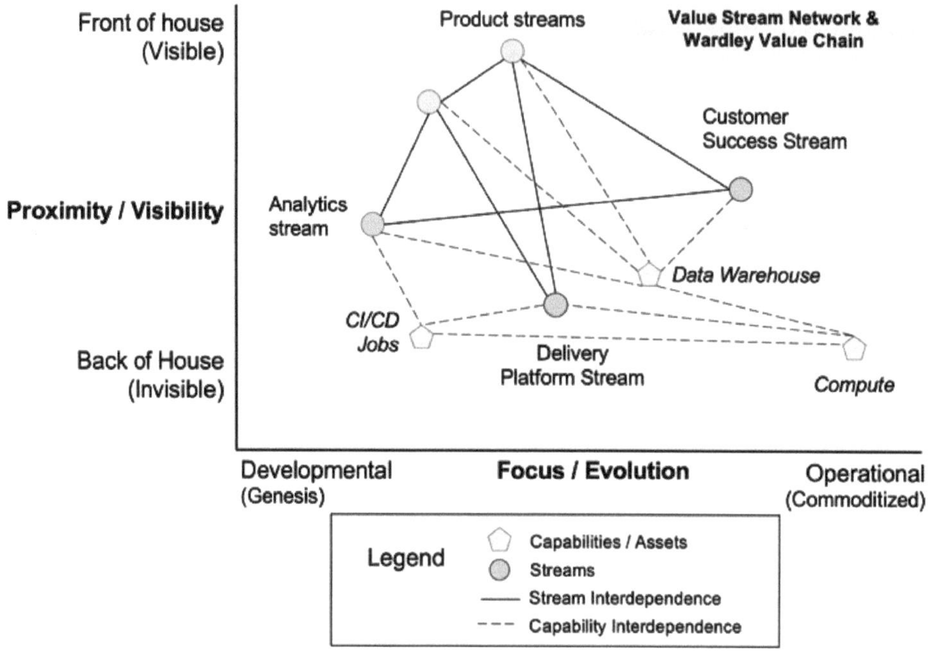

Figure 7.9 – Combining value stream and value chain visualizations

In this graphic, we can see the various capabilities that are used by value streams in the network. To align with our objective, we could define the capabilities from both a producer and consumer perspective, establishing direct connections between capabilities and value streams.

Having seen how the Wardley map integrates with the value stream network to provide strategic direction, it's now time to delve into the finer details of our organizational workflow, visualizing both macro and micro perspectives within our organization's processes.

Evolving the value stream network

As organizations evolve, they increasingly seek a comprehensive understanding of their operational dynamics and how to influence them. Combining the axes of **Customer Proximity** and **Performance Focus** allows leaders to pinpoint each value stream's position relative to its visibility to customers and its performance, as illustrated in *Figure 7.10*.

For example, value streams such as mobile banking are visible to customers and require metrics that are focused on customer satisfaction such as net promoter score (NPS) and customer engagement. These are the front-facing elements of the business where innovation and responsiveness to customer needs are paramount.

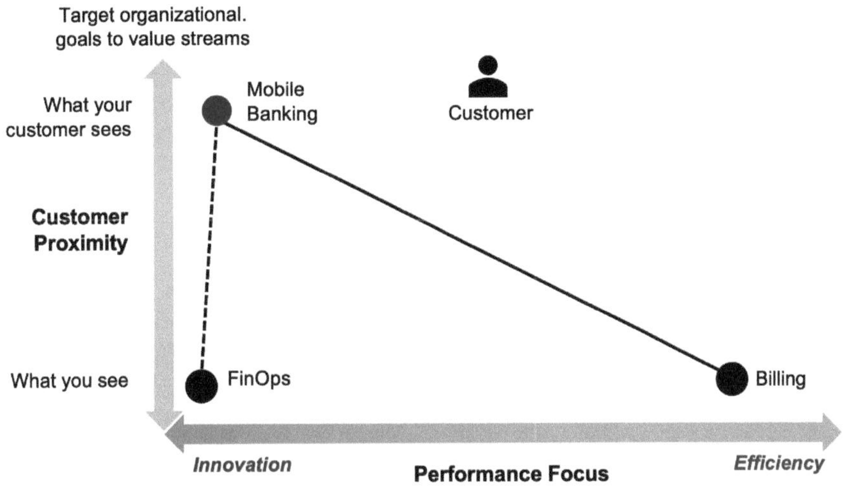

Figure 7.10 – Balancing efficiency and innovation performance focus

Conversely, back-office processes such as billing are invisible to customers and reside in the efficiency range of performance focus. These activities are measured against standards of operational excellence and the metrics include cost, standardization, predictability, and consistency. The strategic considerations for these processes might include the potential for outsourcing to external providers, streamlining operations, or automating to reduce costs.

This dynamic model provides insights into how changes in one area—such as the introduction of FinOps or the automation of platforms—can ripple through the network, affecting adjacent streams. The integration of new capabilities into a value stream such as mobile banking raises questions about adaptation. For example, how should mobile banking adapt to the introduction of automated FinOps platforms? What are the potential impacts on customer experience, and what new efficiencies or innovations might emerge?

The implications for behavior and strategy are profound. Each connection, each node on this map, represents a decision point—a place where the balance between innovation and efficiency, between customer-facing actions and back-end processes, must be carefully managed to maintain an effective value stream network. Understanding these connections and the alignment of internal processes with overarching organizational goals is crucial for strategic agility.

The value stream network is not static; it embodies the potential for movement, reflecting an organization's strategic flexibility. A compelling example of this dynamism is the evolution of **Amazon Web Services** (**AWS**). What began as an internal infrastructure program to support Amazon's operations transformed AWS from an internal capability to an external value stream. This change underscores the significance of measuring and valuing various aspects of the value stream over time, aligning with opportunities and realizing new value.

Organizations must understand where their value streams are positioned and how they can be improved over time. There are many benefits of such strategic movements, from delivering value to customers and optimizing internal processes to maintaining a competitive edge. By understanding and managing this evolutionary path, organizations can unlock new opportunities and create value in ways that were not possible before.

This type of evolution has an impact on our value stream networks, as they, too, must transition. We'll explore this concept in the next subsection.

Improving value streams by performance focus

The decision to improve with sustaining innovation may lead to a reorganization of existing value streams, which should be a deliberate and thoughtful process of evolution rather than a radical disruption. This approach can reduce waste and political risks, as well as leverage existing expertise and capabilities.

Figure 7.11 illustrates the adaptation of a value stream by performance focus, highlighting the shift from innovation to an efficiency focus.

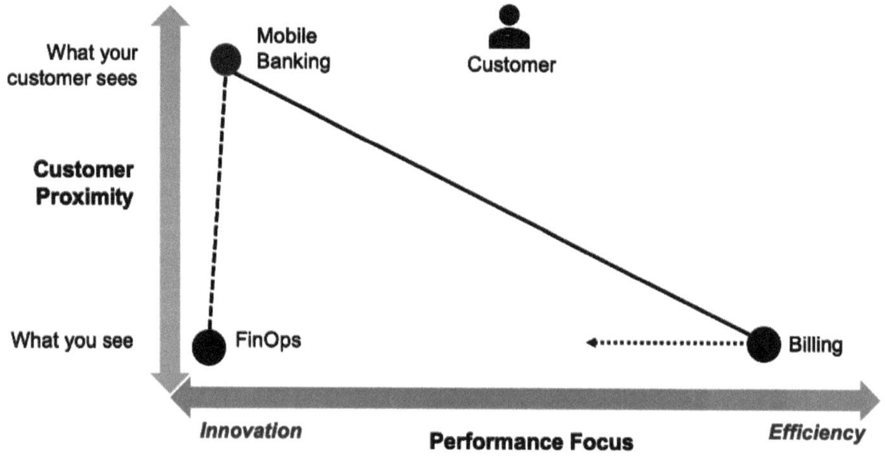

Figure 7.11 – Adapting value streams by performance focus

For many organizations, disruptive innovation—starting afresh with no legacy constraints— is strong. However, this approach often requires significant investment and comes with its own set of risks. Alternatively, by incrementally shifting how an existing process such as billing operates, organizations can evolve their value streams to achieve different, often more innovative outcomes without discarding the underlying systems and processes that have served them well.

This shift involves a conscious decision to move away from established measures and behaviors toward new goals. For example, a billing system traditionally focused on efficiency might begin to incorporate more innovative approaches such as adopting new technologies or modifying workflows to improve the customer experience, automation, or performance. These changes can lead to a more dynamic and responsive billing process that still retains the core advantages of the existing system, such as reliability and predictability.

This transition is about adapting to new environments and challenges while retaining what has proven successful. To be clear, this is the evolution of the operating model, not technology or capability. Leaders, therefore, need to focus on understanding and defining the new metrics that will measure success. By redefining these metrics, the organization encourages behaviors that drive innovation within the context of established value streams.

In summary, by intentionally shifting existing value streams, organizations can find a middle ground that achieves the best of the sustaining and disruptive innovation approaches. In turn, this allows for the evolution of services and processes in a way that is both innovative and grounded in the proven foundations of the past.

Envisioning value stream dynamics

Figure 7.12 again shows a two-dimensional canvas that allows us to plot streams relative to each other and their touchpoint activities.

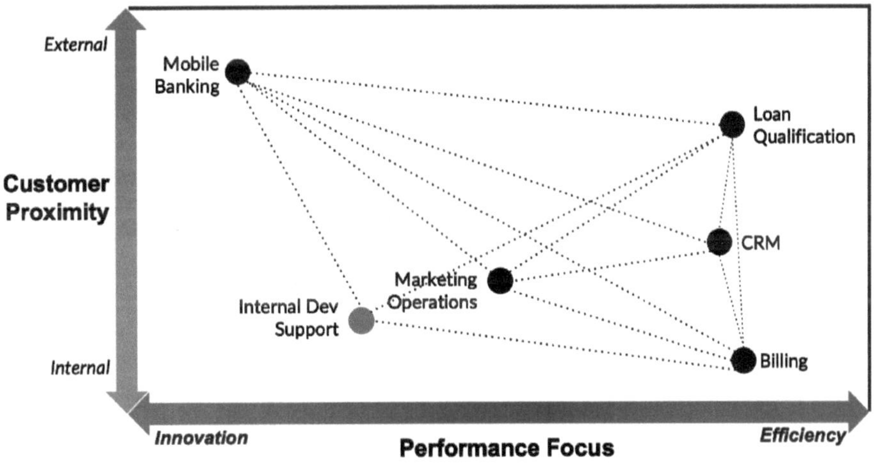

Figure 7.12 – A simplified network of interconnected value streams

Specifically, this diagram depicts a simplified network of interconnected value streams and illustrates the critical nature of these connections.

At the heart of this network lie customer-facing products, such as mobile banking, which may draw support from related streams such as loan qualification services. The proximity of these streams to the customer (external focus) can vary depending on how directly they impact the customer experience.

Diving deeper, the dynamic nature of this network becomes apparent when considering the introduction of modern technologies such as AI in **customer relationship management** (**CRM**). To harness AI effectively, the CRM stream might need to pivot toward innovation, prioritizing metrics that reflect this new focus. Such a shift would naturally drive different behaviors within the teams, pulling the CRM stream closer to the innovation end of the spectrum.

As another example, we may need to assess the experience of our internal developers who can benefit from the use of platforms or learning environments such as dojos. A **dojo** is a structured and collaborative approach to learning that encourages experimentation, skill development, and problem-solving in a practical context. To scale this effectively across the organization, we may decide to move our value streams toward improved efficiencies, measured by the degree of standardization and the consistency of the experience provided to developers.

Understanding that each value stream can encompass multiple teams and functions highlights the complex nature of organizational workflows. The movement of these streams is not arbitrary but is a strategic choice made to drive evolution, leverage opportunities such as AI for enhanced customer outreach, or create efficiencies on that scale.

Through this lens, an organization can begin to see the levers of change and the potential impacts of strategic decisions. By manipulating the metrics that define success within each stream, leaders can guide their teams toward desired outcomes, be they innovation, efficiency, or a blend of both. This approach allows for the intentional design of an organization's value delivery mechanisms, ensuring that they remain agile and responsive to both internal imperatives and market demands.

The evolution of these streams is a dance of strategic repositioning, where each move has the potential to catalyze further transformation. It is this fluidity that empowers organizations to adapt and thrive in a landscape that demands both steadfast reliability and relentless innovation. However, the process of transitioning value streams often requires reorganizing organizational resources to support those transformations. Therefore, we need a way to compare the value streams in our networks. We will look at a way to do so in the next subsection.

Evaluating value stream networks

We can evaluate our value stream networks in a matrix to define key characteristics, allowing us to determine value stream needs. *Figure 7.13* depicts a matrix view that simplifies the comparison of value streams in our network by key attributes, including value stream needs, fulfillment characteristics, network location (from front- to back-of-house), and their primary function (developmental or operational).

In your diagrams and tables, make sure to list, sort, and annotate your streams. If you are ambitious, you might add specific metrics or objectives to each value stream to provide more detail on performance capabilities and goals. You could also define dependencies to indicate common points of leverage or challenge.

Now that we have a way to visualize our value stream network attributes, let's move on to learn how we can use value stream mapping to reveal and address our constraints.

Needs	Fulfillment characteristics	Network Location	Primary function
We need marketing to deliver promotional materials	Marketing defines and delivers after pulling product strategy from PM, and artifacts are pushed to promotional platforms and pulled by customers	Middle	Developmental
Engineering needs to design and deliver new product or service enhancements	Creative and novel, core and developmental activity, pull capabilities, artifacts, and demand from supportive streams	Front to middle	Developmental, but strives to operationalize workflow and waste reduction
The legal department may need to refine its contracts	Produces templates, guidance, and consultation pulled by production streams	Back	Operational
Product management needs to define and refine the product and service requirements and pricing	Pulls from corporate strategy, market insights, and customer success. Pushes requirements and pricing.	Middle	Developmental
Accounting and finance may need to refine their systems to recognize revenues	Pull budgeting needs and forecasts from streams, tracks, and publishes P&L for streams	Back	Operational
Salespeople need to be trained on product enhancements and capabilities and leverage assets to share with prospects and customers	Pull artifacts, leads, and copy from marketing stream; pulls contracting capabilities	Front	Operational but often developmental for new markets and business
Support and customer success assist customers	Pulls from product, sales, ops. Pushes status and metrics	Front to middle	Operational

Figure 7.13 – Comparing value stream attributes

Value stream mapping reveals hidden constraints

With value stream mapping, our objective extends beyond tracing workflows and measuring performance; we seek to identify the hidden bottlenecks that cause inefficiencies. These critical chokepoints are often where dependencies become problematic, revealing the pivotal areas within our processes that most significantly influence the flow of value.

Figure 7.14 encapsulates this comprehensive analysis. It displays a detailed timeline of a process from the initial request to deployment, delineating not only the duration of each step but also the interim delays. This level of transparency is pivotal for identifying where we can gain efficiencies and identify the constraints in our production system.

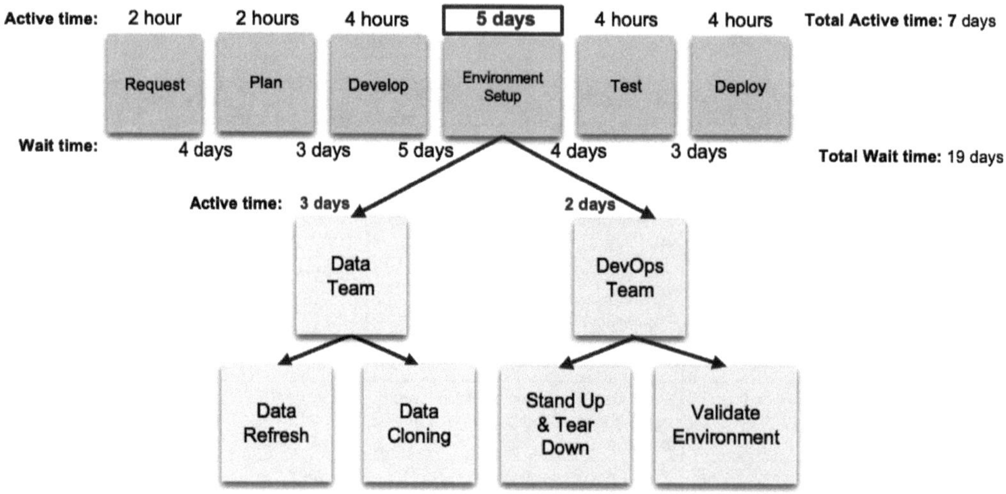

Figure 7.14 – Value stream mapping

Further analysis within this value stream map identifies significant delays: the active time for the environment setup process consumes approximately 71% of the total active time in this value stream. By drilling down into the activities of the environment setup process, we can gain a better understanding of the work performed. Decomposing this step into activities allows us to pinpoint the root cause or causes of delays and formulate targeted strategies for improvement.

Figure 7.14 also reveals how dependencies form the intricate web within our organizational framework. For instance, the environment setup process is part of a collection of collaborative activities involving the data and DevOps teams, along with critical activities such as data cloning and environment validation. Recognizing these interdependencies sheds light on the complex interactions that govern our workflows, which may be ad hoc or interrupt-driven in nature rather than streamlined value streams.

Using this map and digging deeper into flow bottlenecks for activities, we can begin to see the network beyond the value stream and the capabilities that lie even deeper within.

Value stream mapping acts as a lens through which the interconnected nature of cross-departmental workflows becomes apparent and the network emerges. These interdependencies often reflect areas for optimization. For example, manual processes could be automated into a more streamlined self-service workflow, boosting the value stream's efficiency.

However, not every workflow identified through value stream mapping may currently represent a mature value stream. The map is likely to include potential value streams at various stages of maturity and automation. Recognizing these stages allows an organization to prioritize development efforts strategically, focusing on the areas with the most potential for refinement and automation to bolster efficiency and value.

Value stream mapping goes beyond identifying the current workflow. It serves as a diagnostic, enabling us to dissect and comprehend the fabric of our organizational processes. These mapping efforts guide where we can achieve the most impact, turning problems and opportunities into measurable results. So, now that we know that we can use value stream mapping to expose our constraints, let's explore how we can eliminate them to streamline our value flow.

Streamlining product and platform value streams

Figure 7.15 presents a strategic organizational framework that separates product development from platform value streams, enabling efficient decoupling and decentralization within a tech-centric business model:

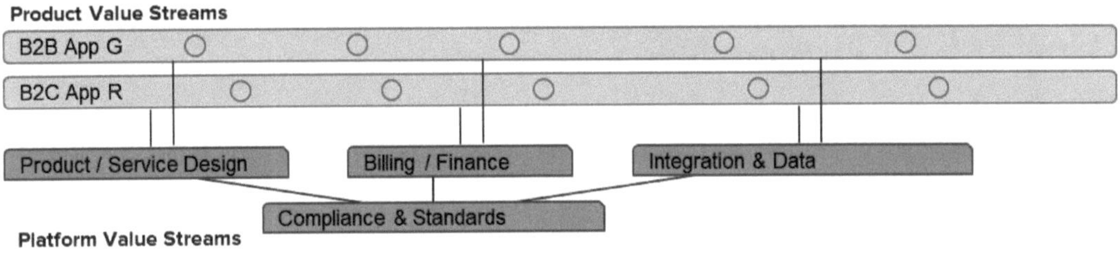

Figure 7.15 – Stream aligning the network view

The central idea revolves around the introduction of a **shared platform** as a means of decoupling team dependencies, allowing teams to operate more independently.

In this example, the product value streams clarify the linear sequences that cater to **business-to-business** (**B2B**) and **business-to-consumer** (**B2C**) markets, highlighting the critical phases that add value and advance the product toward market release. The platform value streams are the supporting structure providing the foundational services that are necessary for product development. They work together to promote a self-service approach, improving agility and reducing time to market.

Now let's pivot away from the overarching concepts of workflow and value realization and delve into the specifics of how these concepts play out within the product and platform value streams of an organization:

- **Product value streams**: *Figure 7.15* shows two paths: B2B App G and B2C App R. These value streams represent the steps required to bring products to market for business clients and individual consumers. Each step adds value and moves the product closer to market readiness.
- **Platform value streams**: These support the product-focused streams. They provide essential services such as design, billing, integration, data management, and compliance, enabling the smooth operation of the product value streams.

The product value streams use the robust infrastructure from the platform value streams seamlessly. This relationship lets product teams use essential services efficiently, speeding up development and simplifying the path from concept to customer.

It should be clear to you by now that this book consistently focuses on delivering the most value to customers. In the next section, we'll explore how to build a customer-centric culture within our value streams.

Cultivating a customer-centric approach

Stream-aligned teams function as internal customers of the shared platform offerings, while platform teams provide self-service capabilities to enhance operational flow and product development. Therefore, platform teams need to adopt a customer service mindset, elevating the quality of service and fostering a culture of excellence and continuous improvement.

The relationship between stream-aligned teams and platform teams is key to our shared-services model. Stream-aligned teams, acting as internal customers, use platform capabilities to improve their operations and product development.

In many organizations, there's a tendency to mandate the use of specific internal software development tools and platforms. However, to avoid counterproductive effects, executive management and platform teams must commit to enabling stream-aligned teams by providing competitive service and capabilities compared to external alternatives.

Rather than treating platform adoption as an obligation, it is essential to approach it with a customer service mindset. Platform teams should deliver their capabilities as if they were serving external customers, ensuring a level of service that rivals or exceeds external alternatives. Alternatively, the organization may consider outsourcing this service to a specialized platform support company. In any case, where there is a customer, there is a customer journey, and care must be taken to support it.

By treating internal deliverables with the same care and attention as products meant for the external market, platform teams can elevate the organization's quality of service. This motivates stream-aligned teams to engage with the platform's offerings, contributing to the overall health of the value stream network and establishing a culture of excellence and continuous improvement.

Summary

We have reached the end of this chapter, where we explored how to analyze value stream networks on a two-dimensional canvas. Let's quickly recap what we covered.

We learned that by detailing and evaluating value streams, we can design them better and communicate more effectively with leaders and contributors, helping them participate in the improvement journey. This chapter outlined the complex and strategic framework of value streams, showing how they integrate people, processes, information, and technology as integrated capabilities to deliver customer value.

The chapter emphasized the importance of optimizing these components to boost productivity, efficiency, and adaptability. It highlighted the need for agility in value stream networks, ensuring organizations can respond to customer needs and maintain a competitive edge in a changing business environment.

Now, we transition to *Part 3, Achieving Lean-Agile and VSM Mastery*. The upcoming chapters will delve deeper into practically applying Lean-Agile and VSM principles at the team of teams and enterprise levels. *Chapter 8* introduces the implementation of **Basic Lean-Agile Solutions Teams** (**BLASTs**), offering insights into coordinating the efforts of multiple teams to address specific areas of work. *Chapter 9* discusses defining a **Business Agility System for the Enterprise** (**BASE**), presenting a blueprint for embedding value-directed agility across the enterprise.

BLAST and BASE will demonstrate how to put the concepts from the first two parts of the book into action, bridging the gap between theory and practice for transformative business practices. Specifically, you will learn how to engage multiple Lean-Agile teams to collaborate in an enterprise-wide model for continuous business transformations while maintaining a focus on delivering customer-centric value through our products and services.

Questions

This section is offered for those readers who want to evaluate their comprehension and retention of the information provided in this chapter. There are four questions. The answers are provided in the subsequent section. Recalling the exact verbiage of the original content is not important. Rather, it's more important that you can recall the concepts and their applications:

1. What is the main objective of integrating value stream network principles in the software development life cycle, and how does this integration enhance efficiency and effectiveness at each stage?
2. How do value stream networks contribute to addressing common organizational challenges such as the need to do more with less, improve quality, deliver more value, keep talent happy, and go faster?
3. In what ways does mapping out value streams using a two-dimensional network model, which includes axes of customer visibility and operational focus, assist organizational leaders in strategic decision-making and maintaining an effective value stream network?
4. How does the concept of stream aligning within an organization's strategic framework facilitate the development and delivery of products and services?

Answers

1. The main objective of integrating value stream network principles into the software development life cycle is to optimize the flow of value from concept to delivery and also in support of the customer journey. This enhances efficiency by minimizing waste, maximizing resource utilization, and improving effectiveness. By focusing on the interplay of people, processes,

information, and technology, this approach facilitates a seamless and adaptable workflow, promoting a culture of continuous improvement and enabling the organization to maintain agility and a competitive edge.

2. Value stream networks help tackle organizational challenges by creating a structured approach to streamline processes, thus facilitating the efficient delivery of value. This method enables doing more with less by optimizing workflows, improving quality through continuous feedback loops, and delivering enhanced customer value by closely aligning outputs with customer expectations.
3. Mapping value streams using a two-dimensional network model, with axes representing customer visibility and operational focus, provides organizational leaders with a strategic tool for decision-making and maintaining an effective value stream network.
4. Stream alignment enhances the development and delivery of products and services by clarifying product and platform value streams. Product value streams focus on activities for specific market segments, ensuring that each step adds value. Platform value streams provide essential services such as design, operational support, and data integration.

Further reading

1. Kersten, M. (2018). From Projects to Products: How to Survive and Thrive in the Age of Digital Disruption with the Flow Framework. IT Revolution Press.
2. Skelton, M., & Pais, M. (2019). Team Topologies: Organizing Business and Technology Teams for Fast Flow.
3. `https://itrevolution.com/articles/the-three-team-interaction-modes`
4. `https://learnwardleymapping.com/`

Part 3: Achieving Lean-Agile and VSM Mastery: For Product-Oriented Business Transformations

In *Part 3* of this book, we delve into two frameworks that empower organizations to address the dual challenge of maintaining Lean and Agile practices while effectively delivering value. Building on insights from *Chapters 8* and *9*, you will learn how to integrate Lean-Agile work practices at a localized or solution level, and on an enterprise scale to drive value to our external customers.

- *Chapter 8, Implementing the Basic Lean-Agile Solution Team (BLAST)*, introduces the BLAST framework, facilitating the development of point solutions by blending Lean efficiency with Agile adaptability across multiple small teams working in collaboration on a particular problem. It underscores the crucial role of domain experts, who often work collaboratively across both Lean-oriented and Agile-oriented teams, in enhancing various processes, products, and systems.
- *Chapter 9, Defining a Business Agility System for the Enterprise (BASE)*, presents the BASE Conceptual Model, which organizes, synchronizes, and integrates work across the enterprise to ensure the successful delivery of value-based products and services to external customers. It enables organizations to navigate evolving market demands by aligning investments with strategic goals and establishing a consistent cadence for product and service delivery.

Throughout *Part 3*, we explore how organizations can achieve Lean-Agile and VSM mastery to drive product-driven business change. These chapters provide actionable insights and practical guidance for harnessing the BLAST Framework to evolve the organization into a Business Agility System for the Enterprise (BASE).

8

Implementing the Basic Lean-Agile Solution Team (BLAST)

Success today requires the agility and speed to constantly innovate, coupled with the efficiency and discipline to deliver value consistently. Integrating Lean and Agile methodologies is the key to achieving this balance.

—Satya Nadella, CEO of Microsoft

The world is changing faster than we could ever imagine, and the pace of change will only accelerate with the rise of **artificial intelligence** (**AI**), **machine learning** (**ML**), and robotics. Automation and digitization have become the norm, allowing individuals to do things more efficiently and faster.

Consequently, competing and thriving in the digital age require sensing and responding to market changes and emerging opportunities. Recognizing this imperative, the **Basic Lean-Agile Solution Team** (**BLAST**) framework is your definitive guide to harmonizing Lean efficiency with Agile adaptability.

While Lean and Agile are based on different foundations, combining them creates unparalleled advantages. For example, Agile-based software delivery organizations have significantly improved their value flows by implementing highly integrated and automated DevOps pipelines. Laggards in DevOps transformation face obsolescence, underlining a hard truth: being solely Agile or Lean is not enough. Tomorrow's leaders will be those who expertly integrate both methodologies, not just in software deliveries but across the organization. By helping to eliminate waste, Lean enables you to unlock more capacity for enhancing products and services, ultimately increasing the bottom line.

BLAST extends conventional Agile methodologies such as Scrum by orchestrating multiple small teams that generate work in continuous flows, yet seamlessly encompasses Agile's iterative and incremental approach to developing new products and services or solving complex business and technical problems.

In this chapter, using BLAST, we detail the mechanics of combining Lean and Agile methods. BLAST's 17 steps (see *Figure 8.1*) illustrate a comprehensive approach from concept to realization, promoting agility and lean efficiency for future-ready organizations. The topics covered in this chapter include the following:

- Harnessing BLAST
- Implementing Basic Lean-Agile Solutions Teams (BLAST)
- Integrating Lean-Agile development concepts
- Optimizing Development Cadences and Value Deliveries
- Embracing Lean-Agile management practices
- Tracing BLAST's history

Technical requirements

There are no technical prerequisites for understanding the content in this chapter. However, you may find value in reviewing the concepts presented in *Chapter 2, Solving Complex Business Problems with Agility*, and *Chapter 3, Establishing Lean Flows to Improve Productivity*.

Harnessing BLAST

If problems were always small and manageable, an organization could simply employ one or two small Agile teams, such as Scrum, to address its business problem-solving or development needs. However, this isn't always the case, especially in larger organizations. Additionally, many of the individuals required to support business processes, systems, product, or service-oriented solutions have operational roles better suited to *Lean-flow practices*.

Following the **iterative and incremental development** (**IID**) model of Agile, other teams within the BLAST collaborate to implement solutions across timeboxed iterations, with varying durations, but always on a set cadence.

The longevity of Blast teams can vary, depending on the scope of work. For instance, a BLAST formed to implement a business process involving data integration across business systems might be relatively short term on the order of weeks to months. Conversely, BLAST teams formed to support ongoing business processes or commercial product and service development activities typically span their economically viable lifecycles, typically measured in years.

Operating within the context of value streams, BLAST implements a team-of-teams concept to synchronize work across either a single value stream or multiple streams with the latter being more common. While some teams and individuals within BLAST adhere to Lean-flow principles and practices for their day-to-day work, others follow Agile's iterative and incremental patterns, using methods such as **Scrum**, **Kanban**, or **eXtreme Programming** (**XP**).

We must also consider hybrid situations where a team employs both Lean and Agile practices simultaneously. This is often seen in modern software delivery organizations that have implemented **continuous integration/continuous delivery** (**CI/CD**) and DevOps toolchains to integrate, streamline, and automate their processes. In modern software delivery pipelines, the BLAST teams operate in dual modes, leveraging Lean's flow for day-to-day operational work while using Agile's timeboxed model for planning , solution development, and delivery purposes. Finally, some domain experts from Lean-oriented operations teams may be called upon to support the efforts of Agile-oriented development teams on an ad hoc or as-needed basis.

Despite employing different work patterns, BLAST guides teams to collaborate in a coordinated manner, aligning their efforts across value streams. Regardless, the Lean-Agile approach emphasizes continuous improvement of the **customer experience** (**CX**) and fosters a value-focused mindset among those involved in planning and execution. In summary, BLAST offers a clear strategy and structure for planning, integrating, and synchronizing solution development efforts across multiple teams, ensuring their collective contribution to organizational goals.

In the next section, we'll delve into the mechanics of BLAST, exploring its role in enhancing collaborative excellence across teams.

Implementing Basic Lean-Agile Solutions Teams (BLAST)

One of the hallmarks of the Scrum framework is its simplicity, with its three pillars, three roles, five events, and three artifacts. This simplicity makes Scrum an ideal Agile framework for individual small teams.

To properly scale Agile across the enterprise, we need to increase the number of teams, not the number of people within each team. While individual teams can retain Scrum's simplicity to support their work, complexity arises when integrating and coordinating work across multiple teams. This is where the BLAST framework becomes crucial – to manage those complexities, as shown in *Figure 8.1*.

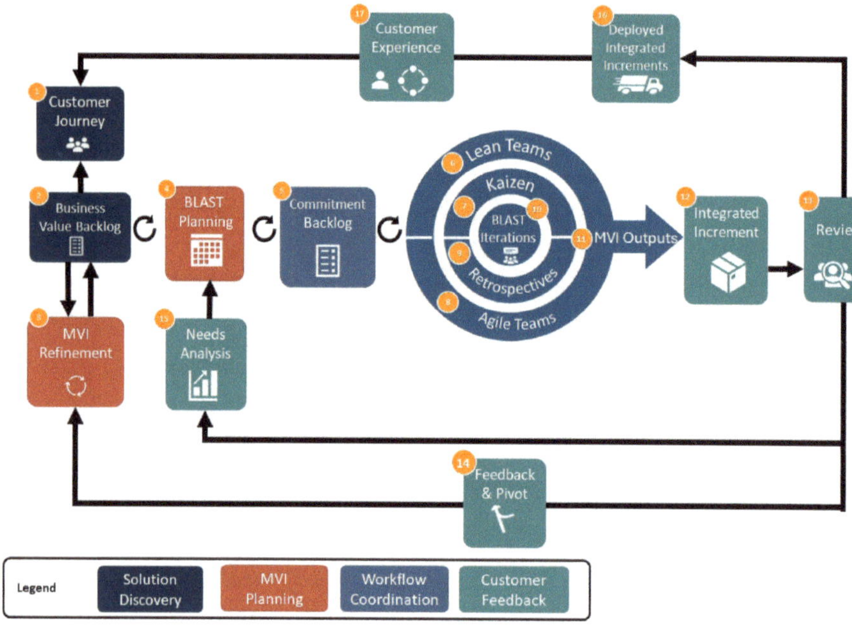

Figure 8.1 – BLAST framework

As you go through this chapter, continue to refer to *Figure 8.1*, which depicts the flow of work conducted by multiple Lean-Agile teams operating within the BLAST.

The authors have endeavored to maintain simplicity in the BLAST framework, but organizing the efforts of multiple teams operating in Lean and Agile modes requires more work. Unlike Scrum, which uses the term *events*, BLAST uses the term *steps* to imply action and progress. As you go through this chapter, you will find that the BLAST framework helps teams coordinate the work of multiple Lean-Agile teams across seventeen steps in four **core domains of work**, with three supporting **roles** and three delivery **artifacts**. We already articulated the goals, foundational principles, and three pillars that make up the Lean-Agile house in *Chapter 1*, so we won't revisit that here.

Categorizing BLAST work activities

As noted previously, BLAST's seventeen (17) activities are grouped into four primary categories:

- **Solution discovery**
- **MVI planning**

- **Workflow coordination**
- **Customer feedback**

The purpose of this grouping is to break the BLAST development cycle down into logical components of work that facilitate our ability to iteratively and incrementally deliver value in a multi-team environment. Equally importantly, BLAST implements a closed-loop and customer-centric flow, ensuring that work progresses smoothly and continuously while maintaining flexibility and adaptability.

Customer centricity entails prioritizing the customer experience in everyone's actions and attitudes. It's a business-wide strategy that requires more than just considering the customer's requirements. Customer-centric enterprises deliver whole-product solutions designed with a profound understanding of customer needs. This approach improves employee alignment, which enhances customer delight and ultimately drives increased revenue and profitability in commercial enterprises. Nonprofits and governments benefit by better serving their beneficiaries and citizens to fulfill their missions.

The subsections that follow describe each of the activities within these four categories, delineating the flow of work in a manner that ensures streamlined integration of Lean and Agile principles. We'll start with the activities that form BLAST's customer-centric foundations involving solutions discovery.

Defining BLAST increments

A BLAST focuses on creating **minimum valuable increments (MVIs)**. However, MVIs are not always released as soon as they are available. Very often, MVIs will be bundled together to create an MVRs. These MVRs may come from one BLAST or from multiple BLASTs. When this occurs, the sequence within which we create the MVIs may be dependent upon their being bundled with other MVIs to create an MVR or integrated increment. Conceptually, an integrated increment is a bundling of MVIs to assemble a complete solution or components of a product release. MVRs are specified in BASE planning activities since they are part of product management-defined releases.

Solution discovery (steps 1 and 2)

Customer-centric enterprises consider customer value, needs, and wants as the most important factors in planning and executing. This philosophy should guide every business decision.

The following foundational steps initiate value-stream improvements for BLAST teams:

1. **Customer journey**: At the core of our approach is a deep understanding of our customers' needs and values. The customer journey encompasses every interaction and touchpoint, from initial awareness to purchase, usage, and beyond, potentially leading to advocacy or repurchase. Achieving positive user experiences and customer satisfaction entails continuous evaluation and enhancement of our value proposition through direct customer engagement.

2. **Business value backlog**: Business value is created by translating customer needs into actionable, prioritized work items that provide comprehensive solutions. The business value backlog starts by identifying potential work items as raw ideas and concepts. Through refinement, these ideas are vetted to fully understand the scope of work involved and prioritize them based on adding the most customer-centric value with the available time and resources. The business value backlog captures this understanding.

BLAST goes beyond theory and supports the use of practices that lead to a profound understanding of customer value and needs. A product is more than the sum of its features; a whole-product approach considers everything involved in the customer journey, from purchase to use and support.

After establishing a customer-centric foundation, the BLAST teams move on to address **MVI planning**, laying the groundwork for value-driven delivery and making commitments.

MVI planning (steps 3 and 4)

This subsection explores how teams collaborate to plan and refine their objectives, strategize their work, and ensure fast value delivery and feedback. Ultimately, we need agreement on the team's short-term goals to manage and eliminate dependencies, integrate requirements, and optimize the workflow:

1. **MVI refinement**: The value manager (product owner) and developers collaborate to refine requirements, architectures, and designs to create the right products, services, or information assets for their customers. This refinement process focuses on three critical areas: decomposing epics into story-level details, addressing architectural and design issues, and determining the lower-level tasks needed to implement the desired features and functionality.

   Epics are simply large stories that have yet to be broken down into refined and actionable user and technical stories. In contrast, stories are detailed enough to build the features and functions needed to implement the requirements.

2. **BLAST planning**: Delivering customer value entails breaking down work into usable, functional increments, often necessitating collaboration among multiple cross-functional teams. This critical activity involves teams coordinating who is responsible for each task and when it will be completed and ensuring synchronization and integration of their efforts. Teams strive for continuous and frequent deliveries on cadence, releasing products and services in collaboration with value managers/product owners and other stakeholders.

Mastering the nuances of BLAST planning ensures that the teams' efforts directly align with customer needs and drive tangible business results. By aligning tactical plans with strategic objectives and making clear commitments, teams can achieve high-quality business outcomes, enhancing their credibility and impact within the organization.

As the BLAST teams shift from planning to action, they move on to the heart of BLAST's operational model. In the next subsection, on **workflow coordination**, we'll learn how teams bring their plans to life, seamlessly integrate workflows, and ensure they can effectively adapt to address challenges during execution.

Workflow coordination (steps 5 to 11)

BLAST emphasizes that robust execution must be in alignment with MVI planning objectives. For BLAST teams, understanding and implementing the steps of execution, integration, and coordination ensures that the planned efforts are effectively realized within the given timebox.\

Modern integrated DevOps toolchains enable automated configuration, builds, testing, and deployment, shifting product development left in the delivery cycle. Agile's iterative and incremental cadences seamlessly integrate with the Lean flow to facilitate planning and release cycles. Automation ensures that every product development step is streamlined, reducing manual errors and enhancing the value flow.

The following section introduces seven steps across two flow operating models for executing and integrating Lean-Agile workflows, as described in the following list:

1. **Commitment backlog**: After reviewing requirements, design, and acceptance criteria, teams commit to completing the scope of work they have reviewed and accepted for the next increment. It's crucial to note that these commitments should be driven by customer needs rather than external influences or driven by team or other stakeholder preferences. Flexibility is key; commitments should not be driven by siloed or traditional project management behavior.

> **Note**
> Commitments cannot be made without sufficient refinement and planning completed in advance. Development teams must be confident that they have the requirements and acceptance criteria sufficiently defined to understand what they need to build. With this understanding and knowledge of their capacity, teams can make informed delivery commitments.

2. **Lean teams**: Teams that perform repetitive work, where productivity, quality, and efficiency are critical concerns, or that want to minimize delays in the workflow, often choose the flow track. In other words, they operate predominantly using Lean-oriented practices, focusing on ensuring the smooth flow of work, people, information, and materials within a business environment.

3. **Kaizen**: In a Lean team, Kaizen events are focused improvement activities to enhance processes, workflows, and outcomes. These events bring together cross-functional team members to analyze specific areas for improvement, identify inefficiencies or bottlenecks, and brainstorm solutions collaboratively.

   By regularly engaging in Kaizen events, BLAST teams foster a culture of continuous improvement, allowing them to refine their practices iteratively, streamline workflows, and optimize performance. This iterative approach enables teams to adapt quickly to changing requirements and market conditions, increasing efficiency, quality, and customer satisfaction in the development process.

4. **Agile teams**: Teams working to solve complex business problems, plan new increments, or develop or enhance processes, products, and services typically choose the timeboxed development track. For example, the timeboxed development approach of Agile practices (e.g., Scrum)

allows teams to iteratively experiment with different concepts and incrementally deploy new features and capabilities.

5. **Retrospectives**: Agile-based teams must rapidly adjust when an issue or impediment blocks the completion of committed work. If an issue arises, teams should have a bias for action and resolve the problem as soon as possible to avoid the accumulation of increasingly complex and challenging problems. A Scrum Master, Value Manager, or equivalent role can help the team resolve impediments, depending on the Agile method employed.
6. **BLAST iterations**: Synchronizing and integrating the work of multiple teams is challenging when some teams use a timeboxed approach while others follow a continuous flow approach. BLAST facilitates cross-team integration via a shared backlog, BLAST planning discussions, and decomposing work into actionable work items. Additionally, implementing cross-team reviews and retrospectives on a regular cadence helps teams align their activities and discover ways to improve their collaboration and work.
7. **MVI outputs**: In mature software delivery organizations, proper team structure and cross-team working agreements reduce the need for synchronization of efforts. However, whole product releases deployed as MVIs may involve teams from disparate business domains working together to coordinate the entire value chain delivery. For example, R&D, legal, product and marketing management, sales, architecture, finance, development, support, and partner management organizations all contribute to a successful MVR release.

Customer feedback (steps 12 to 17)

This stage encompasses the essential customer feedback loops aimed at aligning our future efforts to evolve processes, products, and services in a value-oriented manner. This section will delve into steps 12 through 17 of the BLAST framework, which enable us to evolve and improve continuously to meet our customers' needs:

1. **Integrated increments**: This step is a staging activity for MVIs. Following the workflow coordination stage, which outputs a series of MVIs related to the MVR planned for the current business increment, these MVIs form part of the larger release, though they are often interconnected. The MVI outputs produced across these business functions arrive as needed and may be released at different time intervals. For instance, marketing promotions frequently commence well ahead of a product release. The coordinated and synchronized release of MVIs within an MVR follows the increment release process.
2. **Reviews**: An MVI should not be released to its intended customers without an appropriate review to validate that the outputs meet the requirements specified during refinement in the business value backlog. For example, customers and users are the ultimate arbiters of the value provided by your products and services. However, executives and other stakeholders need to confirm that process and systems updates achieve the business and compliance requirements that justified their investments.

3. **Feedback and pivot**: Integrated increment reviews are ineffective if the value provided fails to achieve its goals and we do not capture feedback and take appropriate action. This activity ensures that bugs (errors in development) and defects (errors in understanding requirements) in the delivered products and services are properly documented and sent back to the MVI refinement process, re-entering the business value backlog for reprioritization. Skipping this step by releasing the product or immediately putting it back into the development stream will certainly cause more problems for the organization.

4. **Needs analysis**: This activity is the BLAST equivalent to Scrum's retrospectives at the team of teams level. Individual teams meet at the end of each BLAST iteration to assess their performance and identify ways to improve in future BLAST cycles. Since BLAST is a team-of-teams concept, each team should appoint a representative who is best qualified to take their findings to a joint meeting with other teams. In these meetings, the representatives collaboratively address integration, synchronization, and dependency issues to enhance future BLAST cycles. Team representatives then share the recommendations from their ToT assessments with their teams to implement the improvements. For complex issues, several iterations may be required to achieve the desired outcomes.

5. **Deployed integrated increments**: This is the path our released MVIs take when judgments from the integrated increment review indicate that the value meets our customers' expectations. MVIs and MVRs typically consist of multiple solution components for customers, and the organization must ensure that each component is fully deployed.

   For example, we cannot release products for resale through our **value-added resellers (VARs)** without fully deploying the necessary communications, promotions, training, product information, and support artifacts required to ensure the success of our partners. From the example provided, it should be clear that an integrated increment may consist of components from multiple BLASTs, coordinated to deliver a cohesive and comprehensive solution.

6. **Customer experience**: After deploying a new product or service to our customers, CX programs are essential to ensure ongoing customer satisfaction and loyalty. These programs should encompass various initiatives to gather feedback, promptly address issues, and continuously enhance the customer journey.

   Examples of relevant CX methods are as follows:

   - Surveys and feedback forms
   - Net promoter score (NPS)
   - Customer journey mapping
   - User testing
   - Social media monitoring
   - Customer support analysis
   - Focus groups

Key components of effective CX programs include customer interviews and sentiment analysis to gain insights into customer satisfaction and preferences. Additionally, proactive customer support and engagement strategies are vital for addressing issues and providing personalized assistance. Regular monitoring of customer interactions helps identify areas for improvement, foster long-term relationships, drive loyalty, and maximize the success of our products or services on the market.

This concludes our walk-through of the BLAST framework. You may notice similarities with other Agile frameworks, particularly Scrum. But the goal of BLAST is to cohesively integrate two fundamental management philosophies: Lean and Agile principles and practices. As always, the details matter. So, let's spend the rest of the chapter understanding BLAST implementation details, starting with a discussion on how to integrate Lean and Agile practices into a multi-team environment.

Integrating Lean-Agile development concepts

BLAST integrates Lean and Agile methods, a strategy designed to empower multiple teams to collaborate effectively on complex business challenges. A fundamental aspect of BLAST is its dual nature: Lean for daily operational efficiency and Agile for fostering innovative product changes.

In many organizations, team members are primarily expected to operate within the Lean framework, as discussed in *Chapter 3*, *Establishing Lean Flows to Improve Productivity*, which aligns with the organization's focus on value delivery. This emphasis on Lean principles forms a foundational element of the BLAST framework. However, BLAST also incorporates Agile components that enable cadence-based business and product planning, driving the development of new products, services, or other business-enabling artifacts.

BLAST is a transformative approach to work aimed at overcoming limiting beliefs and practices that may hinder an organization's full realization of Lean-Agile's potential. Despite BLAST's well-defined processes and activities designed to enhance team collaboration and effectiveness, its methods should be continually tailored to best suit your unique context.

In the subsection that follows, we'll look at how to align the work of multiple teams working together on developing a specific solution.

Aligning teams for collaborative excellence

BLAST operates on a key principle: *When teams align around shared goals to support the organization's value streams, they collaboratively deliver the maximum value efficiently and cost-effectively.*

When aligned, teams can be given more autonomy, go beyond simple coordination, and consistently get better results with less effort. With a mutual goal of enhancing delivery capabilities, the participating teams inherently understand the importance of relentlessly improving products, services, business systems, and processes. They realize that substantial improvements come from optimizing flows, eliminating waste, and focusing on key enhancement opportunities.

A critical aspect of BLAST is the seamless integration of work, ensuring fast feedback. In contrast, lacking harmony and goal alignment can result in fragmented operations, increased overhead, and wasted resources. At the heart of this alignment is a commitment to customer-centricity, emphasizing unrivaled value delivery through innovative products and services.

Combining Lean and Agile practices

While rooted in the principles of Lean Flows, BLAST does not ignore the advantages that Agile IID methodologies offer. It highlights the role of small, adaptable teams that consistently deliver value. Supporting the organization's value streams, BLAST teams embrace Lean values, focusing on maintaining a continuous flow of value, minimizing inefficiencies, and swiftly adapting to changes.

While Lean supports sustained improvements in quality, productivity, and efficiency, adding Agile methods ensures that teams remain flexible in today's global economy. By integrating iterative cycles and responsiveness, BLAST ensures teams respond quickly to changing customer needs and market conditions. Together, Lean's efficiency and Agile's adaptability position organizations to meet customer demands while continuously improving and innovating. Moreover, BLAST's Lean orientation provides improvement insights that feed the organization's holistic VSM initiatives.

In short, BLAST enables teams to achieve maximum efficiency and productivity by employing Lean's flow-oriented concepts, while others opt for Agile's iterative and incremental approach to problem-solving, business planning, and development. Additionally, certain team members, especially domain and technology experts, may be required to support both approaches when assisting multiple teams' efforts.

Yet, even as we recognize the strengths of these combined methods, we must also address where decision-making authority should reside. The next subsection discusses how aligning values helps blend traditional and modern management approaches.

Defining BLAST roles

Note that BLAST does not include the concept of formal *events*. The closest we come is the 17 *steps* defined in BLAST. However, since BLAST is a Lean-Agile methodology, it's more appropriate to consider each step a defined activity within a BLAST-oriented value stream. With this understanding, let's see how BLAST defines its roles.

In BLAST, we approach roles and responsibilities clearly, aiming not to replace terms from other Agile or Lean-Agile disciplines but to offer greater precision. One such role is the *value manager*, functionally equivalent the *product owner* in Scrum. Another is the *value coach* in place of the *scrum master*. But even more importantly, we don't want to change the common terms used in your industry or business domains. So, these roles are meant to be abstractions to define the responsibilities given to individuals within a Lean-Agile enterprise. Renaming these roles is not mandatory, but it brings greater clarity. With this understanding, let's examine the role of the value manager.

Defining the role of value manager

In BLAST, to support the sustainment of Lean-Agile practices within an enterprise, instead of a traditional product owner, we introduce the **value manager**. This renaming isn't about displacing Scrum terminology but clarifying it from a Lean-Agile context. The value manager emphasizes value delivery in all forms, minimizing any misconceptions tied to the Scrum product owner. For example, in large organizations, we have sometimes observed that software is developed but not properly supported because budgets for creating potential customer value were separate from budgets to operate and support the delivered software products.

The value manager balances stakeholder and customer demands, clearly articulating the backlog to guide teams toward high-priority tasks. The name captures the role's essence while sidestepping Scrum-associated pitfalls of focusing solely on product-oriented backlogs. In contrast, the role of a value manager is to evaluate and prioritize all work from a value-added context.

There are varied approaches in BLAST to executing the value manager role and organizations are free to use unique terms for the role to express their responsibilities. The value manager, ideally an executive-level position within the company, provides support and guidance to the chief executives and shareholders, ensuring decisions align with the company's best interests and deliver maximum customer value. They contribute to compliance efforts, financial reporting, risk management, and stakeholder relations within the product line they support, promoting ethical leadership and corporate governance.

Now, let's move on to understanding the role of **developers** in the BLAST framework.

Defining the role of developers

In BLAST, developers are the core individuals who create value in the processes, systems, products, and services they deliver. But they're not just isolated talents—they form a cohesive unit with a shared mission. In other words, they are the value stream team members in a Lean-Agile environment.

So, in BLAST, which can be applied across commercial, government, or non-profit sectors, the term *developer* is not confined to specific roles; rather, it signifies anyone supporting the organization's Lean-Agile value streams. Let's look at some of their defining characteristics:

- **Unified vision**
- **Self-contained**
- **Employs a ToT structure**
- **Clearly defined roles**
- **Cross-functional**
- **Avoids dependencies**
- **Value focused**

Whether it's solving intricate business challenges, devising technical solutions, crafting business artifacts, or delivering products and services for an array of customers (internal or external), all these activities fall under the developer umbrella. Recognizing and valuing this diversity is critical to maximizing the team's potential and output.

Now, let's move on to defining the role of a **value coach** in BLAST.

Defining the role of value coach

The value coach is an essential figure in BLAST, primarily responsible for steering the team toward its goals, facilitating effective communication, and ensuring adherence to best practices.

Often, development teams might focus on individual tasks and overlook the bigger picture. Continuous improvement can be sidelined, and individual commitments might be neglected. A value coach ensures the team remains aligned with its core objectives and constantly evolves.

The value coach role in BLAST encompasses a range of responsibilities crucial to team dynamics and overall progress, including the following:

- Facilitates team growth
- Supports improvements
- Facilitate external communications
- Encourages a Lean-Agile mindset
- Servant leadership style

This completes our discussion on BLAST team roles and responsibilities. The objective is not to enforce terms, roles, and responsibilities that don't align with your industry, domain practices, or organizational preferences. BLAST is a framework to help orchestrate the work of multiple Lean-Agile teams to create solutions. It's not meant to establish rigid rules and procedures. Instead, the aim is to provide clarity on roles and responsibilities that improve the functioning of Lean-Agile work environments and give you the freedom to make it work in your unique business context.

In the next section, we will explore inter-team collaboration in the BLAST framework.

Facilitating inter-team collaboration

In various scaled Agile frameworks, team ambassadors or liaisons serve as communication points between teams to facilitate coordination and alignment.[1] For example, Scrum of Scrums, Scrum at Scale, Nexus, and SAFe® all have roles or other mechanisms to fulfill the liaison role.

In the BLAST framework, we endorse the concept of supporting collaborating teams; however, we refrain from assigning specific names to these roles. We believe that every situation is unique and requires tailored solutions. Additionally, these positions are often dynamic, with individuals being called upon ad hoc as needs arise.

For instance, one or more employees from the accounting department might be summoned to assist a software development team as domain experts in ensuring compliance with financial regulations within a financial application. In such cases, the assignment is both temporary and part time.

We spoke previously about the relevance of management in a Lean-Agile organization, so let's go back to that topic and spend a bit more time reviewing their role.

Balancing decision-making approaches

Traditional management philosophies often favor a top-down approach, guiding organizations through centralized decision-making. In other words, the boss tells us what to do. However, this approach risks being perceived as autocratic, and management may overlook information available only to teams.

In contrast, Agile practices embrace a more participatory, bottom-up approach where the insights and contributions of team members are of higher importance. However, decentralized decision-making across the organization requires more collaboration, and teams may encounter coordination challenges, especially when a team of teams has different viewpoints, goals, and objectives. If we limit our views to these two management extremes, one could argue that a top-down strategy may provide clearer strategic intent even as the decentralized approach can improve the engagement and alignment of employees in their work.

Lean provides a more balanced approach by considering the roles of executive and middle management in supporting the work of multiple teams as they interact across one or more value streams. For example, in a Lean organization, executive managers serve as the architects of organizational strategy, orchestrating the vision and providing a cohesive force that aligns all levels of the company. Middle managers also play a crucial role in Lean organizations as they directly support the value streams. In BLAST, these are our value managers and value coaches. They are often referred to as the "glue" that holds companies together, bridging the gap between top management and lower-level workers.

Therefore, Lean organizations often combine the strengths of top-down and bottom-up paradigms, offering a balanced approach that delivers better business outcomes. This balanced approach, which we refer to as a Middle-Up-Down management strategy, enables a high-level view of what is needed while empowering teams to decide how to work within that context.

In the next subsection, we are going to take a deeper dive into the topic of decentralized decision-making from an Agile-based context at the small team level.

Fostering decentralization

The wider acceptance of Agile-based practices helped start a movement to adopt more streamlined organizational structures. Agile organizational structures foster self-organizing, cross-functional teams that no longer need traditional project managers to push work across silos. Therefore, Agile teams need less daily task direction and rely more on self-management with the assistance of roles such as scrum masters, product owners, and agile coaches.

The list that follows defines the key characteristics of decentralization:

- **Flatter structures**: Agile organizations typically favor flatter structures with self-managed teams that do not require daily task direction.
- **Distributed decision-making**: Don Reinertsen emphasizes the importance of "balancing centralization and decentralization" in his book *The Principles of Product Development Flow: Second Generation Lean Product Development.* [2], [3] Every decision that must be escalated may cause delayed value flow and produce poorer decisions when people are too far from where the information lives. BLAST concurs with Reinertsen and the **Scaled Agile Framework®** (**SAFe®**)[4],[5] that leaders should make and communicate strategic decisions—those that are infrequent, long-lasting, and have significant economies of scale; all other decisions should be decentralized. [6], [7]
- **Servant leadership**: Agile emphasizes facilitation and coaching over traditional hierarchical authority. Servant leaders empower individuals and teams to excel by fostering a culture of responsibility and autonomy. Let's look at two common roles, the agile coach and the scrum master:
  - **Agile Coaches** plan and deliver, facilitate events, establish best practices, advise leadership, and break down barriers between teams
  - **Scrum Masters** ensure the team understands Scrum, facilitate Scrum events, support the goals outlined by the Product Owner, remove team impediments, and shield the team from interference
- **Continuous feedback loop**: The **plan-do-study-act** (**PDSA**) cycle, originally defined by Shewhart and popularized by Deming, is an effective method for gaining faster feedback and controlling unwanted variability during solution development.[8 9,] This loop fosters improvement and development through a consistent and continuous flow of feedback. More frequent and shorter PDSA cycles result in faster learning.

The decentralized decision model of Agile works well in small team environments where the scope of work is constrained. However, as the scope of work increases to involve multiple teams, or agility becomes an enterprise-wide objective, the decentralized model falls short. Fortunately, this is where Lean management practices offer a more compelling management model. Before we get to that topic, let's look more closely at why larger organizations struggle to implement flat structures and decentralized decision-making.

Managing cross-team interactions

A common approach to coordinating the work of multiple teams in scaled Scrum methodologies is to implement team-of-teams structures with representatives facilitating the bulk of the communications between team members and other stakeholders. However, even this approach can become overwhelming. This is one of the reasons why Lean organizations retain middle and upper management positions, ensuring that communication remains effective and manageable.

Embracing Lean leadership

Having flat and decentralized organizational structures is beneficial up to a point. However, as explained in the previous subsection, the number of potential interfaces between team members and stakeholders can become unmanageable. Simply put, more people are needed to facilitate communication and alignment.

In the dynamic landscape of Lean methodologies, organizations work to blend established hierarchical structures with progressive leadership practices. The **Toyota Production System** (**TPS**) offers a prime example of Lean management principles.

Within TPS, traditional management hierarchies remain intact, ensuring a clear chain of command from frontline supervisors to top executives. However, this approach is not rigid "command and control." Instead, Lean leadership emphasizes leading by example, adopting servant leadership, and flattening operational structures to support value streams. The focus shifts from authority to collaboration, continuous improvement, and empowering employees. [10, 11, 12]

Adopting traditional hierarchies with a twist

In Lean organizations, management hierarchies still exist, serving as the framework that supports efficient operations. The TPS model exemplifies this, with distinct layers of management ensuring seamless coordination. TPS integrates hierarchical management with decentralized authority and empowering practices to create a balanced and effective organizational structure. This approach combines clear command structures with the empowerment of frontline workers, fostering a culture of continuous improvement and collaboration.

Implementing key management structures and principles

To successfully blend hierarchical management with decentralized and empowering practices, Lean organizations, like those employing the TPS, have developed a comprehensive approach. This involves maintaining clear command structures while empowering frontline workers and fostering continuous improvement. The following key structures and principles outline how TPS achieves this balance, ensuring that efficiency and innovation coexist harmoniously within the organization.

- **Hierarchical management**:
    - **Clear Chain of Command**: TPS maintains a traditional hierarchy to ensure order and clarity in decision-making, from frontline supervisors to top-level executives
    - **Role of executives**: Executives set strategic direction and foster a culture of continuous improvement and innovation

- **Decentralization and empowerment:**
  - **Gemba walks**: Leaders conduct Gemba walks to observe operations firsthand, stay connected to real-time challenges, and foster continuous improvement
  - **Empowering frontline workers**: Management encourages workers to identify and solve problems, ensuring quality through principles such as *jidoka* (automation with a human touch)
- **Middle management as facilitators**:
  - **Bridge role**: Middle managers translate strategic goals into operational activities, supporting teams with resources and guidance
  - **Servant leadership**: Middle managers function as servant leaders, removing obstacles and supporting team efforts toward operational excellence
- **Team structures**:
  - **Cross-functional teams**: Small, cross-functional teams, working across functional departments and value streams, collaborate to solve problems and implement improvements
  - **Continuous improvement (Kaizen)**: Teams regularly engage in Kaizen assessment activities to enhance processes and eliminate waste
- **Leading by example**:
  - **Going where the work is:** In Lean, leadership involves leading by example through active participation in problem-solving and continuous improvement processes. Practices such as Gemba walks, where leaders visit the actual workplace to observe operations and engage directly with employees, exemplify this approach by fostering firsthand understanding and collaboration.
- **Focused decision-making**:
  - **Strategic alignment**: Although feedback from all levels is essential, strategic decisions typically align with the hierarchical structure to ensure coherence with the organization's broader goals, budget, and schedule considerations. This process is also collaborative.
- **Middle-up-down management**:
  - **Roles**: In the Lean approach, middle managers play a crucial role. They look up to leadership to understand the organization's strategic vision while simultaneously looking down and across value streams to identify how to achieve that vision.
  - **Responsibilities**: Their primary responsibility is to create an environment where the strategic vision can be effectively realized.

By combining these management structures and principles, we can implement a balanced management framework that supports both efficiency and innovation. This creates a dynamic environment where hierarchy coexists with value-based delivery streams and small teams, fostering agility and continuous improvement.

Now that we have a foundational understanding of Lean management, let's move on to explore how BLAST teams are managed.

Conducting Gemba walks for Lean leadership

BLAST, with its Lean orientation, adopts Lean's **middle-up-down management** approach. While hierarchical management structures are retained in Lean organizations, managers do not remain isolated in their offices; instead, they go to where the work takes place to understand the realities of the work environment. They are not there to find fault, but to better understand the issues and how they can help address them. This practice, known as a **Gemba walk**, involves managers and leaders visiting the actual workplace to observe processes firsthand and interact directly with those performing the work.

In virtual or remote work environments, leaders can achieve the essence of Gemba through digital workplace tours and online collaborative discussions, ensuring they remain connected to real-time challenges and nuances of the work.

By encouraging leaders to immerse themselves in the work environment, organizations foster a direct, two-way understanding between management and frontline teams. This hands-on engagement ensures that leaders are informed and deeply connected to daily challenges and opportunities for improving value delivery. It also cultivates a culture of mutual respect, where teams feel their contributions are genuinely recognized and valued. Executives, managers, and team leaders within a BLAST environment prioritize value delivery and work to remove barriers caused by siloed organizational structures.

Managing multi-tiered reviews and communications

For Lean-Agile organizations, the role of the product owner—referred to as the **value manager** in BLAST—leads planning. In a Lean-Agile organization, value is obtained through improvements in processes, infrastructure, tools and equipment, systems, products, and services. Therefore, the value manager role is multi-faceted in its scope and complexity.

This individual also requires strategic foresight to maintain a consistent and relevant flow of work items into the organization's development pipelines. This is not merely about responding to immediate customer needs but involves a deeper alignment with corporate strategy, objectives, and portfolio management, particularly when new circumstances necessitate skills, software, tooling, and equipment changes.

Adopting a multi-tiered planning approach is essential in this context. This involves integrating annual strategic planning cycles with frequent quarterly portfolio and product management planning sessions. These are further supplemented by regular product design and planning activities, creating a cohesive and responsive team planning approach that adapts to the dynamic demands placed on software and product development teams.

For organizations seeking to harness Lean-Agile practices for competitive advantage, understanding and effectively implementing multi-tiered planning cadences ensures that development efforts consistently align with strategic goals, maximizing efficiency and driving innovation. Effective Lean-Agile planning enhances organizational agility and supports sustained competitive success.

Now, let's discuss how team-level planning changes in a Lean-Agile organization.

Improving daily meetings

Have you ever found yourself in a Daily Scrum meeting where the energy is noticeably low, and people's eyes glaze over during the monotonous repetition of information? Do you observe team members multi-tasking or, worse, disengaging and not paying attention to their colleagues' updates? If so, you are not alone. This scenario is more common than you might think and happens for several reasons.

For example, team members often feel sufficiently updated through other communication channels and meetings since the last Daily Scrum. Discussions may delve into excessive detail, shifting focus from quick updates to problem-solving sessions better suited for follow-up discussions. Or are there too many people in your meetings? In our experience, any Scrum meeting with more than seven to nine attendees will become unwieldy, leading to disengagement and discontent.

Recognizing these challenges is the first step toward improving your daily meetings, ensuring they serve their intended purpose—inspecting progress toward the sprint goal, coordinating the day's work, adjusting upcoming planned work, and resolving impediments. The team can use any structure or technique for the Daily Scrum. However, the team should not wait for these daily meetings to adjust. The team should collaboratively adapt, or re-plan work whenever needed. Let's examine some ways to improve:

- **Refine the Daily Scrum process**: Consider reducing the frequency of Daily Scrums to two or three times per week. This change can prevent the meetings from becoming monotonous and make them more dynamic and valuable. As teams become more experienced with Agile practices, they frequently communicate and collaborate to maintain project momentum, making daily meetings less critical.
- **Use a Kanban board**: Integrating a Kanban board into the Daily Scrum process effectively illustrates the team's workflow, the status of work, and the flow of value. The Kanban board efficiently addresses the three questions in the daily meeting so the team can focus more on coordinating the day's work and resolving impediments. This approach aligns well with Lean principles, emphasizing waste removal (in this case, unnecessary discussion) and smooth flow.
- **Use generic language**: Due to differing views on best practices, terms, and the costs associated with training and certification, some organizations may resist adopting specific methodologies and terminology on a large scale. For example, what is typically known as a Daily Scrum could be called a sync meeting or whatever makes sense to your team. You can still implement Scrum's practices without necessarily using its specific jargon—we encourage and support this adaptability if using specific jargon gets in the way of adoption and their supporting value steams.

Use Lean-Agile principles to adapt the Daily Scrum for your context to enhance the effectiveness of it and other Agile events. The evolution of practices requires a mature understanding of Agile methods, emphasizing adaptability and continuous improvement.

Conducting iteration reviews in Lean-Agile environments

In the Lean-Agile development environment, the *Sprint Review* concept undergoes a transformative shift. In BLAST, we prefer *iteration* over the term *Sprint*, though we often use the terms interchangeably in this book. One reason is that the term *iteration* is independent of the team's development approach. Also, the term *Sprint* has the suggestion of running a short but fast race, which is not our intent. Instead, our goal in each iteration is to deliver a new increments of value at a sustainable cadence. We also use the term *integrated increment* over increment to emphasize that the increment is fully integrated from a functional point of view across the teams involved, to fully support a new release.

Timeboxes establish the cadence at which we have agreed to deliver new increments of value. A metronome is a better analogy, as the iterations set the pace for our work and our deliveries. Therefore, the term *integrated increment* more accurately conveys the purpose of this timebox: to produce a new increment of customer-centered value through a new product or value-stream enhancement.

The review of the BLAST integrated increment at the end of each solution development cycle is a structured activity where customers, users, and other stakeholders assess the completeness of the integrated increments for release. For example, an integrated increment might focus on development work across two disparate information systems that simultaneously support changes to existing business processes. The integrated increment may also consist of transformed and migrated data, SQL queries, custom reports, job aids, training materials, and related communications.

Figure 8.2 illustrates the concept of an integrated increment.

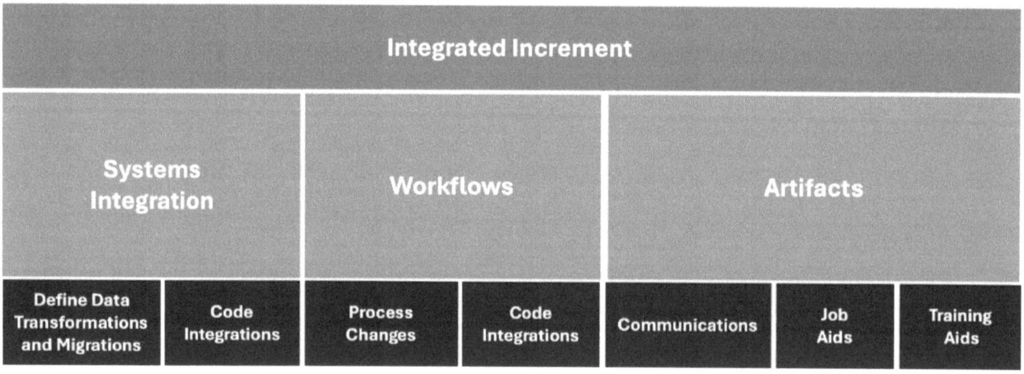

Figure 8.2 – Integrated increment components

The number of incremental releases and the overall timeline for completing the systems integration work are secondary concerns. Instead, the primary focus in MVR planning and BLAST planning is on achieving the increment's goal through the completion of one or more MVIs. The increment's goal provides a clear description of the minimum amount of business value that should be realized from the customer's perspective, detailing all the components required for its release and the acceptance criteria that define their definition of done. In other words, the MVI approach prioritizes delivering tangible, useful, and deployable value in each development cycle.

Additionally, an MVR may include multiple MVIs and follow the same BLAST release cadence. We will explore the relevance of MVIs and MVRs later in this chapter, and again in *Chapter 9, Defining a Business Agility System for the Enterprise (BASE)*.

Now, we will move on to discuss the use of team retrospectives in a Lean-Agile environment.

Enhancing retrospectives with value stream management

In a Lean-Agile organization, the approach to Sprint Retrospectives undergoes a significant transformation. Spending time, money, and resources on non-value-added activities can be detrimental. Well-intentioned retrospectives that lead to local optimizations can harm BLAST performance, resulting in infighting, finger-pointing, fire-fighting, and employee burnout. This often occurs when changes or delivery objectives are dictated without considering their systemic impact. Therefore, in BLAST, we align retrospectives with VSM-based improvement strategies to focus on the most impactful enhancements.

Scrum retrospectives focus on what the development team can directly influence in the forthcoming sprint, aiming for immediate, iterative improvements within the team's local authority and scope. This approach works well in small team settings where the scope is limited to the team's control. However, in large, multi-team settings, individual team improvements can lead to local optimization, overlooking the broader system needs. So, to recap, team-based retrospectives are beneficial for making the team more effective and adaptable but are limited in their capacity for broader, systemic changes due to a lack of visibility and authority over the entire value stream.

In contrast, Lean's VSM practice mandates a broader perspective, examining the entire value stream from concept or request to customer delivery. This helps identify and prioritize enhancements that significantly impact overall flow, productivity, efficiency, and throughput. These improvements directly contribute to increased revenue, reduced costs, and improved quality.

Without systems thinking, optimizations may improve specific teams or processes but miss more impactful changes that benefit the entire value stream. If changes do not address the current bottleneck, considerable effort and resources might be expended with little to no perceptible benefit to customers or the organization. Therefore, VSM practitioners always look for the constraints that hinder flows.

Let's revisit a figure originally introduced in *Chapter 3* as an example of the theory of constraints (see *Figure 8.3*).

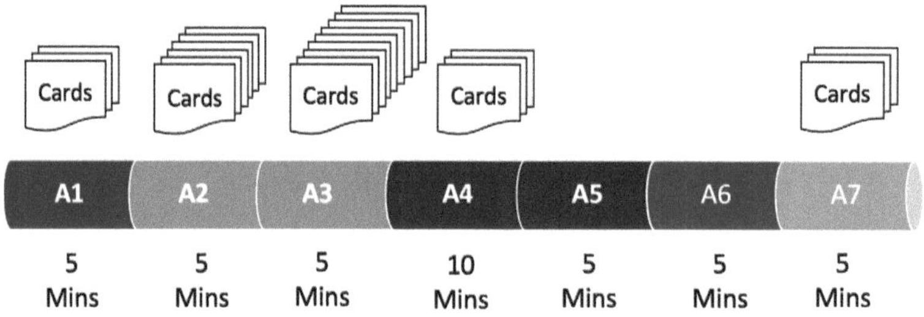

Figure 8.3 – Theory of constraints example

As before, *Figure 8.3* depicts a value stream comprising seven activities, each taking 5 minutes, with one exception: a central activity (A4) that requires 10 minutes. This lengthier activity creates a bottleneck, causing a backlog of work in the steps leading up to it. Meanwhile, subsequent activities lack work, awaiting input from the bottlenecked step. The key issue is that fixing the bottleneck in activity A4 is the primary concern. If another team spends time, money, and effort on reducing their cycle time to 30 seconds, it will be for nothing, as A4 is still the bottleneck. Even with their change, the other six activities cannot support the flow rate of the revised value stream activity.

Therefore, retrospectives in a Lean-Agile organization must be adapted to include a broader VSM perspective. This holistic view fosters a more comprehensive understanding of how value is delivered to customers. By integrating VSM thinking into retrospectives, teams are empowered to make immediate sprint-level improvements and contribute to broader, systemic changes that enhance the overall effectiveness and efficiency of the organization's value delivery.

In this section, we explained how reviews and communications operate differently in a multi-team environment.

Prioritizing value delivery in BLAST artifacts

BLAST stands out with its unique focus on delivering tangible value through its three signature **artifacts**: **minimum viable product** (**MVP**), as defined by Eric Ries, *minimum valuable increment* (*MVI*), and *minimum valuable release* (*MVR*). These artifacts are strategic milestones in the development process that ensure the delivery of actual value to customers while aligning with broader organizational goals. Let's walk through these concepts one at a time.

Minimum viable product (MVP)

The MVP in BLAST is a proven method emphasizing collaboration among integrated value stream teams to create an early version of a new product or service that allows a team to validate a proposed concept or market opportunity. This MVP is a minimal and tangible representation of what can be built and delivered over time. MVPs use an iterative process, allowing teams to gauge the product's viability and adjust based on fast feedback. In his seminal book *The Lean Startup*, Eric Ries describes the MVP as a method to validate whether you have a product that customers need and, if so, what features are needed. In his follow-up book *The Startup Way*, Ries clarifies that MVPs are about addressing all assumptions. That is, MVPs are not just about exploring the product but all the assumptions about the whole product, its marketing, delivery, and support.[13, 14]

Minimum valuable increment (MVI)

This is about delivering new increments of value within a product's life cycle, from concept to end of life. They often integrate the efforts of multiple value stream teams to launch customer-centric products or services. This includes aligning strategies, securing funding, determining market demands, designing, developing, and testing, as well as deployment, promotion, sales, and support. MVIs ensure that each step adds value and aligns with customer needs.

A key principle underpinning both the MVP and MVI is the focus on the rapid delivery of high-value features. However, the defining element of MVIs is that they represent the minimal value that customers expect to meet their needs, delivered in very granular slices. This granularity ensures that each increment is small enough to be quickly developed and deployed, allowing for frequent feedback and continuous improvement. This concept is consistent with Lean-oriented philosophies, which aim to eliminate waste and constraints on activities that customers do not value.

MVIs are identified, prioritized, and refined in the business value backlog. Participating BLAST teams pull their work from the backlog in order of highest priority. Priorities are set based on customers' needs and to ensure that necessary elements to support future value-based deliveries are properly sequenced. Teams that pull lower-priority MVIs engage in a form of local optimization, which may be due to preferences or skills, and this hinders the organization's ability to efficiently deliver the entire increment of value. On the other hand, we cannot expect a marketing team to work on software development tasks. In BLAST, teams pull work items from a single Business Value Backlog. But segmentation within the backlog is necessary to coordinate disparate pieces of work across value streams for each release cycle.

Minimum valuable release (MVR)

While an MVI may offer functionality to customers, there are instances where bundling MVIs together may be more advantageous. This bundling could serve multiple purposes: to reduce the overall transaction cost of the release, to create a more significant functional impact from a marketing perspective, or to make it easier for customers to absorb new capabilities without feeling continuously overwhelmed by new features and functions.

When transaction costs, whether to the customer or the releasing company, are high, bundling MVIs together may be warranted. Additionally, if a larger impact is desired, multiple MVIs may need to be bundled as an integrated solution. Therefore, BLAST implements the MVR concept to coordinate the release of new functions, features, and processes on a planned cadence. Further details on how this works will be explored in the next chapter, *Chapter 9, Defining a Business Agility System for the Enterprise (BASE).*

A significant advantage of BLAST, whether you are working on MVPs, MVIs, or MVRs, is the alignment it creates, enabling quick feedback cycles at low cost. In short, BLAST's MVPs and MVIs ensure that value delivery remains at the forefront, bridging the gap between development ambitions and tangible customer benefits.

This concludes our discussion on BLAST's three artifacts: MVPs, MVIs, and MVRs. This also wraps up our look at the foundational concepts and basic elements of the BLAST Framework, which, in recap, includes marshaling the work of multiple Lean-Agile teams across seventeen steps in four Core Domains of Work, with three supporting roles and three delivery artifacts. The artifacts are the deliverables produced by the BLAST teams to support the incremental release of value by the enterprise to its customers via the BASE Framework, which we will discuss in the next chapter, *Chapter 9, Defining a Business Agility System for the Enterprise (BASE)*. But we have more to cover in this chapter, so let's continue by discussing the rhythms and cadences needed to support value-based deliveries.

Optimizing Development Cadences and Value Deliveries

Cadences in Lean and Agile environments are not new concepts. Agile uses an Iterative and Incremental Development (IID) model to establish a rapid development and delivery cadence, exemplified by the Sprints in Scrum. In contrast, Lean focuses on value stream flows, with a production goal to establish a cadence that matches takt time. The German word *takt* means pulse or beat, conceptually aiming to align production capacities with customer demands.

This is where we begin to see inconsistencies between Scrum and Lean concepts of cadence. For instance, the Scrum Guide suggests a fixed length for Sprints of one month or less, emphasizing consistency in whatever length you choose. In contrast, Lean flows can vary significantly, being much quicker or longer depending on the size and complexity of the development effort. For example, tasks in a modern CI/CD line might be measured in seconds, minutes, or hours, while a Lean production line building large aircraft or ships might be measured in months to years. Moreover, in a Lean environment, takt time dynamically changes based on customer demands.

Synchronizing the concepts of cadence in a Lean-Agile environment becomes a critical concern, and this section shows you how to address it. As a preliminary hint, Lean-Agile organizations establish cadences across planning horizons.

Emphasizing customer centricity in Lean-Agile cadences

Both Scrum and BLAST underscore the paramount importance of the customer. Just as Scrum begins with a product backlog, ordered by priority user stories and features, BLAST incorporates a Business Value Backlog that emphasizes the customer journey, placing customer needs and perceptions at the forefront.

Scrum Guide and SAFe® Distilled

The Scrum Guide at `scrumguides.org/scrum-guide.html` offers more information about sprints and their events, so we needn't repeat them here. Additionally, you may find *SAFe Distilled 5.0: Achieving Business Agility with the Scaled Agile Framework*, authored by Richard Knaster and Dean Leffingwell, an invaluable resource for applying Scrum in a multi-team, scaled environment. It also includes a detailed overview of the Scrum events integrated with Lean concepts.

While Scrum operates with distinct Sprint cycles that incorporate feedback through demos and retrospectives at the end of each cycle, BLAST takes a more continuous approach. Operating as a closed-loop system, BLAST persistently assesses customer needs to guide backlog items and priorities iteratively across a product's economically viable lifecycle, ensuring ongoing alignment with value delivery. This mutual emphasis underscores the shared belief that understanding customer requirements is paramount.

The iterative approach of Agile is reflected in BLAST's dedication to continuous delivery cycles. While BLAST's Timeboxed Teams operate in Scrum-like sprint cycles, there is a key difference. Although Scrum incorporates lean principles to minimize waste, it doesn't fully encompass the Lean concept of flow. In fact, it's easy to argue that Scrum implements a batch process, as the sprint backlog items flow in and out as a batch at the beginning and end of each iteration of the Sprint's set cadence.

In contrast, lean flow concepts emphasize smooth and continuous value delivery with minimal delays or friction. BLAST ensures value is delivered efficiently and mitigates common bottlenecks in traditional development. This commitment to flow reinforces BLAST's comprehensive approach to integrating Lean and Agile practices.

In the next section, we will examine more closely how development and production cycles, as disparate but equally important cadences, work in a Lean-Agile work environment.

Embracing Lean flows in modern software development

As noted in the introduction to this subsection, the Scrum Guide specifies that a sprint is a fixed-length event of one month or less.[15] This recommended duration has not changed. What has changed is the speed of software development due to integrated toolchains and automation capabilities enabled by CI/CD and DevOps pipelines, along with **microservices-based architectures**.

For example, the *Google DORA Accelerate State of DevOps Report 2023* underscores a stark divide in deployment capabilities across performance tiers. Elite performers in DevOps achieve on demand deployment frequencies, maintain a lead time for changes of less than one day have a change failure rate of 5%, and restore service in less than one hour. In stark contrast, low performers deploy on weekly to monthly intervals, grapple with a daunting 64% failure rate, and face failed deployment recovery times that can stretch to an alarming six months.[16] This gap underscores the differences between top-tier developers, who are well versed in the latest software development methods, test automation, and integrated toolchains, and their peers in the lower tier, who may not have fully embraced these advancements.

While the pace and efficiency of software development have undergone profound transformations, it's pivotal to recalibrate our understanding of the purpose of sprints within Agile. As originally conceived, Scrum sprints do not map directly to the end-to-end development cycles typical of Lean-oriented product delivery flows. Instead, they serve a foundational role by providing a consistent cadence for teams to prioritize, plan, execute, and reflect on their work. This rhythm ensures that teams can align their efforts with business needs regularly, make necessary adjustments based on feedback, and deliver incremental value.

So, while Lean emphasizes efficient flows, notably enhanced through integrated systems, tools, and workflow automation, Agile underscores the value of iterative and incremental planning and execution cycles. Thus, in the BLAST framework, the intrinsic nature of a sprint as a cycle of planning and execution remains unchanged, even as the overall delivery speed and flow efficiency improve.

As we've explored the evolving dynamics of software development, it's evident that rhythms and flows are central to modern Lean-Agile practices. With this foundation, we can now fully explore the importance of embracing these rhythms and cadences to harness the power of the Lean-Agile enterprise.

Pursuing a new model for value delivery

In Lean-Agile enterprises, value delivery relies on multiple cadences that span from overarching strategic work to daily operations. The next subsection dives deeper into the planning and execution cycles, highlighting their significance in a successful Lean-Agile enterprise.

To fully understand the Lean-Agile approach to product deliveries, we need a model that illustrates the progression from an idea's inception to its actualization as a process, product, or service. We will get to that model a bit later in this section. Before we get to that, let's introduce some basic concepts.

An integrated Lean-Agile delivery process is anchored in corporate strategy and shaped by market demands and customer insights. Initially, we might be inundated with business and product ideas, but many might not see the light of day. Meanwhile, modern DevOps pipelines enhance software development and delivery capabilities through integrated toolchains and automation. Consequently, the gap between defining requirements and delivering on them has only broadened. The good news is that the BLAST approach clarifies the mechanisms to achieve an efficient software delivery ecosystem.

Conceptually, we can employ a funnel metaphor to illustrate how the *inception phase* for products, services, or business-supporting processes, systems, and artifacts might brim with potential avenues to explore. However, factors such as time, resources, risks, and market dynamics will whittle down these options. Initially, we won't know what products and services we need to deliver, nor the capabilities, features, and functions required. Everything is still fuzzy at this stage. Recognizing this uncertainty is essential to ensure a steady, productive supply to our DevOps pipelines.

To manage this flow of requirements effectively, we utilize different *planning horizons*. These horizons help us structure our approach to requirements assessment and refinement. Long-term planning horizons focus on aligning with corporate strategy and market demands, establishing high-level goals and objectives. Mid-term planning horizons translate these goals into tangible work items, prioritized within backlogs. Short-term planning horizons ensure that teams have well-defined, actionable tasks ready for development. This structured approach ensures that as ideas move through the funnel, they are continuously refined and aligned with strategic objectives, enhancing the efficiency of our delivery processes.

However, defining value through a series of planning horizons isn't exclusive to supporting modern software delivery capabilities. Executives are constantly bombarded with investment ideas to support the business, but there are usually insufficient financial and human resources to pursue every request. Therefore, the organization needs a planning process to properly vet, prioritize, and fund the initiatives that drive the most value. This section fundamentally focuses on defining planning processes to support these vetting and refinement activities. Here, you will learn how to implement the multi-faceted rhythms that drive enterprises holistically across all domains. In a Lean-Agile context, we refer to these rhythms as **cadences**.

We noted that business and product requirements are fuzzy in the early stages of planning. This issue is so significant that we have a name for it: **the fuzzy front-end**.

Taming the fuzzy front-end

The **fuzzy front-end** (**FFE**), a term coined by Smith and Reinertsen in their book *Developing Products in Half the Time*, describes the initial, often opaque stages of requirements discovery and refinement and how they pose a unique challenge in software development.[17] This phase may have high uncertainty, require continuous exploration, and cannot be easily automated. Requirements identification, analysis, and prioritization are just as challenging now as in 1998 when Smith and Reinertsen published their book.

We'll revisit this concept frequently throughout the remainder of this chapter. For the moment, let's turn our attention back to the topic of cadences. We have already touched on this briefly, but we will explore how these cadences extend across various planning horizons, impacting every facet of business domains.

Mastering Lean-Agile Planning and Delivery Cadences

This subsection explains the strategic importance of planning cadences within Lean-Agile enterprises. While iterative planning may seem outdated in today's fast-paced, Lean-Agile environments characterized by continuous flow and rapid delivery, these cadences remain vital for organizations seeking to build and maintain their competitive edge.

Frequent cadence-based planning ensures that organizations can respond swiftly to market demands by consistently replenishing their development pipelines with customer-oriented products, service enhancements, and business process and systems improvements. Moreover, such planning fosters synchronization across multiple teams, promoting alignment and cross-functional coordination, including the management of team dependencies and integrations.

As you work your way through this subsection, refer to *Figure 8.4* for more details on the iterative planning increments necessary to support a modern Lean-Agile software delivery pipeline employing highly integrated and automated CI/CD and DevOps toolchains. These planning processes and horizon concepts apply equally to evaluating all business investment opportunities.

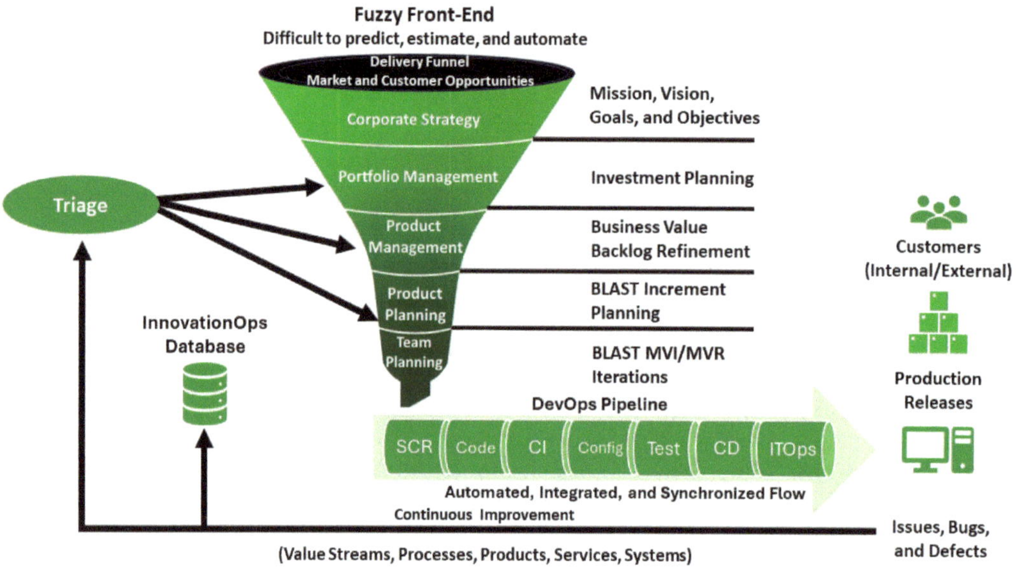

Figure 8.4 – Modern software product life cycle model

Streamlining backlog refinement

We previously introduced the *fuzzy front-end* concept as a critical factor in successfully conducting product requirements analysis. This inception phase represents the initial requirements capture process that resists simplification through automation or systems engineering. In software development organizations, if not effectively addressed, this phase can lead to a shortage of work in the backlog necessary to support highly efficient and accelerated DevOps software development pipelines, starving those lines of work.

Organizations start addressing their fuzzy front-ends with *Corporate Strategy* and *Portfolio Management* activities to establish high-level goals and objectives. However, strategy is not limited to the C-Suite. The function of product management is to have a strategy-level responsibility to refine the executive's product ambitions into tangible work items, usually expressed as epics. Their efforts initiate the *Backlog Refinement* process.

As noted in the *MVI planning (steps 3 and 4)* section, an epic is a large body of work that can be broken down into smaller sets of requirements in the form of user and technical stories. Epics may span multiple iterations or sprints and encompass a significant feature or requirement that delivers substantial business value once completed.

Value managers and product owners support the *BLAST increment planning* process to ensure the epics are decomposed into stories, refined, and prioritized for delivery. They also work with the BLAST teams to plan and provide guidance during the integrated increments.

Developers are responsible for assisting in the refinement process and defining the tasks necessary to build and deliver the solution components. Intentional design and architecture activities must start much earlier during backlog refinement and BLAST increment planning phases.

The concept of backlog refinement in BLAST goes beyond Scrum practices as starting the process earlier is even more important in a highly efficient Lean-Agile organization. Moreover, managing requirements in large enterprises or complex solutions often begins far in advance of actual development.

Managing ideas and innovations

Using the funnel idea previously illustrated in *Figure 8.4*, we conceptualize the refinement process as starting with a broad set of potential value stream processes, product ideas, and infrastructure development options, which are then iteratively narrowed down through successive planning increments.

However, many ideas in the funnel will be discarded or delayed due to cost and priority considerations. This does not necessarily mean they are poor ideas; rather, they may not be relevant in the current timeframe. It is useful to envision our funnel as having leaks where certain ideas and concepts escape our immediate attention. To ensure these ideas are not lost, we can also imagine a drain pan underneath the funnel to catch them for reference at a later date.

Managing these innovative ideas for future consideration requires a structured approach. This is where the concept of an *InnovationOps database* comes into play, serving as the foundation for building and managing a centralized system designed to track innovation-related projects, activities, and data within an organization. While InnovationOps is a crucial aspect of innovation management, a detailed discussion of its implementation is beyond the scope of this book.

Facilitating collaboration and planning during BLAST increments

During the planning and execution phases of the BLAST integrated increments, key players such as the **value manager** (**product owner**), **UI/UX developers**, and **lead developers** engage in deep collaboration. They address critical tasks encompassing usability, design, infrastructure, and architectural considerations. This collaboration also extends to defining user stories and acceptance criteria, and developing UI prototypes for reviewers to evaluate before development begins. This preparatory stage is essential, as these refinements are instrumental in establishing a solid foundation for the upcoming team-based planning sessions.

When it comes time for the development teams to take over, their planning events are designed to be succinct, typically spanning just a few hours. This streamlined planning is only feasible if the preliminary product planning increment work has been thorough. With the refinement details already in hand, development teams can then concentrate on determining the specific tasks and workload for the upcoming BLAST increment, assigning tasks, and clarifying the build requirements and acceptance criteria. It's a straightforward principle: an item from the business value backlog that has not been refined cannot be slated for an upcoming BLAST increment's backlog.

This systematic approach ensures that our development pipeline is consistently fed with well-defined, ready-to-work items, preventing delays in the continuous flow of customer value. By refining the backlog ahead of the integrated increments, we empower our teams to maintain the momentum for Lean-Agile success, fostering a sustainable cycle of delivery that meets and exceeds competitive market demands.

In *Figure 8.4*, there was a note that the fuzzy front end is difficult to predict, estimate, and automate. Not much has changed since Don Reinertsen coined this term in his 1985 article *Blitzkrieg Product Development: Cut Development Time in Half*. However, some strides are being made to address these concerns by utilizing AI.

Embracing AI in discovery

The requirements discovery process is evolving with the help of AI and ML. While AI-based decision-making introduces uncertainties, leveraging algorithms to analyze data and predict outcomes enhances efficiency. Striking a balance between utilizing AI's power and maintaining human oversight is essential.

Here are some examples of how AI is being used to address the challenges of requirements analysis in software development:

- Natural language processing (NLP)
- Automated requirements extraction
- Consistency and conflict-checking
- Prioritization and impact analysis
- Predictive analytics
- Requirements validation

These AI applications enhance the accuracy, efficiency, and effectiveness of requirements analysis in software development. Still, the black-box nature of some AI models raises questions about transparency, interpretability, and accountability. Organizations must navigate this landscape carefully, embracing AI's potential while mitigating risks. Ultimately, the synergy between human intuition and AI-driven insights will shape the future of requirements gathering and innovation.

We've covered the planning cadences needed to effectively transform strategies and ideas into actionable work items. Now, let's get a clearer picture of the time and effort involved.

Exploring planning horizons

In product development and continuous improvement, organizations consistently face the challenge of navigating the ambiguous fuzzy front-end of requirements analysis. As ideas emerge and take form, they naturally evolve from abstract concepts to concrete plans. Without a structured approach, this transition can become chaotic, leading to misaligned efforts and missed opportunities.

> **Important note**
>
> It's essential to add an Agile perspective to planning horizons. For mature processes, systems, products, and services, new customer and business requirements can quickly emerge with high priority. If these changes fit within the approved strategy and portfolio investments, the product management function can expedite them by assigning high priority to the business value backlog.

To address this challenge, it is essential to adopt a planning methodology that leverages planning cadences, as shown in *Figure 8.5*. This approach not only streamlines the development process but also guarantees that value stream improvement initiatives stay attuned to what truly matters for end users, and teams are building the right thing at the right time.

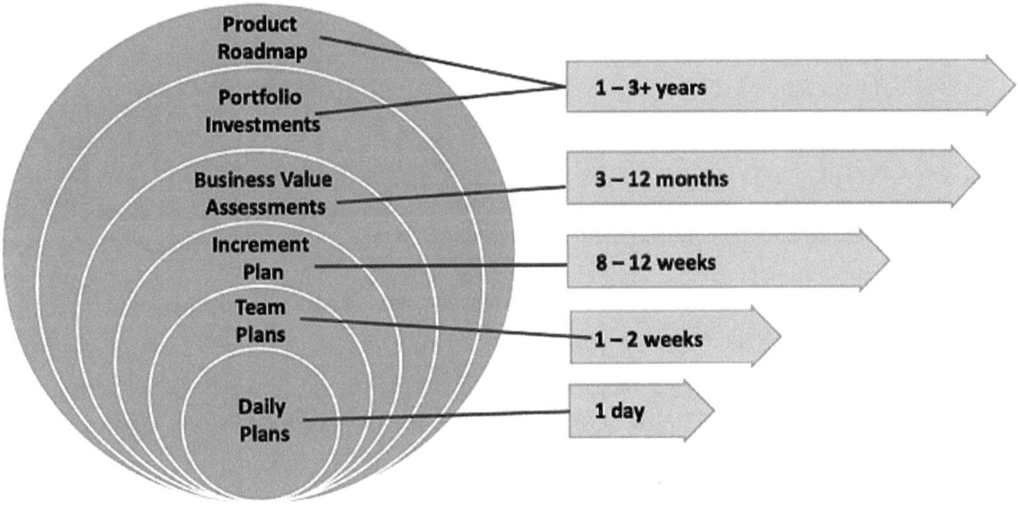

Figure 8.5 – Enterprise planning horizons

Figure 8.5 presents an expanded, timeboxed view that builds on the funnel idea introduced in *Figure 8.4*. This diagram illustrates a clear sequence of planning that enhances the organization's ability to deliver products and services.

With that concern addressed, let's examine the planning horizons depicted in *Figure 8.5*:

- **Product Roadmap and Portfolio Investments (longer term, 1-3+ years ahead)**: Executives maintain the product roadmap, outlining future investments (products and services) vital for achieving the organization's strategic goals. Simultaneously, portfolio management determines the investments needed to support those offerings.
- **Business Value Assessments (mid-term planning within the current fiscal year)**: Converting strategy into actionable plans, product and marketing managers undertake research and collaborate with industry experts, clients, and development teams. Their goal is to identify, define, and prioritize products and services for the business value backlog.

> **Note**
>
> Business and technical architects support this phase by providing preliminary assessments of process, system, infrastructure, and architecture needs.

- **Increment Plan (short-term planning, 8-12 weeks ahead)**: Entering a tactical implementation phase, the value manager (product owner), with input from design and development teams, refines the work items in the backlog in collaboration with stakeholders and clients.
- **Team plans (1-4 weeks out)**: As the requirements become refined and prioritized in the backlog, the development teams need time to assess the requirements and define the tasks to build the work items.
- **Daily plans**: Schedule frequent meetings, as needed, during BLAST solution construction periods to check progress against goals and address any challenges hindering progress. Timebox these meetings to no more than 15 minutes and avoid turning them into working sessions. Hold working sessions separately.

Looking back at *Figure 8.5*, we can see the interconnected nature of these cadences. Each has a vital role in the development of products and services.

The following subsection discusses integrated increments and their importance in synchronizing multiple Lean-Agile teams and multiple BLASTs operating across varied business domains. These concepts are key to understand before we delve into the next chapter, *Chapter 9, Defining a Business Agility System for the Enterprise (BASE)*.

Facilitating collaboration at scale – the team-of-teams approach

In Lean-Agile enterprises, the sheer scale and complexity of business operations can present challenges in ensuring seamless collaboration and alignment across teams. The concept of a team of teams seeks to address this by creating a structured ToT collaboration mechanism.

At the heart of this approach are representatives from individual teams. Previously, we mentioned several scaled Scrum methods that implement similar roles, such as the Ambassador in Scrum of Scrums™ and NITs in the Nexus™ framework. Regardless of what you choose to call them, these representatives come together at periodic intervals, linking disparate teams and forming a collaborative entity that ensures enterprise-wide collaboration. This ToT communications structure facilitates the management of dependencies, seamless integrations, and maintains synchronization across all teams involved. The benefits of this structure include:

- **Addressing dependencies**: As teams work on interrelated tasks, issues related to dependencies, integration, and synchronization inevitably arise. Representatives in the team-of-teams structure ensure these issues are identified early and managed effectively, preventing bottlenecks and ensuring smooth delivery.
- **Ensuring ToTs integration**: Integration points are critical in large-scale projects. BLAST's ToT planning and review sessions should be scheduled with qualified representatives from each team to resolve business and technical integration issues.
- **Aligning/coordinating efforts**: Coordination becomes vital when multiple teams work toward common goals. The team-of-teams approach ensures a synchronized effort, with teams aware of each other's progress, challenges, and upcoming milestones. Coordination tends to be expensive and error-prone. The BLAST framework implements a shared business value backlog to improve the alignment of work and work item prioritization across the BLAST.
- **Shared learning and best practices**: Representatives can share learnings, challenges faced, and best practices adopted by their teams. This collective wisdom improves efficiency and fosters a culture of continuous improvement.
- **Risk mitigation**: Discussing challenges and potential risks at the team-of-teams level can address issues proactively, ensuring that individual teams don't face unexpected roadblocks.
- **Frequent communication**: Regular and clear communication among team members and stakeholders is vital for aligning goals, sharing progress, and addressing any concerns promptly.
- **Continuous improvement**: Teams should regularly review their processes and outcomes to identify opportunities for improvement and implement necessary changes for better efficiency and effectiveness.

BLAST does not define a precise role or set of responsibilities for these representatives. This is because the number and skills of representatives will constantly change in a Lean-Agile organization depending upon the domains and skills involved and the business context of the discussions.

To clarify their role, you may choose to call these BLAST representatives *BLAST coordinators*, or simply *coordinators*; their collaborative working sessions *BLAST meets*; and their socialization networks *BLAST hubs*. However, the choice is yours. Feel free to refer to the representatives and their meetings as you prefer. In short, BLAST implements *coordinators*, *meets*, and *hubs*.

In the next subsection, we'll take a closer look at several common types of issues addressed by the BLAST coordinators.

Ensuring Seamless Project Delivery

In this chapter, and later chapters, we frequently mention that teams and individuals working in a team-of-teams environment must address dependencies, integration, and synchronization issues that arise from managing work across across-team tasks. Let's take a moment to define how these issues manifest in a BLAST or multi-BLAST work environment:

- **Cross-team tasks**: Tasks that are connected or dependent on each other in some way
- **Dependencies**: Situations where one task relies on the completion of another task
- **Integration issues**: Challenges that arise when combining different components or systems to work together
- **Synchronization issues**: Problems that occur when coordinating the timing and sequencing of tasks to ensure they work together seamlessly

By focusing on these critical areas, BLAST teams can enhance their collaboration, minimize obstacles, and drive successful project outcomes, ultimately achieving their strategic goals. The BLAST coordinator approach acts as a bridge, ensuring that while individual teams retain their autonomy and focus, a higher-level collaboration mechanism keeps the entire enterprise aligned, integrated, and moving forward cohesively.

We'll discuss BLAST roles in an upcoming section. But first, we need to understand the concept of increments in BLAST and how they support the life cycles of a process, business system, product, or service.

Understanding increments in life cycle management

In *Figure 8.1*, the term *increments*, and more precisely *increment planning*, stands out as a cornerstone of product life cycle management. Typically spanning 8-12 weeks, this period involves the value manager (or product owner) actively collaborating with stakeholders to refine requirements for near-term enhancements across the business's processes, systems, products, and services.

However, the value manager's role goes beyond merely ensuring the delivery of what customers desire. They also evaluate value through a Lean lens, aiming to eliminate waste, remove constraints, and enhance flow.

As we'll learn in the next section, a product owner's role is not just about embedding desired features; delivering them swiftly and cost-effectively is equally critical. This requires improvements to the organization's value streams. In this context, we prefer to think of the role as a *value delivery manager* or *value manager*, rather than just a product owner.

The significance of increments in the Lean approach extends beyond product development-oriented value streams. The release of new business and customer value often necessitates the orchestration of efforts across multiple domains and value streams, underscoring the comprehensive nature of this concept.

This concludes our discussion on the implementation of Lean-Agile cadences. Now we move on to a discussion on Lean-Agile management practices.

Embracing Lean-Agile management practices

Management, often misunderstood in Agile contexts, holds a multi-faceted role in Lean-Agile work environments, which includes the following:

- **Improving work environments**: Creating a conducive environment for teams to flourish
- **Resource allocation**: Ensuring teams have the necessary people, resources, and information
- **People development**: Offering career guidance and self-improvement
- **Collaboration**: Coordinating with peers to ensure cross-functional efficiency
- **Fiduciary responsibility to shareholders**: Management also has a fiduciary duty to act in the best interests of the company's shareholders, ensuring that decisions and actions align with long-term value creation and sustainable growth

A primary perspective for management in Lean-Agile work environments is recognizing the knowledge and expertise of team members actively involved in tasks. Trusting your teams and individuals is crucial, but it should be balanced with oversight to prevent potential issues.

Championing Lean-Agile management

W. Edwards Deming aptly said, "*A system must be managed. It will not manage itself.*" In an organization, management is the backbone, bridging the strategic vision with the hands-on execution at the Gemba or workplace. They play a central role in aligning organizational goals with actual execution, a concept termed middle-up-down management.

Often perceived as obstacles in Lean-Agile transitions, middle managers can be catalysts for positive change. Their position uniquely positions them to translate overarching strategies into actionable activities, making them vital in transformations and the continuous success of Lean-Agile methods. They communicate strategic visions while also integrating insights from frontline operations.

In BLAST's transformation model, middle management doesn't just oversee the change but actively participates in it, becoming pioneers of the evolving leadership dynamics.

All managers must embrace and champion Lean-Agile practices. Management must take time to understand the issues workers face and ensure a respectful approach focusing on inclusivity and cooperation.

Harnessing middle management for organizational agility

Scrum, first introduced in 1993 by Jeff Sutherland, John Scumniotales, and Jeff McKenna at **Easel Corporation**, was inspired by the HBR article *The New New Product Development Game* (1986) by Takeuchi and Nonaka, which drew parallels between new development strategies and a game of rugby.[18]

The foundational principles of *Middle-Up-Down Management* were detailed in Nonaka's 1988 work *Toward Middle-Up-Down Management: Accelerating Information Creation.* [19] This management approach merges the systematic processing of information—a characteristic of established organizations—with the dynamic information creation typical in Agile entities. Central to this is middle management's role in guiding organizational transformations aligned with business objectives.

Distinctly, the Lean-Agile aspects of BLAST acknowledge and embrace this core aspect of Lean management. In the Lean philosophy, management is viewed as a vital, positive force, not a blocker of progress. This concludes the section on embracing Lean-Agile management practices. Before we end the chapter, let's understand the history of BLAST.

Tracing BLAST's history

BLAST was conceptualized in 2008 during an engagement by Al Shalloway with a client that was using Scrum effectively but couldn't deliver quickly. Although the teams were working on the same product, they operated independently and only attempted integration every two weeks. This led to long final integration times.

By viewing the work as a single value stream instead of separate Agile-based teams, it was quickly determined that a common backlog would create alignment and facilitate full integration after each sprint. The BLAST approach eliminated the need for extensive coordination, expedited integrations, and provided quick feedback across the teams.

This real-world example demonstrates how BLAST can transform team operations and significantly enhance efficiency and delivery speed. Today, this approach also better accommodates the highly accelerated software deliveries enabled via CI/CD and DevOps toolchains.

> **Note:**
> The terms BLAST and BASE were coined by authors Al Shalloway and Gary Rupp in joint working sessions in May 2022.

This brings us to the end of this chapter. But before we move on, let's summarize what you have learned.

Summary

This chapter presented BLAST as a framework and guide to integrating the efficiency of Lean with the adaptability of Agile. Recognizing the imperative of evolving business needs, we discussed how BLAST enhances Agile methodologies, providing an actionable approach from concept to realization. We reviewed the intricacies of harnessing BLAST and its differences from and similarities with Scrum models, as well as gaining an understanding of its roles and artifacts.

Understanding and implementing BLAST is critical for organizations aiming to stay competitive. It ensures timely value delivery at minimized costs.

Looking ahead, in *Chapter 9, Defining a Business Agility System for the Enterprise (BASE)*, we'll transition into the product life cycle in Lean-Agile practices. The focus will be on the development of MVPs, MVIs, and MVRs. The BASE framework defines a systematic cycle of events, ensuring iterative and incremental value delivery through continuous process improvements and product enhancements. You will also learn how BASE facilitates cross-value stream teamwork.

Questions

This section is offered for those of you who want to evaluate your comprehension and retention of the information provided in this chapter. There are 10 questions. The answers are provided in the subsequent section. Recalling the exact verbiage of the original content is not essential. Instead, it's more important to recall the concepts and their applications.

1. What are the three aspects of Lean management?
2. What are the management concepts typified in Agile-based practices?
3. What two steps define the customer-centric foundations of the BLAST framework?
4. What are the three steps within the BLAST framework that define the planning, refinement, and commitment activities?
5. What three BLAST concepts include the six steps for Lean-Agile workflow integrations within the BLAST framework?
6. What three BLAST concepts encompass six steps for evaluating and enhancing product deliverables?
7. What is the fuzzy front-end, and why should you care about it?
8. What are the three primary roles defined in the BLAST framework?
9. What are the three artifacts in the BLAST framework?
10. True or false: the BLAST framework has 17 events.

Answers

1. The three aspects of Lean management are traditional hierarchies may remain, leading by example, and focused decision-making.
2. The management concepts typified in Agile-based practices include flatter structures, distributed decision-making, servant leadership, and continuous feedback loops.
3. The steps defining the customer-centric foundations of the BLAST framework are customer centricity (step 1) and business value backlog (step 2).
4. The BLAST framework steps that define planning, refinement, and commitment activities are MVR refinement (step 3), BLAST planning (step 4), and commitment backlog (step 5).
5. The BLAST framework concepts for Lean-Agile workflow integrations are flow teams and timeboxed teams (steps 6 and 7), daily reviews and review and refinement of workflow tracks (steps 9 and 10), and BLAST integrations (steps 10 and 11).
6. The three BLAST framework concept steps for evaluating and enhancing product deliverables are integrated increments and integrated increment reviews (steps 12 and 13), feedback and pivot (step 14), and BLAST improvements to CX (steps 15 to 17).
7. The fuzzy front-end is important for the following reasons:

   Popularized by Preston Smith and Donald Reinertsen in 1991, the fuzzy front-end refers to a period of ambiguity when determining what needs to be built. Besides requiring more time than we might like, as ideas emerge and take form, there's a natural evolution from abstract concepts to concrete plans. Without a structured approach, this transition can become chaotic, leading to misaligned efforts and missed opportunities.
8. The three BLAST framework roles are value manager, developer, and coach.
9. The three BLAST framework artifacts are **minimum viable product** (**MVP**), **minimum valuable increment** (**MVI**), and **minimum valuable release** (**MVR**).
10. False. However, this is a bit of a trick question. BLAST does not include the concept of events. Instead, BLAST has 17 steps. Unlike Scrum, which uses the term events, BLAST uses the term steps to imply action and progress.

Further reading

1. Knaster, R., & Leffingwell, D. (2020). SAFe Distilled 5.0: Achieving Business Agility with the Scaled Agile Framework. Addison-Wesley Professional.
2. Reinertsen, Donald G. The Principles of Product Development Flow: Second Generation Lean Product Development. Celeritas Publishing, 2009.
3. Reinertsen, Donald G. The Principles of Product Development Flow: Second Generation Lean Product Development. Celeritas Publishing, 2009.
4. `https://scaledagileframework.com/decentralize-decision-making/`. April 2024.
5. SAFe® and Scaled Agile Framework are registered trademarks of Scaled Agile, Inc.
6. `https://scaledagileframework.com/decentralize-decision-making/`. April 2024.
7. SAFe® and Scaled Agile Framework are registered trademarks of Scaled Agile, Inc.
8. Shewhart, W. A. (1931). Economic Control of Quality of Manufactured Product. New York: D. Van Nostrand Company.
9. Deming, W. E. (1986). Out of the Crisis. Cambridge, MA: MIT Press
10. Liker, J. K., & Morgan, J. M. (2006). The Toyota Way in Services: The Case of Lean Product Development. The Academy of Management Perspectives, 20(2), 5–20
11. Liker, Jeffrey K. (2004). The Toyota Way: 14 Management Principles from the World's Greatest Manufacturer. New York: McGraw-Hill
12. Toyota Production Systems: The 'Toyota Way' and Labour–Management Relations. (2006)
13. Ries, E. (2009, September 8). Minimum Viable Product: A guide. Startuplessonslearned.com. Retrieved October 31, 2023, from `https://www.startuplessonslearned.com/2009/08/ minimum-viable-product-guide.html`
14. Ries, E. (2010). The Lean Startup: How Today's Entrepreneurs Use Continuous Innovation to Create Radically Successful Businesses (1st ed.). Crown Business, an Imprint of Crown Publishing Group, a Division of Rando House, Inc, NY.

    Note: If you like to learn more about Scrum and Lean thinking, you can find links to Cecil Rupp's books in the following end notes. Additionally, Al Shalloway's books on AMPLIO available online provide extensive details about BLAST at `https://successengineering.works/books/`.

15. Schwaber, K., & Sutherland, J. (n.d.). The 2020 Scrum Guide (TM). SCRUM GUIDES. Retrieved October 10, 2023, from `https://www.scrum.org/resources/scrum-guide`.
16. DevOps Research and Assessment (DORA). (2023). Accelerate State of DevOps Report. Google Cloud. Retrieved from `https://cloud.google.com/devops/state-of-devops`

17. P. Smith and D. Reinertsen, Developing Products in Half the Time, New York, NY: John Wiley & Sons, 1998.

18. Takeuchi, H., & Nonaka, I. (1986). The New New Product Development Game. Harvard Business Review, 64(1), 1–10.

19. Nonaka, I. (1988). Toward Middle-Up-Down Management: Accelerating Information Creation. Sloan Management Review, 29(3), 9-18.

9

Defining a Business Agility System for the Enterprise (BASE)

"Agility is the ability to adapt and respond to change ... agile organizations view change as an opportunity, not a threat."

–Jim Highsmith

Whether you work in a commercial enterprise, non-profit, or government agency, staying competitive and relevant requires the ability to swiftly adapt and innovate to meet and exceed customer expectations. How can organizations not just survive but thrive amid constant change? This chapter introduces the **Business Agility System for the Enterprise** (**BASE**), a model designed to transform uncertainty into opportunity. The BASE drives continuous improvement by coordinating all facets of a company's resources to enhance business processes, systems, products, and services.

According to the Business Agility Institute, **business agility** is "*a set of organizational capabilities, behaviors, and ways of working that grant businesses the freedom, flexibility, and resilience to achieve their purpose.*" Similarly, **SAFe®** defines business agility as "*the ability to compete and thrive in the digital age by swiftly responding to market changes and emerging opportunities with innovative, digitally-enabled business solutions.*"

Our world is changing rapidly, requiring businesses to adopt an innovative approach to product development. Within the BASE model, Lean's flow-oriented practices improve productivity, efficiency, and quality, while Agile's timeboxed practices help organizations implement a hypothesis-driven approach to innovation, value delivery, and digital transformation. The BASE coordinates the activities of multiple **Basic Lean-Agile Solutions Teams** (**BLASTs**) to deliver new increments of value on cadence. This approach involves continuous cycles of information gathering, informed decision-making, and experimentation to optimize outcomes with available resources.

In this chapter, you will learn how the BASE conceptual model facilitates enterprise-wide collaboration and prioritizes customer-centered value deliveries. BASE also implements a holistic approach to delivering *integrated increments*, coordinating efforts across business functions and value streams. It features a **Virtuous Circle**, where each positive event in the model reinforces the next, driving continuous improvement. This chapter describes how the BASE shapes the enterprise's customer-centric value delivery approach and includes the following topics:

- Understanding the BASE conceptual model
- Establishing customer-centric foundations
- Delivering value across the product life cycle

Technical requirements

There are no technical requirements to understand the content presented in this chapter. However, readers should understand the concepts presented in *Chapter 8, Implementing Basic Lean-Agile Solutions Teams (BLASTs)*, as these teams provide the structure and resources for incrementally implementing new value. Al Shalloway's online books, at `https://successengineering.works/books/`, also provide extensive details on BASE development, including descriptions of the BLAST framework.

Understanding the BASE conceptual model

BASE offers a carefully crafted Lean-Agile **operating model** to promote enterprise business agility. An operating model is a comprehensive framework that defines how an organization operates to deliver value to its customers and achieve its strategic objectives. It encompasses the organization's structure, processes, systems, and culture, detailing the alignment of resources, technology, and workflows to support its goals.

The BASE model supports the dynamic nature of the product life cycle — the continuously changing and often unpredictable stages a product goes through from concept to market release to end of life. This dynamism can be due to many factors, such as evolving customer needs, technological advancements, market competition, regulatory changes, and customer feedback during development. BASE aims to deliver new customer value perpetually, provided it is economically viable to continue supporting the product or service.

A BASE solution typically starts as a **minimal viable product** (**MVP**). Organizations should initially explore new product or service concepts by developing an MVP to design, build, and test a limited set of planned features, functions, and capabilities, and then test them with your customers and in the market. The MVP helps evaluate the product's potential and assesses its viability through fast feedback from one or more customer segments in the target market.

The BASE implements value streams that deliver new increments of business value, starting with an initial MVP followed by a series of **minimum viable increments** (**MVIs**), as illustrated in *Figure 9.1*. Each MVI iteratively and incrementally enhances a business process, information system, a product, or a service, offering customers increased benefits over time. This leads to a higher perceived value and often provides a competitive advantage in the market.

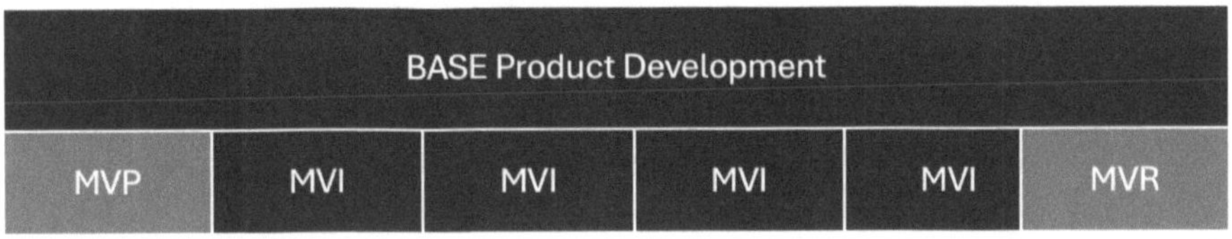

Figure 9.1 – Product development in a BASE value stream

As noted in the previous paragraph, an MVI can also focus on implementing changes in business processes, systems, or other business-enabling artifacts that the organization uses to improve its operations. These changes compete for the organization's limited resources; therefore, business priorities must be assessed alongside enhancements to products and services as part of the business value backlog. This is why we prefer the term "value manager" over "product owner" for the person responsible for managing the business value backlog.

As discussed in *Chapter 8, Implementing Basic Lean-Agile Solutions Teams (BLASTs)*, MVIs often fail to provide a complete solution or may not warrant individual deployment due to cost considerations. Additionally, introducing partial features, functions, or incomplete processes could negatively affect customer satisfaction. Therefore, the BASE conceptual model also incorporates the concept of a **minimum viable release** (**MVR**) to synchronize the rollout of new functions, features, and processes on a regular cadence.

Figure 9.2 illustrates the BASE's conceptual model as a virtuous circle for enterprise improvements, with customers at its core. Customers and their buying journeys enable and fund our business, establishing the requirements that guide our decision-making and business operations. The success of our business hinges on our ability to swiftly meet their needs or desires while managing costs effectively.

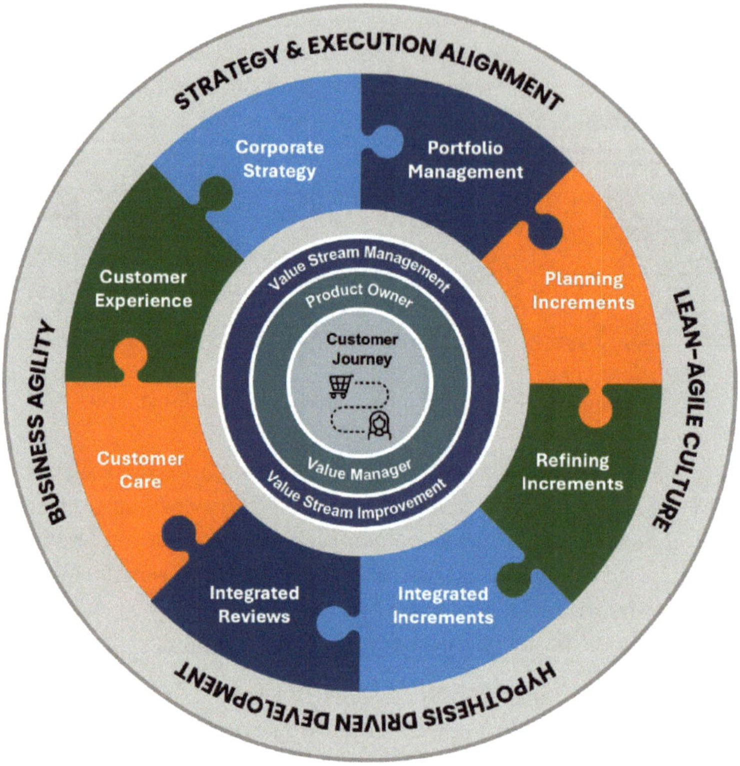

Figure 9.2 – BASE's virtuous circle for enterprise improvement

As we work our way through this section, we will begin with a brief description of the outer ring of the BASE framework representing the four tenets of BASE followed by a more in-depth discussion of each tenet. Then, we will describe the eight BASE core processes (from Portfolio Management to Corporate Strategy) and conclude with the inner BASE core (Value Stream Management, Value Stream Improvement, Product Owner and Value Manager, and the customer journey).

But before we start our review of the tenets and processes defined within the BASE conceptual model, let's first understand why we refer to this model as a Virtuous Circle for Continuous Enterprise Improvements.

Defining the virtuous circle for continuous improvement

A **virtuous circle for continuous enterprise improvements** is a self-reinforcing loop where each positive action leads to further enhancements and benefits. In this context, it means that improvements in one area of the business drive further improvements across the enterprise, creating a cycle of ongoing enhancement and value creation.

For example, an organization invests in analyzing the customer experience within its target market and in marketing to attract more customers who will value its products and services. As the customer base grows, product development budgets increase, allowing further investment in customer-centric product enhancements and related promotional and sales strategies, resulting in even higher revenue and growth. This cyclical process never stops across the life cycles of our products and services. In this example, note how we have kept the customer front and center to ensure we stay on track with our investments and work to meet their needs.

This never-ending loop results in benefits that increase the positive effect of the next item in the loop. Every core virtuous circle activity affects the ability of the value streams to deliver customer-centric value. Consequently, skipping any virtuous circle activity affects the organization's ability to deliver value through value streams that create products and services. A BASE enterprise ensures that its strategy and governance apply a Lean and Agile mindset, principles, and practices to achieve business agility. It enables the enterprise to move quickly and safely and adapt to change. The BASE is also built on two core principles.

Underlying core principles

Before further exploring the virtuous circle, it is essential to grasp two core and integrated principles that inform the BASE model: **first principles** and **systems thinking**. They offer practical insights into decision-making and problem-solving within an organization:

- **First principles**: These represent the fundamental mechanisms of the world, forming the foundation for logical reasoning and decision-making. They are discovered through careful observation and rigorous evaluation.

  In Lean-Agile practices, first principles involve focusing on delivering maximum value to the customer by eliminating waste and continuously improving processes. Ignoring first principles can lead to negative consequences, for example, inefficiencies and overlooked opportunities. Embodying a scientific mindset, first principles involve questioning assumptions, developing theories based on evidence, and testing hypotheses for validation.

- **Systems thinking**: This prompts us to consider the entire system when contemplating change, as issues often originate from the interactions and interfaces among system components, rather than from individual actions. Therefore, focusing solely on individual components or issues within a system is typically ineffective.

  Cross-team challenges frequently arise from external factors, people, and processes within our business as a solution development environment. It's crucial to foster collaboration among these elements to resolve such issues collaboratively rather than in isolation. Moreover, creating a psychologically safe space becomes more achievable when management prioritizes improving systems over attributing blame to people.

The following first principles underpin the BASE conceptual model and guide its implementation:

1. **Satisfying the needs of customers and aligning them with the organization's objectives**: Success is attained by delivering value for both parties. BASE ensures initiatives delivered across the enterprise are prioritized to deliver value as defined by customers. Ignoring this core principle jeopardizes success. Additionally, each virtuous circle activity in the BASE integrates customer feedback to inform decision-making and drive incremental improvements.
2. **Distributing work among small, collaborative teams tasked with delivering customer-centric valuable increments**: Multiple BLAST teams contribute to the BASE's value-creation activities by harmonizing efforts to develop MVPs and a series of MVIs. Information about BLAST was covered in the previous chapter.
3. **Leveraging digital technologies extends to our processes, products, and services**: Digital optimization offers unprecedented opportunities for enhancing operational efficiency, effectiveness, and competitiveness. By prioritizing digital optimization, organizations commit to exploring, adopting, and innovating digital solutions. This commitment elevates performance, delivers superior value to customers, and helps the enterprise maintain a sustainable competitive edge.

With this background in mind, let us take a high-level tour of the BASE virtuous circle and its significant processes. We will start with the four tenets of the BASE.

Understanding the four tenets of the BASE

The outer ring of the BASE diagram in *Figure 9.1* illustrates the four tenets that underpin an organization's Lean-Agile environment. They include **strategy and execution**, **Lean-Agile culture**, **hypothesis-driven development**, and **business agility**:

- Aligning execution with strategy ensures the organization remains focused on achieving its mission and vision
- Establishing a Lean-Agile culture enables the organization to manage competing production and development objectives simultaneously while maintaining operational efficiencies, gaining higher throughput, and quality to adapt and evolve in dynamic business situations
- Hypothesis-driven development using MVPs, MVIs, and MVRs establishes the cadence for producing new increments of value
- Lastly, business agility in an enterprise refers to the organization's capacity to adapt rapidly and effectively to changes in the business environment

Let's take a closer look at these four tenets.

Aligning strategy and execution

Strategy and execution alignment ensures organizational goals get translated into actionable plans, enabling efficient progress, and maintaining focus on the mission and vision. It is critical for success, to ensure employees' daily activities and decisions align with strategic goals, creating a cohesive approach to achieving business objectives.

This alignment bridges the gap between strategic planning and implementation, requiring clear communication of the company's vision, mission, and objectives at all levels. Proper alignment helps employees understand how their roles contribute to broader goals. However, many companies struggle with this, leading to wasted resources and conflicting priorities. Research indicates only a small percentage of senior executives and frontline supervisors can link initiatives to corporate priorities.

To achieve alignment, organizations should focus on clear communications so that strategy is understood at all organizational levels. Align jobs by implementing roles that support strategic objectives. Foster a culture where employees own their contributions to strategy. Regularly review and adjust strategy based on business results and market changes. Use performance management systems to track progress towards goals with systems such as **objectives and key results** (**OKRs**) and **key performance indicators** (**KPIs**).

Focusing on these areas strengthens the link between strategic intent and daily operations, improving strategy execution and enhancing employee engagement. This ongoing process positions organizations to adapt to market changes, outperform competitors, and achieve long-term objectives.

Cultivating a Lean-Agile culture

A Lean-Agile culture fosters a mindset of continuous improvement and adaptability, empowering teams to rapidly respond to change and deliver high-quality value efficiently. It represents a transformative approach to organizational management, rooted in the principles of Lean thinking and Agile methodologies. Moreover, it prioritizes customer value delivery, waste minimization, and the cultivation of a collaborative, adaptive work environment. At its core, it empowers teams through decentralized decision-making, fostering innovation and rapid experimentation.

A Lean-Agile culture is characterized by a customer-centric focus, continuously aligning efforts with customer needs and preferences. It implements iterative improvement through continuous feedback loops for incremental enhancements.

Decentralized decision-making grants teams autonomy to drive innovation and quick problem-solving. Transparency and open communication build trust and alignment across the organization. Cross-functional collaboration breaks down silos to enhance information and idea flow.

The culture favors incremental change, preferring small, frequent updates over large, risky overhauls. Leaders in a Lean-Agile culture serve as facilitators and coaches, not traditional command-and-control managers. They support team empowerment and resource provisioning while championing continuous learning and improvement. This leadership style fosters an environment where adaptability and growth become integral to the organizational DNA.

A Lean-Agile culture enhances organizational resilience and responsiveness, improving the ability to navigate complex business landscapes. It enables faster time-to-market for products and services, increases competitive advantage through continuous innovation, and ensures consistent delivery of exceptional customer value.

By embracing a Lean-Agile culture, organizations position themselves to thrive in the face of rapid market changes, evolving customer expectations, and intense competition. This approach not only streamlines operations but also cultivates a workforce that is engaged, innovative, and aligned with the company's strategic goals. In conclusion, a Lean-Agile culture represents a powerful paradigm shift in organizational thinking and practice. It equips companies with the tools and mindset necessary to excel in today's dynamic business environment, ensuring sustained growth and customer satisfaction.

Implementing hypothesis-driven development

Hypothesis-driven development (**HDD**) is a powerful approach to product development that combines scientific methodology with Agile practices. At its core, it emphasizes the importance of formulating and testing hypotheses about user needs, behaviors, and product features before committing significant resources to development. Hypothesis-driven development is a structured process where assumptions about product features or user needs are rigorously tested. It begins with identifying key assumptions and converting them into clear, measurable statements. Metrics are defined to measure success, and experiments such as prototypes or A/B tests are designed and executed to gather data. The outcomes of these experiments are analyzed to confirm or refute the initial assumptions. Based on the findings, decisions are made to either scale successful solutions or refine and retest. This iterative approach ensures continuous learning and data-driven decision-making in product development. This approach allows teams to make data-driven decisions, reduce risk, and create products that truly meet user needs.

In the context of HDD and the BASE, three key concepts play crucial roles in implementing this iterative and experimental approach:

- **Minimum viable products** (**MVPs**): MVPs are the cornerstone of many lean startup methodologies and play a vital role in HDD. An MVP represents the smallest version of a product that can effectively test core hypotheses about its value proposition. It contains just enough features to gather meaningful feedback from early adopters or potential customers. The primary goal of an MVP is to validate or invalidate key assumptions about the product's market fit, user needs, and potential success with minimal investment of time and resources. By releasing an MVP, teams can quickly learn from real-world usage and adjust their product strategy accordingly.
- **Minimum valuable increments** (**MVIs**): MVIs focus on delivering incremental value to users and support all business development requirements, spanning business processes, systems, artifacts, and enhancements to products and services. An MVI represents a small, discrete piece of functionality or improvement that provides tangible value to the user or the business.

Unlike MVPs, which are typically used at the outset of product development, MVIs are employed throughout the product's development life cycle to continuously deliver value and gather feedback. MVIs allow teams to break down larger features or improvements into smaller, manageable chunks that can be developed, tested, and potentially released more quickly.

This approach supports continuous integration and delivery practices, enabling teams to respond more rapidly to changing requirements or user feedback. Finally, MVIs can be released individually or as part of an MVR.

- **Minimum viable releases (MVRs)**: MVRs extend the iterative approach to the release level, enabling organizations to deliver tangible value while minimizing waste. An MVR represents the smallest set of features or improvements that can be packaged into a release while still providing meaningful value to users or stakeholders.

  MVRs allow teams to release more frequently, gathering feedback and validating hypotheses at regular intervals. This approach helps reduce the risk associated with large, infrequent releases and allows organizations to respond more quickly to market changes or user needs.

By incorporating these three concepts – MVPs, MVIs, and MVRs – into the hypothesis-driven development process, teams can create a highly adaptive and efficient product development cycle. This approach allows for rapid hypothesis testing and validation through MVPs, continuous delivery of value through MVIs, and regular, meaningful releases through MVRs.

This combination supports a culture of experimentation, learning, and continuous improvement. It enables teams to make data-driven decisions, reduce the risk of building features or products that don't meet user needs, and optimize resource allocation by focusing on validated high-value developments. Moreover, this approach fosters closer alignment between development efforts and business objectives. By consistently delivering value in small, measurable increments, teams can demonstrate progress more effectively to stakeholders and adjust course quickly when needed. This agility is particularly valuable in fast-moving markets or when dealing with emerging technologies where a user's needs and market conditions can change rapidly.

Figure 9.3 compares MVPs and MVI across eight areas as these concepts are sometimes confused by people who are new to these terms.

Area	Minimal Viable Products (MVPs)	Minimal Valuable Increments (MVIs)
Investment reason	Discover if a product is viable	Get a return on investment
Focus	Learning and challenging assumptions	Building, delivery, and consumption
Customer Market	Create a new product for early adopters	Extend existing product to a new market segment or improve offerings for an existing market segment
Marketing	Focused interactions with perspective clients	Market through existing channels
Team organization	Start with a dedicated Agile team	Likely requires coordination of several existing Agile teams
How to implement	Start with small features and expand	Decompose into features that only implement the scope of the MVI
Impact on existing offering	Likely little or no impact	Likely to impact with multiple existing solutions
Risks	May not have a viable product	Enhancements may not return sufficient business outcomes or may negatively affect other offerings

Figure 9.3 – Comparing MVPs and MVIs

In summary, hypothesis-driven development, supported by MVPs, MVIs, and MVRs, provides a robust model for modern product development. It combines the rigor of scientific inquiry with the flexibility of Agile methodologies, enabling organizations to innovate more effectively, reduce risk, and consistently deliver value to their users and stakeholders.

Enhancing business agility

In today's rapidly evolving business landscape, the ability to quickly respond to market shifts, customer demands, and competitive pressures is paramount. This capability, known as business agility, forms a critical tenet within the BASE and is essential for organizational success.

Put simply, we define business agility as an organization's capacity to adapt and thrive amidst uncertainty and volatility. It emphasizes flexibility across all business aspects, resilience in the face of challenges, and adaptability in strategy, operations, and customer engagement.

To cultivate business agility, organizations should implement the following key practices:

- Employ decentralized decision-making
- Leverage rapid experimentation and learning
- Focus on making customer-centric decisions

- Practice continuous improvement
- Use value stream management and mapping

These practices enable organizations to anticipate and proactively address emerging challenges and opportunities, staying ahead of the curve in an ever-changing business environment.

Embracing business agility within the BASE also enables organizations to do the following:

- Seize new opportunities quickly
- Navigate uncertainty with confidence
- Foster a culture of innovation and adaptability
- Enhance strategic alignment and improve iterative product development

These benefits position organizations not just to survive but to thrive amidst modern business complexities and challenges. As a vital tenet of the BASE, business agility also empowers organizations to respond effectively to market changes, adapt strategies and operations in real time, engage customers more dynamically, and drive continuous innovation.

In conclusion, business agility, a cornerstone of the BASE, equips organizations with the tools and mindset necessary to navigate today's evolving business environment with confidence and resilience. By adopting Lean-Agile practices and fostering a culture of adaptability, organizations can position themselves for sustained success in an increasingly complex and competitive world.

This completes our discussion on first principles, systems thinking, and the BASE's four core tenets. We will now explore the eight processes within the BASE conceptual model for coordinating work across the enterprise.

Eight BASE business processes

The BASE model outlines eight main processes that define a product delivery strategy for the enterprise to deliver new integrated increments of value in a predictable cadence. These processes can work for any type of organization, including commercial enterprises, non-profits, or government agencies. The BASE model doesn't tell you exactly what kind of work your company needs to do to delivery products and services your external customers want. It also doesn't give step-by-step instructions on how to use Lean-Agile methods to beat your competitors. That hard work belongs to you and your organizations to determine. However, the authors provide the following examples of common business processes and activities that your company might use to get ahead of others in your field:

1. Portfolio management
2. Planning increments
3. Refining increments
4. Integrated increments

5. Integrated reviews
6. Customer care
7. Customer experience
8. Corporate strategy

As you read through the sections that follow, please refer to Appendix 9.1 - Business Processes, Activities and Tasks. In that Appendix, you will find lists of common activities and tasks associated with each of the eight BASE business processes.

Corporate strategy

In the BASE model, corporate strategy encompasses processes to define and communicate the organization's vision, mission, goals, objectives, and priorities. Activities include assessing the products and services the organization can deliver, its target customers, and how the organization can uniquely and profitably deliver value.

C-Suite executives are responsible for developing and refining corporate strategy and governance policies. Chief executives establish governance policies to ensure organizational accountability, ethical conduct, and strategic alignment, fostering trust and sustainable success. Additionally, chief executives are accountable for aligning business unit activities with corporate goals and objectives and making critical business decisions. The establishment of OKRs is a key tool for this alignment.

Ideally, the executives should communicate a new set of OKRs in cadence with each BASE increment. **Objectives and Key Results (OKRs)** is a goal-setting framework used by organizations to define and track objectives and their outcomes. OKRs work by setting clear, measurable goals (Objectives) and specifying key results (Key Results) that indicate progress toward achieving those goals. Objectives are ambitious and qualitative, while Key Results are specific, quantitative, and time-bound, providing a clear metric for success.

The typical recommendation for OKRs is to set 3-5 Objectives per organizational level (e.g., company, division, department), each with 3-5 Key Results. This keeps the focus manageable and ensures that each Objective receives adequate attention. OKRs are usually set and reviewed quarterly, allowing for regular assessment and adjustment while maintaining alignment with longer-term annual goals.

In BASE, the OKR framework encourages alignment, focus, and engagement across the organization, ensuring that all value stream and functional team members work towards common, strategic objectives and can track their progress regularly.

Portfolio management

A Lean-Agile portfolio invests in six fundamental **business enablers**: *people*, *processes*, *information*, *technology*, *products*, and *infrastructure*. In BASE, the portfolio management function oversees these investments and other significant initiatives to achieve the organization's strategic objectives and maximize portfolio value. Chief and Line of Business (LoB) executives determine the funding level for each portfolio and agree on spending for investment themes developed through collaboration between senior portfolio leaders and enterprise executives. These investment themes guide how each portfolio invests in its value streams and contributes to the overall enterprise strategy.

Senior portfolio leaders use investment themes to decide funding for development value streams, prioritize strategic initiatives, allocate resources, and monitor portfolio performance. Collaborating with product management and other business owners, the portfolio identifies significant initiatives to advance from the portfolio's current state to the future state aligned with investment themes.

Business strategy, OKRs, KPIs, and feedback from MVPs, MVIs, and MVRs all serve as tools for data-driven decision-making in portfolio management. Agile teams provide feedback through quantitative metrics and qualitative information enabling collaborative decision-making at both top-down and bottom-up levels.

Portfolio Management within the BASE model encompasses a range of activities aimed at strategically allocating resources, prioritizing initiatives, and maximizing the value delivered by investments across the organization. Key activities include the following:

- Strategic investment prioritization, resource allocation, and budgeting
- Developing Investment themes in alignment with enterprise strategy and monitoring and managing portfolio performance
- Identifying and prioritizing strategic initiatives in collaboration with product management and business owners for initiative selection
- Communicating portfolio strategy, objectives and key results (OKRs, and working with local teams to align their value stream's key performance indicators (KPIs)
- Facilitating top-down and bottom-up collaboration for decision-making, including Integrating feedback from teams using BLAST to support MVPs, MVIs, and MVRs

With Portfolio management considerations accounted for, the next step in our virtuous circle is to plan new increments of value to support the evolution of the portfolio.

Planning increments

This phase entails the meticulous planning and prioritization of work across various domains, including portfolio management, product and marketing management, production, sales, distribution, services, and partner management. The value manager facilitates this process, gathering inputs from customers, stakeholders, domain experts, executives, and team members to assess priorities collaboratively.

While consensus is ideal, it's not always feasible. In such cases, the value manager makes informed decisions based on available information. The BASE model mitigates risks by establishing a consistent cadence, reducing uncertainty with each increment.

Delivering value through integrated increments is paramount in Lean-Agile enterprises, facilitated by coordinating activities through the BLAST framework and BASE conceptual model. Specifically, multiple teams across the enterprise collaborate to assemble essential components, creating integrated increments in the form of MVPs, MVIs, or MVRs to deliver successful value-based releases.

Whether improving value streams, business processes, systems, artifacts, or products and services, a business value backlog is essential in BLAST and the BASE. This backlog spans multiple functions and value streams, requiring input from customers, stakeholders, experts, and executives for prioritization.

An optimal BLAST team size ranges from three to nine individuals, ensuring effective collaboration in addressing dependencies and synchronization issues across teams. Similar considerations apply to the number of participating teams in a BLAST, which should be limited to three to nine teams to facilitate efficient cross-team communication and synchronization management among the sub-team of BLAST representatives. The specific goal of each BLAST is tailored to address specific business needs and the complexity of integrated increments required.

Each BLAST has an assigned value manager responsible for managing its Business Value Backlog and work item prioritization. In multi-BLAST scenarios, a lead value manager oversees cross-BLAST priorities, coordinating efforts with product or portfolio management to produce the desired integrated increments.

The BASE model initiates new planning increments with each cycle, with value managers orchestrating pre-cycle planning sessions. BLAST teams define tasks and activities, and resolve inter-team dependencies. Throughout each BASE cycle, traditional Lean and Agile metrics are monitored to track progress, maintain visibility and ensure timely issue resolution. Simultaneously, the lead value manager collaborates with product managers, marketing managers, and portfolio managers to plan upcoming increments.

Refining increments

The refinement of integrated increments is a continuous activity that occurs in lockstep with the planning increments process. Depending on the required granularity, an integrated increment can include MVPs, one or more MVIs, product features and functions, as well as user and technical stories. Production of an integrated increment may be supported by multiple value streams and various business domains.

Value managers lead the refinement process and work with the BLAST teams and their representatives to better understand and document requirements and acceptance criteria. We recommend the BLAST teams use traditional Agile-based user and technical stories and acceptance criteria formats for documenting the requirements.

With that recommendation made, let's take a quick look at the traditional Agile-based formats for defining epics, user stories, technical stories, and acceptance criteria.

Classically, organizations start defining requirements at a very high level in the form of an Epic. Though normally associated with Agile-based software development, the concept of Epics is easily applied to other requirements assessments, such as process, product, and service improvements.

In Agile methodologies such as Scrum and Kanban, the typical decomposition and relationship between epics, features, functions, stories, and acceptance criteria are structured as follows:

- **Epics**: These are large-scale initiatives or requirements that define broad business goals or customer needs at the outset. Epics are often called large stories, but there is no attempt to format the information beyond organizing it to maintain a logical train of thought.
- **Features and functions**: These represent distinct components or user capabilities derived from epics, focusing on specific customer-facing functionalities (features) or internal operations (functions).
- **User stories**: User stories break down features or functions into smaller, actionable units of work from an end-user perspective, detailing specific tasks that deliver business value. The traditional format is as follows:

  `As a` [*type of user*]`, I want to` [*take action/ achieve a goal or obtain objective*] `so that` [*value-based benefit or outcome*]`.`

  Let's break this down:

  - **As a [type of user]:** This part identifies who the user is. It could be a customer, an admin, a visitor, or any other relevant role.
  - **I want to [take action/achieve a goal or obtain objective]**: Here, we express what the user wants to do. It could be a specific action they need to take or a goal they want to achieve.
  - **So that [value-based benefit or outcome]**: Finally, we explain the purpose behind fulfilling this user need. What benefit or outcome will the user gain from this action?
- **Technical stories**: Technical stories are similar to user stories but focus on technical tasks or activities that are necessary to support the implementation of features or functions. They are written from a technical perspective and outline specific actions or improvements that need to be made within the system or infrastructure. The traditional format is as follows:

  `As a` [*role/persona/user type*]`, I want to` [*goal or action*] `so that` [*desired result from goal/action*]`.`

  Let's break this down:

  - **As a [role/persona/user type]**: Just like in regular user stories, we start by identifying who the user is. However, in technical stories, this user might be a developer, system administrator, or any other technical stakeholder.
  - **I want [goal or action]**: Next, we express what the technical user wants to achieve. This could be related to coding, configuration, infrastructure, deployment, or any other technical task.
  - **So that [desired result from goal/action]**: Finally, we explain the purpose behind fulfilling this technical need. What benefit or outcome will be achieved by completing this technical task?

- **Acceptance criteria**: These are specific conditions that user stories must meet to be considered complete and ready for acceptance by stakeholders, ensuring they fulfill functional and non-functional requirements. The traditional format is as follows:

  `Given: [context or precondition], When: [action or event], Then: [outcome or result]`

  Let's break this down:

  - **Given**: *This sets the context (e.g., being on the product details page with selected items)*
  - **When**: *This describes the action (e.g., clicking the "Checkout" button).*
  - **Then**: *This outlines the expected outcome (e.g., seeing the order summary)*

Fail to define acceptance criteria at your own risk. Two things are guaranteed to happen. First, you will not know the full scope of usage criteria that will impact the successful implementation of the work item. Second, your customers may find fault for not delivering a complete or working solution. Yes, in Agile, we can always put the new criteria into our business value backlog. But, from an efficiency perspective, why not try to catch these requirements in advance? Now that we know how to refine our requirements, let's look at how they progress from epics to acceptance criteria.

Progressing epics

The typical progression in defining and refining requirements moves from broader epics to more detailed features/ functions, stories, and acceptance criteria, as follows:

1. Epics are initially identified to outline major business objectives or customer needs comprehensively.
2. Features and functions are derived from epics, breaking down the broader scope into manageable components aligned with specific business goals or technical requirements.
3. User stories and technical stories are then created based on features or functions respectively, detailing the exact scenarios or tasks users need to perform to achieve desired functionality.
4. Acceptance criteria are developed concurrently with or after defining user stories, specifying measurable conditions that ensure each user story meets stakeholder expectations and functional requirements.

With this progression in mind, we can now move on to understand techniques for prioritizing the work items in our value-based backlogs.

Prioritizing business value backlogs

In this subsection, we will briefly introduce two common strategies for prioritizing the work items in your business value backlogs: **Weighted Shortest Job First** (**WSJF**) and **MoSCoW**. The WSJF approach prioritizes backlog items based on economic value and urgency, emphasizing maximizing returns and minimizing the cost of delay. In contrast, the MoSCoW method categorizes requirements into must-haves, should-haves, could-haves, and won't-haves, focusing on essential features and prioritization based on critical needs and project constraints.

We'll start with WSJF.

Weighted shortest job first (WSJF) prioritization

In *Chapter 4*, we explored how Weighted Shortest Job First (WSJF) serves as a powerful prioritization tool in Agile and Lean environments. By calculating a score based on **Cost of Delay** (**CoD**) and job duration, WSJF helps teams determine which backlog items to tackle first for maximum economic benefit. This method ensures that high-value tasks, which deliver results quickly and incur significant costs if delayed, are given precedence. WSJF aligns with Lean principles by focusing on maximizing value, disregarding sunk costs, and continuously optimizing economic decisions. It's a vital compass for organizations seeking efficient backlog management and prioritization strategies.

MoSCoW prioritization

The MoSCoW method is a prioritization technique widely used in Agile and Scrum methodologies to manage backlog items based on their importance and urgency. The acronym MoSCoW stands for *Must have, Should have, Could have,* and *Won't have (this time).* This method categorizes backlog items into the four MoSCoW categories to guide teams in determining what needs to be delivered immediately versus what can be deferred:

- **Must have**: Essential requirements that must be delivered in the current iteration to meet project objectives or satisfy key stakeholders.
- **Should have**: Important requirements that are not critical for the current iteration but should be included if possible, to enhance the value of the product.
- **Could have**: Desirable requirements that would be nice to have but are not necessary for the current delivery. These items can be considered if time and resources allow.
- **Won't have**: Items that are explicitly excluded from the current scope at this time. If desirable, but not a priority, they may be deferred to future releases or projects.

By using the MoSCoW method, Agile teams can prioritize backlog items collaboratively, ensuring alignment between business priorities and development efforts. This approach helps maximize the delivery of essential features early while maintaining flexibility to adapt to changing requirements throughout the project life cycle.

Integrated increments

We've explained previously that the concept of integrated increments helps us define the work that individual teams and BLAST teams must deliver, and that they take three forms: MVPs, MVIs, and MVRs. This BASE process is where we build, test, and deliver the integrated increments.

This is not a singular process description. For example, the marketing team delivers components of an integrated increment to promote a new product or service which is a much different set of deliverables than those created by a software development team when they build an enhancement to a software application released in the same increment. However, both of these development and operational activities need to be coordinated to support a new MVR. Additionally, there can be other MVIs going through similar integrated increment build cycles in parallel to fulfill all the requirements of the MVR.

With the process automation and integration capabilities available today – recall our CI/CD and DevOps toolchain discussions – many development activities will operate using Lean's flow principles. However, the iterative and incremental release cycle of Agile sets the cadence for increment planning, construction, reviews, and deliveries.

Before we leave this section, let's look at common business processes, activities, and tasks that may contribute to the deliverables produced in a single BASE Cycle.

Forming BLAST teams to deliver integrated increments

Recalling our discussions on how the BASE model establishes a virtuous circle for continuous business improvements, every part of an organization contributes during any given BASE cycle, as depicted in *Appendix 9.1, Table 9.1: Business Processes, Activities, and Tasks.*

In the BASE conceptual model, organizations harness BLAST Teams to effectively execute diverse processes critical to their operations and value streams. Executives may establish multiple BLASTs tailored to support various business processes across different business functions and value streams. For instance, within Corporate Strategy and Portfolio Management, dedicated BLASTs may focus on vision development, strategic planning, performance management, and risk mitigation aligned with specific value streams. Similarly, Product and Marketing Management functions can form BLASTs to manage market intelligence, strategic decision-making, product development, market introduction, and sales support activities that drive value creation across their respective value streams.

The primary objective of these BLAST Teams within the BASE model is to deliver integrated increments of value, presented as MVPs, MVIs, and MVRs, within a single BASE cycle (i.e., one loop of its Virtuous Circle). Some MVIs may be released independently, while others contribute to larger MVRs. The flexibility of the BASE model allows organizations to adjust the number of integrated increments released per cycle based on their size and complexity. Larger organizations typically require multiple BLAST Teams to effectively manage and synchronize these processes, ensuring continuous improvement and alignment with customer-centric goals.

Ultimately, your organization must define the business processes, activities, and tasks necessary to support delivering a new increment of value. It will determine the optimal setup of BLAST teams to support these deliveries in the form of integrated increments. Finally, your organization will decide how and when to release each component of value during each BASE Cycle through its MVPs, MVIs, and MVRs.

As each integrated increment is constructed, it undergoes review for quality and completeness. These activities are detailed in the next core process, Integrated Reviews.

Integrated reviews

Integrated increments from various BLAST teams require synchronization to support a new release. This core BASE process stages the sequencing of integrated increments before their release—for example, coordinating marketing promotions and sales training ahead of product sales and distribution.

SMEs, customers, and stakeholders must review these increments at this stage. They assess whether the integrated increment's goals, user stories, technical requirements, and acceptance criteria have been met.

Any issues identified are processed through the *feedback and pivot* branch of the BLAST Framework. Defects or errors are returned to the *business value backlog* for refinement and prioritization. If urgent and feasible within the current BASE cycle, they are promptly addressed; otherwise, they are scheduled for a future BASE cycle.

At this stage, integrated increments that have been successfully reviewed and deemed ready for release are deployed in proper synchronization with other integrated increments or on demand as needed. Once accepted, the deployed products and services for both internal and external customers must be supported, a topic covered in the next section on customer care.

Customer care

Effective **customer care** is a critical process group within the BASE Model, ensuring that businesses can consistently meet customer needs and expectations across diverse product types and industries. Implementing an exemplary customer support program involves several key practices:

1. **Customer-Centric Approach:** Make it a priority to understand and anticipate customer needs and to provide proactive support and personalized experiences.
2. **Multi-Channel Support:** Offer support across various channels (e.g., phone, email, chat, social media) to accommodate diverse customer preferences and ensure accessibility.
3. **Timely and Responsive Service:** Implement quick response times and resolution to customer inquiries and issues, aiming for high customer satisfaction and retention.
4. **Knowledge Management:** Maintain a centralized knowledge base to empower support agents with accurate information and solutions, ensuring consistency in service delivery.
5. **Continuous Improvement:** Regularly gather customer feedback to identify areas for improvement, iterate on support processes, and enhance overall service quality.
6. **Training and Development:** Invest in training programs to equip support teams with the skills and knowledge needed to handle customer interactions effectively and empathetically.
7. **Integration with Product Development:** Foster collaboration between customer support and product development teams to address recurring issues, prioritize feature requests, and enhance product usability.
8. **Metrics and Analytics**: Utilize metrics such as customer satisfaction scores, response times, and resolution rates to measure performance and drive continuous service improvements.

By incorporating these practices into the BASE Model's Customer Care process, businesses can build strong customer relationships, improve retention rates, and differentiate themselves in competitive markets. Additionally, each product or service release affects the ability to deliver effective customer care processes, necessitating ongoing investments and process improvements to maintain effective customer support capabilities. Next up in our BASE process group is measuring customer experience (CX) and acting on our findings.

Customer experience

Customer experience (CX) embodies the philosophy of prioritizing and enhancing the satisfaction, delight, and loyalty of customers throughout their interactions with a business or brand. This emphasizes flexibility, rapid iteration, and customer feedback to optimize the consumer experience across all touchpoints. By adopting Lean-Agile principles, organizations aim to respond more to customer needs and market changes, enhancing customer satisfaction and loyalty.

Lean-Agile CX in the BASE model requires breaking down large, complex customer experience initiatives into smaller chunks that can fit within a BASE Iteration. During these BASE cadences, cross-functional teams work collaboratively to evaluate changes in the customer experience. These changes could be anything from refining the user interface on a website to streamlining the customer service process. After each iteration, the team reviews the outcomes and gathers feedback from stakeholders, including real customers, to inform the next cycle of product or service improvements. This iterative cycle helps ensure the organization continuously adapts and evolves its strategies to meet customer expectations effectively.

The following five key CX activities are common in many organizations:

1. Conducting customer journey mapping to understand and improve the end-to-end customer experience.
2. Implementing **user interface** (UI)/ **user experience** (UX) design principles to enhance the interactions, usability and accessibility of products and services.
3. Optimizing customer service processes and channels to provide timely and effective support.
4. Personalizing marketing and communication strategies to better resonate with individual customer needs and preferences.
5. Monitoring and analyzing key metrics related to customer satisfaction, loyalty, and retention.

Some organizations may add these additional activities to enhance their customer experience initiatives:

- Continuously iterate and improve CX initiatives based on insights gained from data analysis and customer feedback
- Collaborate cross-functionally to align CX efforts with organizational goals and strategies

- Implement technology solutions such as **customer relationship management** (**CRM**) systems and data analytics tools to enhance CX capabilities
- Train and empower employees to deliver exceptional customer experiences at every touchpoint

These activities are essential for organizations aiming to create positive and memorable experiences for their customers across various interactions and touchpoints. Moreover, Lean-Agile CX fosters a culture of ongoing learning and adaptability. By constantly testing new ideas and gathering feedback through MVPs, MVIs, and MVRs, companies can quickly learn what works and what doesn't, greatly reducing risk. This approach helps refine product offerings and enhances overall service delivery, making companies more competitive and customer centric.

This completes our discussions on the eight core BASE business processes. Now, we are going to move to the core of the BASE conceptual model, which is all about putting our customers first.

Establishing customer-centric foundations

Both Lean and Agile practitioners have stressed the importance of delivering customer-centric value. Therefore, a Lean-Agile conceptual model such as the BASE must similarly place the customer at the center of everything we do.

Figure 9.4, the core of the BASE, provides a graphical perspective of these concepts. The BASE intentionally puts improvements to the customer journey at the center of our enterprise improvement activities. We also show the criticality of having Value Managers and Product Owners orchestrating those efforts.

Figure 9.4 – The core of the BASE conceptual model

To further emphasize the importance of coordinating work to support customers' views on value, the *Value Manager* represents the customer's voice in BASE, signifying their role in overseeing improvements across value streams and products and fostering effective team communication.

While the *Product Owner* role remains a viable option to apply in BASE, we caution against splitting functions between the two roles due to potential conflicts of interest, such as those between value stream improvements and product enhancements. However, if you opt for the title Product Owner, ensure that the individual in this role oversees all aspects of value creation.

Value Stream Management activities are central to the BASE model. In any organization, it's common to face an abundance of tasks and conflicting priorities, which can overwhelm resources and lead to ineffective management. Without a holistic view or prioritization system, this often results in firefighting, conflicts, and unmet expectations.

VSM methods and tools play a crucial role in this context by enabling rigorous evaluation of the most impactful changes to enhance productivity and efficiency across the organization. By taking a systemic view of product delivery activities, VSM ensures that resources are allocated optimally and that each iteration of the BASE cycle benefits from enhanced efficiency, productivity, and adaptability.

Now, let's move on to the last section of this chapter, where we discuss the importance of taking a life cycle view to product development.

Delivering value across the product life cycle

The BASE model embodies the essence of guiding organizations through the complexities of modern business landscapes by emphasizing value delivery across product life cycles. As we delve into practical applications of foundational theories, we explore the intricate processes that form the virtuous circle of BASE. This exploration provides a holistic view of how organizations systematically create, deliver, and enhance value throughout a product's entire lifespan.

At its core, the BASE model is designed to foster a culture of innovation, customer-centricity, and continuous improvement. It offers organizations a structured approach to aligning operations and customer engagement with business strategies, maximizing value creation, and sustaining competitive advantage. BASE stands out for its commitment to leveraging common sense and well-understood business practices avoiding the creation of unnecessary roles or imposition of counterintuitive business activities. While Lean and Agile practices may still be emerging or not fully mature in many organizations, their underlying concepts are proven and robust.

This section dissects the interplay between strategic decision-making, customer insights, and operational excellence. Understanding these elements' convergence enables organizations to develop robust, customer-oriented strategies that drive value creation across every stage of the product life cycle.

From ideation through delivery and beyond, each phase of the product life cycle presents distinct challenges and opportunities. The BASE model equips organizations with principles and practices to navigate these complexities with agility and precision. Readers will gain actionable insights and practical strategies to optimize value creation across product life cycles, positioning themselves for long-term success in today's dynamic business landscape.

Leveraging customer centricity for strategic growth

At the heart of the BASE's customer-centric approach lies the recognition that customer satisfaction and loyalty are pivotal to organizational success. While, theoretically, any core process can serve as an entry point into the BASE model, for this discussion, we begin with Customer Care, which serves as the gateway to successful customer engagements in the BASE model. This function acts as the frontline of interaction between the organization and its customers.

Enhancing customer engagement in the BASE

In a Lean-Agile organization, the commitment to customer centricity is not just a philosophy but a guiding principle that informs every facet of operations. Customer Care, as the front line of customer interaction, extends far beyond mere post-purchase services. It involves a comprehensive suite of activities to ensure ongoing customer satisfaction and loyalty. These activities include providing timely support and assistance, actively soliciting feedback, addressing customer concerns, and identifying opportunities for product or service improvement. Organizations can cultivate strong relationships and foster long-term loyalty by maintaining open lines of communication and demonstrating a genuine commitment to meeting customer needs.

Supporting customer engagements in the BASE

Running through the cycle, customer care encompasses a spectrum of activities, including delivery, support, maintenance, and repair, all aimed at surpassing customer expectations. By actively engaging with customers post-purchase, organizations gain valuable feedback, identify pain points, and stay informed about emerging trends and customer aspirations.

Building upon the foundation of customer care is the customer experience process, which extends beyond basic service provision to proactively engage with customers and understand their holistic experience with the organization's products and services. This involves various initiatives such as outreach programs, reward schemes, and conversational AI technologies designed to capture insights into customer preferences, satisfaction levels, and areas for improvement. Additionally, activities such as customer journey mapping provide a structured approach to understanding the end-to-end customer experience, enabling organizations to identify moments of delight, frustration, and opportunities for optimization.

Corporate strategy integrates insights from customer care and customer experience to shape the organization's future direction. This strategic process involves critical decisions about product extensions, service enhancements, and market expansion initiatives. By aligning corporate strategy with customer needs and preferences, organizations can ensure that their investments and initiatives are strategically aligned to maximize customer value and drive sustainable growth with each delivery cycle.

Beyond CX, customer care, and strategy, the remaining core processes in the BASE model focus on building and delivering integrated increments. The scope of work is dependent upon a myriad of business factors that must be addressed. As the improvement opportunities are identified, the value managers collaborate with BLAST teams, stakeholders, SMEs, and functional area leads to prioritize current initiatives.

Leveraging customer centricity for strategic growth within the BASE necessitates a deep understanding of customer needs, preferences, and behaviors. By prioritizing customer insights and integrating them into strategic decision-making processes, organizations can build competitive advantages, foster customer loyalty, and achieve long-term success in today's dynamic business landscape.

In the next subsection, we delve into the operational aspects of customer engagement within the BASE model. From post-purchase interactions to proactive outreach initiatives, we explore how organizations cultivate meaningful connections with their customers.

Continuously improving value delivery

Value streams play a pivotal role in the BASE, serving as the fundamental path through which value is conceptualized, created, and delivered to customers. These streams encompass interconnected activities and processes spanning the entire product development life cycle, from ideation to delivery and support.

Maintaining a product focus

In larger organizations, operational, development, and support value streams can expand into the hundreds, if not thousands, each with its own set of activities. However, under the BASE model, our goal is simplification. Therefore, we concentrate each BASE cycle on enhancing a product-oriented value stream that delivers a specific type of product or service to our external customers.

In essence, don't lose sight of the big picture. Maintain focus on a product or service that requires improvements. During initial planning, keep your BASE processes defined at a high level, allowing your BLAST teams to delve into the details of how to enhance value delivery. If your organization encompasses multiple product lines—distinguished not merely by variations in make or model but by genuinely different products or services—each should undergo a dedicated BASE cycle to drive improvements in processes, products, and related services.

Indeed, larger organizations may run multiple BASE cycles concurrently by product line. This strategy simplifies and maintains focus on individual product line requirements. Otherwise, consider the challenges involved in making business process, system, product, and service improvements across multiple products—that's far from simple.

By managing and optimizing these product-oriented value streams, organizations can streamline operations, accelerate time-to-market, and gain a competitive edge in today's fast-paced business environment.

Eliminating waste in order of customer impact

One crucial aspect of optimizing value streams is identifying and eliminating waste wherever possible. This process includes conducting thorough value stream mapping exercises to pinpoint inefficiencies, bottlenecks, and areas of redundancy within the workflow.

At times, quality or cost issues may drive decisions on improvement priorities. But often, your constraints will lead you to your most impactful improvement opportunities. Recall our discussions on local optimization. Addressing a waste that is not hindering throughput may have little or no impact when it's not constraining your value stream flows.

Figure 9.5 provides a useful analogy: imagine the owners of this high-performance green Lamborghini. They've invested significantly in this fast car, yet their speed is limited by the traffic around them. Any attempt to push beyond that limit risks undesirable consequences. Put another way, their money is wasted until the bottlenecks and delays constraining it are eliminated.

Figure 9.5 – Stuck in traffic

Organizations can reduce cycle times, improve productivity, and enhance overall operational efficiency by streamlining processes, reducing unnecessary handoffs, and minimizing wait times. This allows organizations to deliver value to customers more quickly, reduces costs, and maximizes resource utilization.

Using metrics to guide decision-making

Effective value stream management involves continuously monitoring and measuring key performance metrics to track progress and identify areas for improvement. By establishing clear performance benchmarks and metrics, organizations can evaluate the effectiveness of their value streams and make data-driven decisions to optimize performance and enhance value delivery. This iterative approach to value stream management enables organizations to adapt and evolve in response to changing market dynamics, customer needs, and business requirements, ensuring that they remain agile and responsive in a rapidly evolving business landscape.

Furthermore, optimizing value streams requires a collaborative and cross-functional approach involving stakeholders across the organization. By breaking down silos and fostering collaboration between different departments and teams, organizations can streamline communication, improve coordination, and enhance alignment toward common goals. This collaborative approach accelerates value delivery and fosters a culture of continuous improvement and innovation, where employees are empowered to identify and implement process improvements to drive organizational success.

Optimizing value streams is essential for organizations seeking to drive sustainable growth and competitive advantage in today's dynamic business environment. By streamlining operations, reducing waste, and fostering collaboration, organizations can enhance their ability to deliver value to customers efficiently and effectively, positioning themselves for long-term success and resilience in the marketplace.

Next up, we delve into our concluding subsection on implementing continuous improvements. There, we will focus on the pivotal role of Value Managers, the adoption of the BLAST framework, and the importance of continuous feedback loops in fostering innovation within the BASE.

Implementing continuous improvement

In the BASE model, driving continuous improvement is a fundamental principle that underpins the organization's ability to adapt, innovate, and thrive in a rapidly changing business landscape. At its core are Value Managers, pivotal in orchestrating work to ensure that value delivery aligns with organizational goals and customer needs.

Value Managers oversee value stream activities, facilitate cross-functional collaboration, and optimize processes to enhance efficiency and effectiveness. They collaborate closely with value stream teams to define objectives, establish performance metrics, and identify improvement opportunities. By providing guidance, support, and resources, Value Managers empower teams to deliver high-quality MVPs and MVIs that meet customer expectations and drive business outcomes.

Lean-Agile teams within the organization leverage the BLAST framework to efficiently deliver new integrated increments. This framework incorporates Lean's flow-oriented processes and Agile's iterative and incremental development model, enabling teams to streamline workflows, accelerate value delivery, and maintain focus on improving customer value.

Continuous feedback and iterative learning are also critical within BASE. Lean-Agile teams regularly solicit feedback from customers, stakeholders, and end users to gather insights, identify improvement opportunities, and validate assumptions. This feedback loop enables teams to iterate on products and processes, refine strategies, and deliver value more effectively over time.

By embracing a culture of experimentation, innovation, and continuous learning, organizations foster a dynamic and adaptive environment where continuous improvement becomes ingrained in the organization's DNA.

Ultimately, driving continuous improvement in the BASE model goes beyond optimizing processes or delivering better products; it cultivates a mindset of continuous learning, adaptation, and innovation. Empowering Value Managers, leveraging the BLAST framework, and embracing continuous feedback and learning position organizations for long-term success and sustainable growth.

This concludes *Chapter 9*. In *Part 4, Driving Sustainable Transformation*, we will explore actionable strategies for sustained digital transformation, simplifying complexity, evolving gradually, and implementing tangible change. But first, let's recap.

Summary

In *Chapter 9*, you delved into the intricacies of the Business Agility System for the Enterprise, also known as the BASE conceptual model (or simply BASE). The chapter unpacked the pivotal concept of the product life cycle, illustrating the dynamism inherent in consistently delivering customer value. You've been introduced to the virtuous circle, a central element representing a continuous, self-reinforcing loop to drive improvements. By exploring the BASE model, you've learned its customer-centric foundations, the importance of aligning portfolio investments with overarching strategies, and how value is delivered throughout a product's life.

The insights from this chapter are paramount as they equip you with a comprehensive understanding of how an enterprise can be Agile, responsive, and always customer-centric. Mastering the BASE empowers you to synchronize multiple teams, ensuring smooth product development and delivery. By internalizing the principles of collaboration, strategy alignment, and customer focus, you can guide your organization toward sustained success and ensure that it remains attuned to the ever-evolving needs of the market and its customers.

In *Part 4, Driving Sustainable Transformation*, we introduce Lean-Agile executive-level strategies.

Appendix 9.1 - Business Processes, Activities, and Tasks

Process	Activities	Tasks
Corporate Strategy	Vision development	Defining mission, goals, and cultural values
	Strategic planning	SWOT analysis, strategy formulation, and resource allocation
	Performance management	Balanced scorecard, KPIs, and continuous monitoring
	Risk Management	Risk assessment, mitigation strategies, and crisis management
	Change management	Change planning, communication, training, and support
Portfolio Management	Portfolio strategy	Strategic alignment, goal setting, prioritization, and flexibility
	Project selection	Criteria development, benefits analysis, feasibility studies, and approval processes
	Resource allocation	Capacity planning, optimal allocation, balancing demand and supply, and monitoring utilization
	Performance monitoring	KPIs, regular reviews, dashboards and reporting, and continuous improvement
	Risk management	Risk identification, assessment, mitigation strategies, and contingency planning

Process	Activities	Tasks
Product and Marketing Management	Market intelligence	Customer insights, validation, competitive analysis, and financial assessments
	Strategic decision	Identify target markets, product strategies, buy/build/partner decisions, pricing and packaging, and business model alignment
	Product development	Personas and scenarios, requirements management, UX design, portfolio management, and product roadmaps
	Market introduction	Product positioning, routes to market, marketing strategies, launch plans, and customer acquisition
	Sales support	Marketing collaterals, lead generation, sales training, thought leadership, and customer relationship management
Sales	Lead generation	Market research, prospecting, and lead qualification
	Customer outreach	Cold calling, email campaigns, and social selling
	Sales negotiation	Value proposition, handling objections, and pricing strategy
	Closing sales	Sales presentations, proposal development, and contract negotiation
	Account management	Customer onboarding, relationship building, upselling, and cross-selling
Legal	Compliance	Regulatory compliance, policy development, and training and awareness
	Contract management	Drafting contracts, negotiation, and review and approval
	Risk mitigation	Risk assessment, management plans, and monitoring and reporting
	Litigation support	Case management, evidence collection, and legal research
	Intellectual property protection	IP strategy, patent filing, and trademark protection

Process	Activities	Tasks
Human Resources	Talent acquisition	Job analysis, recruitment, and selection
	Employee development	Training programs, career pathing, and leadership development
	Performance management	Goal setting, appraisals, feedback, and coaching
	Compensation and benefits	Salary structure, benefits administration, and incentive programs
	Employee relations	Conflict resolution, employee engagement, and compliance
Product Support	Customer support	Helpdesk, ticket management, and customer feedback
	Technical assistance	Technical support, remote support, and on-site support
	Knowledge management	Knowledge base, documentation, and training resources
	Issue resolution	Root cause analysis, problem-solving, and escalation management
	Continuous improvement	Process improvement, performance metrics, and customer satisfaction
Customer Experience	Customer feedback	Collecting, analyzing, and acting on feedback
	Customer journey mapping	Visualizing journeys, identifying touchpoints, and recognizing pain points
	Service design	Customer-centric approach, prototyping and testing, and iterative design
	Customer support	Responsive assistance, multichannel support, and knowledge management
	Customer engagement	Building relationships, personalization, loyalty programs, and community building

Questions

This section is for those readers who want to evaluate comprehension and retention of the information provided in this chapter. There are three questions. The answers are provided in the following section. Recalling the exact verbiage of the original content is not important. Rather, it's more important that you can recall the concepts and their applications. The questions are as follows:

1. What are the four tenets that form the foundation of the BASE, as illustrated in *Figure 9.1 – Base Product Development*?
2. What role does the OKR framework play in the BASE model's approach to corporate strategy?
3. How does the BASE model facilitate customer-centricity and continuous improvement throughout the product life cycle?

Answers

1. The four tenets of the BASE model are strategy and execution, Lean-Agile culture, hypothesis-driven development, and business agility.
2. The role of the OKR framework in the BASE model serves to align business unit activities with corporate goals and objectives. It helps define and track clear, measurable objectives and their key results, ensuring focus, alignment, and engagement across the organization.
3. The BASE model facilitates customer-centricity and continuous improvement throughout the product life cycle by emphasizing continuous value delivery. It starts with customer care as a pivotal entry point, ensuring ongoing customer satisfaction through proactive engagement, feedback incorporation, and product/service enhancement initiatives.

Further reading

1. `https://scaledagileframework.com/business-agility/`

Part 4: Driving Sustainable Transformation: Strategies to Achieve Lean-Agile Mastery

Welcome to the final section of our book. Throughout the preceding chapters, we've explored a diverse range of principles, practices, and frameworks related to Lean-Agile methodologies and value stream management. If you're feeling a bit overwhelmed by the breadth of information covered so far, fear not. In this section, we bring everything together into actionable strategies.

In this section, our aim is to distill the knowledge you've acquired into actionable strategies for implementing and sustaining Lean-Agile transformations with digital enhancements. These strategies are crafted to facilitate easier adoption and cultivate habits that support ongoing improvement. We'll emphasize the importance of gradual evolution over abrupt changes, while ensuring alignment with business objectives, strategies, and customer needs.

Consider this last segment of our book as a practical toolkit for translating theoretical knowledge into tangible implementation approaches. Our focus is on constructing a versatile business methodology that seamlessly adapts to the dynamic demands of modern enterprises, spanning commercial industries, non-profits, and government agencies. Our ultimate goal is to establish sustainable practices for continuous business transformation.

Chapter 10 serves as the gateway to this section, introducing methods to enhance decision-making within Lean-Agile organizations. You'll be introduced to BRIA and QIDA concepts, which help define critical business questions to extract actionable insights from data. This underscores the vital role of information as the lifeblood of organizational adaptability, highlighting the significance of effective management in driving enhancements across all operational domains.

Moving on to *Chapter 11*, we transition from theory to practice, providing a pragmatic roadmap for implementing Lean-Agile and VSM strategies that facilitate continuous organizational transformations.

Finally, *Chapter 12* offers a comprehensive recap of the preceding chapters before delving into five cross-cutting themes that provide coherence and continuity to our discussion of Lean-Agile mastery. We conclude with three real-world reference stories showcasing successful applications of Lean-Agile and VSM concepts presented in this book.

Part 4 is not merely about absorbing information; it's about taking decisive action, driving evolution, and fostering leadership to support change. This section equips leaders and teams with a Lean-Agile mindset to ensure their organizations can make a lasting and positive impact in the digital era. Within these pages lies a roadmap for those ready to innovate, streamline operations, and lead—your journey awaits.

Chapters within *Part 4* are as follows:

- *Chapter 10, Enhancing Decision-Making in the Lean-Agile Organization*
- *Chapter 11, Implementing Strategies for Organizational Transformation*
- *Chapter 12, Building Lean-Agile and VSM Mastery*

10

Enhancing Decision-Making in the Lean-Agile Organization

"In today's data-driven world, success belongs to those who can transform information into insights, and insights into action."

- Satya Nadella, CEO of Microsoft

Our digital age, with its vast oceans of data teeming with swirling currents of information, presents a challenging business voyage. Metaphorically, navigating these waters is about seizing opportunities and avoiding perils. Do we know our market position amid these vast expanses? Are we equipped with the right information to guide our destination? If not, what data is needed to make the proper course corrections?

In this chapter, we provide a map for a crucial journey toward organizational success, experienced differently by executives and employees. Executives operate at a strategic level, setting the course to guide the organization's direction through competitive seas. Meanwhile, employees operate at a tactical level, managing daily operations to keep all systems functioning smoothly and efficiently. Both perspectives are essential, ensuring that every aspect of the organization's value streams works together toward achieving corporate goals.

However, organizations face a unique paradox: while data is abundant, they often struggle to find the right data on demand to uncover actionable insights. The proliferation of data often obscures the insights needed to make timely and informed course adjustments. This chapter addresses this challenge by guiding you through methods to distill vast data into actionable, relevant information.

By the end of the chapter, you'll possess strategies to convert raw data into tangible insights that steer decisions, shaping the efficiency and trajectory of your organization's value streams.

In this chapter, you'll learn how these practices work together to deliver customer-centric value. The topics covered include the following:

- Understanding data's true potential
- Organizing business objectives with BRIA
- Facilitating informed decision-making through QIDA
- Conducting BRIA workshops for strategic alignment
- Leveraging AI-based tools to support BRIA workshops

Technical requirements

You do not need expertise in data management to grasp the concepts discussed in this chapter and to understand their role in specifying data and information requirements. However, **Database Management System** (**DBMS**) specialists are essential to implement these concepts within your organization's business systems. DBMS specialists can look at the *Further reading* section at the end of the chapter for relevant books on data management from Packt. Finally, those who want to dive more deeply into the BRIA/QIDA concepts covered in this chapter should read the book *Climbing the Ladder of Business Intelligence* by James E. Cates, Sam S. Gill, and Natalie Zeituny.[1]

Understanding data's true potential

Navigating today's vast oceans of data can be overwhelming, whether you're an IT expert charting the depths or a senior operational leader merely skimming the surface. In today's data-rich world, IT leaders, practitioners, and those outside the tech domain face a shared challenge: knowing where to find the information they need when we need it most.

Whether you're an information consumer or producer, you must understand how to distinguish the nuances between facts, data, and information. Recognizing the power of asking the right questions to sift through data to unearth high-value insights effectively becomes paramount. Grasping these principles equips you to collaboratively ensure that business strategies are data-informed, empowering you to contribute more significantly to your organization's success.

As you progress through this chapter, you'll grasp the dilemma: too much data can slow decision-making, while too little reduces the ability to make informed decisions. You'll learn to curate and refine data by aligning it closely with specific business objectives and by focusing on asking the right questions—emphasizing quality over quantity through the following approaches:

- **Business Role Intelligence Analysis** (**BRIA**) process
- **Question, Information, Decision, Action** (**QIDA**) concept.

So, let's start this understanding by looking at current statistics highlighting this challenge's scope.

Addressing Data challenges and opportunities

In our digital age, our world is inundated with a seemingly endless stream of data. From clicks on a web page to real-time analytics spanning business and financial transactions, every second gives birth to vast amounts of data. This presents both an opportunity and a challenge: with such immense volumes of data at our fingertips, how do we unlock its true potential?

Zippia's recent report reveals some thought-provoking insights:[2]

- A staggering 2.5 quintillion bytes of data are produced daily
- Yet, companies only harness and analyze 37–40% of their data
- Despite 97.2% of businesses heavily investing in big data and AI, an alarming 60–73% of data remains untouched and unanalyzed

These statistics underscore a paradox: there's an overflow of data but a significant shortfall in its meaningful use. The vast seas of data remain largely uncharted for most organizations, concealing valuable insights beneath their depths. So, it should be obvious we need to start figuring out how to discover and use this data most effectively.

Charting a course for data utilization

At its core, data's true potential is not in its volume but in its applicability. More explicitly, it's about knowing which questions are pivotal to your organization's success, and what data is necessary to answer those questions. Where can you locate the data? And how can you transform raw data into actionable insights that propel decision-making? Let's break this process down into three parts:

1. **Refining data**: Suppose your data was oil. The number of oil barrels is less important than the refining process's quality and efficiency, which enable the oil to be converted into something of value, such as gasoline, diesel, or asphalt, and then distributed to customers.
2. **Asking the right questions**: Every strategic initiative should begin with the right questions. What do you need to know? These questions act as the compass pointing toward the data that matters.
3. **Knowledge management**: Once you've identified the right questions, you must know where to find the answers. This involves diving into databases, discerning patterns, and distinguishing between relevant, irrelevant, and redundant data.

Completing this journey from question to actionable insight is the essence of realizing data's true potential. Organizations that stand out in this ever-evolving digital landscape will master this navigational skill, converting vast data into information that informs our business decisions and allows us to take appropriate actions. By continually refining the process, prioritizing the right questions, and effectively harnessing data, businesses can chart a course to their strategic objectives, ensuring that every decision is grounded in the most relevant, actionable insights.

As you move forward, remember that data is your ally – a tool that, when used aptly, can forge the path to sustained growth and innovation. So, now, let's move on to understand how we transform raw data into actionable insights.

Transforming data into insights

Capturing and assessing data is merely the initial step in a larger journey. The real mastery emerges in its transformation – specifically, converting raw data into information-rich insights. Through a combination of analytical tools, methodologies, and, at times, intuitive judgment, one can sculpt this raw material into actionable insights, unlocking the profound potential that data holds for guiding decisions and crafting strategies.

This chapter invites you to see beyond the overwhelming expanse of data and focus on its essence. This means distinguishing between data that adds value versus data that overwhelms without a positive effect. For the aspiring professionals, it's about ensuring that organizational strategies tap into the heart of data, extracting insights that align with and drive business objectives.

Understanding and harnessing the true potential of data is more than professional competency; it's a game-changer. However, capturing and assessing data is merely the initial step in a more comprehensive journey. Transforming raw data into insights is achieved through a blend of analytical tools, methodologies, and, at times, intuitive judgment.

The concept of BRIA paves the way in the realm of business intelligence as a moniker for how we define information needs. The BRIA concept is simple. Data requirements are defined by the type of business or business domain in which we work and by our roles and responsibilities. Therefore, the business and roles affect the type of information we need to take appropriate and timely actions.

As you make your way through this chapter, please refer to Figure 10.1, The BRIA Process. This roadmap will help your organization navigate the boundless oceans of data to uncover the insights needed to make informed, near real-time decisions and take more effective actions.

The BRIA Process	
1	Identify value streams and their core processes.
2	Identify key roles and decide which of these need the RIA.
3	Define the business role responsibilities.
4	Address the key business questions that the business role needs to be answered to be successful.
5	Identify the information required to answer those questions.
6	Identify quality data sources needed to generate the information to answer the questions.
7	Evaluate the time-frequency. How often does the business rule need the information to be successful?
8	Decide how the information will be displayed (for example, table, chart).
9	Decide where the information will be displayed (for example, mobile app, email, online report)
10	Identify the core processes that support the RIA/QIDA assessments.
11	Determine any additional business roles involved.
12	Document their RIA/QIDA needs. The goal is to ensure that when they have a critical question that must be answered, the information required to make an informed decision and take appropriate action is available on demand.
13	Climb the Ladder of Business Intelligence (LOB) to create an intelligent business.

Figure 10.1 – The BRIA process

But BRIA is only part of an effective data management strategy. Its refined and subsequently extended counterpart, QIDA, takes BRIA a step further as we come to understand that it's the questions we need to be able to answer that drive the decisions and actions we need to take. Also, we cannot forget that data requirements change by roles and responsibilities. So, together, the combined insights of BRIA and QIDA are implemented through the intelligent business model via BRIDAI tables and workshops. **BRIDAI** is the acronym for **Business, Role, Information, Decision, Action, Impact**. This acronym spells out the columns in the BRIDAI tables, shown later in Figure 10.2 - BRIDAI Table Elements and in the examples included in this chapter's Appendix.

As we delve deeper into this chapter, we will unpack and explore these interconnected processes and their profound implications for modern businesses. We'll start by defining the concepts behind BRIA.

Organizing business objectives

Navigating the dynamic business landscape, you'll often find the need to align organizational endeavors with data-driven insights relevant to the role of the individual or organization. This section introduces the BRIA framework, a tailored approach designed to seamlessly connect your role's tasks with the broader business objectives.

Specifically, we'll focus on the structure and application of BRIA emphasizing how this methodology guides organizations to align their information needs with overarching business objectives. This alignment applies whether you operate in the C-Suite, in a managerial capacity, or directly within a value stream.

By embracing these insights, you'll grasp not just the theoretical aspects but also the hands-on utility of the BRIA-based executive and value stream workshops. As you integrate these learnings, you'll be better poised to shape and influence business strategies with clarity and confidence, ensuring that every step you take is rooted in data-centric wisdom.

In the next subsection, we will describe the BRIA process, outlined in *Figure 10.1* and originally described in the book *Climbing the Ladder of Business Intelligence* by James E. Cates, Sam S. Gill, and Natalie Zeituny.[1]

Creating intelligent businesses

The essence of creating an *intelligent business* lies in its ability to ask – and, more importantly – answer intelligent questions. In other words, we apply critical thinking and inquiry in the context of business intelligence to answer the organization's most challenging questions. Specifically, we implement a systematic approach to transform data into actionable insights. These insights are also tailored to specific roles within an organization. This ensures that every decision-maker has the precise information they need. This intelligent business journey, known as BRIA, unfolds as follows:

Starting at the top of the list shown in *Figure 10.1*, we pinpoint the organization's core processes and value streams. These are the essential operations that keep the business running, forming the backbone of every other action and decision. Once these processes are crystal clear, the focus shifts to the key players – the roles that execute the information requests. Not all roles need an in-depth analysis, so it's vital to discern which ones do – or at least start your BRIA assessments with the highest priority business domains and roles that have the most impact in decision making in your Lean-Agile organization.

As always, at the value steam level, prioritize based on eliminating your constraints, lowering costs and improving quality. In contrast, sales and marketing will focus on identifying the right customers, their needs, and their journeys. And chief and LOB executives will prioritize the information they need to build and drive their strategies while ensuring compliance with legal and financial constraints.

Upon identifying these pivotal roles, they're clearly defined by name and organization - for example, John in accounting, Mary in customer support, or Jose in fulfillment. But merely naming a role and business function isn't enough. To truly empower each role, uncovering the burning questions they need answered to succeed in their responsibilities is essential. In other words, what do they need to know daily? What information can drive their decision-making to the next level?

These questions lead to the next phase: discerning the exact information to provide those answers. To get that information, you need reliable, high-quality data sources. Identifying these sources ensures that the derived information is accurate and relevant. Data often needs to be combined or changed to become useful information. This process, called data transformation, involves cleaning, checking, and preparing the data for different uses.

Yet, the quest doesn't end at merely sourcing the right data. It's equally crucial to understand the role's scope of responsibilities. How frequently do they need this information? Is it a daily lookup or dashboard glance, a weekly report, or a monthly analysis?

Then comes the mode of presentation. In our technologically driven era, the medium can often influence the effectiveness of the message. Whether the information is channeled through an email, displayed on a mobile device, or integrated into an application, dashboard, or report, it has to suit the preferences and responsibilities of the role.

The next consideration circles back to the core processes identified at the outset. It's about understanding how the role interacts with these processes. What are the inputs and outputs unique to this role concerning the core processes? Additionally, recognizing other business roles that intersect with the one being analyzed can provide a holistic view of the organization's data ecosystem.

Lastly, and perhaps most crucially, there's a need to ascertain the current position of the role on the organizational structure and envision where it ideally should be. Think about this from a value stream perspective. If the person's role was originally defined in a traditional hierarchical structure, but their responsibilities support a specific value stream, their focus and responsibilities will change. In turn, that knowledge aids in understanding potential changes in responsibilities and ensuring that the information needs evolve in tandem.

The BRIA process offers a proven roadmap to creating an intelligent business environment. For IT experts, it's a window into the intricate dance of data and decisions, while for executives, it offers a strategic lens to seamlessly align data with business objectives.

Now that you understand RIA's foundational concepts, we can evaluate how that framework gets extended through QIDA.

Facilitating informed decision-making

Plumbing the depths of business intelligence can often seem daunting, but the BRIA framework, with its integrated QIDA approach, provides the diving gear for clarity. The QIDA extension to BRIA empowers professionals at all levels – from the C-Suite to managerial tiers to those embedded operationally within value streams – to discern essential questions that lead to informed decisions and purposeful actions. Without this structured inquiry, one might swim against the tide of overwhelming data without the precise insights needed to make informed decisions and take appropriate and timely actions.

So, let's dive in to see how QIDA refines the BRIA business intelligence model.

Navigating the surge of modern data

Businesses have been inundated with data largely due to rapid technological advancements, the rise of digital transactions, the proliferation of connected devices, and an ever-growing online user base. The digital era has given birth to many tools and platforms that track, measure, and store every conceivable metric.

From the Zippia list of *22 Stunning Big Data Statistics [2023]*, it's evident that the granularity with which we can now monitor business operations and consumer behaviors is unprecedented. For example, here are three relevant findings from the Zippia report that make this point clear that we have become very good at capturing data, but most of the data is inaccessible or at least unused: [2]

- *"90% of the world's data has been created in the last two years."*
- *"The average company doesn't use 60-73% of its data for analytics. This means that almost three-quarters of the data companies collect goes unanalyzed and, as a result, unused."*
- *"95% of businesses consider the need to manage unstructured data a problem they face."*

Online interactions, social media activity, e-commerce transactions, and even device-to-device communications produce vast amounts of data daily. Moreover, businesses, in their quest to be more data-driven, have adopted systems that capture and store this data, hoping to derive insights and competitive advantages. However, a BRIA assessment will likely determine that we don't need all the data; instead, we need the right data at the right time to answer our most pressing questions. In other words, without the right frameworks and strategies in place, our executives and employees often find themselves overwhelmed not by a lack of data, but by its overabundance.

Managing data overload

While modern enterprise applications empower organizations to amass vast amounts of information, they also present a dilemma: an overabundance of data can lead to information overload, obscuring clear decision-making. Overcoming these tumultuous waters demands a structured, strategic approach to extracting meaningful insights.

Enter QIDA, the operational sequence designed to harness factual business intelligence. Its foundational premise lies in transforming raw data into real-time, on-demand information. With QIDA, the emphasis shifts to harnessing that data to answer specific questions – the kind of questions that propel action and drive desirable business outcomes when answered with the right information.

The sequential steps of QIDA can be broken down as follows:

1. **Questions**: What are the pivotal queries that need quick answers?
2. **Information**: How should the data be organized, derived, calculated, formatted, and displayed to address our critical questions?
3. **Decision**: Leveraging the derived information to make informed decisions
4. **Action**: Having accurate and timely information is necessary to take the right actions to address current issues

Consider the following pharmaceutical industry example of how a QIDA assessment might play out, but purposely specified at a high level to simplify:

- **Questions**: In the pharmaceutical industry, pivotal queries might include: What are the test criteria for a new drug? When are the review meetings scheduled? What are the preliminary test results?

- **Information**: To address these critical questions, data must be organized effectively: test criteria and results should be entered into a centralized management tool, meeting schedules should be maintained on shared calendars, and summarized reports should be created for quick reference.
- **Decision**: Leveraging this organized information, informed decisions can be made. For example, adjustments to the test criteria can be based on preliminary results, or modifications to the drug release schedule can be determined.
- **Action**: Accurate and timely information enables the right actions, such as implementing changes in the drug release plan to minimize delays and rescheduling meetings to ensure all stakeholders can attend.

Crafting actionable intelligence

In our previous example, the pharmaceutical company had determined the need to collect facts and organize its data. However, information emerges when one understands the completion timelines of specific analyses, their review periods, and approval processes, all crucial to deciding on the product's release. The pinnacle is in knowing that all decision criteria have been satisfied, pushing the button on that final decision.

At the heart of this approach lies the concept that not all questions are created equal. Trivial questions yield minimal impact, while pivotal ones can reshape organizational trajectories. In short, the information consumer (by Role) is better off focusing on identifying their 3 to 5 most critical questions rather than trying to think of every possible question. From a Lean-Agile perspective, we can always come back and add more questions as business needs arise or evolve.

Moreover, the distinction between **facts, data,** and **information** is paramount. Facts are standalone, representing real-world events or measurements. Organizing these facts, such as in a structured database or worksheet tables, gives rise to data. But it is when this data is tailored to answer specific questions that it evolves into actionable information.

In the context of crafting actionable intelligence, knowledge also plays a crucial role in understanding and interpreting the organized data. While facts and data provide the foundation, knowledge encompasses the comprehension of the significance of that information. Understanding completion timelines, review periods, and approval processes, for instance, requires knowledge of the industry standards and regulatory requirements. This knowledge is essential for making informed decisions regarding product release, ensuring that all the necessary criteria are met. Thus, knowledge bridges the gap between raw data and actionable information, enabling organizations to leverage data effectively for decision-making.

Our goal, with a QIDA-enriched BRIA strategy, is to guide organizations in their quest for this actionable information. Instead of getting swamped in oceans of data, we equip businesses to mine valuable insights by addressing their most critical questions. After all, in an age of information overload, it's not the organization that collects the most facts and data but the one that harnesses it most effectively that emerges victorious.

This last passage bears repeating: *Information matters more than the underlying facts or data.* Equally important is the application of acquired knowledge to make informed decisions and take appropriate actions based on insights gained.

The following clarifies the distinctions:

- **Facts**: Standalone recordings of events or real-world measurements, unorganized
- **Data**: Organized facts categorized without a specific purpose
- **Information**: Data that is organized and often transformed to address a particular question
- **Knowledge**: Comprehension and interpretation of organized data, integrating industry expertise, regulatory understanding, and contextual awareness to extract actionable insights

This ends our discussion on facilitating informed decision-making and action-taking by applying the concepts of QIDA. Put succinctly, questions drive the need for information that, in turn, enables decision-making and taking appropriate actions based on the user's knowledge. Moreover, this section illustrated how harnessing the power of the QIDA concept can transform vast data reservoirs into streamlined channels of actionable intelligence. By mastering this concept, you're better equipped to chart a course that successfully navigates the challenges and steers you toward your goals in business and life.

The following section is the heart of this chapter: how to conduct a BRIA-based workshop.

Conducting BRIA workshops for strategic alignment

BRIA workshops guide the work to enable business intelligence, helping professionals steer a proper course to achieve their business strategies, goals, and objectives. Based on the BRIDAI format, shown in Figure 10.2, these workshops are pivotal for decisions at both executive and operational levels.

BRIDAI TABLE ELEMENTS	
B	Business domain
R	Role & questions
I	Information need
D	Decisions to be made
A	Actions to be Taken
I	Impact expected to business

Figure 10.2 – BRIDAI table elements

As you can infer from the table, *BRIDAI* is an acronym that defines the work involved in the combined BRIA/QIDA process. We select a domain to support and identify the critical roles and the questions those folks need to be able to answer. From there, we determine the information they require to support the decisions they need to make. Ultimately, the BRIA workshop's purpose is to have the right information to make informed decisions and to take responsive actions to achieve expected or desired outcomes. Six examples of completed BRIDAI tables are provided in *Appendices 10.1* through *10.2*.

The next subsection will introduce the BRIA workshop sessions that support the BRIA/QIDA process.

Defining the BRIA/QIDA workshop sessions

Organizations that elect to conduct an BRIA/QIDA assessment should plan on conducting a series of workshops across three different session types:

1. **Session 1 workshops**: Uncovering business outcome questions
2. **Session 2 workshops**: Conducting facilitated discussions with executives and domain experts
3. **Session 3 workshops**: Creating BRIDAI tables, action items, and assignments

The BRIA workshops kick off at the executive level, aligning everyone with organizational goals and ensuring that executives have the right data to evaluate performance against corporate objectives. As executive BRIA workshops evolve, continuing workshops focus on operational-level decision-making, leading to more workshops tailored to business operations at the domain and value stream levels. In other words, these three sessions occur at the executive, operational, and domain levels.

Let's explore these three session types.

Defining Session 1 workshops

These commence with executive-level BRIA workshops, pinpointing desired business outcomes and defining the roles, questions, information, and decisions vital for achieving these outcomes. While these workshops also occur at the operating level, the distinction lies in having a mid-level manager or team lead steer those BRIA discussions.

Defining Session 2 workshops

This session offers domain and DBMS experts a platform to probe and understand the prerequisites for delivering the information outlined in Session 1. They delve deep, asking questions and clarifying the intricacies of the information requirements. As part of this activity, they assess whether they already have the data or information and where it lives. If they don't have it, they assess which systems should be used to capture and transpose the data into actionable information. They also explore the best approaches to make the information both available and visible.

The BRIA working teams may need to conduct additional meetings to work through all the details fully.

Defining Session 3 workshops

The aim of this session is to identify action items, establish priorities, set timelines, and delegate assignments to expand the targeted databases and applications. Moreover, if process enhancements are needed to attain the targeted results, the team also undertakes planning and task allocation for such improvements.

Now that you know what workshops are required to support an BRIA/QIDA assessment, let's explore the topic of workshop preparations.

Preparing to conduct BRIA workshops

This section further explores the BRIA/QIDA framework and implementation of the BRIA workshops. Each workshop focuses on a specific business domain, which must be identified and described for all workshop participants. The active involvement of both the **Executive Sponsor** and domain experts is vital. Moreover, BRIA workshops are divided into executive, domain, and value-stream levels to optimize outcomes.

Given the significant investment of time and resources in BRIA workshops, ensuring strong support is crucial. Inevitably, this requires one or more C-Suite or **Line of Business** (**LOB**) executives to step forward as executive sponsors to support, encourage, and fund the effort.

Traditionally, an experienced **Business Analyst** (**BA**) leads the BRIA workshop, supported by the expertise of DBMS professionals. These DBMS experts must be well-acquainted with the specific business system of the domain in focus. For larger domains involving multiple workshops across various business departments and value stream teams, a facilitator may be required to help schedule and coordinate the workshop events.

The following steps define the BRIA process.

Scoping the BRIA assessment

The following activities are necessary to help identify business domains and value streams that define the scope of the BRIA/QIDA assessment, and must be completed prior to conducting the first workshop:

- The Executive Sponsor determines which business domains and value streams need assistance. While multiple domains may be identified, priority is given to those aligned with the organization's strategic objectives.
- The BA identifies the key executives required for the BRIA workshops within their domains.
- The workshop lead initiates communication with the appropriate executive, ensuring that they are equipped to explain the domain's objectives, roles, responsibilities, primary questions –preferably, no more than three to five questions per executive, and projected actions and outcomes.

- Executives are responsible for identifying their domain experts to participate in the BRIA workshops.
- The designated BRIA workshop lead schedules the subsequent sessions and sends out the relevant meeting invitations.

Preparing for Session 1 BRIA Workshop

The purpose of session 1 BRIA/QIDA workshop is to discuss and clarify business questions that the organization's key executives must be able to answer at a moment's notice to successfully run their businesses. The preparation activities include:

- Decision-makers come prepared to discuss their business questions identified earlier
- Use a whiteboard (digital or physical) to facilitate discussions of the domain's objectives, roles and responsibilities, key questions, and ensuing decisions and actions
- Domain experts analyze the discussions and ask clarifying questions, setting the stage for Session 2

Let's move on to introduce the Session 2 preparation activities.

Preparing for a Session 2 BRIA workshop

Session 2 is where the business domain and technology specialists join the executives to discuss decision-making needs and identify relevant data sources, and should include these activities:

- The domain experts, the BA, and the DBMS experts engage with the executives, refining their comprehension and probing the nuances of their decision-making needs
- The group also analyzes the executive questions and information needs and helping identify the potential sources and availability of data Once Session 2 workshops are completed, we can move on to prepare for Session 3.

Preparing for a Session 3 BRIA workshop

The Session 3 workshop is where we create the BRIDAI tables and includes the following activities:

- The BRIA workshop lead unveils the comprehensive BRIDAI table to the executives and their teams. This table delineates the business domain, role/questions, information, decision, action, and impact. This blueprint aids in crafting impactful business intelligence strategies.
- After this session, a list of prioritized actions will be integrated into the BRIA work schedule. The BA consolidates all insights into a BRIDAI table, showcased in a final session with the domain's team and executives to create action plans, schedules, and responsibilities.

While the previous discussions focused on executive-level BRIA workshops, the steps remain consistent for departmental or value-stream level workshops. The key distinction lies in the source of the questions, which now arise from the area managers' or team leads' perspectives.

It's essential to remember that this book revolves around Lean-Agile practices. At its core is the conviction that the insights necessary to operate and enhance our business are embedded within the individuals executing the work. Therefore, every BRIA workshop should actively seek feedback from the team members and employees in the respective areas.

This ends our introduction to the BRIA workshop sessions. As you progress through this chapter, you'll gain the expertise to adeptly guide these workshops, fostering collaboration between executives and frontline teams and ultimately leading to organizational success. Next, we'll delve into the preparations for a successful BRIA workshop.

Assembling the BRIA team

Assembling the BRIA team can begin once the executive sponsor signs off on the BRIA workshops. Some organizations may establish executive steering committees to oversee larger-scale information improvement activities, such as the installation of new information systems to support business processes or value stream improvements. Like it or not, budget, scope, resource constraints, and concerns over return on investment (ROI) will always require some degree of executive oversight.

Selecting the workshop lead

The executive sponsor or their representatives appoint a workshop lead, ideally someone with a BA background familiar with DBMSs. Once identified and onboarded, the lead collaborates with the executive sponsor to identify key business domains that need enhanced data management capabilities. Insight from VSM team leads on identified improvement opportunities and priorities, as detailed in *Chapter 4, Driving Improvements with Value Stream Management (VSM)*, can be invaluable here.

Allocating workshop resources

During preparations, it's essential to identify key business systems and the necessary DBMS experts. Following the concepts discussed in our BLAST framework (see *Chapter 8*), the BRIA team participants will come from various domains and functional groups across the organization. Have the executive sponsor select domain experts who are knowledgeable about operations in the target domain.

The DBMS experts play a critical role. Ultimately, their job is designing system updates and programming the SQL queries vital for new data management requirements identified in the BRIA workshops.

Likewise, the domain experts are equally important as they provide invaluable insights, from workflow dynamics to areas needing enhancement. While larger teams can participate in BRIA workshops, efficiency will quickly decrease with more than 20 participants. Research on optimal team size recommends 4 to 6 people for problem-solving, increasing to 7 for decision-making, and 10 to 20 for brainstorming.[3]

Now, let's discuss the three types of BRIA workshop sessions.

Scheduling and conducting BRIA workshops

After clarifying the participants' roles, the workshop lead or PM sets the schedule. In Session 1, executives outline domain objectives, roles, responsibilities, and key questions using a linear format – detailed in the upcoming *'Conducting Session1 BRIA workshops'* subsection. A BRIDAI form is shared before the session, allowing targeted questions to be pre-recorded.

This session lasts at least 30 minutes. Session 2 lasts 50 minutes to 2 hours and dives deep into data needs, integrations, and transformations, all necessary for executive queries. By Session 3, the team reviews the BRIDAI table, transitioning from linear-horizontal to a concise vertical table format.

This wraps up BRIA workshop preparations. The next subsection delves into the details of conducting Session 1 workshops with the goal to identify the role's critical business questions.

Conducting Session 1 BRIA workshops

The purpose of Session 1 BRIA workshops is to identify critical business questions, which we can also refer to as business outcome questions. In other words, all questions are designed to pull the information needed to create a desired business outcome through informed decision-making.

The BRIA workshop facilitator will spend a few moments on introductions and explaining the BRIA, BRIDAI, and QIDA concepts (suggested timebox: 30 minutes).

Ideally, to conserve time, the executive sponsors will come to the BRIA workshop prepared with three to five key business questions they want to always be able to answer and the type of information they believe is necessary to answer those questions. If the executives don't know what information they need, they can just bring the questions they want to be able to answer. They should also be able to discuss the types of decisions and actions they expect to make with each question.

The inaugural session of the BRIA workshop tailored for executives focuses on extracting the most pressing questions crucial to an organization's strategic aims and operations. Typically, the company's Executive Sponsors or the designated facilitator will list these questions – no more than five per role, on a whiteboard – physical or electronic – following a linear format. This format combines the BRIA and QIDA formats, and is essential for categorizing questions and their related information. Participants then delve into each question, spending roughly 10 minutes elucidating the rationale behind their queries to the larger group. This thorough explanation of the *Questions, Information, Decisions*, and (optional) *Actions* (**QIDA**) is vital for a comprehensive understanding of why these questions are important. The session primes the team for clarity, ensuring that everyone is aligned with the company's strategic vision and tactical objectives.

Session 1 asks the primary decision makers to step forward and describe the top three to five questions about their business that keep them up at night. On a whiteboard, the lead decision maker presents information about the business domain they oversee, their specific roles and responsibilities, key questions they must be able to answer at a moment's notice, and the potential decisions and actions they need to take. Their teams listen as the executives explain the relevance of this information to their operations.

Session 1 (suggested timebox: 50 minutes)

1. The Executive Sponsors or the facilitator will write the five questions out on a physical or electronic whiteboard in a linear format. (Use Executive Team – Sample BRIA – QIDA Model – Linear Format as shown in Figure 10.3.)
2. The executive Sponsors should spend up to 10 minutes describing the QIDA reasoning behind their questions to the entire group.
3. Continue to use the BRIA-QIDA format (i.e., linear list format) to display the information captured over the course of the workshops.
4. The BRIA-QIDA table in the linear format includes the following columns: Business, Role, Key Questions, Decisions, Actions, Reasons, Information, Data Sources, Exists (Y/N).

Conducting Session 2 BRIA workshops

The purpose of Session 2 BRIA workshops is to bring in other domain experts so that the lead can facilitate a collaborative exchange of ideas on what information and data transformations are required to support the identified business questions. We also need to identify whether the data and information already exist and are available in the right form. So, the second session is where collaboration and idea generation take the front seat.

Various brainstorming techniques help simplify this facilitation process:

- **Mind mapping** offers a visual exploration of concepts. Starting from a central point and branching out, it captures related subtopics or pivotal ideas visually.
- The **Delphi technique** is an approach to collect expert inputs while retaining the participants' anonymity. This iterative method thrives on group dynamics and is excellent for reaching a consensus.
- The **Nominal Group Method** (**NGM**) is a step-by-step brainstorming technique in which participants jot down ideas and then share them individually, facilitating a collaborative discussion. Eventually, the group prioritizes the ideas, resulting in collective decisions.

Session 2 – (suggested timebox: 50 minutes)

In Session 2, the executive's team members ask questions to refine their understanding of this information. They must understand the motivations and reasoning that guide executive decision-making. Moreover, the team begins to get more granular about the information requirements and discuss whether or where the required information exists.

1. Pivot to group discussion sessions to dive deeper into evaluating the identified key questions regarding data and information requirements, potential data sources, and data availability. (Use Executive Team – Sample BRIA-QIDA Model – Linear Format.)
2. To complete the rows used to capture information across specific business roles, participants can use brainstorming techniques such as mind mapping, the Delphi technique, or NGM.

3. Ten minutes are allotted per question spread across one 50-minute or two 30-minute sessions.
4. For larger groups, teams can be split by interests to include a mix of SMEs from the organization in the represented business domains.

These techniques ensure that every participant contributes effectively to the discussions regardless of position or expertise.

Session 3 – (suggested timebox: 50 minutes)

Conducting Session 3 BRIA Workshops

The purpose of the Session 3 workshops is to create comprehensive BRIA-QIDA information displays (see Figure 10.3) for each business role, presented in a horizontal format known as BRIDAI tables. These tables serve as blueprints for defining the organization's most critical business questions, identifying related data and information needs, and determining the appropriate actions to support business decisions. The goal of this exercise is to ensure the most important information is available in proper context, instantly, on-demand, and at a moment's notice.

The primary activities associated with conduction the session 3 workshop include the following:

- Prior to the workshop, the BRIA workshop facilitator summarizes findings in BRIDAI tables and either discusses them in a group session or emails them to all workshop participants to prior to the Session 3 workshop.
- BRIA workshop participants can add columns to the BRIA table as necessary. In other words, the team can extend the BRIA-QIDA formats. For example, they may add sections to capture question/information context, data tables and fields, metrics, and any necessary data transformations.
- The BRIA workshop facilitator passes the information along to the business's DBMS and applications experts to create prototypes to present later in demo and approval sessions.

In the third session, the BRIA workshop lead presents the information in a BRIDAI table format, as illustrated in *Figure 10.3*. Also, refer to *Appendices 10.1* through *10.2.* to see additional examples of completed BRIDAI tables. This format provides a clear and concise plan of action to build the business intelligence your executives and team members need to make informed decisions, take appropriate actions supporting your organization's strategic objectives, and quickly respond to operational issues.

Post discussions, the workshop's primary output is the completed BRIDAI table. The BRIDAI format encourages teams to focus exclusively on one business role at a time, ensuring a thorough investigation of information needs and action items to make the information available.

Let's look at an example to see how questioning in one business function or domain area can lead to follow-up questions in other areas. We have created a linear BRIDAI table for this example, as shown in *Figure 10.3*. In this case, the CFO needs to assess whether they have sufficient funds to cover their costs over the next period. However, to answer that question, they will need input from the executives managing the organization's sales and marketing functions.

Role	Key Questions	Decisions, Actions, and Reasons	Information	Data Sources	Data Sources Exist?
CFO	How much new revenue from sales can I count on in the next quarter? How accurate are previous forecasts? Will we have sufficient revenues to pay our expenses? What should I tell shareholders and investors to expect in the upcoming earnings report?	Decision to maintain cash or take a short-term loan to meet our debt obligations Perform cash flow analysis To ensure the organization's financial stability and liquidity To ensure they have the data to answer shareholder and investor data and meet compliance requirements.	Sales forecast for the next quarter The probability of closing our forecasted sales A historical record of actual sales performance versus forecast	Financial management software or Enterprise Financial Management (EFM) systems Salesforce – Opportunities and forecasts from CRM	1) Yes 2) Yes
VP Sales	What are the projected sales for the staff I have? Do I need more salespeople? Do we have sufficient time to hire and develop salespeople? Will sales from the new release offset increased costs and reduced margins from hiring more salespeople?	Decision to hire, when, and how Use internal or external recruiting sources to hire Cost versus time and hiring consideration	Pipeline forecasts versus target quotas Salesperson close proficiency Sales team capacity	1) Total revenue in sales from CRM 2) Sales team's historic performance against forecasts from CRM	1) Yes 2) No

Role	Key Questions	Decisions, Actions, and Reasons	Information	Data Sources	Data Sources Exist?
VP Marketing	What revenue opportunities and demographic insights, including the Total Addressable Market (TAM), should be understood for the next release?	Decide whether the market supports company revenue goals Conduct market research and competitive analysis To craft effective market expansion strategies, leveraging strengths, mitigating risks, and seizing growth opportunities	Data on market trends, customer preferences, competitor analysis, sales projections, and marketing strategies.	1) Market research surveys 2) Research from industry analysts 3) Sales projections from CRM 4) In-house tools and data for competitive analysis and SWOT analysis	1) Yes 2) Yes 3) Yes 4) TBD

Figure 10.3 – Sample BRIDAI table, linear QIDA format

These BRIDAI format tabulations encapsulate the result from a series of workshops across three domains – Finance, Sales, and Marketing – and provides an actionable roadmap. It represents the organization's intelligence requirements, guiding decisions and actions in alignment with strategic objectives. This table is particularly valuable as it can be continuously updated and adapted. Furthermore, participants can augment the table with additional columns for deeper insights, such as specific data sources, metrics or transformation needs.

The BRIDAI table, therefore, is not just a workshop's outcome; they serve as living documents propelling the company forward. Moreover, this effort will directly inform the activities of IT, as discussed in the next subsection.

Translating insights into IT strategy

After charting the course with BRIA workshops, it's time to implement the insights, ensuring our organization is well equipped to embark on its journey to actionable decision-making. We cannot overstate the critical role of the IT department in bringing to life the insights identified during the BRIA process.

Like a seasoned crew preparing for a new voyage, IT now takes the helm, transforming the BRIA-derived insights into actionable IT strategies and solutions. These changes may encompass new data fields, UDFs, data transformations, or even the introduction of entirely new information systems.

Whether you're an executive setting the strategic direction, a manager overseeing operations, or a team member executing tasks, it's essential to understand how these IT decisions directly impact the flow of information and the organization's overall performance. Essentially, it's about ensuring the organization sails steadily toward its goals, fully informed and effectively powered by its IT systems.

In the next section, we'll explore a specific example of how AI tools and technologies are evolving to support BRIA workshop activities.

Leveraging AI-based tools to support BRIA workshops

The originator of the 'Ladder of Business Intelligence' (LOBI now LOBAI – Ladder of Business and Artificial Intelligence) concepts outlined in this chapter is James E. Cates. He has an impressive background that includes:

- Co-founder of Watson Group at IBM and its underlying technologies.
- Former global head of Software R&D at IBM
- Former CIO at Brocade, Silicon Graphics, Synopsys, and Altera

With this background, you might imagine that he is attempting to apply modern AI-based technologies to support this approach to creating the *Intelligent Business*, and you would be correct. He is a co-founder of **Quarrio** and guides this company's technology to support the LOBAI strategy along with another co-founder Earl Sacerdoti, who has similarly impressive credentials:

- Former associate director of artificial intelligence at **Stanford Research Institute** (**SRI**) where he was involved with the development of Apple's Siri technology
- Co-founder of the American Association of Artificial Intelligence
- Co-founded Symantec and built their first product; held bottom-line responsibility up to IPO

Their's is but one approach in the AI community to make information immediately available, relevant, and accurate. In their approach, Quarrio's software integrates **Natural Language Understanding** (**NLU**) capabilities and a user interface that appears to offer functionalities similar to **Generative Pre-trained Transformer** (**GPT**) and **Large Language Model** (**LLM**) tools such as ChatGPT. However, their underlying mechanisms operate in distinctly different ways.

For instance, ChatGPT relies on deep-learning **neural network** structures, utilizing **machine learning** methodologies for pre-training on extensive and varied digital data and linguistic resources within datasets. Subsequently, it undergoes fine-tuning to accommodate specific tasks related to information retrieval. In the realm of machine learning, a prevalent objective involves developing algorithms capable of learning from data and making predictions. This can be termed a **bottom-up approach**, where the machine looks for patterns in large amounts of data to create pattern recognition and prediction.

In contrast, Quarrio adopts a multi-level **semantic grammar** approach, also known as a **symbolic** approach, to information retrieval. This method diverges from the probabilistic pattern recognition of models such as ChatGPT by instructing computing systems about the semantics – meaning of words and phrases – and the grammar rules of natural languages such as English.

Quarrio's approach addresses a fundamental challenge in NLU systems, commonly referred to as an "AI-hard" problem, which Quarrio is tackling. Quarrio's software operates on a **top-down approach**, utilizing a grammatical simulation to precisely interpret user requests and generate SQL queries, in contrast to the probabilistic methodologies employed by models such as GPT and other LLMs, which rely more on statistical inference. This emphasis on accuracy and precision is particularly valuable in regulated industries or functions where these qualities are critical, ensuring that outcomes meet stringent regulatory standards.

This distinction is crucial; unlike approaches that rely on probabilistic guesswork to interpret user queries, Quarrio leverages the user's natural language input to dynamically generate a SQL query. This method ensures that the query retrieves and displays information from trusted data sources, directly relevant to the user's request. The output follows a **deterministic pattern**, meaning it produces consistent and predictable results every time, which can be crucial in environments requiring high reliability and traceability.

In addition, the deterministic nature of the output allows for thorough validation through audit trails and other methods. This ensures consistency and accuracy in the information retrieval process. Furthermore, both users and DBMS experts have the option to toggle a feature on or off to see how the user's sentences were interpreted and the SQL queries it generated. This feature enhances the system's transparency and assures users of the accuracy of the results.

However, a significant challenge with symbolic tools such as Quarrio is the potential for ambiguity, as different industries, domains, and even individual users may interpret the same or similar language terms differently in specific contexts. To address this, Quarrio utilizes a *multi-level grammar architecture* designed to incorporate these variances and has developed a configuration tool that enables non-technical users to map language terms and business concepts to their specific uses within the domain's data stores. This strategy ensures accurate mapping of terms to concepts and effective information retrieval. Ultimately, the precision of the retrieved information depends solely on the organization's data and its repository of domain-specific semantic mappings.

This does not imply that GPT/LLM-based technologies are more accurate than symbolic approaches; in fact, it's quite the opposite. GPT/LLM-based tools rely on statistical inference and are fundamentally probabilistic. This means that, at best, they can achieve high levels of accuracy but can never be completely precise. Nor will they return the same result predictably.

Moreover, GPT-based tools are known to experience episodes of **hallucinating**, where they generate nonsensical, irrelevant, or even misleading responses. This phenomenon can occur due to various factors, including a lack of context, ambiguity in the user's language, biases in training data, and limitations in the model's understanding of semantic meanings.

Users often cannot detect when GPT-based AI tools *hallucinate* unless the errors are obvious, and the opaque nature of these systems complicates understanding how responses are generated. Consequently, while useful for general queries, GPT-based tools should not be used for critical decision-making or automating vital business processes without external checks.

In contrast, Quarrio's deterministic approach, based on clear semantic mappings and grammar rules, ensures reliable and traceable outputs, making it trustworthy for sectors such as healthcare, finance, and legal, where accuracy and traceability are crucial and errors can have severe consequences.

While Quarrio's tools are currently being launched onto the market, they remain in the early stages of commercialization and have yet to be extensively market-tested. For full disclosure, one of our authors, Gary Rupp, has provided consulting support to Quarrio's executive team.

Summary

This chapter delved into the vast sea of data that organizations continuously collect, highlighting the challenge of navigating this abundance to find essential information for business operations. It shed light on the importance of clearly defining the information needs of executives responsible for data retrieval, as well as the team members who fine-tune daily operations, by introducing the QIDA concepts embodied in the BRIA process to bridge this gap.

Exploring our digital age, characterized by vast volumes of data in which we can easily get lost, this chapter served as a navigational chart through two critical journeys. Firstly, it outlined the importance of strategic objectives and profitability markers for executives, emphasizing their role in guiding the organization's direction. Secondly, it underscored the significance of operational teams in ensuring the harmonious alignment of value streams toward corporate goals.

These insights are crucial as organizations often struggle to extract actionable insights from vast datasets, hindering informed decision-making. This chapter offered methods to distill and harness vast amounts of data into actionable information, empowering you to help shape the efficiency and trajectory of your organization's value streams.

Building upon these foundations, the next chapter, Implementing Strategies for Organizational Transformation, serves as a practical guide for executives and VSM teams seeking to implement Lean-Agile practices throughout their organization. There you will gain further insights into creating a sustainable culture of continuous improvement by exploring practical strategies for implementing Lean-Agile and value stream management practices.

Appendices

Appendix 10.1 – Value Stream Manager BRIDAI results

This BRIDAI table offers an example for a value manager overseeing a value stream that supports the development of a commercial product.

Specifically, this table provides a framework for a Value Stream Manager to make data-informed decisions regarding commercial product development. The data sources listed are common tools and databases a manager might use, though specific software/tools can vary depending on the organization.

Role	Key Questions	Decisions, Actions, and Reasons	Information	Data Sources	Data Sources Exist?
Value Stream Manager	What stages in the development process are causing delays?	Allocate more resources to bottlenecked stages to streamline the process.	1) Stage-by-stage breakdown of time spent 2) Resource allocation at each stage	1) Project management software 2) Resource allocation tool	1) Yes 2) Yes
	Are there any quality issues identified in the process?	Investigate and resolve identified quality issues.	1) Quality reports for each stage 2) Feedback from QA teams	1) Quality assurance reporting tools 2) Feedback systems	1) Yes 2) Yes
	How aligned is the current development with customer needs?	Modify product features based on customer feedback and requirements.	1) Customer feedback and reviews 2) Market research reports	1) Customer feedback system 2) Market research databases	1) Yes 2) Yes
	Are there sufficient resources to meet the development timeline?	Hire or reallocate resources if there's a projected deficit.	1) Current team size and roles 2) Projected resource needs for upcoming stages	1) HR software 2) Project management software	1) Yes 2) Yes

Role	Key Questions	Decisions, Actions, and Reasons	Information	Data Sources	Data Sources Exist?
	How do current expenditures compare with the budget?	Re-evaluate allocations or request more funds if exceeding budget.	1) Detailed breakdown of expenditures 2) Allocated budget for the value stream	1) Accounting software 2) Budget planning tool	1) Yes 2) Yes

Appendix 10.2 – CEO's BRIDAI results

Here's a BRIDAI table for the CEO of a company overseeing the development of a commercial product.

This table equips the CEO with the critical data-driven insights they need to have a holistic view of their company's performance and growth. It ensures that they have the information necessary to steer the company in line with its strategic objectives at any given moment.

Role	Key Questions	Decisions, Actions, and Reasons	Information	Data Sources	Data Sources Exist?
CEO	How are we performing financially compared to our targets?	Adjust operational or financial strategies based on performance gaps.	1) Current financial statements 2) Yearly targets and KPIs 3) Comparisons to past performances	1) Financial management software 2) Strategic plan documents	1) Yes 2) Yes
	Are our products aligning with market demand and trends?	Reassess product strategies or invest in R&D for new products.	1) Market research data 2) Competitive analysis reports 3) Sales and customer feedback	1) Market research databases 2) Sales analytics platform	1) Yes 2) Yes

Role	Key Questions	Decisions, Actions, and Reasons	Information	Data Sources	Data Sources Exist?
	How are our employee satisfaction and retention rates?	Implement HR initiatives or strategies to improve company culture.	1) Employee feedback and surveys 2) Turnover rates and reasons	1) HR software 2) Employee feedback system	1) Yes 2) Yes
	Are there any emerging risks or threats to our business?	Create mitigation plans or diversify business strategies.	1) Risk assessment reports 2) Industry news and alerts	1) Risk management tools 2) Industry news platforms	1) Yes 2) Yes
	How well are we progressing toward our long-term goals?	Redirect resources or adjust priorities based on goal progression.	1) Strategic goal tracking. 2) Reports on company-wide initiatives	1) Goal tracking software 2) Annual report documents	1) Yes 2) Yes

Appendix 10.3 – CFO's BRIDAI table

Here's a BRIDAI table for the CFO of a public company with concerns about cash flow, financial planning, taxation, financial reporting, and SOX compliance.

The table provides the CFO with a structured approach to key financial concerns, ensuring that the public company consistently maintains financial health, compliance, and reporting standards.

Role	Key Questions	Decisions, Actions, and Reasons	Information	Data Sources	Data Sources Exist?
CFO	Is our current cash flow sufficient to cover operational costs?	Prioritize expenses, consider financing options, or cut costs if needed.	1) Current cash flow statements 2) Upcoming operational expenses	1) Accounting software 2) Departmental budgets	1) Yes 2) Yes

Role	Key Questions	Decisions, Actions, and Reasons	Information	Data Sources	Data Sources Exist?
	Are we meeting our financial projections and targets?	Adjust budgets and financial strategies, or revise projections if necessary.	1) Current financial statements 2) Set financial targets 3) Comparisons to past performances	1) Financial modeling software 2) Historical financial records	1) Yes 2) Yes
	Are there potential SOX compliance issues?	Implement corrective actions or enhance controls to ensure compliance.	1) Internal audit reports 2) External audit feedback 3) SOX compliance checklist	1) SOX compliance software 2) External auditor feedback	1) Yes 2) Yes
	How effective are our tax strategies in minimizing liability?	Consider alternative tax strategies or consult with tax advisors.	1) Current tax liabilities 2) Potential tax-saving avenues 3) Comparative tax analyses	1) Tax software 2) Tax advisory consultations 3) International tax databases	1) Yes 2) Yes 3) Yes
	Are our financial reports accurate and up to financial standards?	Ensure data integrity and initiate any corrective measures if needed.	1) Financial reports and statements. 2) Validation and verification records.	1) Financial reporting system 2) Internal and external audit results	1) Yes 2) Yes

Appendix 10.4 – CIO's BRIDAI table

Here is a sample BRIDAI table tailored to the CIO's roles and responsibilities.

The table serves as a holistic guide for the CIO to consistently ensure that the company's IT strategies and systems meet the current needs and are forward-looking and aligned with the company's broader objectives:

Role	Key Questions	Decisions, Actions, and Reasons	Information	Data Sources	Data Sources Exist?
CIO	Are our current IT systems aligned with the company's objectives?	Consider system upgrades or replacements if current tech doesn't meet business needs.	1) IT system capabilities 2) Company objectives and strategic goals	1) IT system documentation 2) Company strategic plan	1) Yes 2) Yes
	How can emerging technologies benefit our business processes?	Invest in research and development or partnerships to leverage new tech.	1) Analysis of emerging technologies 2) Potential benefits and ROI	1) Technology market research 2) ROI projection tools	1) Yes 2) Yes
	Is our IT infrastructure secure and compliant with industry standards?	Enhance security measures or consider technology overhauls to ensure compliance.	1) Security audit reports 2) Compliance checklists against industry standards	1) Security assessment tools 2) Industry standard documentation	1) Yes 2) Yes
	How are we preparing for IT workforce needs in the future?	Develop training programs, hire new talent, or contract with third parties if needed.	1) Current IT workforce capabilities 2) Forecast of future tech needs and skills required	1) HR talent assessment tools 2) IT industry trends analysis	1) Yes 2) Yes

Role	Key Questions	Decisions, Actions, and Reasons	Information	Data Sources	Data Sources Exist?
	Are we maximizing the ROI from our IT investments?	Reallocate budget or resources to high-ROI areas or reassess current tech investments.	1) Current IT expenses and investments 2) Returns and benefits realized from these investments	1) Financial tracking tools for IT 2) Performance metrics and KPIs for implemented tech solutions	1) Yes 2) Yes

Appendix 10.5 – VP/Chief of Sales BRIDAI table

This is a BRIDAI table tailored to the VP/Chief of Sales and their responsibilities.

This table will provide the VP/Chief of Sales with a structured way to continually monitor and adjust sales strategies, ensuring that the sales department is operating at peak efficiency and effectively responding to market dynamics:

Role	Key Questions	Decisions, Actions, and Reasons	Information	Data Sources	Data Sources Exist?
VP/ Chief of Sales	How are we tracking against our sales goals for the quarter/year?	Adjust sales strategies or reallocate resources based on progress toward goals.	1) Current sales figures 2) Quarterly/ yearly sales targets	1) Sales tracking software 2) Annual sales plan	1) Yes 2) Yes
	Which products/ services are underperforming in sales?	Focus marketing efforts or reevaluate the sales approach for those specific products/ services.	1) Sales figures by product/ service 2) Market demand for each product/ service	1) Product-specific sales reports 2) Market research data	1) Yes 2) Yes

Role	Key Questions	Decisions, Actions, and Reasons	Information	Data Sources	Data Sources Exist?
	What feedback are we getting from our top clients about our products/ services?	Incorporate feedback into product development or address specific concerns.	1) Client feedback reports 2) Insights from sales meetings	1) Customer Relationship Management (CRM) system 2) Meeting notes/ minutes	1) Yes 2) Yes
	Are our sales teams equipped with the right tools and training to succeed?	Invest in new tools or training programs if current resources are deemed insufficient.	1) Sales performance by team 2) Feedback from sales staff on tools and training	1) Sales performance tracking software 2) Internal surveys or feedback collection tools	1) Yes 2) Yes
	How do our sales promotion efforts correlate with actual sales results?	Adjust promotional strategies based on their effectiveness in driving sales.	1) Sales figures during/after promotional periods 2) Details of promotions and campaigns run	1) Sales analytics tools (before, during, and after campaigns) 2) Marketing and promotion details/ records	1) Yes 2) Yes

Appendix 10.6 – VP/ Chief of Marketing BRIDAI table

Here's a BRIDAI table tailored for the VP/Chief of Marketing given their responsibilities.

This table equips the VP/Chief of Marketing with insights to make strategic decisions, optimize campaigns, and lead their team in alignment with the company's broader objectives:

Role	Key Questions	Decisions, Actions, and Reasons	Information	Data Sources	Data Sources Exist?
VP/Chief of Marketing	How is our brand perception evolving in the market?	Adjust brand strategy or campaigns based on current brand perception.	1) Brand sentiment analysis 2) Feedback from customers and stakeholders	1) Social media monitoring tools 2) Customer feedback surveys	1) Yes 2) Yes
	Are our marketing campaigns yielding a positive ROI?	Evaluate the effectiveness of campaigns; consider pivoting strategies or reallocating budget.	1) ROI for each campaign 2) KPIs related to campaigns	1) Marketing analytics software 2) Campaign-specific tracking tools	1) Yes 2) Yes
	How are we performing against our set marketing goals?	Modify current strategies or implement new tactics to meet goals.	1) Progress against set goals 2) Performance metrics of marketing initiatives	1) Marketing performance dashboards 2) Goal tracking platforms	1) Yes 2) Yes
	How are market dynamics and competitor activities influencing our market share?	Refine marketing plan and positioning to compete and maintain/ grow market share effectively.	1) Market share analysis 2) Competitor activity and performance reports	1) Market research reports 2) Competitive intelligence tools	1) Yes 2) Yes

Role	Key Questions	Decisions, Actions, and Reasons	Information	Data Sources	Data Sources Exist?
	How well are we utilizing our marketing budget, and are there areas where funds can be reallocated for better use?	Optimize budget allocation to areas showing potential or higher returns.	1) Budget spending versus results 2) Performance metrics of various marketing channels/efforts	1) Financial management systems showing budget allocations and spending 2) Performance metrics from analytics tools	1) Yes 2) Yes
	What feedback or suggestions do internal teams have about marketing support or collaboration?	Improve inter-departmental collaboration and align marketing efforts with company-wide objectives.	1) Feedback from sales, product, and other teams 2) Collaboration metrics (if any)	1) Inter-departmental meetings/ feedback sessions 2) Collaboration tools with feedback functionalities	1) Yes 2) Maybe

Questions

This section is offered for those of you who want to evaluate comprehension and retention of the information provided in this chapter. There are 10 questions. The answers can be found in the following subsection. Recalling the exact verbiage of the original content is not important. Rather, it's more important that you can recall the concepts and their applications.

1. What is the paradox highlighted by Zippia's report regarding data usage in businesses?
2. How do the BRIA and QIDA models contribute to transforming data into actionable insights?
3. What is the main focus of the BRIA framework in aligning organizational endeavors?
4. How does the BRIA process contribute to the creation of an intelligent business environment?
5. How does the QIDA extension to the BRIA framework assist professionals in making informed decisions and taking purposeful actions?

6. What are the key differences between facts, data, and information as outlined in the QIDA-enriched BRIA strategy?
7. What is the primary objective of conducting BRIA workshops, and how do they align with business strategies?
8. What are the key phases in the BRIA workshop process and their significance?
9. How does the BRIA workshop contribute to creating a comprehensive business intelligence strategy?
10. What role does the IT department play following the BRIA workshops, and why is it crucial?

Answers

1. Zippia's report reveals that while businesses produce 2.5 quintillion bytes of data daily and heavily invest in big data and AI, 60-73% of this data remains unanalyzed, highlighting a gap between data availability and effective utilization.
2. The BRIA process defines the workshop approach while the QIDA concept emphasizes that key questions drive decisions and actions. Together, they align data analysis with business needs, turning raw data into actionable insights using the linear (BRIA-QIDA) and vertical (BRIDAI) tables.
3. The BRIA process aligns an organization's information needs with its business objectives across all roles, ensuring decision-makers have the necessary data-driven insights to shape and influence strategies effectively.
4. The BRIA process identifies core processes and value streams, defines key roles, and determines the specific information needs of each role, ensuring tailored, relevant insights support informed decision-making.
5. QIDA structures the approach to business intelligence by identifying essential questions and gathering relevant data, leading to informed decisions and purposeful actions.
6. Facts are basic recorded events, data organizes these facts, and information emerges when data is analyzed to answer specific questions, making it actionable for decision-making.
7. BRIA Workshops align professional roles with business domains to ensure data-driven decisions at all levels, using the BRIDAI format to connect roles with business strategies.
8. The BRIA Workshop process includes the Preparatory Phase, Session 1 (discussing business questions), Session 2 (engaging domain experts), and Session 3 (presenting the BRIDAI table), ensuring systematic alignment from needs to actions.
9. BRIA Workshops involve key decision-makers in identifying core processes, defining roles, and organizing information needs, crafting a BRIDAI table as a blueprint for impactful business intelligence strategies.
10. The IT department implements BRIA-derived insights into actionable IT strategies and solutions, ensuring the IT infrastructure supports the flow of information and aligns with strategic directions.

Further reading

1. Cates, J. E., Gill, S. S., & Zeituny, N. (2007). Climbing the Ladder of Business Intelligence: Enabled Intuition, Understanding Knowledge Information, Data and Facts (1st ed., pp. 85-86, 169). Mitchell Levy. `https://www.abebooks.com/9781600050435/Climbing-Ladder-Business-Intelligence-Happy-1600050433/plp`
2. McCain, A. (223, January 16). 26 STUNNING BIG DATA STATISTICS [2023]: MARKET SIZE, TRENDS, AND FACTS. Zippia - The Career Expert. Retrieved October 5, 2023, from `https://www.zippia.com/advice/big-data-statistics/`
3. Stone, M., & Shellenbarger, S. (2018, July 3). Who should be at the table? Tips for selecting your meeting attendees. Atlassian Work Life Blog Post. Retrieved October 6, 2013, from `https://www.atlassian.com/blog/teamwork/who-should-be-at-the-table-tips-for-selecting-your-meeting-attendees`

11

Implementing Strategies for Organizational Transformation

"The rate of change is not going to slow down anytime soon. If anything, competition in most industries will probably speed up even more in the next few decades."

– John P. Kotter

This chapter explores modern approaches for revolutionizing business transformations. It offers several practices for executive leaders to adopt, implement, and sustain continuous improvement. Consider this chapter an executive primer, providing a quick and comprehensive overview of Lean-Agile implementation strategies for those with limited time to dive into the details. Here, you will learn actionable strategies to drive innovation, enhance efficiency, and unlock your organization's full potential, ensuring it stays competitive in this unprecedented, rapidly evolving, and digitized business climate.

Understanding how to build a roadmap for transformative change is essential. This includes leveraging proven change management frameworks, implementing **value stream management** (**VSM**) methods and tools, fostering a culture of continuous learning, using metrics to track progress and business results, and building collaborative cross-functional Lean-Agile teams (and teams of teams).

In this chapter, the following topics will be covered:

- Simplifying complexity: navigating Lean-Agile implementation challenges
- Lean and Agile: two sides of the coin
- Building cross-functional teams and encouraging collaboration
- Leveraging data and analytics for decision-making
- Adopting a change management framework

Simplifying complexity – navigating Lean-Agile implementation challenges

A common theme throughout this book is that the journey toward achieving organizational agility and operational excellence can be realized through the adoption of Lean-Agile principles and methods. However, this path is often fraught with complexity, especially when applying the new paradigm within enterprise environments where people are resistant to change.

The art of simplifying complexity lies at the heart of effective Lean-Agile implementation. By eliminating organizational silos, we enhance work and information flows via value streams. We get increasingly better over time by identifying and eliminating activities that do not add value to our products or services. That's the Lean part of a Lean-Agile Enterprise.

But that's only half the story. Organizations must also be willing and able to continuously adapt and evolve to address changes in business requirements, market dynamics, and customer needs. By breaking up the complexity of change into smaller increments and iteratively finding new ways to improve, we get better with each new incremental delivery. That is the essence of Agile-based practices.

Let's quickly explore what Lean-Agile practices entail at their most fundamental levels.

Applying Lean-Agile practices – streamlining processes and enhancing agility

The fundamental principles of Lean-Agile practices are straightforward. First, organize people, processes, technology, and information to facilitate seamless product delivery flows, eliminating organizational silos common in hierarchical structures. Second, identify and eliminate waste in activities that don't add value from the customer's perspective. This reduces costs, improves quality, and increases throughput. Eliminating constraints is equally crucial; an organization can only move as fast as its slowest activity. Trying to force more work into the system increases costs, bottlenecks, delays, and hidden defects. Finally, small, cross-functional teams should be implemented to tackle business problems, planning, and developing solutions iteratively and incrementally. For example, employ small cross-functional teams to resolve your constraints and other wastes. By following these practices, organizations can become both lean and agile.

While Lean-Agile practices are relatively simple to understand and learn, the complexity lies in changing the culture and mindset of the organization without tearing it apart in the process. So, next, we'll look at customizing Lean-Agile practices to facilitate organizational transformation.

Customizing Lean-Agile practices for organizational transformation

A primary concern in Lean-Agile transformations is the potential mismatch between the proposed methods and the organization's existing hierarchical or flattened structures and legacy practices. Hierarchies encourage siloed business activities, while flattened organizations often lack the structure to coordinate work and information flows. Neither of these extremes is ideal.

Without a thoughtful, context-sensitive approach, companies might be entangled in expensive and complex implementations that do more to disrupt than improve. This reality underscores the importance of a customized adaptation of Lean-Agile practices (or frameworks) tailored to the organization's unique DNA.

Regardless of the Lean-Agile framework you choose, there is no out-of-the-box solution for your organization. Tailoring the use of methods and tools is always critical. You may find it more beneficial to mix and match practices to meet your needs situationally. While vendors will happily promote their knowledge bases, practices, and training, it may be more than you need and still not directly fit your needs. Meanwhile, your executive management team is responsible for finding cost-effective solutions for implementation, training, mentoring, and coaching. This requires full engagement from the executive sponsors.

When navigating the challenges of Lean-Agile implementation, it is crucial to acknowledge and respect the diversity of existing organizational landscapes. Each enterprise has its history, culture, and established processes, which must be considered when designing the transformation strategy.

Executives must deeply understand their operations to avoid common pitfalls such as misaligned roles and outdated enterprise-wide processes. This book has stressed the importance of GEMBA Walks, which involve going to where the work is being done to see firsthand how things work and what the issues are. Talking to the people doing the work is essential, as they best understand the problems and opportunities.

The insights gained serve as a compass for refining the implementation of Lean-Agile practices, ensuring they meet the organization's needs for change while driving maximum efficiency and value delivery. Consequently, simplifying complexity isn't about applying Lean-Agile principles by the book; it's about interpreting them in the language of the organization. It's a strategic exercise in customizing frameworks, tools, and practices to fit within the organization while propelling it forward.

Lean-Agile thus becomes a strategic asset underpinning the organization's continual quest for excellence and growth. It's considered "*strategic*" because Lean-Agile mastery contributes significantly to achieving strategic goals and objectives and is often central to the company's value proposition.

Lean and Agile – two sides of the coin

Lean and Agile are complementary but distinct areas of focus for your operating model and should be balanced against each other to ensure smooth progress and performance. We discussed the developmental and operational spectrum of value streams in *Chapter 6*, with a deeper understanding of value streams as interconnected networks of people, processes, information, and technology in *Chapter 7*.

With its focus on adaptation and rapid delivery, agile techniques sit on the developmental side, striving for increased effectiveness with the associated uncertainty and inconsistency. Conversely, lean techniques emphasize the minimization of waste and the implementation of pull production control strategies and standardization where possible. Each balances the other to enable sustainable value delivery. The challenge is to leverage value stream concepts intelligently, applying Lean principles where appropriate to improve productivity and quality, and using Agile's iterative and incremental development methods to drive change.

As a leader, your challenge is to ensure value streams are defined and the work is aligned with the tasks at hand. For day-to-day operational work, the goal is to create efficient and sustainable business practices that meet customer demands with high quality. However, other value streams must use Agile's IID practices to create new solutions for improving business processes, systems, products, and services. Additionally, you need to ensure that your subject matter experts (SMEs) have time to support the development teams with their expertise.

Modern digital technologies integrate, automate, and synchronize work across traditional development boundaries, tremendously accelerating deliveries. For example, IT's CI/CD and DevOps pipelines have reduced software development cycle times from months to days, or even less. In these situations, Agile practices set the stage for planning and analysis, while the actual development activities operate as Lean-oriented flows.

Fostering a culture of continuous learning and improvement

Leaders should create an organizational culture that values continuous learning and improvement. This involves encouraging experimentation, tolerating failures (but failing small) as learning opportunities, and regularly providing training and development resources. Such a culture supports Lean-Agile principles and practices by empowering employees to seek out inefficiencies and propose innovative solutions.

In the current business climate, the only constant is change. For organizations to thrive and stay competitive, they must embrace a culture of continuous learning and improvement. This culture is not a natural byproduct of daily operations; it must be cultivated and nurtured. Leaders play a pivotal role in weaving the new culture into the company's fabric. Here are some ways leaders can achieve this:

- **Implement Lean-Agile principles**: Adopt Lean-Agile methodologies emphasizing customer value, efficiency, and employee empowerment. These principles naturally encourage continuous improvement and learning.
- **Leading by example**: Leadership starts at the top. Leaders must not only endorse continuous learning but also actively participate in it. By engaging in learning activities themselves, leaders set a precedent for all employees to follow.
- **Embedding learning in strategy**: Make continuous learning integral to the company's strategic objectives. This requires clear communication on the value of learning and its direct impact on achieving business goals.
- **Establish psychological safety**: Encourage employees to experiment by creating a safe space where genuine efforts and sincere failures are not frowned upon but seen as a stepping stone to innovation. Reward efforts and learning, not just successful outcomes.

- **Failing small and early**: Recognize that one of the key benefits of Agile's iterative and incremental development approach is risk reduction, enabling teams to fail small, fast, and early, and using the failures for course corrections and learning experiences.
- **Embrace experimentation**: Instead of penalizing failures, dissect them to understand their root cause. This will transform them into powerful lessons for the organization and prevent future repetition of the same missteps.
- **Provide training and development resources**: Invest in diverse training programs that cater to different learning styles and professional paths. Ensure employees have the time and resources to engage with these learning opportunities.
- **Encourage knowledge sharing**: Promote an environment where knowledge sharing is a norm. Tools such as internal messaging, wikis, regular "lunch and learn" sessions, and collaborative projects can facilitate this exchange.
- **Empower employees**: Give employees the autonomy to identify inefficiencies and propose solutions. When individuals feel their input is valued, they are more likely to contribute proactively.
- **Frequent feedback cycles**: Integrate regular feedback mechanisms to allow employees to understand how they are performing and where they can improve.
- **Recognize and reward**: Publicly acknowledge individuals and teams who exemplify the spirit of continuous learning and improvement. Rewards can be intrinsic, such as recognition, or extrinsic, such as bonuses.
- **Use technology to enhance learning**: Leverage commercial and in-house training platforms to provide easy access to educational resources.
- **Continuously reflect and adapt**: Encourage regular reflection on both personal and organizational practices and be willing to adapt based on what is learned.

By embedding these principles into the organizational DNA, leaders will create a skilled and adaptable workforce and foster an environment where continuous improvement is the norm. This environment supports Lean-Agile principles for a responsive and resilient organization. It leads to a virtuous cycle where learning leads to improvement, and improvement opens new avenues for learning, ensuring that the organization survives and thrives in an unpredictable world.

Building cross-functional teams and encouraging collaboration

The siloed nature of traditional organizational structures can hinder the effective implementation of complex business processes. Leaders can drive change by fostering cross-functional teams that bring diverse skills and perspectives together within a value stream to deliver specific components of an integrated increment. Recall from *Chapter 8* (BLAST) and *Chapter 9* (BASE) that integrated increments take the form of **minimum viable products (MVPs)**, **minimum valuable increments (MVIs)**, and

minimum valuable releases (**MVRs**). Encouraging collaboration through BLAST teams and teams of teams enhances problem-solving and innovation, making the organization more adaptable to change.

Traditional organizational structures often compartmentalize expertise within distinct departments, leading to what is commonly referred to as **silos**. These silos can create barriers to communication and workflow, impeding the organization's ability to implement complex business processes efficiently and effectively. Worse, departments can become bloated in large part due to the inefficiencies of managing cross-departmental workflows and disconnect from the primary purpose of the organization – which is to deliver value to their customers through their products and services.

To combat this, leaders can champion the formation of cross-functional teams, which are collaborative groups of people with varied expertise and perspectives from across the organization. Building cross-functional teams is a strategic initiative that promotes a holistic approach to tackling business problems. Drawing together diverse skill sets, these teams are better equipped to view problems from multiple angles, leading to more robust solutions. This diversity of thought is particularly valuable in problem-solving and innovation, as it encourages out-of-the-box thinking and synthesizing ideas from different domains.

Encouraging collaboration within and across teams is essential. Collaboration can be fostered through various means, such as shared goals, joint projects, and team-building activities. Moreover, collaboration tools and platforms can facilitate more effective communication and idea-sharing among team members, irrespective of their physical location.

One of the key benefits of cross-functional teams is their ability to make an organization more adaptable to change. Since these teams have a comprehensive understanding of the organization's functions, they can anticipate the impacts of changes across the board and help to navigate the transition more smoothly. Moreover, because they are not confined to the limited view of a single department, cross-functional teams can often execute change initiatives with a greater appreciation for how each piece of the organization fits into the larger puzzle.

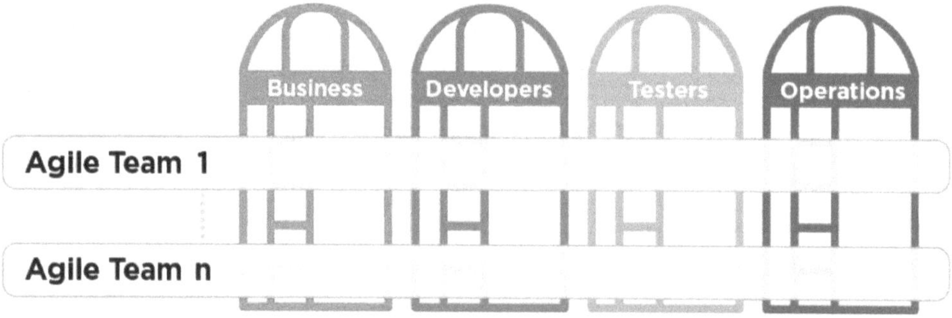

Figure 11.1 – Agile teams are cross-functional and are designed to break silos

For leaders looking to drive change, investing in developing dedicated cross-functional teams is a powerful strategy. It requires a commitment to reshaping the organizational culture that values and rewards cross-departmental collaboration. By doing so, they lay the foundation for an organization that is more innovative, more cohesive, better aligned, and better prepared for the challenges of the modern business environment.

In previous chapters, we've noted that small teams are best. Let's explore that topic in more depth.

Debunking the myth that large teams are more productive

When organizations attempt to assemble larger teams, they often encounter various challenges that can hinder productivity and effectiveness:

One common issue is communication overload. In larger teams, it becomes increasingly difficult to ensure efficient communication among members. With more voices in the mix, important messages may be lost, leading to misunderstandings and delays.

Another challenge is coordination difficulties. Managing activities and decision-making processes within a large group can be cumbersome. Decision-making becomes slower, and reaching a consensus takes more time. Furthermore, scheduling meetings that accommodate everyone's availability becomes increasingly challenging.

Social loafing is also a concern in larger teams. Individuals may feel less accountable for their contributions, leading to reduced effort and productivity. Some team members may rely on others to carry the workload, further exacerbating the issue.

While diversity of thought is valuable, larger teams may struggle to align on a common vision or approach. Balancing diverse perspectives with cohesive decision-making becomes crucial to maintain productivity and effectiveness.

Additionally, larger teams may naturally form cliques or subgroups, hindering overall collaboration and creating silos. This can limit the flow of information between different parts of the team and impede progress.

Leadership challenges also arise when leading a large team. Strong management skills are required to ensure that everyone feels heard, motivated, and engaged. Maintaining team morale becomes more complex in a larger group setting.

Resource allocation is another issue to consider in larger teams. Allocating resources such as budget, time, and personnel across a large team can be tricky. Prioritizing projects and managing dependencies becomes essential to avoid inefficiencies.

In summary, while larger teams may bring diverse expertise, they require careful management to mitigate challenges and maintain effectiveness. Striking a balance between team size and collaboration dynamics is essential for optimizing team performance.

Navigating the complexities of collaboration and integration among multiple small teams is paramount for successfully executing large-scale projects, programs, and value streams. That's the topic we'll discuss next.

Addressing collaboration and integration challenges in small team environments

Collaboration and synchronization of activities are essential in small team environments for successfully executing large projects or programs. However, integrating the work of multiple small teams can pose significant challenges. Here, we'll address these challenges and explore strategies for overcoming them effectively:

- **Collaboration**: Collaborating effectively among multiple small teams requires clear communication channels, shared goals, and alignment of efforts. Each team must understand its role within the larger project or program and work collaboratively towards common objectives. Regular reviews, meeting events, and collaborative tools can facilitate team communication and coordination. Collaboration isn't always an intuitive instinct so it should be facilitated and supported intentionally.
- **Synchronization of activities**: Synchronizing activities across multiple small teams involves aligning timelines, milestones, and deliverables to ensure smooth progress and avoid bottlenecks. Establishing a common cadence for activities, such as BLAST integrated increment planning sessions and retrospectives, can help teams synchronize their efforts and maintain momentum. Additionally, regular cross-team meetings and stand-ups can provide opportunities to identify dependencies and address any issues promptly. The benefits of this coordination is a considerable factor in managing and eliminating dependencies across teams, products, and capabilities.
- **Team-of-teams working and planning sessions**: While multiple teams can come together in a single meeting, that should not be the normal practice for all the reasons previously cited about the challenges of communication and participation in large team settings. Bluntly speaking, large meetings should be limited to information dissemination rather than planning or working sessions. For the most part, each team should appoint one representative to attend a BLAST team-of-teams working or planning session. The ToT representatives form a small group that works in parallel with their assigned teams. This is why BLASTs should not have more than nine teams: to ensure that BLAST representatives can collaborate effectively in small team sessions. If you need more teams, set up additional BLASTs. The assigned representatives can vary across meetings depending on the skills and knowledge required.
- **Integration of work**: Integrating the work of multiple small teams requires careful planning and coordination to ensure that individual contributions come together seamlessly to achieve work or product delivery objectives. This involves establishing interfaces and integration points between teams, defining clear standards and guidelines for work integration, and conducting regular integration testing to validate interoperability.
- **Managing dependencies**: Managing dependencies between multiple small teams is critical to avoid delays and ensure that project milestones are met. Teams must identify and prioritize dependencies early in the project lifecycle, establish mechanisms for tracking and resolving dependencies, and communicate dependencies transparently across teams. Regular dependency

management meetings and dependency mapping exercises can help teams proactively address dependencies and minimize their impact on project timelines.

By addressing these collaboration and integration challenges proactively, organizations can harness the collective capabilities of multiple small teams to deliver integrated increments of new value effectively and efficiently. In summary, effective collaboration, synchronization of activities, integration of work, and management of dependencies are key pillars of success in small team environments, enabling organizations to achieve their strategic objectives and drive business growth. Next, we'll explore how integrating data and analytics serves as a cornerstone for mastering Lean-Agile principles and effective VSM.

Leveraging data and analytics for decision-making

In the previous chapter, *Enhancing Decision-Making in the Lean-Agile Enterprise*, we addressed the prevalent issue of organizations being inundated with vast amounts of data. We introduced the **BRIA-QIDA** (**Business-Role-Information-Action and Question-Information- Decision-Action**) approach to assist organizations in assessing the necessary information for making informed decisions and executing timely actions. Now, let's look into the tools and platforms that facilitate the transformation of this data deluge into actionable insights.

In the era of big data, leveraging analytics for strategic decision-making is crucial. Leaders should invest in analytics platforms that provide real-time insights into operational processes, customer behaviors, and market trends. Data-driven decision-making enables organizations to be more agile, responsive, and competitive. Executives should sponsor the BRIA workshops to ensure the development of capabilities that provide immediate access to the information needed to answer our most pressing business questions.

Leveraging data and analytics is fundamental to mastering Lean-Agile principles and effective value stream management practices. In the current technical environment, characterized by large and diverse data sets, harnessing this information becomes a significant competitive advantage.

In Lean-Agile environments, where responsiveness and adaptability are key, data analytics platforms can provide actionable insights rapidly. These insights are crucial for understanding customer needs and behaviors, enabling organizations to deliver value optimally. By closely monitoring and analyzing performance metrics, waste can be minimized through continuous improvement – a core Lean principle.

For VSM, data analytics facilitates a comprehensive view of the value stream, allowing for the identification of bottlenecks and inefficiencies. Real-time data feeds into VSM tools enabling teams to track the flow of value from concept to customer, ensuring that every step in the process contributes positively to the overall outcome. In order to succeed with this approach, data needs to be accessible, organized, high quality, consistent, and relevant. It's not enough to simply connect your tools to a value stream management platform and trust that insights will arise out of your data. In the 2023 Value Stream Management Consortium's *State of Value Stream Management Report*, only 4% of respondents had connected their data to a VSM platform, the lowest of any step in the implementation roadmap.

Leaders should invest in robust analytics platforms and foster a culture where data-driven decision-making is the norm. Executives and employees alike need timely access to the information required to make informed decisions and take appropriate actions. Teams should be empowered to use data insights to guide their work, experiment with new ideas, and pivot quickly based on feedback and changing market conditions.

This data-centric approach aligns with the Agile principle of delivering working solutions frequently. It ensures that decisions are not based on gut feelings or outdated reports but on current, relevant data that reflects the true state of affairs.

In summary, integrating data and analytics into decision-making processes for Lean-Agile and VSM can lead to the following:

- Improved efficiency and productivity through the elimination of waste
- Enhanced customer satisfaction by quickly responding to their needs and behaviors
- Greater market adaptability by understanding and reacting to trends
- Better risk management by anticipating and mitigating potential issues before they escalate
- Increased return on investment by making informed strategic decisions that align with the organization's goals and customer value

For organizations striving to be at the forefront of their industries, the mastery of data and analytics is not just a strategic asset; it's a necessity.

Implementing VSM to align IT development activities

Recall that value stream management, as a methodology, is about identifying improvement opportunities, prioritizing the work to have the most value-added impact, and creating and executing a Kaizen Plan to achieve our priorities. In *Chapter 4, Driving Improvements with Value Stream Management (VSM)*, we introduced the nine-step VSM methodology for this purpose. Then, in *Chapter 5, Introducing the VSM Implementation Roadmap*, we discussed the **Value Stream Management Consortium's** (**VSMC**) approach to implementing VSM to align IT with the organization's value stream improvements.

In the journey toward organizational agility and operational improvement with Lean and Agile, there are two dimensions highlighted by the VSMC's research: **flow** and **value realization**. VSM is tailored to improve both. In service of building an effective VSM capability, the VSM implementation roadmap was created to guide leaders and practitioners through the process of standing up VSM within an organization and sustaining the practice. *Chapter 5* steps through the roadmap in detail, and we'll summarize it briefly here. As depicted in *Figure 11.2*, the VSM Roadmap begins with the assumption that any current state is a viable starting point, and then steps through each activity required to establish, build, deploy, and maintain the value stream improvement activities.

Figure 11.2 – VSM implementation roadmap

The VSM Roadmap outlines the steps and strategies for effectively implementing VSM within an organization to improve efficiency and value delivery. This roadmap serves as a guide for executives and managers looking to streamline their processes and maximize the value of their operations. While it can be applied in any value steam improvement initiative, it was specifically developed to support knowledge work and IT.

By following the VSM implementation roadmap, organizations can identify and eliminate waste to optimize their value streams flows, and enhance their overall agility. Let's review each step:

Step	Description
Start	Get started from wherever you are, on the right foot. Understand the basics.
Assess	Understand your current state, scope, and context.
Vision	Set a compelling target vision to establish buy-in and build clarity and enthusiasm.
Identify	Identify your relevant value streams – anything that delivers a product or service.
Organize	Assemble the people accountable for every step in each value stream.
Map	Lay out each activity and its performance, working backward from delivered value.
Connect	Bring together data to uncover insights into your value stream's flow.
Inspect	Review performance insights and potential improvements.
Adapt	Use insights to design and perform experiments that optimize flow and value.

Overall, the VSM implementation roadmap offers a comprehensive and clear approach to implementing value stream management, aligned with the principles of lean and agile methodologies. It provides a clear path for executives and managers to enable continuous improvement and maximize the value delivered to customers. By leveraging the implementation roadmap, you can establish a solid foundation and process for effective adoption of VSM tooling, without stumbling over the challenges involved in that effort.

Implementing VSM tools

Modern VSM tools support DevOps-based software delivery processes by visualizing the flow of work across the end-to-end activities constituting the software delivery value stream and measuring the success of each delivery cycle. In other words, VSM tools help visualize and analyze the flow of materials (for example, code and other assets) and information required to bring a product or service to customers. By identifying bottlenecks, waste, and opportunities for improvement, these tools support Lean and Agile initiatives, enabling better decision-making and prioritization based on customer value.

Through 'what-if' analysis, VSM tools are instrumental in optimizing the processes involved in delivering a product or service to customers. These tools play a vital role in visualizing and analyzing value flow. By mapping each step of the product development lifecycle, VSM tools allow teams to identify and understand the value of each action, spotting bottlenecks, redundant tasks, and any form of waste that may exist – be it overproduction, waiting times, unnecessary transportation, over-processing, excess inventory, unnecessary movement, or defects.

Implementing VSM tools is particularly beneficial when used with Lean-Agile initiatives and methodologies. Specifically, VSM tools enhance Lean-Agile solution delivery activities by providing clear insights into how actual work aligns with these principles and how it contributes to the organization's overall goals.

These data-driven insights enable better decision-making and prioritization of people and functionality. By understanding where value is created and where it is diminished, teams can make informed choices that align their efforts with customer value. Prioritization becomes less about who shouts the loudest and more about objective measures of what will deliver the greatest benefit to the consumer and, consequently, to the business.

In software delivery, as with any other value stream, various metrics are utilized to determine the business value and efficiency of the delivery pipeline:

- **Lead time**: The total time it takes from a customer request to the delivery of the final product. It's a measure of the efficiency of the entire process.
- **Cycle time**: This measures the time it takes to complete one activity within the value stream, which helps establish the measurement of performance within each stage.
- **Throughput**: The number of units of work a system can deliver in a certain period of time. This metric can reflect a team's or a process's capacity.
- **Wait time**: The actual time spent waiting between stages of the value stream.
- **Work-in-Progress (WIP)**: The amount of work that has started but not yet completed. High WIP levels can indicate issues with bottlenecks and overloading of team capacity. High volumes of WIP also tend to hide errors and defects, accumulating more technical debt in the process.
- **Defect rate**: The frequency of errors in the deliverables. This can be used to gauge the quality of output and the effectiveness of quality control processes.
- **Value stream flow efficiency**: The ratio of process time to lead time indicates how much of the overall cycle time is spent adding value. A low-value stream efficiency indicates significant waste and delays in the value stream steps.
- **Feedback loop speed**: The time it takes for information or issues to be communicated to the development team for action, exemplified by the rapid iteration cycle of code deployment, testing, and refinement in software engineering through continuous integration and deployment pipelines.

The successful implementation of VSM tools allows an organization to shift its focus from merely being busy to being productive. It helps create a continuous improvement culture where decision-making is driven by data and customer value, not by flawed assumptions or inertia. By embracing VSM tools, companies can make the necessary strides toward delivering their products and services in the most efficient, effective, and customer-centric way possible.

VSM tools are essential for organizations that aim to optimize value delivery through their software development processes. VSM tools enable these organizations to align around common goals, identify bottlenecks, and improve efficiency. By establishing clear value streams within an organization, VSM tools facilitate the measurement of key **DORA** metrics such as deployment frequency, lead time for changes, mean time to recovery, and change failure rate, which are crucial for assessing performance and implementing Agile and DevOps methods.

The VSM tools in the market vary widely, and they generally provide capabilities to connect disparate teams and tools, visualize workflows, measure performance metrics, and align organizational structures with customer needs. These tools help break down silos, create a shared understanding of workflow, and automate the collection of performance data to drive continuous improvement.

The authors of this book propose extending the concept of VSM tools to effectively '*instrument*' all organizational value streams. This concept diverges from workflow systems, which originated from the business process reengineering and improvement fields to instantiate standardized processes. Workflow systems promote a mindset focused on controlling process and information flows, while VSM goes beyond this functionality. VSM not only facilitates process and information flow control but also aids in identifying areas for improvement and experimenting with potential value stream flow enhancements in near real time.

Now, let's transition from our discussion on leveraging data to exploring change frameworks that support our Lean-Agile and VSM implementation initiatives.

Enhancing software delivery through Flow Metrics

Flow Metrics, coined by Dr. Mik Kersten in the Flow Framework, are pivotal business-level metrics tailored to illuminate the software delivery process. They serve to connect business objectives with IT operations by focusing on the flow of value through product value streams. The key Flow Metrics include:

1. **Flow Velocity**: Quantifies the number of work items completed within a specific timeframe, offering insights into team delivery speed and capacity.
2. **Flow Efficiency**: Reflects the ratio of active time spent on work items versus the total time taken, highlighting operational efficiency.
3. **Flow Time**: Measures the comprehensive duration from work initiation to completion, encompassing both active work and waiting periods.
4. **Flow Load**: Indicates the aggregate number of work items in progress at any given moment, pinpointing potential bottlenecks and workload issues.

Though not technically a single metric, **Flow Distribution** is similarly critical to track as these measures Illustrate the composition of work items (e.g., features, defects) in progress, ensuring a balanced flow of value.

These metrics are indispensable for organizations aiming to refine software delivery processes and harmonize them with business goals. They provide a unified language for business and IT leaders to drive informed decisions and continuous improvement.

While both Flow Metrics and traditional lean-oriented metrics strive to enhance efficiency and value delivery, they diverge in focus and application:

- **Focus and Scope**: Flow Metrics are purpose-built for software development, concentrating on value stream flow to bridge business-IT gaps. In contrast, traditional lean metrics, originating from manufacturing, target waste reduction and process enhancement across industries.
- **Key Metrics**: Flow Metrics center on metrics like Flow Velocity, Efficiency, Time, Load, and Distribution and are specifically tailored for software delivery contexts. Traditional lean metrics encompass Cycle Time, Lead Time, Throughput, Work In Progress (WIP), and First Pass Yield (FPY), which are applicable broadly across various industry and domain sectors.
- **Application**: Flow Metrics are primarily deployed in software development to align IT with business objectives and enhance value delivery. Traditional lean metrics find application in manufacturing and beyond, optimizing processes and reducing waste.
- **Measurement Approach**: Flow Metrics emphasize end-to-end value flow, integrating active and idle times to prioritize business value delivery. In contrast, traditional lean metrics target specific process steps for efficiency gains and waste minimization.

In summary, while both metric frameworks aim to optimize efficiency and value delivery, Flow Metrics are tailored to software contexts, emphasizing continuous value flow. Traditional lean metrics, broader in scope, focus on process refinement and waste reduction across industries.

Adopting a change management framework

Organizational change can be disorienting and cause negative disruption if not properly managed. Instead of using an unproven or ad-hoc process, leaders can turn to established change management frameworks to guide their organizations through the turbulence of change. Kotter's 8-step process for leading change and the **ADKAR** change model are two of the most prominent and proven frameworks. They support planning, implementing, and sustaining change and are briefly discussed in the following subsections.

Kotter's 8-step process for leading change

John Kotter, professor emeritus at the Harvard Business School and the founder of Kotter International, a management consulting company, has authored numerous books and articles on leadership and change, including the highly influential book, *Leading Change*. His seminal works presented the 8-step process for leading change, designed to help organizations overcome the resistance often accompanying significant change and foster acceptance and engagement. Kotter has significantly inspired and impacted how organizations manage and adapt to change, emphasizing the importance of urgency, vision, communication, and making change stick within the organizational culture. Kotter's contributions have made him one of the leading voices in organizational behavior and leadership studies.

Figure 11.3 illustrates Kotter's model and is followed by a brief description of each element.

Figure 11.3 – Kotter's eight-step change model

1. **Create a sense of urgency**: Inspire people to act by communicating the need for change that appeals to people's heads and hearts. This need must be sufficiently compelling to move people out of their comfort zones and escape the inertia of the status quo. It requires open discussions about what's at stake and the opportunities change presents. For change to succeed, it must inspire and align people to make the change a reality.
2. **Build a guiding coalition**: Assemble a volunteer team of effective people from within the organization who can guide, coordinate, and communicate change activities. They must have the power, energy, and influence to support collaborative change.
3. **Form a strategic vision**: Craft a vision to direct the change effort and develop strategic initiatives to achieve that vision. Clarify how the future state will differ from the past and get buy-in to make the change a reality through initiatives linked directly to the vision.

4. **Enlist a volunteer army**: Significant change can only occur when many people rally around a shared challenge or opportunity. Enlist people who want to actively engage and make a difference. These volunteers must want to collaborate to achieve the goal together.
5. **Enable action by removing barriers**: Identify and remove obstacles that hinder the change effort, whether organizational structures, skill deficits, legacy policies, and practices, or anything else that prevents employees from executing the vision.
6. **Generate short-term wins**: Plan, define, and execute visible and unambiguous opportunities for success as soon as possible. Short-term wins prove that sacrifices are paying off, which can silence detractors and energize supporters. Ensure wins are real and can be recognized, collected, and widely communicated – early and often – to track progress and energize people to persevere and prevent returning to legacy thinking and acting.
7. **Sustain acceleration**: Use the credibility gained from early wins to progressively tackle bigger, more difficult changes. After every win, analyze what went right and needs improving, and then set more ambitious goals. Relentlessly initiate change until the vision becomes a reality, having a bias for action.
8. **Institute change**: Anchor the changes into the culture to ensure they become the norm and replace old habits. Communicate and celebrate how the new behaviors and attitudes have improved performance and resulted in wins. Use systems thinking to evaluate systems and processes to avoid expensive and ineffective local optimizations and ensure management practices reinforce the new behaviors, mindsets, and ways of working.

Change initiatives often fail because they don't address the human element, such as how individuals in the organization feel about the change. Consequently, success with Kotter's process requires focusing on the people side of change. By following these eight steps, leaders can confidently steer their organizations through the choppy waters of change and emerge stronger and more prepared for the future.

The ADKAR® change model

The **ADKAR model**, developed by Jeff Hiatt, founder of Prosci in 1994, is a cornerstone of the Prosci method, a comprehensive approach to change management. Hiatt, a former engineer and program manager at Bell Labs, designed this model after studying change management practices across over 700 organizations. ADKAR, an acronym for **Awareness**, **Desire**, **Knowledge**, **Ability**, and **Reinforcement**, was created to address the human side of change and has seen widespread adoption. Hiatt's contributions to change management extend beyond the ADKAR model, reflecting his extensive research and writing in the field.

ADKAR represents a bottom-up approach, focusing on the transitions individuals need to make for a change to be successful. *Figure 11.4 – Prosci ADKAR change model*, provides a high-level overview of each component, and a brief description of each element follows.

Figure 11.4 – Prosci ADKAR change model

- **Awareness**: Make sure that employees understand the need for change. This means communicating the nature of the change and the rationale behind it.
- **Desire**: Encourage a desire to participate in and support the change. This involves engaging with employees on an emotional level and addressing their motivations.
- **Knowledge**: Provide the training and education necessary to enable employees to realize the change. This can be through workshops, seminars, or hands-on training.
- **Ability**: Give employees the tools, resources, and support they need to implement change effectively. This includes time, budget, and changes to their daily routines.
- **Reinforcement**: Implement measures to ensure the change sticks. This includes ongoing support, recognizing success, and embedding change into the organization's culture.

The ADKAR model is known for its simplicity and effectiveness, allowing leaders to diagnose gaps in their change process and provide targeted interventions at different stages of employee adaptation. It's a tool that can be used for personal change and enterprise organizational change management initiatives.

ADKAR and Kotter's model offer two distinct approaches to managing organizational change. Kotter focuses on the *strategic* aspect of change, prioritizing leadership buy-in and the steps necessary to facilitate effective change management. It starts with establishing a sense of urgency and is followed by creating a guiding coalition, developing a vision and strategy, communicating the change vision, empowering broad-based action, generating short-term wins, consolidating gains, producing more change, and finally, anchoring new approaches in the culture.

In contrast, the ADKAR emphasizes an *individual's* journey through change, highlighting key stages of awareness, desire, knowledge, ability, and reinforcement.

Moreover, Kotter's approach is strategic and top-down, while ADKAR is a bottom-up approach that is more individual-centric, focusing on personal readiness and support for change. Leaders can use these frameworks independently or together to guide their change initiatives, ensuring they are thoughtful, well executed, and ultimately successful.

Summary

In *Chapter 11*, we have presented executive-level strategies for successful organizational transformation through Lean-Agile principles and practices. This executive summary provided actionable insights to drive innovation, enhance efficiency, and maintain competitiveness in today's dynamic business environment. Specifically, the chapter focused on practical approaches for implementing Lean-Agile principles as a continuous business transformation strategy, ensuring you have the tools and knowledge to effectively lead your organization through change.

Key takeaways include building a roadmap for transformative change, leveraging change management frameworks, implementing value stream management methods, fostering a culture of continuous learning, using metrics for tracking progress, and building collaborative cross- functional Agile teams.

These insights are crucial for executives seeking to streamline processes and drive sustainable organizational growth. One final thought before we conclude this chapter: This chapter provided a high-level overview of the information and concepts covered in previous chapters as a recap of critical concepts contained within this book. However, as an executive, you need to be aware of the details from those chapters to effectively facilitate the transition to a Lean-Agile organization.

In the next chapter, we'll consolidate the key concepts and lessons learned throughout this book as a set of cross-cutting themes, offering practical guidance on implementing these strategies effectively within your organization.

Questions

This section is offered for those of you who want to evaluate your comprehension and retention of the information provided in this chapter. There are five questions. The answers are provided in the next section. Recalling the exact verbiage of the original content is not essential. Instead, it's more important to recall the concepts and their applications.

1. What are two established change management frameworks discussed in this chapter?
2. What are the eight steps in Kotter's model for leading change?
3. What does the ADKAR change model stand for and what are its components?
4. How does Kotter's approach to managing organizational change differ from the ADKAR model?
5. What are some key takeaways from *Chapter 11* regarding organizational transformation through Lean-Agile principles and practices?

Answers

1. The two established change management frameworks discussed in the document are Kotter's 8- step process for leading change and the ADKAR change model.
2. The eight steps in Kotter's 8-step process for leading change are:
   1) Create a sense of urgency
   2) Build a guiding coalition
   3) Form a strategic vision
   4) Enlist a volunteer army
   5) Enable action by removing barriers
   6) Generate short-term wins
   7) Sustain acceleration
   8) Institute change
3. The ADKAR change model stands for Awareness, Desire, Knowledge, Ability, and Reinforcement.
4. Kotter's 8-step process differs from the ADKAR model as follows: Kotter's approach is a strategic top-down approach which is focused on leadership buy-in and the steps necessary to facilitate effective change management. In contrast, the ADKAR model is more individual-centric, focusing on an individual's journey through change and highlighting key stages of awareness, desire, knowledge, ability, and reinforcement.
5. Some key takeaways from *Chapter 11* regarding organizational transformation include building a roadmap for transformative change, leveraging change management frameworks, implementing value stream management methods, fostering a culture of continuous learning, using metrics for tracking progress, and building collaborative cross-functional Agile teams.

12
Building Lean-Agile and VSM Mastery

Widespread lean adoption would make the US more competitive.

Industry Week, September 2023 [1]

Congratulations! You've acquired a wealth of knowledge on driving competitive advantage through continuous business transformations with Lean-Agile and **Value Stream Management** (**VSM**) practices. However, our journey doesn't end here. It's time to consolidate your learnings and start your journey to Lean-Agile mastery by applying what you have learned.

The goal of this final chapter is to empower you with a comprehensive understanding of Lean-Agile and VSM practices and their application in real-world scenarios. By consolidating your learning and providing practical guidance, our objective is to equip you with the tools and strategies needed to drive transformative change within your organization.

Here, we will recap the key learnings from each section of the book and provide actionable strategies to embed these practices within your organization, fostering continuous business transformation that enhances competitiveness and customer-centricity. Specifically, you'll gain insights into how Lean, Agile, and VSM principles work in concert to drive value-centric customer delivery and sustainable organizational excellence.

In today's dynamic business landscape, where competition is fierce and change is constant, mastering Lean-Agile and VSM practices is essential for staying ahead. This chapter will cover the following topics:

- Addressing labor's declining share of GDP
- Recapping the main concepts and essential takeaways
- Connecting themes and real-world examples
- Applying real-world illustrations
- Empowering change: a call to action for organizational excellence

Addressing labor's declining share of GDP

Did you know that the U.S. market share for manufactured goods by domestic producers has been declining steadily for the past 20 years? According to the CPA Domestic Market Share Index, it reached a record low of 66% in 2022. A critical issue cited is a two-thirds fall in labor's share of U.S. GDP. Economists cite three main factors contributing to this decline:

1. **Weak productivity growth**: Sluggish productivity growth significantly impacts labor's share, accounting for half of the decline. [2]
2. **Income inequality**: The widening gap between average and median wages contributes to the decline, representing 19% of the overall gap in labor's share. [3]
3. **Technological progress**: Unequal effects on labor and capital due to biased technological change play a role. Capital deepening (increased capital relative to labor) is a contributing mechanism. [4]

This alarming trend underscores the pressing need for organizations to return to the basics of Lean production practices. Additionally, they must incorporate Agile practices that originated within the software industry to adapt and evolve through digital innovations across products, services, and business-enabling systems. Together, these strategies help organizations navigate the complexities of the global economy effectively and remain competitive.

That's a bold statement and a tall task to undertake. So, let's explore how responsible Lean-Agile enterprises and society can collaborate to address these vital challenges.

Promoting corporate responsibility through Lean-Agile practices

Henry Ford famously understood the importance of fair wages for his employees, recognizing that they needed to be able to afford the products they were creating. Otherwise, he would have no customers for his automobiles. This principle of enlightened management is crucial today, where businesses must bear responsibility for broader societal issues such as income deficiencies and technological disruptions. Lean-Agile practices offer a framework for addressing these challenges while also driving business success.

Addressing income inequality

Leaders and shareholders in Lean-Agile enterprises should recognize their responsibility to pay fair wages based on the skills and expertise of their employees. Fair compensation is not only a moral obligation but also a strategic necessity. By ensuring that their employees are fairly compensated, companies help foster a robust economy filled with prospective customers who have the financial resources to purchase their products and services. Additionally, by ensuring that employees are fairly compensated, businesses can foster a more motivated and loyal workforce, ultimately contributing to a more stable and prosperous outcome. This approach recognizes that the very people who contribute to the company's success are also its customers, sustaining the market for their products and services.

Navigating technological progress

While Lean-Agile enterprises can leverage technology to enhance efficiency and value delivery, society must address the broader implications of technological progress. Ensuring that technology does not displace workers at the expense of the economy is a collective challenge. Businesses, policymakers, and communities need to work together to create solutions that balance technological advancement with job security and economic stability. This collaborative effort will help mitigate the risks of automation and ensure that technological progress benefits everyone.

The employment of Lean practices, combined with technology enhancements, helps businesses eliminate inefficiencies, reduce unnecessary inventories, minimize defects, and empower employees to participate in problem-solving and decision-making. Additionally, the adaptability of Agile practices ensures that these types of improvements become a continuous process. This holistic approach ensures that organizations contribute positively to society while achieving their strategic goals, ultimately fostering a sustainable and prosperous future for both the company and its customers. The key to continuity is understanding that technology, including AI, cannot be viewed as a replacement for people but as an enabler for them. People drive our economy through their purchases, so we need to view technology as a means to expand our economy by freeing up resources to deliver new products and services that we haven't yet thought of.

Having addressed the two-thirds decline in labor's share of U.S. GDP and how Lean-Agile enterprises can respond, let's conclude this book with a recap of what you have learned, including cross-cutting themes. We will also provide three real-world case studies where Lean-Agile practices have improved business operations.

Recapping the main concepts and essential takeaways

In this section, we will quickly summarize the key points covered in the four parts and twelve chapters of this book. We'll start with the first three chapters, which comprise *Part 1*.

Part 1: Summarizing Lean-Agile foundations

In *Part 1*, we explored the foundational aspects of Lean-Agile and Value Stream Management (VSM). The importance of not just surviving but leading in a rapidly changing digital landscape was emphasized. Lean, Agile, and VSM practices were highlighted as crucial for optimizing value streams, refining processes, and fostering collaboration.

Navigating digital transformations

Chapter 1, Navigating Lean-Agile Transformations, introduced Lean-Agile methodologies, underscoring their significance in today's digital landscape. Key insights included the following:

- The necessity of Lean-Agile mastery
- Fundamental principles and practical applications
- Enhancing organizational performance through Lean-Agile practices

Solving complex business problems

Chapter 2, Solving Complex Business Problems with Agility, delved into Agile methodologies. Key points covered were as follows:

- Agile's iterative and incremental development
- Collaboration techniques and Scrum methodologies
- The team-of-teams approach for breaking down organizational silos
- Strategies for continuous improvement and process streamlining

Establishing efficient flows

Chapter 3, Establishing Lean Flows to Improve Productivity, examined Lean principles focusing on the following:

- Productivity enhancement, efficiency optimization, and waste elimination
- Implementation strategies and standard terminologies
- Embedding Lean principles into organizational culture for sustained growth

This concludes our summary of *Part 1, Implementing Lean-Agile Foundations*. Next, we will explore the key points from *Part 2, Making Value Stream Improvements*.

Part 2: Insightful approaches to value stream improvement

Part 2 of this book focuses on Value Stream Management (VSM) and its role in enhancing Lean-Agile principles within organizations. It provides practical strategies to optimize processes, drive improvements, and foster a culture of continuous enhancement. This section equips you with the tools to drive meaningful change and achieve Lean-Agile mastery.

Driving improvements with the nine-step VSM methodology

Chapter 4, Driving Improvements with Value Stream Management, introduced the transformative potential of VSM through the nine-step VSM methodology. The chapter emphasized a mindset of continuous improvement essential for thriving in today's competitive landscape. Key insights included the following:

- The nine-step VSM methodology for assessing improvement opportunities
- VSM as a strategic approach to perpetual improvement
- Practical strategies for identifying and prioritizing value streams
- A roadmap for leveraging VSM for sustained success through operational excellence

By adopting this methodology, you gained a framework to systematically assess improvement opportunities and execute effective initiatives, mitigating risks of stagnation and decline.

Implementing the VSM roadmap

Chapter 5, Introducing the VSM Implementation Roadmap, explored the practical approach of the **Value Stream Management Consortium** (**VSMC**) for implementing VSM principles. Building on *Chapter 4*, it presented a nine-step framework: Start, Assess, Vision, Identify, Organize, Map, Connect, Inspect, and Adapt. Key insights included the following:

- A comprehensive framework to drive transformative change by aligning IT efforts with ongoing value stream improvement opportunities
- A roadmap to integrate Lean and Agile practices to optimize value streams
- Ensuring IT alignments with strategic objectives and customer-centric value delivery

This roadmap provided structured guidance for navigating complex business transformations with confidence and agility.

Achieving streamlined value streams

Chapter 6, Navigating Value Stream Optimization, delved into the intricacies of value stream optimization. It explored both macro and micro levels of operational dynamics, highlighting the quest for seamless flow within organizations. Key points included the following:

- The significance of Lean flow principles and Agile's iterative planning
- Addressing challenges disrupting streamlined workflows
- Transitioning from traditional hierarchical structures to a value stream perspective
- Optimizing flow to enhance operational efficiency

The chapter emphasized the importance of intentional workflow design and strategic resource alignment for fostering collaboration and continuous improvement.

Enhancing organizational flows with value stream networks

Chapter 7, Connecting the Value Stream Network, examined the interconnected flows within organizations from inception to customer delivery. Acknowledging insights from Mik Kersten's book, *From Project to Product*, we highlighted the need for lifecycle, product-oriented thinking and the importance of aligning our efforts with customer needs. Key insights included the following:

- Understanding the interconnected flows of work items
- Integrating people, processes, information, and capabilities to optimize value delivery
- Shifting from project-centric to product-centric and customer-focused perspectives

- Anchoring value streams to customer journeys for better organization and visualization
- Emphasizing the importance of ongoing management and refinement to ensure continuous improvement and adaptability

By mastering the principles outlined in *Part 2*, you are equipped to navigate the complexities of value stream optimization and propel your organization toward sustained success and innovation in today's competitive landscape. Now let's move on to recapping the topics covered in *Part 3*.

Part 3: Coordinating Lean-Agile teams for enterprise value delivery

Part 3 of this book explores how organizations can drive continuous value delivery through the BLAST framework and the BASE Conceptual Model. The BLAST Framework coordinates the work of multiple Lean-Agile teams collaborating on solution-oriented tasks, while the BASE Conceptual Model orchestrates multiple BLAST teams to incrementally deliver value at the enterprise level. This section introduces strategies for integrating these approaches to foster continuous business transformations and enhance overall organizational efficiency.

Implementing the BLAST framework

Chapter 8, Implementing the Basic Lean-Agile Solution Team (BLAST) , introduced a comprehensive approach to integrating the work of multiple collaborating teams on larger projects. It highlighted the need for actionable methodologies in modern business, combining Lean efficiency with Agile adaptability. Key insights included the following:

- The BLAST framework integrates work across multiple Lean and Agile teams on larger projects and programs
- It harmonizes Lean efficiency with Agile's iterative development
- Some BLAST teams follow a flow track, while others follow the Agile timeboxed track
- Situationally, teams may employ both Lean and Agile tracks, such as IT departments that leverage Agile's timeboxed approach to manage planning and work cadences while taking advantage of Lean's flow concepts to improve flow via integrated and automated CI/CD and DevOps pipelines
- BLAST implements four core processes, seventeen steps, enterprise cadences, three roles, and three artifacts

In conclusion, *Chapter 8* provided a deep dive into Lean-Agile integration through the BLAST framework, offering valuable insights into orchestrating multiple small teams within a continuous flow environment.

Achieving enterprise excellence with BASE

Chapter 9, Defining a Business Agility System for the Enterprise (BASE), explored the BASE conceptual model. BASE is not a prescriptive Lean-Agile framework or methodology. Instead, it specifies a cyclical series of common processes and activities that help an organization coordinate the work of multiple BLASTs to deliver new integrated increments on a predictable cadence. BASE does not explain how the work is to be performed, as the organization must determine what adds value and how to achieve maximal value at the lowest practical cost. Key insights included the following:

- The BASE Model emphasizes collaboration and continuous improvement through feedback loops
- It focuses on the "product or service lifecycle" to deliver new customer value continuously
- The purpose of the BASE model is to define a "Virtuous Circle for continuous enterprise improvements" that revolves around customer-centric practices
- BASE specifies four tenets of the Lean-Agile enterprise and eight core processes
- BASE puts the customer journey at the center of its focus, with product owners and value managers representing their customers' interests
- BASE employs value stream management practices to help accelerate the delivery of value
- Having a focus on delivering Integrated Increments (i.e., MVPs, MVIs, and MVRs) ensures organizations concentrate on generating sufficient value to meet customer needs while minimizing waste.

In conclusion, *Chapter 9* emphasized the importance of customer-centric practices and maintaining the "Virtuous Circle" within the BASE Framework to adapt to market changes swiftly and deliver incremental value.

Summarizing organizational excellence: implementing BLAST and BASE frameworks

The BLAST Framework and BASE conceptual model presented in *Part 3* of this book are crucial for driving rapid innovation, peak efficiency, and continuous value delivery within organizations. The BLAST Framework facilitates adaptive iterations to create integrated increments while eliminating waste and constraints, and the BASE Framework focuses on customer-centric value delivery and navigating the product lifecycle with precision. Together, they provide organizations with the tools and methodologies necessary to thrive in today's dynamic business landscape.

Part 4: Reflecting on Lean-Agile mastery

In this section, we recap the key points covered in *Chapters 10, Enhancing Decision-Making in the Lean-Agile Enterprise* and *Chapter 11, Implementing Strategies for Organizational Transformation. Chapter 12* is the chapter you are currently reading and therefore does not need to be recapped.

First, we'll recall the advanced concepts for refining decision-making processes in today's digital and profit-driven economy, exploring how BRIA and QIDA concepts empower organizations with sharper insights and strategic choices. Next, we'll revisit guidance for implementing Lean-Agile and VSM practices, demystifying complex methodologies, and offering clear pathways for effective adoption. Together, these chapters offer a holistic perspective on navigating modern business environments while driving continuous improvement and transformational change. Let's review the key points from *Chapter 10*.

Sailing through the oceans of data to master decision-making

Chapter 10, Enhancing Decision-Making in the Lean-Agile Enterprise, focused on uncovering critical business questions that unlock data to drive meaningful insights. Key points included the following:

- The chapter introduces the **Business Role Intelligence Analysis** (**BRIA**) and **Question–Information–Decision–Action** (**QIDA**) processes to help refine data and align it with business objectives
- How the digital age presents both opportunities and challenges due to vast data availability
- Noted that organizations often struggle to derive actionable insights despite abundant data
- The BRIA process helps distill and harness vast data reserves into actionable information
- The chapter emphasized converting raw data into tangible insights to improve business decisions and improve value stream efficiency

Simplifying organizational transformation

Chapter 11, Implementing Strategies for Organizational Transformation, offered practical strategies for executives to support and sustain the adoption of Lean-Agile and VSM practices. Key points included the following:

- The rapid pace of change in industries necessitates modern approaches to drive innovation and competitiveness
- Noted that simplifying processes, eliminating waste, and adapting to shifting business requirements are essential
- Emphasized the need to cultivate a culture of continuous learning and improvement, fostering experimentation, and providing resources for employee development
- Building cross-functional teams enhances collaboration and problem-solving, with a focus on the advantages of smaller teams
- Data-driven decision-making is crucial for mastering Lean-Agile and VSM principles and practices, identifying customer needs, and enhancing efficiency

- Implementing VSM tools is indispensable for visualizing workflows, pinpointing bottlenecks, and optimizing value delivery
- Kotter's 8-Step Process and the ADKAR change model were introduced as established frameworks for managing organizational change

Now that we've recapped the key points and insights presented in the previous chapters, let's shift our focus to examining this book's cross-cutting themes plus real-world examples.

Connecting cross-cutting themes and real-world examples

In this book, we've thoroughly explored the depths of Lean-Agile mastery - as we know them today, uncovering fundamental principles guiding organizational transformation. This section examines the core themes that serve as threads weaving the Lean-Agile concepts together seamlessly, providing coherence and insight into driving organizational success.

The cross-cutting themes presented here enrich our understanding of Lean-Agile and Value Stream Management (VSM) practices, offering invaluable perspectives on how successful organizations apply these concepts to drive business improvements. We will analyze how they connect—through *agility, adaptability*, *continuous improvement*, *customer-centricity*, and *breaking down silos*—and their profound impact on organizational excellence.

Through this lens, we will assess their significance, gaining insights that illuminate pathways for organizations to thrive amid change and uncertainty. Once this solid foundation is laid, we will transition to exploring real-world examples where these principles and practices helped several organizations reshape their ability to compete in their respective industries.

Examining cross-cutting themes

In this subsection, we examine the fundamental concepts or principles that serve as cross-cutting themes throughout this book. These themes provide coherence and continuity to the overall topic of Lean-Agile mastery. Identifying and understanding these cross-cutting themes is essential for exploring the connections and patterns that emerge across the chapters. With this understanding, we identify the following cross-cutting themes as applied to the principles and practices outlined in this book:

- **Emphasis on agility and adaptability**: Each chapter underscores the importance of agility and adaptability in today's dynamic business environment. Whether it's navigating digital transformations, solving complex business problems, establishing lean flows, driving improvements with VSM, or implementing frameworks such as BLAST and BASE, agility is highlighted as a crucial competency for success.
- **Integration of Lean-Agile practices**: The integration of Lean and Agile practices is a recurring theme throughout the chapters. Whether it's exploring Lean-Agile principles, discussing VSM methodologies for productivity improvement, or implementing frameworks such as BLAST and BASE, the fusion of Lean efficiency with Agile adaptability is emphasized as a key strategy for maximizing value delivery and operational excellence.

- **Continuous improvement**: Throughout the chapters, continuous improvement is emphasized. Improvements come from Lean's productivity and efficiency enhancements, Agile's flexibility to adapt to market shifts, VSM's prioritization of customer value-driven improvements, and frameworks such as BLAST and BASE integrating lean and agile practices on an enterprise scale for value-based product and service releases. The importance of ongoing enhancements, iterative problem-solving, and the pursuit of operational excellence is consistently emphasized.
- **Customer-centricity**: The focus on delivering maximum customer value is another cross-cutting theme. All organizations, regardless of their size or industry, ultimately deliver value to their paying customers through their products and services. Whether it's through the adoption of Lean-Agile concepts, VSM methodologies, and tools, or frameworks such as BLAST and BASE, the emphasis is on crafting enterprise excellence by prioritizing customer-centric value delivery and aligning organizational efforts with customer needs.
- **Breaking down silos for streamlined value streams**: The chapters consistently emphasize value stream optimization. Whether through Lean and Agile principles to reduce waste and focus on essentials, VSM-based improvement prioritization, or frameworks such as BLAST and BASE to efficiently coordinate organizational resources for continuous value delivery, the imperative of breaking down silos and organizing work, information, materials, and processes into streamlined flows is underscored. This holistic approach aims to enhance operational efficiency, streamline processes, and maximize value delivery.

Overall, these cross-cutting themes highlight the need to integrate Lean, Agile, VSM, and frameworks such as BLAST and BASE in driving organizational success, fostering innovation, and delivering continuous value.

Analyzing the impact

Reflecting on the themes of agility and adaptability, integration of Lean and Agile practices, continuous improvement, customer-centricity, and breaking down silos, we see how these concepts enrich the understanding of Lean-Agile and VSM practices. They play a pivotal role in shaping the book's focus by emphasizing the importance of agility, adaptability, and customer-centricity in achieving operational excellence.

Evaluating the significance

The recurring and cross-cutting themes hold significant importance in the context of organizational transformation. They influence strategies and concepts for improving processes and efficiency by highlighting the necessity of embracing change, fostering collaboration, prioritizing customer value, and optimizing value streams. These themes serve as guiding principles for organizations seeking to navigate digital transformations, drive improvements, and achieve lasting competitive advantage.

Concluding with insights

In conclusion, the analysis of cross-cutting themes underscores the critical role of agility, adaptability, customer-centricity, and continuous improvement in Lean-Agile and VSM practices. By understanding and leveraging these themes, organizations can better navigate the complexities of today's business landscape, drive sustainable transformation, and deliver continuous value to their customers. The insights gained from this thematic analysis provide valuable guidance for real-world implementations, emphasizing the importance of holistic approaches that integrate Lean, Agile, VSM, and frameworks such as BLAST and BASE to drive organizational excellence.

Now that you have a solid foundation of knowledge to build upon, let's look at some real-world examples of where organizations have applied Lean-Agile and VSM principles and practices to improve their business performance.

Reviewing real-world case studies

In this section, we provide three real-world case studies where the cross-cutting themes of Lean-Agile practices and principles led to critical improvements across the organization. We'll start with the Lean-Agile Center of Excellence established within Amadeus, a leading technology provider in the global travel and tourism industry.

Amadeus Lean-Agile Center of Excellence (LACE) case study

The **Amadeus Lean-Agile Center of Excellence** (**LACE**) team guides organizational transformation for the company, embodying a steadfast commitment to excellence and adaptability in today's dynamic business landscape. With a resolute mission to catalyze change and foster sustainable cultural shifts, the LACE team serves as the vanguard of enterprise agility within Amadeus.

Fostering organizational transformation

At the heart of the LACE's mission is the relentless pursuit of high performance and sustainability, achieved through enduring cultural change and leadership in enterprise agility initiatives. With responsibilities ranging from assessing and driving transformations to training and coaching organizations in Lean-Agile practices, the LACE team acts as a cornerstone for organizational evolution. Their tight integration with **People & Culture** (**P&C**) ensures alignment with global Lean-Agile practices, safeguarding the organization's journey toward agility and efficiency.

Driving continuous improvement

The success of the LACE is measured by a series of key performance indicators, including employee net promoter scores, predictability, quality, and time to market. These metrics serve as barometers of organizational health and effectiveness, reflecting the tangible impact of Lean-Agile practices on Amadeus' operations and outcomes.

Collaborating across locations

Spanning across multiple locations, including Sophia-Antipolis, France; Bangalore, India; and Bad Homburg, Germany, the LACE team comprises dedicated professionals committed to driving transformational change. With a diverse array of talents and expertise, the team collaborates seamlessly to deliver impactful outcomes and support the organization's agility journey.

Facilitating effective communication

The LACE team engages in a cadence of activities, including weekly meetings and participation in enterprise agility events such as PI planning and ART sync sessions. Leveraging communication platforms such as Yammer and SharePoint, the team fosters collaboration and knowledge-sharing, enabling widespread adoption of Lean-Agile principles and practices.

Championing key organizational themes

Throughout its endeavors, the Amadeus LACE exemplifies five overarching themes critical to organizational success: emphasizing agility and adaptability, integrating Lean and Agile practices, committing to continuous improvement, maintaining unwavering customer-centricity, and breaking down silos for streamlined value streams. These themes underpin the LACE's strategic initiatives and guide its efforts toward driving transformative change and operational excellence within Amadeus.

Applying cross-cutting themes to Amadeus

- **Emphasizing Agility and adaptability**: The establishment of the Lean-Agile Center of Excellence (LACE) offered flexibility in response to dynamic market conditions and evolving organizational needs. By adapting methodologies such as SAFe® and Agile Release Trains, the LACE demonstrates its commitment to agility and adaptability in driving organizational transformation.
- **Integrating Lean and Agile practices**: The seamless integration of Lean principles such as waste reduction and value stream optimization with Agile methodologies such as Scrum and DevOps fostered a balanced approach to efficiency and adaptability, ensuring alignment and optimizing value delivery across the organization.
- **Pursuing continuous improvement**: Continuous improvement was a central theme in the organization's iterative approach to LACE setup and transformation. By prioritizing skills development, experimentation, and learning, the organization fostered a culture of innovation and agility, enabling it to evolve and adapt in response to emerging challenges and changing market dynamics.
- **Prioritizing customer-centricity**: The organization's commitment to customer-centricity was achieved by aligning transformation goals with strategic business outcomes and customer needs. Through the inclusion of HR, finance, and other business functions in the LACE team, the organization prioritizes initiatives that directly impact customer satisfaction and long-term value creation.

- **Breaking down silos for streamlining value streams**: With the adoption of a hub-and-spoke LACE model involving representatives from various business units, the organization promotes alignment, transparency, and knowledge-sharing across departments. This streamlined approach to value stream management enhances operational efficiency, eliminates waste, and maximizes value delivery, ultimately improving customer satisfaction and organizational effectiveness.

Leonardo Worldwide VSM case study

We now offer a second case study – that of a software technology firm, **Leonardo Worldwide**, supporting the travel industry. In this case, the company provides content management and distribution software.

A travel tech leader's leap toward Agile efficiency

This case study depicts a performance improvement effort within a larger, long-term transformation that was struggling to deliver compelling business results. The company needed a way to improve prioritization and accelerate execution to learn, build, and refactor faster. The executives couldn't see what was delaying progress, or how individual contributions were impacting the transformation effort. As an experiment, they aimed to dramatically improve an eight-month process to satisfy critical customer requests, which came with a serious churn risk and opportunity cost. Utilizing the capabilities of Leonardo Worldwide's travel technology platform, the transformation team worked to reduce their Enterprise Feature Request process from 8 months to 3 months with just a few hours of lean value stream mapping

Challenge encountered

Leonardo Worldwide helps hotels and travel channels source, manage, and distribute their content. Transformation within Leonardo was nearing the end of its planned 1.5-year transformation journey, and yet many milestones were still beyond the horizon. The company's time-to-market metrics were not sufficient to address demand, which was impacting morale.

The current state operating model represented agile cycles inside a waterfall process. As a result, QA, operations, marketing, and support were involved too late in the planning process. There were many meetings, handoffs, and activities involving simple manual work. The company had developed ideal world process documentation, but the reality of their situation was twice as complicated as described in the documented processes.

Recognizing that large-scale change is daunting and prone to failure, the executives and transformation team elected to start small, with a **Lean Value Stream Mapping** (**LVSM**) methodology selected as the catalyst to spark awareness, visibility, and change.

Lean IT with a VSM approach

The company embarked on a Lean IT initiative employing Value Stream Mapping to scrutinize and refine its enterprise partner integration process. Simple, lean value stream mapping – completed in a few short hours – was leveraged to identify, and eliminate non-value-adding activities, streamline workflow, and ultimately reduce delivery lead time.

Implementation

The team initiated the process using just a whiteboard and marker, gradually refining their approach over a couple of hours. They then transitioned to utilizing common enterprise productivity software such as Excel and Google Sheets to develop dynamic dashboards, enabling visualization of gaps, tracking progress, and sharing successes.

They opted for a lightweight approach, steering clear of commercial VSM tools. Recognizing that even simple spreadsheets could introduce unintended complexity and impede progress, they utilized existing, accessible worksheets and document creation and collaboration tools. This allowed them to maintain a delicate balance between structure and simplicity.

To secure executive buy-in and align efforts, the transformation team strategically engaged with business leaders whose key performance indicators were directly impacted by the process. Moreover, they involved other stakeholders who had expressed concerns about the process, fostering buy-in among the remaining skeptics.

Despite their active involvement in transformation discussions, many participants had limited day-to-day interaction with colleagues outside their specific areas of work. This led to surprising discoveries about the significant contributions of other departments to the flow of work and information within the targeted value stream.

Outcomes achieved

The application of VSM and Lean IT principles enabled Leonardo to achieve remarkable improvements in its SDLC process. Let's explore those improvements in the context of the organization's critical performance metrics:

- **Reduced lead time**: The streamlined process saw a reduction from 8 months on average and 12 months in the worst case, to a consistent three-month flow with sufficient buffering. The reduction marks a 62.5% decrease in typical delivery time and a 75% decrease from the worst-case lead time.
- **Enhanced efficiency**: The team condensed the process from 23 sequential steps with numerous handoffs to just 6 phases involving parallel activities. They streamlined the number of process reviewers from 12 to 2 individuals – a primary and a backup approver, clarifying roles and ownership. Furthermore, optimizing workflow enabled a reduction in team size from 12 contributors to just 4, facilitating the execution of three parallel efforts concurrently.
- **Cost savings and additional revenue**: The team demonstrated fully loaded cost savings of 150k /year over 3 years. Additionally, the ability to execute three additional Change Request cycles per year over 3 years presented an additional $720,000 revenue improvement opportunity.

Applying the cross-cutting themes to Leonardo Worldwide

Now let's look at the transformation team's outcomes in the context of the cross-cutting themes identified previously in this chapter:

- **Emphasizing Agility and adaptability**: Within the context of the VSM case, Leonardo recognized the necessity of agility and adaptability in its IT operations, enabling swift responses to changing demands and improvement opportunities. This focus led to the adoption of flexible processes that could be rapidly adjusted or scaled according to requirements and business needs.
- **Integrating Lean and Agile practices**: The integration of Lean and Agile practices allowed Leonardo to enhance its software development lifecycle by combining Lean's efficiency in measuring value streams with Agile's iterative approach to management. This holistic strategy ensured a seamless flow of work and improved collaboration across teams.
- **Pursuing continuous improvement**: Leonardo Worldwide's journey with Value Stream Mapping was underpinned by a commitment to continuous improvement, systematically identifying and eliminating waste in their SDLC process. This ongoing pursuit of operational excellence resulted in significant reductions in delivery time, increased contributor satisfaction, and increased revenue opportunities.
- **Prioritizing customer-centricity**: By adopting a Lean-Agile IT approach, Leonardo placed a strong emphasis on customer-centricity, ensuring that every phase of the software development process was aligned with delivering maximum value to customers by maximizing value-added time. This focus led to more efficient service deliveries and products that more closely met customer needs and expectations, in addition to higher efficiency.
- **Breaking down silos for streamlining value streams**: Leonardo tackled the challenge of organizational silos by breaking down value stream steps and clearly identifying costly handoffs, which often hindered efficient workflow and information exchange. Through value stream mapping, the company identified and removed painful bottlenecks and smoothed handoffs, fostering a culture of collaboration, and enabling more streamlined and efficient value delivery across departments.

Conclusion and insights

After the initial value stream transformation session, team members departed feeling energized and clear about the goals and next steps, with ample energy remaining to fuel the subsequent improvement efforts. Participants expressed surprise at the complexity of the process and the burden it placed on others, emphasizing the widespread presence of waste, delays, and inadequate visibility and measurement.

This case exemplifies a successful application of value stream mapping within a complex enterprise IT environment, highlighting the versatility and effectiveness of Lean-Agile methodologies in enhancing software development processes. Moreover, it underscores the strategic value of embracing a continuous improvement mindset in today's dynamic business landscape, showcasing not only the tangible benefits, such as reduced cycle times and improved operational efficiency, but also the broader organizational advantages.

BLAST case study

The **Basic Lean-Agile Solutions Team** (**BLAST**) framework revolutionizes how multiple Lean and Agile teams collaborate on developing solutions. Born out of the necessity to address challenges faced by one of Al Shalloway's clients, BLAST emerged when they initially attempted to employ a Scaled Scrum approach for orchestrating the work of numerous teams on a sizable software development program.

However, devoid of Lean-oriented concepts, they struggled with discipline, synchronization, and integration of their work. From a Lean-Agile perspective, they lacked both cadence and flow. By analogy, imagine a combustion engine that is not firing in a synchronized manner across all its cylinders. The engine will misfire and potentially seize.

BLAST offers a structured yet flexible approach, emphasizing the alignment of team backlogs to foster a cohesive environment that mitigates delays and enhances workflow efficiency.

Overview: utilizing alignment for multi-team collaboration

BLAST is a value stream-based approach that leverages the alignment of business value backlog to facilitate collaboration among multiple teams. This alignment serves as a cost-effective method of coordinating teams compared to external coordination, fostering a cohesive sense of a larger team, and minimizing delays in workflows between teams.

One of the primary challenges in product development is the occurrence of delays in the workflow. These delays hindered the timely feedback, which is essential for minimizing rework and other unplanned tasks. To address this challenge, the Basic Lean Agile Team employs a combination of **Minimum Value Increments** (**MVIs**), coordinated backlogs, and a shared goal. These elements ensure effective collaboration among teams with diverse skills and responsibilities.

Furthermore, BLAST implements the Lean-oriented concept of value streams and flows. By incorporating workflows, process automation and integration, and standard Lean practices, BLAST significantly accelerates the delivery of customer-centric value through the organization's products and services. This approach not only enhances quality, productivity, and efficiency but also ensures a relentless focus on meeting customer needs and expectations.

The genesis of BLAST can be traced back to a pivotal two-day consulting engagement led by Al Shalloway. The next section delves into the circumstances surrounding BLAST's inception during collaboration with a company experienced in Scrum methodologies at scale yet encountering challenges in realizing value efficiently.

Discovering the genesis of BLAST

BLAST originated during a two-day consulting engagement led by Al Shalloway, involving a company proficient in Scrum methodologies, characterized by two-week sprints, and utilizing practices akin to Al's original concepts around **Minimum Valuable Increments** (**MVIs**). In other words, the product teams had the goal of releasing full increments of value as complete features or solutions. Despite receiving training from a well-known, leading Scrum consultant, the client's product and component teams encountered difficulties in delivering value through their products efficiently.

Their development organization, comprising approximately 150 individuals, was organized into approximately 20 teams, with 2-3 product lines, each encompassing 2-3 products. Additionally, their people had just been reorganized into application teams, components teams supporting the application teams, and a component team supporting all applications (see *Figure 12.1* as an example of the team orientations).

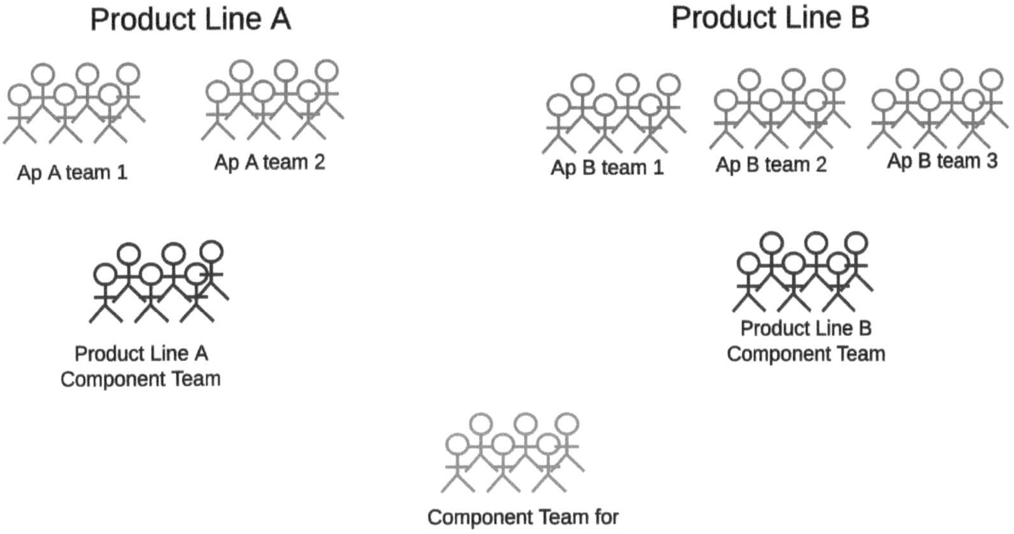

Figure 12.1 – Team compositions and structures

The teams found themselves in a perplexing situation where each team could complete their sprints but struggled to release software solutions promptly. Upon closer examination, they discovered that the teams were diligently performing the tasks they had been instructed to do. Consequently, they were baffled by the significant delays in releasing the new enhancements they were collectively building as integrated solutions.

After a swift value stream mapping session, a practice not commonly emphasized in Scrum-based methodologies, their issue became apparent. Despite each team performing their tasks competently, prolonged product enhancement projects spanning more than two sprints resulted in considerable time and effort dedicated to component integrations. The root of the problem lay in each team pulling work from the product backlog while selecting tasks optimized for their skills, resources, and availability.

Unfortunately, this approach led to fragmented integration of work across teams, as each team focused on implementing distinct capabilities and failed to coordinate their efforts effectively. This resulted in the delivery of partial components of multiple features within a sprint, rather than complete, customer-centric features. It became evident that they required a more effective approach to planning, coordinating, and integrating their work to deliver value to the customer.

As a side note, it's important to mention that the client likely needed to reassess its reliance on component teams, as opposed to feature teams. A **feature team**, known for its cross-functional and cross-component nature, is responsible for building and providing end-to-end customer features or slices of features. Conversely, a **component team** is a specialized team focused on specific components, such as UI, backend development, frontend development, APIs, QA, and testing.

Many organizations opt for component teams based on their existing skills or domain-based organizational structures. However, as a general rule, feature teams tend to work best, facilitating the generation of flow across continuous integration/continuous delivery (CI/CD) and DevOps-based software delivery pipelines.

But let's get back to our story on the genesis of the BLAST framework. The lack of customer feedback was only part of the problem. The absence of a defined increment of product-oriented value meant that any misunderstandings between the teams could not be detected at the end of the sprint because full features were not completely implemented.

Figure 12.2 illustrates the disconnect created by this component team approach to development across multiple teams.

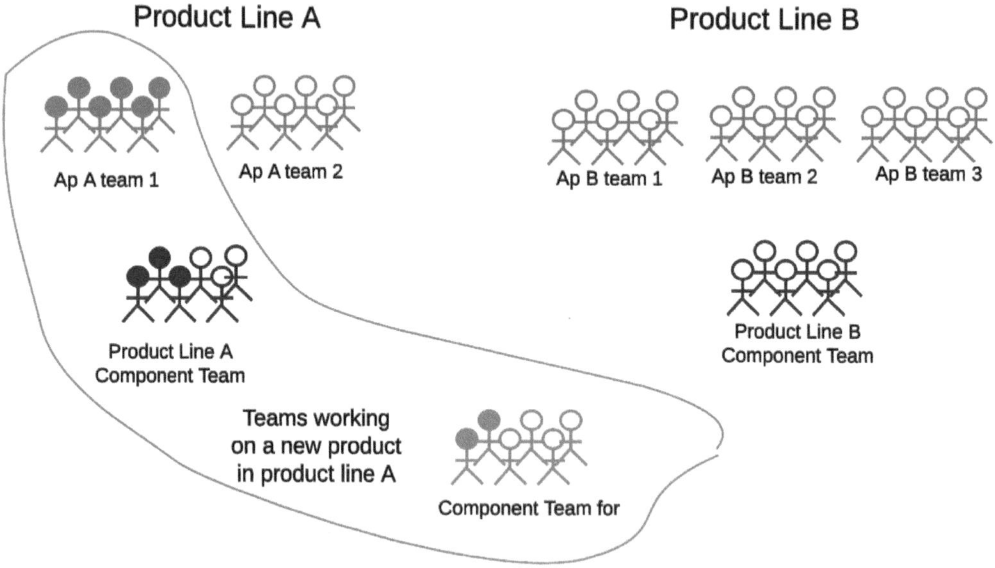

Figure 12.2 – Disconnected product team efforts

Each team pulled work off the product backlog based on what was easiest for them to implement with the skills and resources available in their component-based teams. Consequently, different parts of the required features were pulled regardless of priority. As a result, at the end of each sprint, very little real integration could be achieved, as a complete solution was not available for release. When each team completed their work, they attempted to integrate the entire system, only to discover errors and incorrect assumptions, requiring significant unplanned work.

Additionally, new projects in the pipeline meant that any delays on one project adversely affected many others. This introduced further delays and extra, unplanned work.

This client situation became a case study of having quality individuals working at the team level but failing to translate their efforts into delivering quality components across a group of teams building integrated and value-added solutions. Despite genuine efforts to coordinate work across teams, the result created a culture of unproductive micro-management and finger-pointing. Instead, what was needed was for teams to learn to work together naturally.

The key to addressing this was for teams to autonomously pull the required tasks to complete features in a coordinated manner.

The product teams found themselves in this situation by following a process originally designed to support the efforts of one or maybe two Scrum teams working against a single backlog. In this model, the Scrum teams remain reasonably autonomous, cross-functional, and self-managing. However, when multiple teams were tasked with pulling from the same product backlog, they pulled in a way that accelerated value delivery across individual teams but not for the collective of teams tasked with delivering value-added solutions.

The bottom line is individual team delivery isn't the point; the goal is to deliver value to customers. Using a single-team approach to coordinate multiple teams with different focuses is rarely successful.

Leveraging the BLAST framework for team synergy and value delivery

The BLAST framework enables multiple teams to work together to deliver value-added solutions. In the BLAST model, some teams use Lean-oriented practices to deliver products and services efficiently, rapidly, and with high quality in a repeatable manner. Meanwhile, other teams adopt Agile's iterative and incremental development models to solve complex problems, plan new increments and releases, develop new product and service enhancements, and improve business processes and systems.

The BLAST framework also facilitates collaboration with domain experts who support the Agile-based teams where their expertise is needed for requirements gathering, testing, and feedback.

A prime example of this collaboration is modern DevOps software development teams. DevOps builds upon the continuous integration / continuous delivery (CI/CD) pipeline concepts developed to support the software development process. Both CI/CD and DevOps pipelines utilize technology to integrate, automate, and synchronize software development, delivery, and support processes, end to end. While this approach aligns closely with Lean-oriented development models, new work enters the pipeline on a cadence using Agile's **Iterative and Incremental Development** (**IID**) approach to gathering requirements, planning feature releases, refining the backlog, and releasing new enhancements to customers.

In our modern software delivery model, the DevOps team collaborates with domain experts, stakeholders, and customers to support their solution delivery efforts. These domain experts also likely work in Lean-oriented work environments to maximize their ability to deliver value in their areas of work. Effectively, they are loaned out to the Agile-based teams on an ad hoc and as-needed basis.

Aligning with the principles of agility and adaptability, the BLAST framework emphasizes the importance of teams collaborating on a shared backlog to determine which features to prioritize and develop collectively. This approach fosters cohesion among teams, enabling them to focus on interconnected aspects of the product, complete feature components required for integration, and prompt gathering of customer feedback.

This suggests that teams should collaborate on a shared backlog, pulling features together to determine their collective priorities. By doing so, teams can focus on interrelated aspects of the product, ensuring the completion of feature components necessary for integration and facilitating prompt customer feedback. Additionally, this approach minimizes the amount of integration work carried over to subsequent sprints. This type of collaboration creates alignment automatically, thereby reducing the need to coordinate teams. The effect is lower costs while achieving greater efficiency.

So, with this understanding, let's examine our five cross-cutting Lean-Agile themes to find a better approach for this client to deliver high-value products and services efficiently, rapidly, and with high quality.

Maximizing value delivery through cross-cutting Lean-Agile themes

In the domain of Lean-Agile practices, the pursuit of maximizing value delivery with the available resources is the primary imperative. Embedded within this endeavor are the five cross-cutting themes meticulously discussed throughout our Lean-Agile Mastery book. These themes not only guide the principles of the BLAST framework but also serve as pillars for effective Lean-Agile implementation.

As we observe these themes applied to this client's situation, it becomes evident how they intertwine with the fabric of BLAST, driving its efficiency and success in delivering value to customers. Let's delve into each theme, uncovering their significance in shaping Lean-Agile practices within the BLAST framework:

- **Integration of Lean and Agile practices**: Coordinated pulling of work items minimized workflow delays between teams, resulting in reduced workloads
- **Continuous improvement**: Collaborative efforts allowed teams to enhance their alignment and coordination methods continually
- **Customer-centricity**: Teams shifted their focus from individual responsibilities to prioritizing customer value
- **Breaking down silos with streamlined value streams**: Teams ceased operating in isolation and instead collaborated to deliver value to the customer more efficiently

Essentially, BLAST was born! An interesting observation is what prompted the client to recognize the necessary course of action and why it wasn't apparent to them earlier.

One reason is that Scrum lacks an in-depth theory about the first principles of knowledge work. An example of the first principle of knowledge work is understanding how information is processed and utilized within a team or organization to achieve its objectives. Instead, Scrum relies on predetermined practices such as sprints, cross-functional teams, events, and values. A mantra of Scrum is that teams are self-managing, focusing on what's best for the team individually.

So, this approach led to local optimization within the client's product and component teams, resulting in high integration costs. On the positive side, as team leaders realized this was working against them, they saw the value in considering themselves as part of "one big team."

Presenting them with a value stream map illustrating their workflow and the benefits of alignment through a common backlog provided the insights needed to change their approach.

The following list highlights BLAST's scaling approach:

- BLAST emphasizes alignment, ensuring that teams are synchronized in their efforts.
- BLAST advocates for clearly defined agreements within and across teams to avoid confusion and foster effective collaboration.
- BLAST promotes the use of minimum valuable increments (MVIs) within the product backlog, outlining the next valuable increment for release. This clarity in defining releasable increments aids in creating alignment among teams.
- BLAST accommodates various team structures, including Scrum, Kanban, or any other type, as long as they adhere to the coordination cadence.

In conclusion, the BLAST framework emerges as a robust approach to maximizing value delivery within Lean-Agile practices. Through the lens of our Lean-Agile Mastery book, we have explored five cross-cutting themes that underpin BLAST's effectiveness, each contributing to its success in delivering value to customers. As we reflect on how these themes intersect with the fabric of BLAST, it becomes evident how they drive efficiency and efficacy within the framework.

The genesis of BLAST stemmed from a pivotal moment when the client recognized the need for a shift in approach, shedding light on the limitations of traditional Scrum methodologies. By emphasizing alignment, fostering clear agreements, defining minimum valuable Increments, and accommodating diverse Lean and Agile team structures, BLAST offers a comprehensive solution for organizations seeking to scale Agile practices effectively. This underscores the evolution of Agile at Scale and distinguishes BLAST as a trailblazer in Lean-Agile implementation.

Summarizing the success of alignment with BLAST

BLAST's adoption was swift and successful due to the executive managers' ability to recognize the transformative shift from coordinating teams to aligning them around a backlog of features. This coordinated approach fostered alignment and circumvented the challenges previously encountered.

This ends our section containing real-world case studies. We can now move on to wrap up both this chapter and this book.

Empowering change for operational excellence

Reflecting on key messages

As we wrap up our journey through this chapter, it's time to take stock of the valuable insights we've gained. Each chapter has provided practical strategies aimed at fostering organizational excellence in today's fast-paced business world.

We started by understanding the importance of mastering Lean-Agile and Value Stream Management (VSM) principles, essential for navigating digital transformations and solving complex business problems. These foundational chapters set the stage for implementing Lean-Agile practices effectively.

Moving forward, we delved into Value Stream Management (VSM, exploring methodologies such as the 9-Step VSM methodology and the VSM Implementation Roadmap. These insights equipped us to drive continuous improvement and streamline value delivery across organizational workflows.

Additionally, we explored executive-level strategies for implementing enduring Lean-Agile practices and enhancing decision-making in the digital era. By embracing frameworks such as the BLAST framework and the BASE conceptual model organizations can drive continuous value delivery, fostering sustainable growth and innovation.

In conclusion, achieving organizational excellence is a never-ending journey. Now, it's your turn to enter this journey to empower change and drive organizational excellence.

Summarizing the main takeaways

Throughout this exploration of what it means to achieve Lean-Agile mastery, we've uncovered a wealth of insights aimed at driving organizational excellence. Let's consolidate the main takeaways from this learning journey:

- **Mastering Lean-Agile and VSM principles**: Understand the core principles to streamline processes and foster continuous improvement
- **Navigating digital transformations**: Embrace agility to thrive amid constant change in the digital landscape
- **Solving complex business problems with Agility**: Drive productivity and innovation through iterative development, incremental deliveries, and cross-team collaboration
- **Establishing efficient workflows**: Optimize productivity by focusing on process optimization through the elimination of waste and constraints
- **Making value stream improvements**: Drive meaningful and value-based change with strategic approaches such as the 9-Step VSM methodology

- **Driving continuous value delivery**: Achieve lasting competitive advantage by harmonizing Lean efficiency with Agile adaptability
- **Enhancing decision-making in the digital era**: Distill vast data reserves into actionable insights to guide strategic decision-making
- **Simplifying Lean-Agile implementations**: Streamline adoption processes and drive sustainable growth by embracing change and collaboration

By embracing the principles, strategies, and practices outlined in this book, you can drive meaningful change, foster innovation, and propel your organization toward unparalleled success.

A call to action

Now equipped with invaluable insights and practical strategies, it's time to act. Embrace the principles of Lean-Agile and VSM to drive transformative change within your organization. Continuously experiment until you find the right formula to streamline processes, enhance productivity, and foster a culture of ongoing improvement. Share your experiences and insights with others, contributing to a community of learning and collaboration. Working within collaborative Lean-Agile business environments, you and your teams can help propel your organizations toward excellence in today's dynamic business world.

Looking ahead, organizations need to heed this call to action. Executives must lead by championing a culture of operational efficiency while retaining agility and innovation. Teams must collaborate seamlessly, breaking down silos and aligning efforts toward common goals. Individuals at all levels must embrace a mindset of lifelong learning, adapt to change, and drive positive transformation.

Questions

This section is offered for those readers who want to evaluate comprehension and retention of the information provided in this chapter. There are five questions. The answers are provided in the following section. Recalling the exact verbiage of the original content is not important. Rather, it's more important that you can recall the concepts and their applications.

1. Why is the cross-cutting theme of Agility and adaptability an important concept?
2. Why is the integration of Lean and Agile practices an important concept?
3. Why is continuous improvement an important concept in Lean-Agile practices?
4. Why is customer-centricity an important concept in Lean-Agile practices?
5. Why is breaking down silos to streamline value streams an important Lean-Agile concept?

Answers

1. The cross-cutting theme of Agility and adaptability is crucial for digital transformations and complex business problems.
2. The integration of Lean and Agile practices highlights the fusion of Lean efficiency with Agile adaptability to maximize value delivery and operational excellence.
3. Continuous improvement as a concept stresses the need for ongoing enhancements and iterative problem-solving for productivity, efficiency, and flexibility.
4. Customer-centricity focuses on delivering maximum value to customers by aligning organizational efforts with customer needs.
5. Breaking down silos promotes value stream optimization by reducing waste, coordinating resources efficiently, and more effective organization of work.

Further reading

1. Berger, D. (2023, June 15). Widespread Lean Adoption Would Make the US More Competitive. Industry Week. Retrieved from `https://www.industryweek.com/operations/continuousimprovement/article/21267990/widespread-lean-adoption-would-makethe-us-more-competitive`

2. Coalition for a Prosperous America (CPA) Report: Coalition for a Prosperous America (CPA). (2023). U.S. Producers Recapture Substantial Domestic Market Share in Q1, China Loses Share. Retrieved from CPA Report

3. Wang et al. (2019) Report: Wang, Y., Ash, J., Zhuang, Y., Zhibin, L., Zeng, Z., Hajbabaie, A., Hajibabai, L., & Tajalli, M. (2019). Understanding Opportunities with Connected Vehicles in the Smart Cities Context (Report No. WA-RD 885.1). Washington State Department of Transportation. Retrieved from Report

4. Europeana Task Force on Metadata Quality Report: Europeana Task Force on Metadata Quality. (2015). Report and Recommendations from the Task Force on Metadata Quality. Europeana. Retrieved from Report

Index

A

B

C

D

E

F

G

H

I

K

L

M

N

O

P

Q

R

S

T

W

X

Other Books You May Enjoy

If you enjoyed this book, you may be interested in these other books by Packt:

SAFe® Coaches Handbook

Darren Wilmshurst, Lindy Quick

ISBN: 978-1-83921-045-7

- Discover how to set up Agile Teams to attain maximum effectiveness
- Avoid common mistakes organizations make with SAFe®
- Find out how to set up the Agile Release Train
- Discover common mistakes enterprises make that affect the success of the ART
- Understand the importance of Value Streams and learn how to work with them successfully
- Start using the best ways to measure the progress of Teams and ARTs at an Enterprise level
- Recognize the impact of successful SAFe® adoption on Enterprise strategy and organizational structure

Driving DevOps with Value Stream Management

Cecil 'Gary' Rupp

ISBN: 978-1-80107-806-1

- Integrate Agile, systems thinking, and lean development to deliver customer-centric value
- Find out how to choose the most appropriate value stream for your initial and follow-on VSM projects
- Establish better flows with integrated, automated, and orchestrated DevOps and CI/CD pipelines
- Apply a proven eight-step VSM methodology to drive lean IT value stream improvements
- Discover the key strengths of modern VSM tools and their customer use case scenarios
- Understand how VSM drives DevOps pipeline improvements and value delivery transformations across enterprises

Scaling Scrum Across Modern Enterprises

Cecil 'Gary' Rupp

ISBN: 978-1-83921-647-3

- Understand the limitations of traditional Scrum practices
- Explore the roles and responsibilities in a scaled Scrum and Lean-Agile development environment
- Tailor your Scrum approach to support portfolio and large product development needs
- Apply systems thinking to evaluate the impacts of changes in the interdependent parts of a larger development and delivery system
- Scale Scrum practices at both the program and portfolio levels of management
- Understand how DevOps, test automation, and CI/CD capabilities help in scaling Scrum practices

Packt is searching for authors like you

If you're interested in becoming an author for Packt, please visit `authors.packtpub.com` and apply today. We have worked with thousands of developers and tech professionals, just like you, to help them share their insight with the global tech community. You can make a general application, apply for a specific hot topic that we are recruiting an author for, or submit your own idea.

Share Your Thoughts

Now you've finished *The Lean-Agile Way*, we'd love to hear your thoughts! Scan the QR code below to go straight to the Amazon review page for this book and share your feedback or leave a review on the site that you purchased it from.

`https://packt.link/r/1835461875`

Your review is important to us and the tech community and will help us make sure we're delivering excellent quality content.

Download a free PDF copy of this book

Thanks for purchasing this book!

Do you like to read on the go but are unable to carry your print books everywhere?

Is your eBook purchase not compatible with the device of your choice?

Don't worry, now with every Packt book you get a DRM-free PDF version of that book at no cost.

Read anywhere, any place, on any device. Search, copy, and paste code from your favorite technical books directly into your application.

The perks don't stop there, you can get exclusive access to discounts, newsletters, and great free content in your inbox daily

Follow these simple steps to get the benefits:

1. Scan the QR code or visit the link below

`https://packt.link/free-ebook/978-1-83546-187-7`

2. Submit your proof of purchase
3. That's it! We'll send your free PDF and other benefits to your email directly

Printed in Poland
by Amazon Fulfillment
Poland Sp. z o.o., Wrocław

50030481R00214